On Racial Frontiers

The New Culture of Frederick Douglass,
Ralph Ellison, and Bob Marley

Frederick Douglass, Ralph Ellison, and Bob Marley each inhabited the shared but contested space at the frontiers of race. Gregory Stephens shows how their interactions with mixed audiences made them key figures in a previously hidden interracial consciousness and culture. They are integrative ancestors who can be claimed by more than one "racial" or national group.

Frederick Douglass was "something of an Irishman as well as a Negro." The world's most famous abolitionist, he was also a critic of black racialism. He demonstrated his multiple allegiances by marrying a white feminist. Ralph Ellison's *Invisible Man* is a landmark of modernity and black literature which illustrates "the true interrelatedness of blackness and whiteness." Bob Marley claimed sole allegiance to neither blacks nor whites but to "God's side, who cause me to come from black and white." His Bible-based *Songs of Freedom* envision a world in which black liberation and multiracial redemption coexist.

The lives of these three men illustrate how our notions of "race" have been constructed out of a repression of the interracial. This has profound political and educational implications. In addition to the multiracial publics of their own time, they also speak to subsequent generations for whom racial language is inadequate. In their different ways, they promoted a multiracial "imagined community" at the brink of what Nelson Mandela has called a "nonracial democracy."

GREGORY STEPHENS is Visiting Assistant Professor in Human Relations at the University of Oklahoma. An award-winning songwriter before returning to academia, he has published in *Whole Earth Review*, *Village Voice*, and *Reggae and African Beat*.

On Racial Frontiers

The New Culture of Frederick Douglass,
Ralph Ellison, and Bob Marley

Gregory Stephens

CAMBRIDGE
UNIVERSITY PRESS

PUBLISHED BY THE PRESS SYNDICATE OF THE UNIVERSITY OF CAMBRIDGE
The Pitt Building, Trumpington Street, Cambridge, United Kingdom

CAMBRIDGE UNIVERSITY PRESS
The Edinburgh Building, Cambridge CB2 2RU, UK
40 West 20th Street, New York, NY 10011–4211, USA
10 Stamford Road, Oakleigh, VIC 3166, Australia
Ruiz de Alarcón 13, 28014 Madrid, Spain
Dock House, The Waterfront, Cape Town 8001, South Africa

http://www.cambridge.org

First published 1999
Reprinted 2000

Printed in the United Kingdom at the University Press, Cambridge

Typeset in Plantin 10/12pt [VN]

A catalogue record for this book is available from the British Library

ISBN 0 521 64352 X hardback
ISBN 0 521 64393 7 paperback

this book is for
Sela and Samuel
my most important (co-)creations
on the racial frontier

Contents

Illustrations

Preface

The reader glancing at the cover of this book might reasonably be expected to ask: what do Frederick Douglass, Ralph Ellison, and Bob Marley have in common? Or what claims is the author making by putting them together in a book about "racial frontiers"? I begin trying to answer those questions at length in the introduction, but it would be only fair to give readers a preview of the direction I intend to take.

Douglass, Ellison, and Marley were all of mixed heritage – "racially" and culturally.

All were enormously successful in using the media of their day to address a multi"racial" audience. Both their mixed heritage and their interaction with a mixed public had a profound impact on their identity, and on the style and content of their communication.

All grew up without their biological fathers. Which is surely an important reason why they lifted their eyes to a more distant horizon, in order to imagine families, communities, and nations of a more inclusive character.

As public figures who spoke to more than one community, who employed more than one style of communication, and who did not limit themselves to one ideology, all were accused within their day of being a "sellout," insufficiently radical, etc. Their responses were similar. "You be your kind of militant and I'll be my kind of militant," Ellison said. Marley asked what it meant to be a "real revolutionary." Douglass chided those who struck oppositional poses that only looked good "on paper."[1]

All were inheritors of, and co-creators of, a "new culture" that was often racialized in its origins, and yet spoke to multi-ethnic and multinational audiences of the present and of the future, for whom racial language would be inadequate.

While researching and writing this book, educational and political questions have been foremost in my mind. If iconic figures such as Douglass, Ellison, and Marley were presented in our school books, and in the popular imagination, as "integrative ancestors" who can be claimed by more than one ethno-racial group, would this help us to build a democracy in which commonality and difference could coexist?[2]

I have written this book, first, for educators in both the humanities and the social sciences, in a language that I hope will allow them to assign it to their students. As a writer who had careers as a journalist, songwriter, and publicist before entering graduate school, I also hope to reach nonacademic readers. Those readers who are primarily interested in one of the figures presented here should feel free to skip ahead. They can later return to the other case studies, time and interest permitting, hopefully drawn by the common themes which echo throughout this text.

This book is in part about the inadequacy of "racial" and disciplinary boxes to describe the complexities of the sociocultural, psychological, and political realities in which we live. Its interdisciplinary nature is in part a product of my training in the Communication Department at the University of California-San Diego. This was a program which during my stay had no faculty trained in Communication. Communication was envisioned as a sort of unitary meta-discipline. This enforced institutional interdisciplinarity has both its strengths and its weaknesses. I have to ask a great deal of scholars who make their living within the strictures of one academic discipline or another.

My book is of course a form of cultural studies, broadly defined, and is affiliated with ethnic studies, although I am often critical of current practice in both of those domains. Indeed, I think that the work of scholars of interraciality has "devastating implications for ... ethnic studies," as Werner Sollors remarks regarding the book *Invention of Tradition*.[3] If our notions of "race" have been *invented*, or constructed, out of a repression of the interracial, then the very legitimacy of "racial" categories must be questioned. I do not believe that the study of interracial or multi-ethnic domains can be done effectively within the confines of one disciplinary or "ethnic" box. My alternative is communication-centered: I conceptualize this domain as *the communicative culture of multiracial audiences*.[4] That is, my object of study is the "new culture" which is created through the process of communicating to a multiracial audience.

This is a work of synthesis, and I am indebted to the pioneering work of many scholars on whose foundations I have built. I hope that these scholars will pardon my amateurism, or at least understand the impossibility of "covering all the bases" in a work of this nature. When I use evidence they supply to support conclusions with which they do not agree, I hope they will remember that "one repays a teacher badly if one remains only a pupil," as Jung once said to Freud, quoting Nietzsche.[5] My attempts to map a "new paradigm" are offered with the humble under-standing that there are always two sides to every story, at least. My own story must remain preliminary and incomplete.

Gregory Stephens
El Cerrito, California

Introduction: the contemporary rear-view mirror

Frederick Douglass, Ralph Ellison, and Bob Marley: three giants of our political, literary, and cultural heritage. They were three of the most widely acclaimed speakers, writers, and singers of their respective eras, whose contributions to a common moral vision and cultural critique (constructive criticism rooted in a living culture) form the subject of this book. They are the means through which I discuss two core ideas. First, I engage Douglass, Ellison, and Marley as key figures in a "previously hidden" *interracial consciousness and culture*.[1] Second, I use their work to argue for the need to address how *multiracial audiences* have long shaped public sphere discourse. In broadest terms, these men helped push a multiracial "imagined community" towards the horizon of what Nelson Mandela has called a "nonracial democracy."

Douglass, Ellison, and Marley all believed that the problems of race could not be solved with the language of race. They understood that racism and racialism are rooted in the language of race itself. Scientists at the dawn of the twenty-first century agree: "Race has no biological justification," the Association for the Advancement of Science states. The American Anthropological Association has called for the elimination of racial categories by the 2010 census. Kwame Appiah, a philosopher born to an English mother and a Ghanian father, has exposed the illusory foundations of "racialism." Still, we cling to our "color complex," or "color-phobia," as Douglass called racialism, with the entrenched institutional support of an "ethno-racial pentagon."[2] The debate about "race" is often polarized, in public sphere discourse, in such a way that those who insist that racialism should be resisted "regardless of color" will be beaten about the head with something called "history," and accused of being naive, if not reactionary.

This context has impressed upon me the need for a truly historicized identity politics: the need to move beyond action–reaction cycles, and towards a synthesis: a reenvisioning of his-story as our-story.[3] This is not to erase the history of "race," or the endurance of racial formations. But it is an insistence on the need to understand that our very conceptions of

1

"race" grew out of interracial contexts – and most specifically, with the repression of interraciality, in order to construct racial privilege. The notion of racial privilege has roots in white supremacist thought, but it is increasingly used now across the spectrum, whether in overt or covert form.[4]

Douglass, Ellison, and Marley were all deeply involved, in their own way, with criticizing our "color complex" and trying to create alternatives. In critiquing racialism, they became even further embedded in racialized thinking, in one sense, yet in another way all three paid tribute to their interracial foundations, and tried to envision a postracial future.

Frederick Douglass, who described himself as "something of an Irishman as well as a Negro," was the world's most famous "man of color" during the nineteenth century. He was a hugely popular speaker on both sides of the Atlantic whose public career spanned six decades. Women of all colors saw him both as a sex symbol and as a model of intellectual growth; presidents employed him as a diplomat in the Caribbean. Douglass is best known as a hero in the struggle against slavery and white racism. Yet he was also a persistent critic of black racialism, decrying in later years "the everlasting cultivation of race" as a "false foundation." His late interracial marriage demonstrated his multiple allegiances.[5]

Ralph Ellison was a jazz musician, novelist, and essayist, born and bred in the frontier state, Oklahoma. His life work was in some sense an extended meditation on "the true inter-relatedness of blackness and whiteness." His novel *Invisible Man* is not only a classic of "black literature" but a landmark of modernity. Its richly vernacular voice illustrates why, as Ellison's peer Albert Murray would say, "the mainstream in America is not white but mulatto."[6]

Bob Marley, quite possibly the most enduringly influential popular songwriter of the twentieth century, claimed sole allegiance neither to the black side nor the white side of his heritage, but to "God's side, who cause me to come from black and white." Marley used a Bible-based, postcolonial poetry in his "Songs of Freedom" which envisioned, and popularized globally, a world in which *black liberation* and *multiracial redemption* were part of the same process, neither of which could succeed without the other.[7] He called the form of consciousness required to create this new culture *Rasta*.

Douglass, Ellison, and Marley were the offspring (biological and cultural) of interracial relations. They were both the symbols of, and the producers of, a culture that emerged from a racialized history, and yet was also something more than the sum of its "racial" parts. What shall we call its name? I have sometimes referred to this culture as "biracial," yet as with all racial language, this term is problematic. In the era in which I write, *biracial* is often used to signify a hybrid offspring of black and white parents, or more broadly, the fusion of any racial or cultural traditions. I mean to convey this sense of synthesis when I later refer to Douglass and Marley as "biracial black culture heroes." Yet for most of the twentieth century, biracial seems to have been used to refer to a system of racial binaries, rather than a synthesis. So in searching for a term that conveys a sense of the ways in which Douglass, Ellison, and Marley spoke to a transracial imagined community, *as well as* to black people, or diasporic Africans, I have taken my cue from E. Franklin Frazier. The preeminent mid-century Afro-American[8] sociologist, Frazier was trained by Robert Park to think of racial frontiers as a contact zone in which hybrid cultures emerged. "It is on the frontiers of race relations where multiracial communities have grown up that the emergence of *new peoples* and *new cultures* is most apparent," Frazier wrote.[9]

In the "naming and framing" of a book dedicated to the troubling of racialism, it seems best to resist the temptation to be more specific. Douglass, Ellison, and Marley contributed to the creation of a "new culture," a communicative culture which transcends racial, national, and temporal boundaries. In the long term, it may still be too early to name this culture, to foretell the ways in which interpretive communities of the future will respond to its call. My use of racial terminology should be understood as provisional. None of the terms I employ are fully satisfactory. Yet although the terminology may at times seem confusing, I think the reader can detect a progression through the course of the book. In the early historical survey, I primarily use *interracial* to indicate the interaction between different groups. *Interraciality* indicates that this interaction has become an ongoing process. The varieties of interracial or interethnic relations produce biracial or multiethnic individuals (many of which, in accordance with the dominant racial mythology, continue to define themselves in mono-racial or mono-ethnic terms). *Multiracial* indicates public spheres in which participants have a variety of individual identities and group allegiances. I mean for multiracial to point towards the need to move beyond thinking of publics in black and white. When I specifically want to indicate publics that include Latinos, Asians, and other groups which do not fit in a black–white binary I sometimes use multiethnic, although in general I mean for multiracial to carry the same meaning. Finally, as I begin to discuss the larger implications of these case studies, I sometimes use the term *transracial*. This indicates transitional forms of communication that have origins in racial formations and racial mythology, yet are directed towards multiethnic and multinational audiences in a way that seems to indicate movement *towards* a postracial language.

I ask readers to think of Douglass, Ellison, and Marley as *integrative ancestors*. That is, people from more than one ethnic or national group can claim them as "their own." They can act as a common icon or shared antecedent, an "integrating personality" through whom diverse groups trace many of their ideological beliefs, their expressive style, or their model of identity and cultural rootedness. Douglass, Ellison, and Marley are cornerstones in what Eric Sundquist has called "the expressive heritage of a biracial culture." (Biracial as a synthesis, not as a binary system.) In this sense, this book is part of a mapping process of a mestizo-style culture, which is a burgeoning domain of scholarly inquiry and popular expression.[10]

Douglass, Ellison, and Marley function for me something like prominent peaks in this landscape. This is not to say these case studies are exercises in hero worship. I speak of Douglass, Ellison, and Marley as giants because of their stature in these domains: abolitionist politics, American literature, and popular music. To say that they tower over this terrain is not to be uncritical. To the contrary. Let us apply our critical faculties to the paradox that three iconic figures so central to "black history" and culture were thoroughly immersed in interracial networks and a transracial consciousness. Should not this give us food for thought? As Johann Herder wrote back in 1785, racial divisions are arbitrary because "Complexions run into each other."[11] There have been forward-thinking men and women in every age who, like Douglass, Ellison, and Marley, have tried (and often failed) to put this transracial consciousness into practice.

Learning to see these familiar figures as part of a transracial "new culture" can itself be a form of critical thinking – if the concept of interraciality is the beginning, rather than the end, of our critique of racialism. Interracial culture could be defined narrowly (in academic terms) as *representations of a multiracial imagined community, as they evolve over time, through use by multiracial speech communities.* If we look at the relationship between this system of representations, and the communities in which it is situated, it becomes clear that interracial culture is located not only in words and images, but in human beings and their institutions. To borrow an ancient scripture for a different purpose: "the word became flesh and dwelt among us."[12] Through our imaginings and re-imaginings of a multiracial imagined community, we also create members of a new generation who are the embodiment of this collective imagining.

This is not a merely utopian project: this "new culture" may be an interracial co-creation, but it emerges typically through a sort of "antagonistic cooperation," in Ellison's words. Whether one chooses to focus more on the *cooperation* or the *antagonism* in this process, the fact remains that interracial culture (the "mulatto mainstream") is usually produced by individuals who are enmeshed in long-standing interracial networks. These interactions cannot be reduced to a temporary "Jungle Fever," in street coin. To do so is itself an exhibition of historical amnesia. Yet this tendency to pathologize or "scapegoat interracial dynamics that challenge the color line" has been as pervasive in the scholarly world (at least in North America) as it has in popular culture, as George Hutchinson makes abundantly clear.[13]

In interpreting the systems of representations produced by interracial relations, we cannot ignore the power imbalances that have so often been characteristic of race relations. But neither can we accurately portray the authors of these representations as if they lived solely within a self-contained racial group whose borders were well marked and seldom crossed. *Racial formations* have had a major structuring role in cultural production and political discourse, to be sure. They are psychological and institutional realities. But much as we have replicated racial formations, so have we engendered *multiracial formations*. They take shape in multi-centered public spheres which cannot always be mapped along color lines.[14]

The time has come to remove our binary racial blinders, and give multiracial formations their due. As Paul Gilroy insists, these multiracial structures give us multiracial "claims to ownership" which we dismiss at our own loss.[15] Multiracial institutions and representations are our co-creations, whether we want to lay claim or assign blame. Speaking in procreative terms, we share the responsibility to recognize and raise our offspring, rather than merely assigning blame for how they came into being.

I write from within an era and a geographical space in which changing demographics has radically shifted the nature of this debate. "Non-whites" are now a majority in California, and students of European descent are not even the biggest minority at the University of California. Such demographic shifts preview a cultural diversification happening, on a smaller scale, in the rest of the US, and in European countries such as England, France, Germany, the Netherlands, and Italy. But whereas tensions in Europe have centered on the exclusion, or assimilation, of nonwhites, among younger Californians, the tension has often centered on whether or not to "allow" whites to participate in multiethnic coalitions.[16] This tension derives from a racial mythology, widely taught with institutional support, in which whites are portrayed as collective op-pressors, and "people of color" as collective victims. (Although this can be read as tongue-in-cheek, it is barely a parody of the level at which this mythology is often regurgitated by students. My first chapter sketches the far more complex history of racial ambiguity in the United States.)

One result of this racial mythology has been an obsessive (and rather fashionable) oppositionality to all things "white" or European.[17] In this climate, Angela Davis gave the keynote address to a 1993 conference at the University of California-San Diego titled "Building Coalitions among Students of Color." Ms. Davis, Bob Marley's avowed model of black womanhood, was an icon of the 1960s Black Power movement, and is a widely respected scholar on the Cultural Studies "holy trinity" of race, class, and gender. She used these credentials to engage in a critique of the antiwhite rhetoric which had preceded her. A functional multicultural coalition, advised Davis, should be one *"in which white people are neither centered nor excluded."*[18]

That struck me as wise advice, both for coalition-building, and for cultural criticism. In California, as in the larger world, demographic shifts and multiple networks of economic and cultural exchange are leveling out the long period of European dominance. Some people, terrified of that change, try to protect a privileged position for European people and culture. Others seem terrified of a world without a European/white "other" against which to define themselves. Yet a decentered, multiethnic politics and cultural practice cannot afford to center on any one group. Binary models no longer suffice. To seek "pure opposition" is to center what one opposes. There are two forms of subservience, David Hackett Fischer once wrote: "slavish imitation and obsessive refutation." Either extreme is a form of "mental slavery," in Marley's words.[19]

I have repeated Davis' words often to my own students, in an effort to find common ground. Conventional wisdom has it that our educational texts are still relentlessly Eurocentric, an opinion these students voice reflexively. And yet almost all of them have emerged (in California, mind you) from a "reaction cycle" in higher education which has inverted previous racial mythologies. These students have absorbed a worldview in which a binary opposition between an oppressive white center, and marginalized "people of color" who occupy heroic "sites of opposition," is so complete that historical interracial relations short of rape and genocide are unimaginable.[20]

One realizes the political and educational futility of moving directly from critiquing racialism to advocating "postracialism." Racial categories are still used as a tool to safeguard against discriminatory patterns in areas such as public housing, for instance. As a scholar, one is faced with the belief that "the people who invented the hierarchy of 'race' when it was convenient for them ought not to be the ones to explain it away, now that it does not suit their purposes for it to exist," as Toni Morrison has said.[21] And as an educator, one must take seriously the *psychological realities* of students who are often deeply invested in "racial" definitions of personal and collective identity.

Something rarely tabled in United States discussion of "race" is the issue of scale. Almost 300 million people from around the globe now live within its borders. Now, where is the center to that collective? Ah yes, the center will not hold. 300 million people is not a nation but an empire. An "imperial democracy," as Octavio Paz put it. So, why should we not cling to the tribe of our birth, and hold the corner of our invention? An upsurge in voluntary segregation (or ethnic self-affirmation) is probably an inevitable consequence when national identities are writ on such a large scale. "Racial" identity can be an attractive alternative when national identity is too grand to grasp, or has been written off as "the white man's country" to begin with.[22]

So while I endorse Mandela's ideal of a *nonracial democracy* as a horizon worth aiming for, I do not promise a "postraciality" in this work. I opt for starting-point-definitions which are more politically achievable. My focus is upon forms of communication addressed to multiracial audiences, which arise on racial frontiers – spaces which cannot be *owned* by any one group, and whose fluid boundaries point to the socially constructed nature of racial categories. By studying communicative acts that take place within interracial or multiethnic contexts, we should be able to glimpse the possibility of a transracial, if not a postracial, style of communication, leading to the creation of "new cultures" which cannot always be defined in racial language. In narrowest terms, I would define my area of emphasis – a proposed domain of shared interest – as: *the development of multiple allegiances in multiracial public spheres in which no one group is either centered or excluded.* Such an "ideal speech community" may be presently unattainable, but it is an orienting horizon, I agree with public sphere theorists, which must be continually redefined and reaffirmed.[23] Douglass, Ellison, and Marley are flawed but still inspiring attempts to enact such a "multicentric" approach.

Such transitional concepts are the most we can hope for, for now, I think, if we are serious about finding common ground in the challenge of creating "systems of survival." However, I clearly see Douglass, Ellison, and Marley as figures who provide important lessons in our ongoing struggle to build a "true democracy" – more inclusive and more tolerant varieties of political, cultural, and religious practice. And I try to forward their example by troubling racialized language and thinking wherever possible.[24]

Each case study in this book is a "story" and a self-contained scholarly inquiry in its own right. Yet read together, with the historical context of chapter 1, these case studies should give a clear sense of the common historical and cultural currents which fed Douglass, Ellison, and Marley, and which they in turn helped recreate for multiracial audiences. I try to situate each figure as a part of specific historical moments. Yet I also view them through a "historical rear-view mirror," as it were. Because each of these figures continues to influence contemporary culture, they must be understood as something more than mere historical monuments. Douglass, Ellison, and Marley are a living part of the popular imagination of our time. My approach to them is influenced by the diverse ways in which people continue to engage in dialogue with them: to define themselves with, and against, their legacies.

For instance, my understanding of Douglass is altered by the fact that people from rappers like KRS-One to Supreme Court Justice Clarence Thomas to political theorists such as Michael Lind still cite Douglass for contradictory political purposes. Our understanding of Ellison's writing continues to be broadened by the work of scholars such as Shelly Fishkin and George Hutchinson, who map in great detail the interracial networks out of which much of our best literature has emerged. And my perspective on Marley continues to be reshaped by hearing scores of artists from many genres who "cover" (reinterpret) Marley's songs each new year.[25]

A subject like *interracial culture* is part of an intensely contested domain, and I would be less than honest if I did not offer an appraisal of how my own "positionality" shapes my approach. My interest in multiracial audiences grows out of "participant observation" in this realm over many years: as a journalist, songwriter, and publicist always working in multicultural contexts. My understanding that cultural critique must be accompanied by self-critique arose, in part, because during the 1980s, I was a journalist writing about primarily "black" and Latino art forms, and readers questioned what right I had to criticize "their" culture. That made me question why I felt "their" culture was also "our" culture; and yes, sometimes even a co-creation.

Similarly, my understanding of "black" cultural forms as an essentially multiracial phenomenon was deeply influenced by the experience of being a songwriter during the 1980s for a band in Austin, Texas, that played "black" styles of music (funk, reggae, and blues), and yet both the band itself and our audience were thoroughly multiethnic, and multinational, in composition.[26]

When I claim Douglass, Ellison, and Marley as "integrative ancestors," this too is rooted in personal experience as well as scholarship. Being the father of two biracial children, I have a vested interest in exposing them to a history and a cultural heritage that their mother and father both share. Furthermore, I only speak and read Spanish with my children, so they are growing up laying claim not only to Europe and

Africa as ancestral homelands, but to *mestizaje* – the hybrid mixture of European, African, and indigenous peoples and cultures in Ibero-America.[27] So when my daughter Sela greets the life-size portraits of Douglass and Marley above my desk, she calls them "abuelo Frederick" and "tio Bob." They are a part of her cultural heritage, and her psychological structure.

We have "familial relations," in a cultural sense, with a multiethnic community. My family is part of the world that Douglass, Ellison, and Marley imagined. We are descended from the same families they married into or were born into. The communities their children grew up in now help educate my own children. As I write, the children of parents who come from different cultural backgrounds are truly becoming the new cultural mainstream.[28] Census figures tell us that over 3 million people in the United States alone are partners in an interracial marriage. The children of such "mixed" couples certainly number in the tens of millions, and depending on how one wants to define "biracial" or "multiethnic," could easily be a majority (especially if we factor in Latinos, the true majority in the Americas, and soon to be the largest US "minority"). "Mestizo" or mixed-race people have long been a majority in countries such as Mexico and Brazil. And now biracial children are a rapidly growing demographic group in former colonial powers such as France and Great Britain.

Therefore, when I refer to Douglass, Ellison, and Marley as "integrative ancestors," and call on them as spokespersons for a transracial "new culture," my perspective is personal, but cannot be *merely* personal. At a few points during the course of this book, I pause to comment briefly on how my "positionality" ("relationship to field of study") affects my approach to the subject at hand. This strategy rings alarms for some academic scholars. I share a distaste for what is often an excessive use of personal voice in cultural studies. Yet what has been called the "self-reflexive turn" in ethnography is a justifiable strategy, I think, for scholars studying and participating in intersubjective realms. To be "self-reflective" is to acknowledge that one's own ethnicity, gender, language, age, etc., will have an impact on the object being studied. Self-reflexive ethnographers deny that a completely objective position of observation is possible. The act of observation, they assert, is in fact a form of participation which changes the nature of what is being studied in fundamental ways. Therefore, it is better to try to be conscious of one's "positionality," to the greatest degree possible, and to understand the ways that this both imposes humbling limitations, and provides challenging insights.[29]

Since this study grows out of a lived experience, as well as scholarly research, I think it is important to acknowledge that there are sources of knowledge (and legitimacy) outside of academic channels. To some degree a cultural domain only becomes apparent to those who live in it. Those of us who document our encounters with the world in one form or another are often "unconscious ethnographers," writing ethnography without knowing it.[30] I certainly see this as being the case in my career as a journalist, in which I wrote about popular culture and racial politics for a decade before entering graduate school. Although I wear the hat of a scholar here, I still draw on worldviews developed through careers as a journalist and songwriter.

No doubt to this experience goes the credit or blame for my various uses and abuses of academic "language games." Efforts to find a mode of expression engaging all of these speech communities usually satisfy none. Yet this too, I believe, is an effort worth making. "In order for criticism to be responsible, it must always be addressed to someone who can contest it," wrote Talal Asad. So every now and then it helps to break things down to basics. "Tell the children the truth," Bob Marley sang over and over, and that has always seemed like something worth bearing in mind.[31]

Many of the cultures from which I have drawn inspiration prior to, and during, my academic training are hostile to academic discourse. Marley once said: "I don't have education, I have inspiration – if I had [only] education I would be a damn fool." A part of me still feels that way. Having roots in popular culture, I know that academic language is "impenetrable" for most of the public which I believe I should try to reach. In reframing this book, I have tried to balance education and inspiration. I hope that the nonacademic cultures which have nourished me, and the scholarship which has inspired me, will both be in evidence.

One could call this project a form of "American Studies," if this term is understood as referring to a more inclusive "*nuestra América*," as José Martí envisioned the Americas in hemispheric, multilingual form.[32] A part of this book is in fact an effort to rethink "race" in American culture: to illustrate "the emergence of 'race' out of the denial of . . . 'interracial' and 'biracial' realms," as Werner Sollors has written. Yet I agree with Sollors that the explosion of scholarly and popular interest in biracial identity and interracial culture "may mark a turning point in the racial symbolism of the United States, which may be moving in the direction of the Latin American models at this moment."[33]

A North American frame cannot fully contain this map. With two of my three case studies, their stays in Europe restructured their cultural, psychological, and political development. It would be impossible to understand Douglass without grasping how his sojourns in Ireland and England reshaped his thinking. Great Britain was Douglass' "postracial" horizon. Similarly, one cannot understand how Marley constructed a contemporary "Exodus" myth without seeing how it emerged during "exile" in London. His collaboration with British punk-rockers was essential to his strategies for speaking to a multiracial audience, and led to fusions which still inform much of contemporary popular music (ska, jungle, Brazilian samba-reggae, etc.).

Let me come at this America/not-America dilemma from another angle. Ralph Ellison often advised white youth that instead of talking about "black men in a white society, they should ask themselves how black *they* are." Similarly, Robert Farris Thompson insisted: "If you don't know how black you are, you don't know how American you are." C. Vann Woodward remarked that "as far as their culture is concerned, all Americans are part Negro." And John Edward Philips has argued that a systematic study of African retentions reveals that "as much African culture survives now among whites as among blacks in the U.S." These comments were made in an era in which we (North Americans) thought in black and white. But now we are forced to make the transition from black and white to living color. All ethnicities in America should learn the extent to which they are, culturally, "black." Yet "black" and "white" and all shades of brown have always, in the New World, been constructed out of the interracial. To say that one cannot be American without being black is also to say that one cannot live in the Americas without being multiracial, or mestizo. This line of thinking has much broader implications. As Simon Frith points out, "America" is now more of a cultural myth than a geographic entity, since "its very cultural forms are now everywhere available." If you participate in, or consume, cultures from the *Americas* – including the Caribbean and Latin America – then you are also part of a cultural heritage that, from its deepest roots to its contemporary fruits, is fundamentally interracial, multiethnic, mestizo: a fusion of African, European, and Native American cultural traditions. Which is why I think, on some frequencies, Douglass, Ellison, and Marley speak to "all of we."[34]

1 Interraciality in historical context: return of the repressed

Among the obvious reasons for the Revolution's failure to cope with slavery were *an inability to imagine a genuinely multiracial society*, and an over-scrupulous regard for private property. (Staughton Lynd 1967: 180)

Nations reel and stagger on their way; they make hideous mistakes; they commit frightful wrongs; they do great and beautiful things. And shall we not best guide humanity by telling the truth about all this, so far as the truth is ascertainable? (Du Bois, *Black Reconstruction*, 714)

Can a country be born in a day
or a nation be brought forth in a moment? (Isaiah 66:8)

The genealogy of racial frontiers

The three principal subjects of this book were public figures – political, artistic, and religious – who lived within interracial domains, and who consistently addressed themselves to multiracial and multinational audiences. To think in a nonreductive way about the kinds of language they used, and the ways that their interaction with a multiracial public reshaped their identities (or at least their personas), requires us to find a way to imagine a social arena outside the racial hall of mirrors. I call this arena a racial frontier.

The concept of a "frontier" carries a problematic history, much of it rooted in how Frederick Jackson Turner used the term. Writing about the closing of the "old frontier" in 1893, he tried to foreclose the significance of slavery. "When American history comes to be rightly viewed, it will be seen that the slavery question is an incident," he argued. In constructing his myth of the American (South)West, Turner presented a narrative of "progress" in which the resistance of indigenous peoples was seen primarily as an obstacle to European settlers. Some post-1960s historians have reacted by coining new terms for the history of the West, such as the "rendezvous model." Others have argued that the frontier is a valid concept only in situations of domination. John Cell believes that the frontier ceases to exist after one group establishes political control over another. Lamar and Thompson speak of a termination of struggle for control of a frontier contact zone, after which "the frontier ceases to exist."[1]

It is right to note that the "frontier" was a home to many peoples long before Europeans arrived. However, the insistence that a frontier can exist only under conditions of domination seems to be a reaction to the chauvinism of earlier, Eurocentric concepts of the frontier. A frontier could just as easily exist under conditions of partial control, where the struggle for domination continues indefinitely, or even as a state of equilibrium between neighboring states or tribes. This sense of ongoing struggle for, and resistance to, domination, evolving into an uneasy equilibrium, informs Quintard Taylor's history of Afro-Americans in the West, *In Search of the Racial Frontier* (1998).

"The notion of race has played a role in the way Americans think about their history similar to that once played by the frontier," Barbara Fields has observed, and is, "if anything, more durable." By combining these terms, and designating the frontier as *racial*, I mean to convey several things. I am reaffirming the centrality of slavery in the Americas – not only its continuing sociopolitical relevance, but its connection with our very notions of freedom. In a broad sense, I mean the term *racial frontier* to evoke an arena of interracial interaction and contestation, both within geographic and nongeographic domains. The racial frontier may have begun within specific historical and geographical circumstances – i.e., person-to-person contact on a plantation, or between slave and nonslave states. But it has increasingly manifested itself through texts which circulate among multiracial audiences in multinational contexts, and more recently as symbolic interaction within electronically mediated domains. Thus, Frederick Douglass' and Ralph Ellison's writings about the racial frontier have been distributed and consumed primarily within what Paul Gilroy calls the *Black Atlantic*. (This domain in fact maps a modernity defined in multiracial, multi-national terms. It centers on the contributions of the African diaspora, from slavery to twenty-first-century popular music.) And Bob Marley's music, most immediately about black liberation, has been reframed by the singer and his corporate producers and delivered to a global, multiethnic audience, which in turn "reads" these texts in ways often far removed from their original "racial" context.[2]

Residents of racial frontiers participate in a culture which has been transmitted across generations. As Bob Marley's songs testify, the culture of this domain can speak in multiple voices, which can be read by different portions of its audience in racial, multiracial, and postracial fashion. So, by "racial frontiers" I mean to convey a sense in which its residents often live in a liminal zone between racial, and postracial, definitions of identity and community. "Frontier" carries a sense of the unknown, the unsettled, the partially unexplored. When we approach a frontier, we do not always know what lies "beyond the boundary." Thus, while I am often obliged to use "racial" language in describing racial frontiers, I hope that readers will come to share a sense that, as Charles Chesnutt wrote a century ago, the residents of this contested space are often a "new people" with a "new culture." This people and their culture sometimes transcend the descriptive power of racial language, even if they cannot escape the structuring power of racial history.[3]

Racial frontiers is similar to the concept of *borderlands*, which has been applied to the Anglo-Latino frontier by writers such as Gloria Anzaldúa, Renato Rosaldo, and José David Saldívar, performing artists like Guillermo Gomez-Peña, and by novelists such as Carlos Fuentes. Anzaldúa defines borderlands as an area of cross-pollination "where people of different races occupy the same territory." She and Saldivar locate borderlands in geographical space – not only national borders but a hemispheric "nuestra America." But borderland writers also recognize that this domain is a "psychological borderland," which Anzaldúa believes has the potential to "uproot . . . dualistic thinking in the individual and collective consciousness." My use of racial frontiers, inflected by this view of borderlands, also parallels Mary Pratt's concept of a "contact zone." I endorse Pratt's call for a "linguistics of contact" focused on "the operation of language across lines of social differentiation." Yet I want to distinguish my approach from that of Pratt and other postcolonial theorists, with its emphasis on "contact between dominant and dominated groups." While Pratt wants to define this "zone of contact" as "processes of appropriation, penetration or co-optation of one group's language by another," I aspire to a more interactive model. The model I have in mind is closer to Robert Park's accent on "an *interpenetration* of peoples and a fusion of cultures."[4]

Park and his students such as Everett Hughes and E. Franklin Frazier have most explicitly articulated the concept of "racial frontiers." This theory, which I apply to the history of interracial communication, must itself be seen as an interracial co-creation. It was also voiced, in similar ways, by many social scientists and cultural critics of the early twentieth century, as varied as Max Weber, Franz Boas, and Alain Locke.[5]

Park, a "founding father" of American sociology, felt that prejudice and racial identity were not unchanging, but could be transformed through migration, intermarriage, and other processes. Park popularized the notion of the "Marginal Man" who existed between two racial groups, a "cultural hybrid" which he thought signified "the end of one epoch in human and racial relations and ... the beginning of another."[6]

Park's student Everett Hughes pursued the idea of expanding margins between races in *Where Peoples Meet: Racial and Ethnic Frontiers*. Hughes believed that "the true unit of race and ethnic relations is not the single ethnic group, but the *situation*, embracing all of the diverse groups who live in the community or region." He called these domains "racial or cultural frontiers."[7]

E. Franklin Frazier engaged in a global survey of the sorts of "multi-racial communities" which had emerged on racial frontiers under, or in spite of, European imperialism. He also applied Park's theory of the "Marginal Man" to anticolonial movements, observing that, particularly in Africa, "the cultural hybrid has become the leader in the nationalist movement."[8]

This context-specific view of "racial or cultural frontiers" as being the most appropriate unit of analysis for "race or ethnic relations" has largely been the path not taken in social science and the humanities. Michael Banton, in *Racial Theories*, noted that "sociologists were slow to follow Hughes's lead. The 'race problem' was perceived [only] as a problem of conflict." Herbert Blumer observed in 1958 that most research on race relations was fixated on a "prejudice-discrimination axis."[9]

Forty years later, Blumer's assessment seems more true than ever. US writers on race, in particular, often get caught up in "a game of competitive disillusionment, and are quick to accuse each other of being too optimistic," as David Hollinger notes. For instance, in *Blackface, White Noise* Michael Rogin derides Eric Lott, a scholar of nineteenth-century blackface, for being "anxious ... to find points of identification across racial lines."[10]

The sheer terror which many American intellectuals exhibit toward the prospect of being called optimistic or utopian about race relations is a psychosocial phenomenon that is "ripe for the picking." This discourse seems to be driven by a belief in white racism as a sort of biological inheritance. Those who declare for the "permanence" of (white) racism and the impermeability of the Racial Divide acquire an instant legitimation: they assume that they have, and are widely assumed to have, the weight of history on their side. People who consider themselves progressive (or radical) wind up in a reactionary position quite similar to white supremacist thought: resistance to, repression of, and pathologizing of "interracial life" – the denial of the very possibility of an interraciality which residents on racial frontiers have adopted by choice.[11]

Not surprisingly, "racially hybrid" individuals and culture are very threatening to the binary racial status quo. They are "as upsetting to a right-wing segregationists's as ... to a left-wing relativist's need for contained cultures," as Werner Sollors writes. The only appropriate response to binary racial myopia, whether from the "left" or the "right," is to do what Sollors and his peers have done: lay out the pervasiveness of this repressed or denied interracial life, and the culture and consciousness it has spawned, in all its encyclopedic detail.[12]

• • •

The growth of "social constructionist" scholarship on race was an interracial enterprise, linked (in opposition) to a "high stage" of white supremacist thought and practice (1890–1920).[13] The racial hysteria (and national amnesia) of this era had an enduring impact on artistic discourse, political activism, and scholarly research that would echo throughout the twentieth century. For instance, the National Association for the Advancement of Colored People (NAACP) was founded, most directly, as a response to 1908 race riots in Springfield, Illinois (among other factors). Some writers who came of age in this era, such as W. E. B. Du Bois, became convinced that its racism represented an inevitable norm for "white America." Others researched the roots of this racism and determined that racial attitudes had passed through numerous, rather fluid stages. Social and cultural critics such as Alain Locke, Franz Boas, and later C. Vann Woodward detailed the ways in which racism changed over time in response to demographic, economic, and political forces. This historicism had consequences for those who sought to "imagine a genuinely multiracial society." If racism was "diseased imagination," as Douglass once commented, then the disease had its causes, its mediums of contagion, its periods of epidemic and relative remission. If it could not be "cured," it could be kept in check by providing the imagination with more compelling alternatives.[14]

The revolution in scholarly treatment of race (replacing nineteenth-century so-called "scientific racism") has been a long process. As the "bloody field" of Reconstruction historiography makes clear, old racial mythologies have died hard. Historians prone to "overzealousness in revising earlier misconceptions," as Ann Malone writes, have created reactive counter-myths. The "new boss" is often about the same as the old boss, and it is hard to claim that we have yet arrived at a synthesis. Yet since the 1960s mainstream scholarship has paid great attention to slavery, to the central roles of African and indigenous peoples in creating "new cultures" in the Americas, and to the dominance of the African diaspora in the making of "modernity." One can safely say that the institutionalization of this new paradigm had *begun* by 1920. It was after this date that educators such as Park and Boas and their students gathered momentum in pushing a "social constructionist" perspective, both in academia and within popular culture.[15]   But this paradigm shift began earlier. Max Weber, following a line of thought dating back to Vico and Herder, argued that there were *"no immutable ethnic frontiers."* Weber emphasized the fluidity of ethnic boundaries, the "diverse origins" and the "gradual transitions" of cultural customs. He concluded that "the concept of [a self-contained] 'ethnic' group . . . is unsuitable for a really rigorous analysis."[16]

A common benchmark for scholars involved in this paradigm shift was Franz Boas' 1911 speech at the Universal Race Congress in London, "The Instability of Race Types," and Boas' book *The Mind of Primitive Man* (1911), which "revolutionized theories of race and culture," as Jeffrey Stewart comments. Boas rejected the notion that "races" could be ranked on a scale. He argued for the mental plasticity of immigrants from areas then considered inferior, and stressed the importance of studying cultural interaction and diffusion.[17]

Several influential works by Anglo-Americans and Jews in this era also emerged through exposure to interethnic "contact zones." Most early twentieth-century scholars who tried to adjust to diversity used an Aryan-Jewish binary as the principal marker of difference. For instance, both Freud and Jung constructed their psychologies around a Jewish/Aryan "racial divide." For American writers, the main location of the Racial Divide was in transition – from the European-Indian division of the Western frontier, to a concern with Anglo-Jewish difference, occasioned by massive immigration from East Europe, to a preoccupation with a black–white binary, which had become predominant by the Harlem Renaissance. Those who theorized diversity saw Afro-Americans as everything from an unblendable "other," to model Americans. Israel Zangwill, who wrote the 1908 play *The Melting Pot*, was "a universalist-feminist Jew who believed passionately in miscegenation," as Todd Gitlin notes. But Zangwill later felt compelled to clarify, under pressure from white supremacists, that his model of miscegenation did not include Negroes. Horace Kallen's theory of "cultural pluralism" was inspired by his talks with Afro-American scholar Alain Locke. Randolph Bourne, who wrote the famous essay "Trans-National America" in 1916, cited Boas as an antiracist model, and endorsed an emerging Negro Theatre as an alternative to an imperialistic Anglocentrism. Both Kallen and Bourne wrote in opposition to Zangwill's model of immigrants being poured into a preexisting Anglo-Protestant mold. Kallen's pluralism envisioned transplanted groups acting like separate instruments in a symphony or-chestra. As David Hollinger notes, this is the "mosaic" model of 1990s multiculturalism, with a tendency towards essentialized (although cooperative) racial groupings. In Bourne's "cosmopolitan" model, citizens were capable of maintaining multiple allegiances. Ethno-racial affiliations were partly voluntary, potentially multicentered, and not over-determined.[18]

In this scholarship, one can see four stages of efforts to envision diversity. In Zangwill's meltdown model, Afro-Americans were not quite ready for prime time. In a second stage, Kallen expressed commitment to an inclusive pluralism. But in order for Kallen's unhyphenated ethno-racial orchestra to stay in tune, hybridity had to be stamped out. The "race-self" had to be pure. In his view, "an Irishman is always an Irishman, a Jew always a Jew." By contrast, Bourne's "Trans-America" allowed for "hyphenated diversity." He saw dual citizens (Jewish-American; Afro-American) as an antidote to provincialism, and even as a potential "salvation." But Bourne was no more accepting of "racial hybridity" than Kallen. Bourne was in fact hostile to "Marginal Men," viewing them, in Biblical terms, like salt which had lost its savor. In this context, emerging theories of a "racial frontier" represented an advance. This model not only allowed for hyphenated "dual citizens," but presented mixed-race "marginal men" as harbingers of a "new era" of race relations.[19]

If we look at these four models from the vantage of the end of the century (Du Bois' "problem of the color-line" century), then it would seem that we have not progressed far beyond the first two stages. Most arguments in the United States, at least, are stuck at the Zangwill vs. Kallen stage. We hear competing demands, each provincial in its own way. Nationalists demand that we be "just American" (an affirmation of the melting pot), while multiculturalists assert that primary allegiance should be to one's ethno-racial block, usually defined in essentialist terms. A minority of multiculturalists envision diversity in terms closer to Bourne, in which "hyphenated" identity and patriotism coexist. But the racial frontier model, in which racial hybridity is normative, since "colors run into each other," seems only to have entered the margins of public sphere debate in the late 1990s.[20]

• • •

It should be clear that there are no pure or "correct" ideological origins to help us "know what diversity means." All of our efforts to deal with difference are fated to use language, and human antecedents, which are ambiguous, or troubling to our contemporary perspective. Such is the case in the circumstances and manner in which Robert Park began to articulate a theory of racial frontiers. Park probably had more interracial experience than any other Euro-American scholar of his generation. Park got his philosophical moorings primarily from John Dewey and William James. But his biggest influences, prior to his late career as a sociologist, were his journalism during the 1890s, and his work from 1905 to 1912 as a ghostwriter for Booker T. Washington. While doing research for Washington, Park had extensive contacts with black Southerners. Park certainly had Washington in mind when he began writing about racial frontiers and the "Marginal Man" (although his articulation of these ideas became more nuanced after he traveled and taught in Asia, and developed ties to Northern black intellectuals and artists).[21]

I cannot fully discuss here what Louis Harlan has called Washington's "ambiguous legacy." But in a book about racial frontiers which uses Douglass, Ellison, and Marley as case studies, we must briefly consider the Park–Washington relationship, for two main reasons: Washington's claims to be the successor of Frederick Douglass, and Ralph Ellison's own comments about the "ambiguous legacy" of both Park and Washington.[22]

James Olney has compared the relationship between Washington's *Up From Slavery* (1901) and Douglass' first two autobiographies, to the relationship between the Constitution and the Declaration of Independence. Douglass' autobiographies and the Declaration were revolutionary assertions of equal rights. "Slaveholders' claims have no legitimacy in Douglass' *Narrative*, just as the English king's claims have no legitimacy in the Declaration; but Washington clearly could not proceed in this revolutionary mode in his time and his place and given his temperament and intentions," Olney writes. But to point out that Washington's autobiography marked a compromise with white supremacists, as the Constitution compromised with slaveholders, is not to say that either text was without its tools or strategies of resistance. Douglass argued that the Constitution, properly interpreted, was an antislavery document. And nationalists from around the globe found in Washington's story inspiration for their own resistance to imperialism. Even Marcus Garvey credited *Up From Slavery* with inspiring his black nationalist crusade.[23]

Just as Douglass "rewrote" the founding fathers to position abolitionists as the *truer* American revolutionaries, Washington revised Douglass to legitimate his own claim to black leadership. He actually published a biography of Douglass under his name in 1907. W. E. B. Du Bois had originally been assigned the honor of writing this Douglass biography. But Washington apparently had rights of first refusal, and claimed the biography for himself. This "exceedingly bland" biography served two purposes – it cast Douglass in the image of "the Wizard of Tuskegee," and it kept Washington's main rival, Du Bois, from using this project to present himself as the "heir apparent" to Douglass. Washington published a second memoir in 1911, *My Larger Education*, in which he tried to reinforce public perception of himself as "the Douglass of his day and the Moses of his people."[24]

Washington's biographer Louis Harlan notes that Robert Park, the future sociologist of racial frontiers, "researched, drafted, or revised most of Washington's writings for publication between 1905 and 1912." This included putting the "final polish" on the Douglass book (which other writers had drafted), and shepherding *My Larger Education*. He also wrote many of Washington's letters, and revised his communiques to President Roosevelt. Through this partnership, "Washington came to treat Park as an equal, something he rarely did," remarks Harlan. Park, who had spontaneously gone to work at Tuskegee because he was "disgusted" with academic life, in his turn felt that "I probably learned more about human nature and society, in the South under Booker Washington, than I had learned elsewhere in all my previous studies."[25]

Such was the reputation that Park acquired through his work for Washington that Ralph Ellison, writing as a young man in 1944, called Park "the man responsible for inflating Tuskegee into a national symbol, and who is sometimes spoken of as the 'power behind Washington's throne'." This hyperbole need not be taken seriously, but it does reflect a historical ambivalence among progressive intellectuals towards the legacies of both Park and Washington. Ellison's comments appear in a rather scathing review of Myrdal's *An American Dilemma*, the most famous book on race relations ever to appear in the United States. His specific point concerned the fact that most of the black sociologists who worked with Myrdal were in fact trained by Park. Ellison seems to feel that some of the preconceptions about race to which he objects in Myrdal's study have their origins in Park's partnership with Washington. Yet at the same time he acknowledges that "American Negroes have benefited greatly" from the research done by Park and his students. Ellison's feelings about Washington were similarly divided. He was critical of Washington's accommodation to Jim Crow laws, and yet he was sympathetic to his emphasis on self-reliance. Ellison had received what he saw as a first-rate musical education at Washington's Tuskegee Institute from 1933 to 1936. Many of his experiences there would be immortalized in *Invisible Man*. Late in life Ellison would muse on the irony that "two reasonably literate writers," he and Albert Murray, had emerged from Booker Washington's supposedly vocational school.[26]

• • •

There are three core ideas in Park's writings with which I want to express general agreement, before noting some limitations for my own study of racial frontiers:

(1) *there is no biological transmission of racial characteristics*;
(2) *racial hybridity is a norm, rather than an aberration*;[27]
(3) *contact on racial frontiers as an appropriate area of study.*

What Park meant by areas of cultural or racial contact, and what contemporary theorists mean by "contact zones," are quite different. Park is more interested in the consequences of cultural fusions than in the assignation of blame for "forced diffusion," or in quixotic quests to recover, preserve, or recreate a "pure" ethnic culture. He pays significant attention to "cultural conflict," and is far from blind to the role that European imperialism has played.[28] But Park does not discuss slavery, or slave revolts, in his writing on interracial conflict. He has little to say about "the relations of power between black and white." In fact, Michael Banton points out, "his writing, like that of most of his contemporaries, neglects this dimension in a fashion that must astonish a later generation." However, Banton credits Park with asking, in later years, "why anyone should expect racial peace before there was racial justice." And it is "of particular importance that he moved the emphasis in the expression 'race relations' from the first word to the second." "Any assessment of Park's contribution to race relations studies," Banton believes, "must give a high place to his leadership in formulating an alternative to prevailing conceptions of race relations as biological relations." Brace, Meier, and Rudwick surmise that "no other person could have facilitated the transition of mainstream sociology's stance from racism to an attempt at objectivity in racial studies as easily as Robert E. Park." Park's later essays are often quite farsighted. He concluded "The Nature of Race Relations," published in 1939, by predicting that "race conflicts in the modern world ... will be more and more in the future confused with, and eventually superseded by, the conflicts of classes." This is a position that anticipates the work of contemporary Afro-American and Afro-Caribbean sociologists such as W. J. Wilson and Orlando Patterson.[29]

There are two strains of Park's theory of racial and cultural contact from which I must dissent, to distinguish it from my own approach to racial frontiers. Park outlined a four-stage "race relations cycle": "contacts, competition, accommodation, and eventual assimilation." Movement through these stages was "apparently progressive and irreversible," he thought. Few social scientists would agree now with assimilation as the inevitable outcome of intercultural contact. They have criticized a tendency in the Anglo-American tradition to assume assimilation into Eurocentric, patriarchal norms.[30] Park does often assume Anglo models into which American immigrants would assimilate, although those norms are at least strongly inflected by a black presence. This is not dissimilar from Du Bois' cultural Eurocentrism.[31]

The "accommodation" arrived at in race relations cycles may in fact be a more or less permanent form of resistance or opposition. This must be qualified by noting that "pure opposition" is a material and rhetorical impossibility in "intensely miscegenated," electronically mediated societies. This point is still too seldom understood in the "oppositional utopias" of cultural studies.[32]

I have cited a term Ellison uses, "antagonistic cooperation," as a useful way of thinking about how opposition and mediation often coexist in race and culture contacts, and I will return to it often during the course of my study. The concept probably derives from an article by George Devereux and Edwin Loeb titled "Antagonistic Acculturation." Devereux and Loeb provide a typology of resistance to cultural borrowing and lending. They employ a broad range of examples that range from Biblical history to relations between neighboring Malaysian tribal groups.[33]

"Resistance," they note, "forms the foundation of the process of antagonistic acculturation." Resistance can be to *borrowing* from or *lending* cultural items to another group. And resistance can be either to borrowing or lending of a *specific cultural item*, or it can be resistance towards an *entire group*. Yet resistance to acculturation is rarely total, since even "overt hostility . . . seems to impose very little bar to cultural borrowing." I am reminded of Weber's comment that "attraction and repulsion" typically coexist in interethnic relations, as when two "mutually despising groups" employ the same chosen people mythology.[34]

The ability to distinguish between resistance to a cultural tradition or artifact, and hostility towards an entire out-group, is evident in the "antagonistic acculturation" employed by Douglass, Ellison, and Marley. Their strategies of resistance seem to indicate at least partial agreement with Molefi Asante's view, that "symbol imperialism, rather than institutional racism," is the main long-term problem facing multiethnic societies. To rebuild institutions which perpetuate racialism, one has to change the symbols which structure the thinking which sustains the institutions. For Douglass, learning to read was an act of resistance, as was physical resistance to the slave-breaker Covey. He endorsed both verbal and physical resistance, but he emphasized opposition to "symbol imperialism": reclaiming liberatory elements in the Bible and the Constitution, which had previously been used to justify racial oppression. For Ellison, learning to write and think in a "nonracial" tradition was an act of resistance to both black and white racialists. Bob Marley saw himself as a "revolutionary – fighting single-handed with music" – and the cornerstone of that music-as-weapon was a restructuring of Biblical symbolism.

Douglass, Ellison, and Marley were all intensely resistant to racism, and the culture of racialism. Yet they also embraced certain political or cultural traditions from Europe, even though many in their own in-group viewed whites as a racial enemy.[35]

Oppositional thinking is a relative thing. Paul Gilroy stresses that the role of diasporic Africans in constructing modernity was so central that "Even our gestures of disaffiliation can unwittingly confirm just how Western and modern we are." He concludes that Du Bois' notion of two "warring racial selves" may itself be a form of mental slavery, to paraphrase via Marley. The implications of this line of thinking are that the concept of "doubleness" is a reaction to a particular stage of interracial contact. Its continuing appeal speaks not only to the enduring power of racial formations to make "other" (marginalize) nonwhites, but also to a personal and collective investment in "doubleness" or marginality as a racial mythology. This mythology acts as a self-fulfilling prophecy, on some levels. While as part of a psychological structure, it may provide validation or even be perceived as liberatory, on a collective and structural level, this racial mythology often prevents those who helped build the structures of modernity from claiming their rightful (co-)ownership.[36]

Which brings me to my second and more serious critique of Park: the exceptionalism, and even racial heirarchies, underlying his writings on the "Marginal Man" and "racial hybrids." Using a concept of marginality that included, but was not limited to, interraciality, Park wrote that people living between two worlds faced worst case/best case scenarios: such individuals "might be ground between their conflicting subcultures, but if quick-witted might be able to thrive by playing off the elements of their complex environment against one another." The Marginal Man is someone who lives in a liminal state, which Park, quoting Simmel's "discursus" on the "Stranger," believes has its advantages: "He is the freer man, practically and theoretically."[37]

This is fine as far as it goes. One finds similar claims about the special talents of those who live on borderlands, for instance in the writing of the Mexican-American poet Gloria Anzaldúa, and in Nigerian novelist Chinua Achebe. Remembering his upbringing on the crossroads between "traditional" Yoruba society and the "modern" cultural forms imposed by British colonizers, Achebe saw such frontiers as sites of both danger and opportunity: "a man might perish there wrestling with multiple-headed spirits, but also he might be lucky and return to his people with the boon of prophetic vision." This is, again, very similar to Du Bois' claim that the American Negro was born with "second sight."[38]

Yet when Park analyzes the "Mentality of Racial Hybrids" as a sub-type of the Marginal Man, he engages in "mulatto elitism." He speaks of "the actual superiority of the mulatto in comparison to the Negro," and makes only fleeting references to the role that "the relative status of each in the existing social order" may play in their success. We find Park claiming that mulattos are "more enterprising than the Negroes, more restless, aggressive, and ambitious" (in expressive behavior, rather than innate capacity). He speculates that this is a result of their "double inheritance, biological and cultural," and of having been "more stimulated" by living between two races in conflict.[39]

I hope to make it clear that my own focus on interraciality does not arise from any belief, or desire to prove, that "racial hybrids" are "superior" in any way, on any scale. Still, I believe that we should try to resist the temptation to project the values of the present on to the past. About Park, Banton notes: "It is important not to pillory an author by picking out passages that convey an untruthful impression." It would be a mistake to claim this element of Park's thought as representing the whole. For the most part, his writings on interraciality represent a relatively enlightened moment in a skewed historical discourse on mixed-race people, whose other extreme is to portray them as *inferior* to both parent cultures. Park wrote during an era in which some leading mulattos, reacting to the ways in which the larger culture on both sides of the Racial Divide pathologized them, claimed to be "composite men" who were "unexcelled in . . . mental endowment," and even the "only true Americans outside the Indians."[40]

I am using this discourse on racial frontiers, and the offspring engendered thereon, as a starting point to meditate on what it means to be the product of a double/multiple inheritance. Ellison, who was not directly the offspring of an interracial relationship, claimed to be the inheritor of a double literary and cultural heritage. He saw this as an advantage which could be claimed in theory by someone of any race. Most people in Park's day tended to equate this "double heritage" more specifically with direct racial hybridity. Thus, in the course of outlining what was a sort of "popular psychology" of mulattos, Park quoted a poem called "The Mulatto to His Critics" by Robert Curlin:

> Ashamed of my race?
> And of what race am I? I am many in one.
> Through my veins there flows the blood
> Of Red Man, Black Man, Briton, Celt, and Scot,
> In Warring clash and tumultuous riot.[41]

This myth of a "warring clash" in the blood of mixed-race individuals was a dominant trope of the literature of the "Tragic Mulatto," as Sollors and others have documented.[42] This literature was written by authors across the racial spectrum for a variety of ideological aims: both to defend and criticize slavery and segregation. It reflects a national obsession about where to draw, or whether to erase, the color line that marked the Racial Divide.

This "warring clash" is also central to Du Bois' writing. Park quoted his famous passage about the "two warring ideals" of an unreconciled "double-consciousness," words clearly informed by Du Bois' own "racial ambiguity."[43] Yet they have come to resonate across an entire century for Afro-Americans. They have also spoken eloquently for Americans of many ethnicities who have shared the sense of being "divided selves," as William James wrote, in words that inspired Du Bois and other writers of his generation.[44]

Americans "of color" have long been symbols of our "unreconciled strivings" – notably, the strivings to bridge the racial divide, which has been the "stumbling stone" which has prevented us from putting our demo- cratic ideals into inclusive practice. And so often, it has been people of mixed race who have expressed that striving most elequently. Why is that?

Consider: it was during the era when stereotypes about blacks and mulattos were most virulent – during the early Jim Crow years – that we also witnessed a peak in treatment of race-mixing in our literature, much of it an effort at rehabilitation. Social science discourse about racial frontiers emerged from the ironies of this national schizophrenia. The 1910 census listed over 2 million mulattos, yet in this year the *American Journal of Sociology* published an article asserting that racial hybrids were "sterile or relatively infertile." This was not just a white construction: "mulatto-baiting" was common among Afro-American spokespersons from the Reconstruction on. It seems to have been particularly intense around 1900–10, with journals such as the *Colored American* voicing the conventional wisdom that mulattos were debilitated hybrids, and troublemakers. Against this climate, Franz Boas began proving from 1909 on that scientists in fact knew nothing about "mulatto fertility." One of Park's students, Edward Reuter, published a study of *The Mulatto in the United States* in 1918. Park began publishing his own essays on racial frontiers and hybridity in the 1920s. And in 1933 Park's student E. Franklin Frazier felt compelled to publish evidence in the *American Journal of Sociology* that mulattos were as "fecund" as any other group. Yet the myth of the infertility, inferiority, or tragic nature of mixed-race people has lived on – in oral tradition, in literature, and in film. It still finds expression in the era in which I write, such as in Spike Lee's film *Jungle Fever*.[45]

Boas, Park, and their associates were the first generation of scholars to look critically at what had long been a national obsession with the off-

spring of life on racial frontiers. Their theories were sometimes, understandably, an overreaction to the racial stereotypes against which they
struggled. But we now have the benefit of a rich body of scholarship which
has reconstructed the histories of interracial communication, of miscegenation, of co-created religious traditions, and of representations of
interracial life in our literature and political discourse. It is now clear that
what Park and his students were witnessing, and struggling to come to
terms with, was a recurrent phenomenon in American history: the return
of a repressed interracial culture.

The repression of our biracial offspring

A belief in "the degeneration and eventual extinction of mixed-race
people," Eric Sundquist writes, enjoyed "overwhelming acceptance" in
the late nineteenth and early twentieth centuries, both in the social
sciences and in folk culture. This pathologizing of mixed-race (or biracial) people flourished in spite of pervasive evidence that they were not
only surviving, they were "replenishing the earth" at such a rapid pace
that the color line was becoming an unsustainable fiction.[46]

The United States Census tried to enumerate people of mixed race,
generically classed as mulattos, from 1850 to 1920. These numbers were
low, as they relied on visual ability to distinguish between black and
mixed-race Americans. Officially, mulattos grew from about 400,000 in
1850 to over 2 million in 1910, as we have seen, then dropped off to 1.6
million in 1920. Joel Williamson, in the pioneering study *New People:
Miscegenation and Mulattoes in the United States* (1980), offers two main
reasons for this drop. One is that large numbers of lighter mixed-race
people were "passing" over into "whiteness." This phenomenon was a
popular theme in the literature of the era, and was also studied by social
scientists, including Park's student Charles Johnson. But a more important factor in the lowering numbers of mulattos was that by 1920, the
mixed-race population had entered the final stages of a merger with a
larger Afro-American population.[47]

Williamson's study illustrates a cyclical pattern in our history with three
phases: (1) a period of widespread race-mixing (miscegenation); (2)
attempts to ban or repress further race-mixing, along with a sustained
effort to discredit or deny the very existence of the human and cultural
offspring of the previous period of race-mixing; (3) the forceful reappearance or return of this repressed mixed-race population.

In his essay "Repression," Freud makes two points which I use to
adapt this concept to the psychosocial domain of interracial relations.
First, repression is an ongoing process which "demands a persistent

expenditure of force." Second, repressed psychic contents are "exceeding *mobile*." The greater force we use in repressing a forbidden or taboo subject or psychic content, the greater will be the force of its return, often in mutated or disguised form, in unexpected places and unanticipated moments.[48]

There is about the cycle of repression a compulsive pattern: we "repeat to complete," in lay terms, returning to the scene of the crime, as if to assure ourselves that what we are repressing is no longer an immediate threat, and yet still requires our continued vigilance. One fascinating example of this, regarding America's repression of the interracial, has been outlined in Tilden Edelstein's essay "*Othello* in America: The Drama of Interracial Marriage." *Othello* has been one of the most popular of Shakespeare's plays in the United States, in spite of, or more likely because of, its interracial theme. Edelstein notes that during the colonial era, *Othello* was advertised as a parable of the dangers of not following the Christian ideal of color-blind "One Blood." But after the revolutionary era, with white racism on the rise, the play began to cause unease among white audiences. By the Jacksonian era, a black Moor as a nobleman was a tough sell. So the white actors in black face who portrayed Othello responded by lightening their makeup. The period between 1820 and the Civil War became known as the "bronze age of *Othello*." After the Civil War, Othello was very popular, but with an ever-lighter face. And explicit references to race were stricken from the play. The play was at the height of its popularity during the 1880s (in "octoroon" face), then was rarely performed from 1890 to 1920, during the peak of Jim Crow. The tradition of bleached Othellos continued well into the twentieth century. It was not until 1942 that a black man (Paul Robeson) could play Othello in "mainstream" productions.[49]

Here we see, within the realm of public performance, an example of the repression of the African content of an interracial artform. This repressed content apparently returned primarily in the form of popular literature on the consequences of race-mixing. Since it was read in the private sphere, this literature was not subject to the same level of censorship. Repression of real-life interracial relations followed a parallel path to the whitewashing of Othello. Williamson points out that before 1850, there was a much greater tendency to allow mixed-race people to claim a status as a sort of intermediate race. Some Southern judges still defined "the privileges of a white man" more by reputation than by mere "mixture of negro blood." There were a significant number of mulatto slaveholders. Some, such as the large Metoyer clan of Louisiana, "rejected identification with any established racial order ... and achieved recognition as a distinct racial ethnic group," according to Gary Mills.[50]

But during the 1850s, "agitation against free mulattoes was virulent," Williamson writes, "throughout the slave South." States such as South Carolina and Louisiana, which had been lax about interracial relations, suddenly sought to drive affluent mulattos from their midst, to outlaw interracial sexuality, and to define white privilege more precisely. Whites had seemed "unconcerned about white blood mixing with black and being held in slavery," Williamson observes bitingly. "On the other hand, they went into a rage against white blood mixed with black and being free."[51]

Mulatto slaves, a growing presence in the 1850s, were even more of a threat to the "peculiar institution," as an ideological weapon. European visitors such as Fredricka Bremer commented on the "white children of slavery." This revealed inconsistencies in the white supremacist argument. As Williamson writes: "If whites be human and fitted only for freedom and blacks be somehow subhuman and made for slavery, what then is a mulatto? How does one justify the enslavement of white blood?" The reality that "many slaves were more white than black, was a fact with which the proslavery argument could not cope." Douglass, as we will see, also used mulattos as a weapon in his antislavery argument.[52]

After the war, agitation against mulattos continued. Perhaps, for Southerners, mulattos were a symbol of its defeat, and a living reminder of a now-repressed prewar miscegenation. In any case, the prewar "tri-racial" society was increasingly reduced to a binary construction, and white supremacists went to ever more irrational lengths to maintain, or claim, racial purity. The *Plessy* Supreme Court decision of 1896 is best known for having established the policy of "separate but equal," but it also gave official sanction to the so-called "One Drop" rule – the folk belief that any admixture of African blood, no matter how remote, made one irrevocably black. Homer Plessy, the plaintiff, was one eighth black, according to the calculus of color. With the appearance of a white man but the legal status of a black man, he had been chosen as a test case to challenge segregation on Louisiana trains precisely because it was thought that his "racial ambiguity" would dramatize the irrationality of Jim Crow laws.

Plessy "naturalized" a mass psychosis no longer subject to reason. There is of course nothing "natural" about someone whose ancestry is seven-eighths European and one eighth African being classified as "black," any more than it is "natural" for someone whose ancestry is seven-eighths African and one eighth European to claim to be "white." The "One Drop" ideology is an American fascism rooted in white supremacist fears about the "taint" of "black blood." It is a racialized Puritanism taken to its logical extreme, in which the repression of the interracial and the repression of the sexual were deeply intertwined. Lillian Smith, the Southern author of *Strange Fruit*, was born a year after *Plessy*, and remembered growing up in an era in which legalized segregation "was only a logical extension of the lessons on sex and white superiority and God." Contact with Negroes and with "forbidden areas of our body" were closely linked, particularly for Southern white women, as part of a system of taboos, banned wishes "which we learned early to send to the Dark-town of our unconscious." ("We were pushed to the back of the head, to the underside of the mind," Ellison said.) Lynching and a hysterical fear of miscegenation were two core symptoms of this repression. The cult of pure white womanhood was a cornerstone of the religion of white supremacy, and the lynching of black men was its most horrible fruit. The victims of these "necktie parties" were usually accused of having raped white women. Douglass and Ida B. Wells took it for granted that consensual sex often *had* taken place between the white women and the black men charged with raping them. The responses of white men reflected their own violently repressed or denied interracial urges. And white Southerners, unable or unwilling to claim their own mixed-race offspring (whether directly or indirectly), then projected their own pathology on to people of mixed race.[53]

The pathologizing of mixed-race Americans by whites had its parallel on the black side of the Racial Divide, with sustained "mulatto-baiting" among some editors, and "whispering campaigns," as Marcus Garvey would call for, in the private sphere. These mass projections had their consequences. Mixed-race families themselves developed "an artificially exaggerated animus against interracial unions," as Caroline Bond Day found, especially between white men and light-skinned Negro women. A growing number of Americans of mixed race began to abandon their claims to a "third space," and to identify themselves as Negroes. Williamson believes this trend became finalized between 1905 and 1925. During the early twentieth century, Afro-Americans themselves internalized the "One Drop" rule. Black–white miscegenation was primarily replaced by what some social scientists called "internal miscegenation," and the "New Negro" was born.[54]

The return of the "mulatto mainstream"

There was a direct link between many of the writers, artists, and intellectuals of the Harlem Renaissance, and the so-called "mulatto elite" of the nineteenth century. An abbreviated list of the mixed-race writers who took the lead in "representing" black culture to America, from the first decade of the twentieth century through the Great Depression, would include W. E. B. Du Bois, Charles Chesnutt, Pauline Hopkins, James Weldon Johnson, Jean Toomer, Nella Larsen, Countee Cullen, and Langston Hughes. Williamson emphasizes that these writers were "the direct and legitimate heir[s] to a long tradition of mulatto culture in America."[55]

There is a kind of poetic justice in the process by which this repressed mulatto offspring returned as the "mulatto mainstream." Rejected by most white Americans, they sought refuge with black Americans (where their acceptance, though certainly not complete, was greater). In the process, they not only played a central role in defining "blackness," they also often articulated, on a national stage, what was most uniquely American.

Most mixed-race Southerners had origins in concubinage, interracial rape, or the ambiguous "back door" relations of slavery, which produced offspring which white fathers often (but certainly not always) refused to recognize. Some of these white fathers (often under pressure from their wives) sold their own mulatto children, south into slavery. This was part of the process through which the "Black Belt" was converted into the "Mulatto Belt."[56] Another important role in this transformation was played by Northern mulattos. They often had roots in much older, less coercive patterns of interracial relations. During the antebellum years Northern mulattos had often been either white-identified, or as in Douglass' case, self-designated mediators between black and white communities. From the Reconstruction years on they increasingly identified themselves with Southern blacks. Many engaged in a missionary "racial uplift" activity – going south to teach the recently freed slaves. Often they intermarried with blacks. Even more important, culturally speaking, these sojourns of Northern mulattos among Southern blacks produced many of our most influential definitions of "black culture."

Two of the most lyrical, enduringly influential portraits of Southern black culture, *The Souls of Black Folk*, and *Cane*, were authored by men of mixed race, who were raised in Northern, almost entirely Euro-American environments. Their classics were written after they had "gone south" to teach Southern blacks and, in essence, discover their own "blackness." Du Bois himself admitted, in his autobiography *Dusk of Dawn*, that his familial customs and cultural patterns came from New England. Although he claimed to write as an American Negro, his philosophical groundings were European. Just prior to teaching at Fisk, which provided him with much of the raw material for *Souls of Black Folk*, Du Bois had been living in Berlin, pursuing a doctorate and drinking at the fount of German Romanticism. As Sundquist observes, in writing *Souls* "he connected himself for the first substantial time to a folk with whom he did not have a great deal in common." Similarly, Toomer wrote *Cane* after teaching briefly in rural Georgia, whose black folk culture he romanticized. Toomer had grown up in an aristocratic environment he remembered as "mid-way between the white and Negro worlds." In Williamson's view, he seems to have "hardly even understood that he was Negro." His outsider-ness to the rural black culture he described is part of what lends *Cane* its haunting beauty.[57]

The inescapably interracial origin of much of American literature, be it "black," "brown," or "white," is not my main point here. I am more interested in how these early twentieth-century authors of mixed race not only claimed to speak for a black collective, but also made explicit claims to represent what was most truly American.

In *Souls*, Du Bois asserted that "there are to-day no truer exponents of the pure human spirit of the Declaration of Independence than the American Negroes." This echoes Douglass' claim that Afro-Americans are the "truer" sons and daughters of the revolution. On one level, Du Bois seeks equal recognition, of the Negro as "a co-worker in the kingdom of culture." On another level, he makes exceptionalist claims. His assertion that the only "true American music" has "black" roots would hardly be contested now. However, in his work as editor for the NAACP organ *The Crisis* he often makes claims for the superior democratic spirit and expressive capacity of Afro-Americans, by contrasting them with the undemocratic spirit, and the comparative artistic poverty, of Euro-Americans. He casts Afro-Americans in a "chosen people" role, in which they would "redeem" America, which has both black nationalist overtones, and is part of a very mainstream "redeemer nation" ideology. During his *Crisis* years, Du Bois sometimes took quite assimilationist stances, especially in opposition to Marcus Garvey (who as we will see in the Marley chapter, was culturally even more Eurocentric than Du Bois).[58]

Du Bois' life and work dramatize the limits of terms like "assimilationist" and "separatist." *The Crisis* was in some ways "assimilationist" in its long-term vision of the United States, writes Hutchinson, but "its idea of assimilation entailed *the 'blackening' of the national culture*, a process it recognized as having begun before the founding of the nation itself and apparently accelerating in the early twentieth century, despite a simultaneous intensification of racism." This is the same perspective we will see with Ellison, who insisted that "From the very beginnings of the nation Afro-Americans were contributing to the evolution of a specifically *American* culture."[59]

Du Bois' "field organizer" for the NAACP, James Weldon Johnson, made even stronger claims for Negro contributions to American culture. In a 1917 speech to a conference of the Intercollegiate Socialist Society,

Johnson proclaimed: "the only things artistic in America that have sprung from American soil, permeated American life, and been universally acknowledged as distinctively American, had been the creations of the American Negro." This claim dates to the abolitionists. But in 1917, Johnson's speech was reported in the *New York Times*, and portions of this article were reprinted by periodicals around the world. The reporter, Herbert Seligmann, was promptly hired by the NAACP as its director of publicity![60]

Johnson's life and career also dramatize the difficulties of drawing firm racial or ideological lines between "black" and "white" cultures. His 1912 novel on passing, *Autobiography of an Ex-Colored Man*, reflected some of his own racial ambiguity. A fair-skinned man who had entry to both white and black cultural and political circles, Johnson exemplified the relativity of passing. As Zora Neale Hurston later wrote with characteristic wit, he was "a man white enough to suit Hitler" who had been "passing for colored for years." Johnson was also an acclaimed songwriter, whose credits include "You're All Right, Teddy," Theodore Roosevelt's 1904 campaign song (which led to a seven-year diplomatic career in Venezuela and Nicaragua), as well as "Lift Every Voice and Sing," the "black national anthem."[61]

From the early twentieth century through the 1930s, then, Afro-Americans were being claimed as the "truer Americans," in black, white, and interracial forums. The 1920 census showed that more Negros were American-born, in fact, than any other group, including Native Americans. According to research done by Melville Herskovits during the 1920s, 27 percent of Negroes claimed Indian ancestry, and 72 percent white ancestry. These factors certainly lent authenticity to the claims of being representative Americans. And it was most specifically people who had previously been called mulattos who acted as the primary black voice during this era. By 1925, Charles Johnson could write about "The Vanishing Mulatto" because of the extent to which people of mixed race had, for the most part, either "passed" into whiteness, or merged with Afro-Americans. By the 1930s, this merger was so evident that the term "Brown America" came into wide use to refer to Afro-Americans as a whole, although a "mulatto elite" continued to function in some cities. Both Afro-American and Euro-American diversity were reduced to a black–white binary by the Census after 1920.[62]

• • •

Fast-forwarding through the twentieth century, we can see that "Brown America" disappeared during the 1960s, repressed by demands for racial solidarity. A similar consciousness did not reappear until the 1990s, when the offspring of a post-Civil Rights wave of race-mixing began coming of age. (It was not until 1967 that the Supreme Court's *Loving* decision struck down anti-miscegenation laws still on the books in seventeen states.) Williamson's history of miscegenation is often superb, but his view of contemporary race-mixing is off the mark. Writing in the late 1970s, he can assert: "The great fact about miscegenation today is that it is minimal, and further has been minimal since 1865." In fact, census records show interracial marriages growing 225 percent from 1970 to 1990: from 310,000 to 1 million. 1995 estimates of 1.3 million mixed marriages indicate that by by the year 2,000 over 3 million Americans will be partners in an interracial marriage.[63]

A torrent of literature about interracial or multiethnic families and offspring has come off the presses in the 1990s. A sub-category of this genre concerns "hidden" interraciality: whites who discover repressed black ancestry; blacks who trace or uncover the white side of their family tree; the reconstruction of families previously separated along racial lines by "passing." The theme of the "return of a repressed" interracial ancestry has also appeared in two excellent films, *A Family Thing* (1995) and *Secrets and Lies* (1996). Shirlee Taylor Haizlip's memoir *The Sweeter the Juice*, a classic of this genre, reveals just how complicated the history of interracial families can be. It also confounds stereotypes about "white privilege," as the families who "passed" or repressed their "black side" sometimes turn out to have been less successful, socioeconomically (a dynamic also evident in *Secrets and Lies*).[64]

An engagement with the popular literature on multiethnicity or inter-raciality is beyond the scope of the present book, but I do want to make three observations about the challenges that this context poses for my study. First, the most virulent opposition to the notion that people of mixed race can carve out an identity that is neither black nor white is now coming from Afro-Americans. Mixed-ethnicity children who do not have a black parent are not subject to the same "One Drop" rule, but for those with a black parent, there is often intense pressure to "cleave to the black," and accusations of racial betrayal if the individual chooses not to choose to be "only black." Surely it is a significant irony that, one century after Euro-Americans were trying to write mulattos out of existence, the repression is now coming from Afro-essentialists. It seems we are witnessing another instance of the construction of the "racial" out of the denial of the "interracial," to repeat Sollors' phrase.[65]

A second phenomenon, which surely must be taken into consideration by the scholar venturing interpretations of the history of interracial relations, is a belief that black culture is "the property and possession of black people," as August Wilson wrote in the *New York Times*. This possessiveness about Afro-American cultural traditions has increased in proportion to growth of nonblack interest in these cultures. This has produced some bizarre dynamics. In a phenomenon I have previously studied, the more that black rap musicians have insisted that they are "real" blacks who are only speaking to "the black community," the more it has been Anglo, Latino, and Asian youth who buy their records.[66]

In academic circles, there has been an "explosion of interest in black women as literary and historical subjects," Ann duCille writes. There are several factors which have contributed to this explosion, such as the institutionalization of multicultural curriculum in higher education, Toni Morrison's Nobel Prize, and the phenomenal increases of sales in books by black women writers (among others) occasioned by talk show host Oprah Winfrey's Book Club recommendations. The flood of critical interest in black women writers has occasioned a great deal of resentment, and assertions of territorial rights. The fear of "being trampled by the 'rainbow coalition' of critics" which Ms. duCille voices is partly a demand that those "invading" this terrain educate themselves about its "scholarly genealogy," a concern I endorse. But one also sees in the obsessive policing of the borders of "black culture" a historically myopic claim of racial ownership.[67]

Finally, the intersections of these two contested realms – the issue of multiracial identity, and "outsider" claims to interpret "black" culture – are a bone of contention. Jon Michael Spencer, a scholar of black musical traditions, has accused "multiracialists" of trying to "steal black history" by "claiming parts of black history to be multiracial history." Such a charge, which expresses widespread fears and suspicions, deserves a response. I would confirm that I do claim parts of *what have been thought of* as black history, as *also* a part of a multiracial history. There is a problem here in the distinction between *either/or* and *both/and* thinking. Spencer believes he sees in "the mixed-race movement" a "wish to leave black behind." I understand that such accusations reflect a pain and anger rooted in the belief that black people have never "gotten their due." Yet I take a both/and approach. Rather than trying to "leave black behind," I am trying to call even more attention to the contributions of peoples of the African diaspora. And I think that the best way to do that is to locate them in multiple traditions: *both* as a part of what we have called "black history" and culture, *and* as a part of a co-created multiracial tradition, *and moreover* as contributors to a "new culture" whose relevance extends far beyond the language of black and white. To claim "black" figures for such larger traditions is not to diminish their blackness, it is to expand their humanity.[68]

That said, I want to reemphasize once more, as explicitly as possible, that "black history" and "black culture" are not my subject matter. My focus is rather on the kinds of language and culture that have developed in interracial contact zones: on racial frontiers. And although the three figures of my case studies are "Negro" or of mixed race, I pay attention to their alliances with European people and culture at every step, to their participation in a culture of "equal rights and justice" that has always been multiracial. As Nathan Huggins wrote in an oft-quoted passage that is worth repeating: "there can be no white history or black history, nor can there be an integrated history that does not begin to comprehend that slavery and freedom, white and black, are joined at the hip."[69]

Racial ambiguity in early American history

To get a fuller sense of the "true inter-relatedness of blackness and whiteness," and of slavery and freedom, we need to dig a little deeper. Let us follow the suggestion of Du Bois and Ellison that the "blackening" of American culture began long before the United States ever became a nation. To fully understand the meaning of our "inability to imagine a genuinely multiracial society," and the contributions that Douglass, Ellison, and Marley made towards correcting that imaginative poverty, we must look at the racial hybridity that was present in our very foundations, and persistent attempts to repress it. So let us make a preliminary foray through pre-Civil War American history, and highlight some of the most striking instances of the ambiguity that Americans have long exhibited towards bodily and cultural "race"-mixing.

Most of the men who joined to found the United States "had inherited both their slaves and their attachment to freedom from an earlier generation," Edmund Morgan notes. "The rise of liberty and equality in America had been accompanied by the rise of slavery." He calls this "the central paradox of American history." Just as our notion of "racial" identity arose through repression of the interracial, so our concepts of freedom came through a close encounter with the negation of freedom: slavery.[70]

But slaveholders were a small elite. It may help here to once again clear off the residue of racial mythology from our historical rear-view mirrors. In the South, "slave owners always constituted a minority of the white population," Peter Kolchin emphasizes. Just how small this slaveholding elite actually was may surprise us, given the endurance of *Gone With the Wind*-type images of Southern life, and the stranglehold that slaveholders had on national policy for almost a century. William Freehling, an acclaimed historian of nineteenth-century history and culture, gives us these numbers: just prior to the Civil War, 70 percent of US whites lived outside the South, and 70 percent of Southern whites did not own slaves. Which means that in the late-antebellum era, only about 10 percent of Euro-Americans owned slaves. What was the attitude of the other 90 percent? This was of course the audience which abolitionists sought to "convert." We need to know something about their historical interactions with Afro-Americans.[71]

The history of nonelites is not so easy to describe in black-and-white. The further back we look in American history, in fact, the lower the percentage of slaveholders becomes, and the less distinction we find between blacks and poor whites, who often came to the Americas as indentured servants. In the colonial era there was extensive economic, cultural, and sexual exchange among poor blacks and whites. The existence of interracial alliances, and elite attempts to destroy these alliances, is an old story. In the seventeenth century, it was common for white servants and black slaves to "run away together, steal hogs together," and even "to make love together," Morgan observes. "The very fact that laws had to be passed after a while to forbid such relations indicates the strength of that tendency," remarks Howard Zinn.[72]

Elite whites often tried to stop or limit interracial interaction, and not only of a sexual variety. "Only one fear was greater than the fear of black rebellion in the new American colonies," Zinn writes. "That was the fear that discontented whites would join black slaves to overthrow the existing order." In Bacon's Rebellion of 1676, "one of the last groups to surrender was a mixed band of eighty negroes and twenty English servants." Some of the most restrictive laws against interracial congress seem to have been passed either in reaction to or in fear of such multiracial rebellions. The strategy, writes Morgan, was to "separate dangerous free whites from dangerous slave blacks by *a screen of racial contempt*."[73]

In the eighteenth century, opposition to interracial exchange was often economic. Many poor whites and blacks found themselves in daily contact, and black slaves often sold surplus or stolen goods to poor whites. George Washington recognized that without "their connexion with my Negroes," neighboring poor whites "would be unable to live upon the miserable land they occupy." So white elites often moved to curtail such interactions. Even so, there remained spheres of sanctioned interracial transactions. Mechal Sobel notes that as white artisans trained blacks, these whites found themselves "in an increasingly black world of work," a reality attested to by Jefferson and other colonists.[74]

Scholarship on colonial-era interracial sexuality paints a very different picture from the antebellum era. Colonial authorities sought ways to curtail or punish miscegenation, primarily among the poor, almost from the beginning. The Virginia legislature passed a number of laws from 1662 on which discouraged interracial sexuality, and defined the legal status of mulattos. While Virginia's colonial authorities never explicitly prohibited interracial marriages, they did pass a series of increasingly punitive measures. A 1691 law required that whites who entered inter-racial marriages be expelled from the colony with three months. A 1705 law sentenced them to six months in jail. Most of the colonies went through a similar sequence. The severity of anti-miscegenation laws seems to have been a response to the frequency with which it was practiced. After a large number of mulattos settled in Philadelphia, in 1725 Pennsylvania outlawed all interracial unions, and sentenced mu-latto children of white women to servitude for thirty-one years. In these examples we see that a "repression of our mulatto offspring" was a key factor in how an emerging definition of "white privilege" was construc-ted. But there were exceptions and ambiguities in the pattern: Maryland reclassified mulatto offspring of white women as free, after masters had begun "pushing" their white servant women to marry Negro slaves in an effort to breed more servants.[75]

In fact, some white women were freely choosing black partners through most of the colonial era. Anti-miscegenation laws largely kept white women from marrying black men, but it did not prevent them from becoming their lovers. Ira Berlin estimates that in seventeenth-century Virginia "one-quarter to one-third of the bastard children born to white women were mulattoes." "Illegitimate mulatto children of white women appear on record throughout the colonial period," Mechal Sobel affirms. In a study of southern miscegenation, James Johnston cites colonial records which show numerous white women giving birth to mulatto children through the 1720s. Dickson Preston observes a similar trend in Maryland, Frederick Douglass' home state.[76]

The stereotype about mixed-race children born during the days of slavery is that they were all the result of the rape of black women by white men. Yet here we see evidence that substantial numbers of white women and black men came together of their own free will. This was seen as a threat or an offense in three ways: (1) it would lead to a breakdown in the social order, or produce alliances, and offspring, that could lead to an uprising; (2) it would undermine the boundaries of racial privilege; (3) it was revolting to racist sensibilities. Such concerns led to a string of legislation against those who joined in, or performed, "such shameful matches." Revulsion against such matches was clearly felt more among the moneyed class than the servants and the poor. And there was more outrage concerning the union of white women and black men that any other variety of race-mixing.[77]

Of course, not all of the mulatto children of the colonial era were born to white women. Given the degree of interaction between blacks and poor whites during this time, it is a reasonable inference that not all relations between white men and black women were forced. But let us turn our attention to the antebellum era, for which we have much more documentary and oral evidence. Again, racial mythology and the evidence do not always match. Significantly, most Southern miscegenation took place in cities and towns, not on plantations or farms, as Eugene Genovese emphasizes. Such interracial relations often began as a form of concubinage, but court records show that they sometimes evolved into a more permanent character. We have, even more importantly, the testimony of ex-slaves themselves, which indicate a range of behaviors in antebellum miscegenation: from white men violating black women, and selling their offspring into slavery, at one end of the spectrum, to a surprising number of white men who engaged in lifelong partnerships with black women, and who recognized, nurtured, and freed their offspring.[78]

Our view of this issue is slanted by a selective history that has been transformed into racial mythology, and then projected back on to history. As a result, stereotypes that all sexual relations between white men and black women are a form of rape have continued to the present day, as Arnold Rampersad has observed.[79] Just as evidence of historical attraction between white women and black men has been largely tuned out, our view of relations between white men and black women have been reduced to a myth of original sin – a collective rape which caused a national stain, a racial guilt which can never be washed away.

A more balanced view would acknowledge that sexual relations between whites and blacks almost always took place under unequal power relations, but on a spectrum. Rape was a dominant phenomenon within that spectrum, but "attraction and repulsion," to repeat the wording of Weber and Mukerjee, was more common. And one must concede that, at the far end of the spectrum from rape, there were some interracial relationships that grew out of, or led to, love.

Aside from this sexual attraction, cultural curiosity and the natural openness of children was much in evidence. An English "gentleman" touring America in 1736 criticized colonial parenting skills, observing of their children that "they suffer them too much to prowl among the young Negroes, which insensibly causes them to imbibe their Manners and broken Speech." Adults and teachers sometimes recorded their disapproval when their children crossed the Racial Divide in too explicit a way. For instance, the Northern tutor Fithia wrote in his journal of 1774 that he disciplined his charges when he found them "dancing with abandon among blacks in the school-room."[80]

At the same time, adults indulged and institutionalized their interracial curiosity to some degree. Whites often closed their cotillions with a "Negro jig," paralleling the way that slaves parodied white dances. The dances of slaves "intrigued their white masters . . . from the beginning," writes James Haskins. Isaac Jefferson, a slave at Thomas Jefferson's Monticello plantation, recalled that Thomas' brother Randolph "used to come out among black people, play the fiddle, and dance half the night." This was a sort of cultural borrowing under unequal power relations, whose characteristic ambivalence is summed up in the title to Eric Lott's study of blackface and minstrelsy: *Love and Theft.*[81]

Interracial and intercultural interpenetrations were evident to many visitors in the early nineteenth century. One of the most famous, Tocqueville, observed in 1833 that in parts of the United States "European and Negro blood are so crossed that one cannot find a man who is either completely white or completely black." In truth, he believed, "one can really say that . . . there is a *third race* derived from these two, but not precisely one or the other." Cultural miscegenation, despite repression of bodily miscegenation, grew to such an extent that the journalist Sidney Andrews, traveling the US in 1866, remarked that "the language of the whites is so much like that of the negroes that it is difficult to say where the English ends and the African begins."[82]

• • •

This brief sketch of themes of racial ambiguity in early American history is meant not to deny that many or most people could be located near one end of the spectrum or the other. But it is meant to illustrate that there were significant areas of interlap between "black" and "white" cultures and people. What was created in this area of interpenetration, over time, took on a life of its own, which was – despite all efforts to repress it – interracial in character and complexion. This cultural and biological interraciality, embodied by growing numbers of mixed-race Americans, caused persistent confusion and anxiety among Euro-American elites, regarding where to draw the line defining who would be granted the privileges of full American citizenship.

What happened to the "repressed mulatto" offspring of the colonial era? We know that some of them, forced from the colonies, emigrated to the Caribbean, to Canada, and to Europe. Some intermarried with whites or Native Americans and "merged" with those populations. Many joined the growing pool of free blacks in Northern cities. Their children and grandchildren ran the first black-owned businesses, built the first black institutions, and agitated against slavery within the narrow slices of the young nation's public sphere which were then available to them.

Close calls and "could-have-beens"

The antislavery movement known as abolitionism was one of the great "secular churches" of the Western world. Abolitionism found its first truly international voice in Frederick Douglass, just as Martin Luther King later became the spokesman for the Civil Rights movement on a national and global stage. But as Douglass was happy to confess, he was a latecomer to a very old tradition. "In fact, the rights of the Negro ... began to be asserted with the earliest American Colonial history," he noted.[83]

The roots of abolitionism are in a thoroughly multiracial eighteenth-century Protestant revival movement. It spawned the fiercest public critiques of slavery in preRevolutionary America. To illustrate why I feel colonial-era religious expression within multiracial contexts is important, I want to begin by highlighting some of its more dramatic "consequences." For the abolitionism which grew out of the "Great Awakening" revivals did succeed at times in changing the course of American history. At other moments it came within an eyelash of fundamentally altering the "racial formations" which would later result in the Civil War.[84]

In 1784, Thomas Jefferson's Southwest Ordinance, which would have outlawed slavery in the Alabama and Mississippi territories, lost in the Continental Congress by just one vote, "that of a New Jerseyite who lay ill at home."[85] What might have happened if that Congressman had not been ill on that day in 1784, and the Southwest Ordinance had passed? Would that have altered the balance of power between slaveholding states, and antislavery activists? Would the framers of the Constitution have felt emboldened three years later to call the bluff of South Carolina and Georgia delegates, who threated to pull out of the fledgling Union if pro-slavery provisions were not written into the Constitution? Would church leaders have been able to maintain their multiracial constituency, instead of drifting towards segregated congregations, as increasingly became the trend after 1790? Or was the emergence of a white supremacist ideology and political practice a tide that could not have been stemmed?

Wondering about other outcomes to the American Revolution might seem naive. After all, freedom and slavery were always paired off, twins in memory and in practice. As Edmund Morgan puts it: "To a large degree it may be said that Americans bought their independence with slave labor." We paid for our freedom with tobacco, harvested by masters, grown by slaves.[86]

The fact that most American founders owned slaves inevitably shaped the language they used to describe the ideals of liberty and equality. In adapting "radical theories of the right of a people to judge their rulers" to the New World, colonists justified their defiance with the spectre of slavery. Americans were "resolved to die freemen rather than to live slaves," the Continental Congress declared in 1774. In 1776 George Washington grieved that "the once happy and peaceful plains of America are either to be drenched with Blood, or inhabited by Slaves." Most colonists did not seem concerned with the bloody removal of Indians from the "peaceful plains of America," nor shy to compare their "enslavement" to that of 500,000 Africans in their midst. "To warn against slavery was the way Britons raised questions about constitutionality," John Phillip Reid remarks. However, an increasing number of American colonists came to believe that they would have to endorse abolition if they were to remain true to revolutionary principles. They were spurred on by the clergy's warnings that "British tyranny was divine punishment for the sin of slavery," and to a lesser degree by Enlightenment equal rights rhetoric.[87]

There was a clear reservoir of antislavery sentiment in the years between the Declaration of Independence (1776) and the 1787 writing of the US Constitution. US antislavery activism, far from being an isolated phenomenon, was part of a resurgent European abolitionism (and a subsequent wave of slave revolts in the Caribbean) during the 1780s and early 1790s. In these years, the outcome of the battle over America as a "White Republic" was not a foregone conclusion. Sometimes antiracist sentiments won out. Congress did ban slavery from the future states of Ohio, Illinois, Michigan, and Wisconsin in the 1787 Northwest Ordinance. When the New York legislature passed a law in 1785 denying free blacks the vote and prohibiting interracial marriages, the state's Council of Revision vetoed the bill. The council wrote that the measure created "an aristocracy of the most dangerous and malignant kind, rendering power permanent and hereditary in the hands of those persons who deduce their origin through white ancestors only."[88]

Between 1776 and 1787, North American antislavery sentiment peaked. Many politicians, including Jefferson, were convinced that slavery would disappear in the short term. Vermont, Massachusetts, Rhode Island, Pennsylvania, Connecticut all passed abolition laws within this period. Criticism of slavery from American clergy was intense, with churches in many states publicly opposing slavery. Baptist, Methodist, and Quaker groups did not succeed in changing Southern policy, but they did propel a growing trend towards private manumissions, which became a minority fashion, particularly in border states such as Virginia and Maryland.[89]

Antislavery discourse mixed Enlightenment philosophy and scripture.

The abolitionism of Protestant revivalism, and a "natural rights" anti-slavery ideology, were part of the same discursive environment. For instance, Montesquieu, whose influence on the "framers" was enormous, was explicitly opposed to slavery. He wrote on the title page of his widely circulated *Spirit of the Laws* (1748): "Slavery not only violates the Laws of Nature, and of civil Society, it also wounds the best Forms of Government; in a Democracy, where all Men are equal, Slavery is contrary to the Spirit of the Constitution." This passage was quoted often by abolitionist leaders, along with Biblical passages that seemed to argue for inherent equality (as we will see with Douglass).[90]

But while most literate colonists read the Bible, few read Montesquieu. Church antislavery agitation preceded political zeal for natural rights. So to understand the source of abolitionism it is necessary to trace its emergence from the waves of religious revivalism known as the "Great Awakening." These constituted the principal public sphere during 1740–90 from within which citizens, having formulated a conception of multiracial redemption and an incipient conception of a biracial republican society, could criticize the pro-slavery compromises of the founders.

The Great Awakening: eighteenth-century multiracial abolitionism

The role of eighteenth-century revivalism in shaping antislavery attitudes and in constructing an interracial culture has been largely ignored by historians. The reason for this unwillingness or inability to "take religious excitement seriously" seems connected to the influence of Marxist views of religion as "the opiate of the people," and to the Freudian tendency to pathologize religious experience.[91] But beyond this tendency to tune out religious dimensions of our expressive heritage, I suspect the lack of attention to the "Great Awakening" is also caused by our binary filters. We are so accustomed to seeing "black" and "white" cultures and histories as mutually exclusive that evidence which challenges this black-and-white worldview tends to be overlooked.

Yet the mass fervor associated with the various Great Awakening revivals, the widespread multiracial participation in these revivals, and the political and economic impact that these revivals had, were a dominant feature of eighteenth-century North America. In reality, "virtually all 18th-century Baptist and Methodist churches were mixed churches," Mechal Sobel maintains. "Almost by definition a religious revival was inclusive," writes Jordan: preachers saw themselves as shepherds gathering lost sheep, whether black, white, or Indian. The presence of blacks at revivals was testitified to by many observers, both pro and con, including preachers such as George Whitefield, Thomas Price, and Samuel Davies. Revivals sometimes had blacks preaching to whites, and always had blacks and whites testifying, singing, and sharing ecstatic experiences together. Power relations varied from church to church, with a "last among equals" status for blacks being a common mode of operation. But in many churches blacks were able to criticize and in some cases bring censure against their masters, or even bring about excommunication, if the masters refused repentance. In general "blacks functioned as full members in early churches," notes Sobel. After black preachers began addressing mixed and white congregations, they were responsible for converting many whites. Some black preachers could engage white preachers in debate and be considered "victorious."[92]

What is known as the First Great Awakening peaked around 1742, as one of the recurrent waves of Protestant revivalism that swept the populace beginning in the 1720s and continued until the Civil War. There is also documentation for a large wave of revivalism that began in 1785 and peaked between 1787 and 1789 – the time of the Constitutional Convention. At the peaks of these Awakenings "mass hysteria was clearly reached," writes Sobel. There were widespread reports of jerking, fainting, and crying, and sometimes even of "barking, shaking, running, chanting, humming, laughing, shouting, and losing consciousness." These symptoms sound similar to those of a wide variety of trance or vision states among the African diaspora, which go by the name of Santeria in Cuba, Macumba in Brazil, Voodoo in Haiti, and "sanctified" among African Methodist and Baptist churches in the United States and Great Britain. Documentation of this sort of behavior is available from the colonial days up to the present: one can see behavior like "jerking, . . . laughing, shouting and losing consciousness" in the Brazilian movie *Black Orpheus*, in Maya Deren's documentary of Haitian voodoo, *The Divine Horsemen*, or read about it in James Baldwin's *Go Tell It on the Mountain*.[93]

If these descriptions of eighteenth-century revival behavior remind us of trance rituals observed in cultures of the African diaspora, this should not be surprising. Sobel emphasizes: "Blacks began to participate in revivals in the South at a very early date and no doubt influenced the emerging so-called white patterns. It is therefore *difficult to find a preblack Baptist pattern . . .* " Blacks were usually welcomed by whites to revival meetings because "blacks clearly helped to build the emotional excitement and to bring down the spirit."[94]

These "Awakenings" rose in part out of dissatisfaction with Anglicanism, the main form of Christianity then extant in the colonies. Anglicanism was an elite religion: blacks were excluded, and the lower classes were marginalized. When George Whitefield began the first of his hugely popular revival tours, most Anglican ministers followed an unwritten rule against attempting to convert slaves. But Whitefield's journals reveal that he was deeply affected by the emotional participation of blacks in his meetings. He challenged whites to rethink their racial preconceptions: "Think you, your children are in any way better by nature than the poor negroes? No! In no wise! [Both blacks and whites] I am persuaded, are naturally capable of the same improvement."[95]

Whitefield was in the habit of staying among the slaves on the plantations he visited. As slaves flocked to hear him throughout the colonies, he began to see them as, in a sense, chosen. In his journal he wrote: "God will highly favour them . . . to wipe off their reproach, and shew that He is no respecter of persons." Whitefield's published attacks on slaveholders were reprinted by Ben Franklin and other colonial presses. He was accused of giving "great countenance" to the so-called "Great Negro Plot" in the New York plot of 1741 (actually a multiracial conspiracy) by publishing a plea for black conversion.[96]

Whitefield converted many other preachers, both black and white, who extended his influence throughout the colonies, and into Canada and the Caribbean. Whitefield and the egalitarian evangelists who followed in his wake helped change the language which much of the population used to talk about people of African descent. They expanded the margins of the Christian "imagined community," and publicized a multiracial concept of redemption, by using scripture to broaden the range of Americans who saw in the Bible a legitimation of an inclusive "equal rights."

There were other, more radical egalitarians during the Great Awakening. The Quakers were early and sometimes influential opponents of slavery. John Woolman journeyed to Virginia in 1746 at age twenty-six, and then spent several years researching and meditating on slavery. In 1754 he published a small book called *Some Considerations on the Keeping of Negroes* that reached a wide audience. The book was distributed to all attendants of the yearly meetings of Quakers in America, as well as to the English Friends. As Thomas Paine's *Common Sense* put democratic ideals into a simple language which widely influenced colonists who often had read little besides the Bible, so Woolman framed slavery in simplest form. "Did not He that made us make Them?" he asked. Woolman and his fellow reformers convinced the Quaker polity to condemn slave trading in 1758 and to essentially "ban" any Quaker ownership of slaves in 1776.[97]

Another Quaker abolitionist whose impact exceeded Woolman's was Anthony Benezet. Benezet was responsible for the "conversion" to abolitionism of Benjamin Rush, who went on to play a major role in building early black religious and educational institutions. Benezet's writings inspired British abolitionists such as Thomas Clarkson, and helped pave the way for abolition in the British West Indies in 1833. And black speakers and writers continued to ritually invoke Benezet as a patron saint of abolitionism well into the nineteenth century.[98]

The teaching that blacks were not only equals, but in a sense God's chosen people, was adapted by a range of other evangelists, including Presbyterian minister Samuel Davies, who became the most influential preacher in Virginia during the Great Awakening. Like other preachers addressing multiracial congregants, Davies sought Biblical legitimation for an emerging theology of multiracial redemption. In 1750 Davies held out the hope that "Ethiopia will soon stretch out her hand unto God for a considerable number of Negroes have not only been proselytized to Christianity and baptized, but seem to be the genuine seed of Abraham by faith." Whites such as Davies and Benezet publicized evidence of African agency in the Bible. Gradually, Biblical narratives relating the deliverance of Hebrews from Egyptian slavery, and their Babylonian exile, became a "sacred topography" for black Christians. Characters from the Bible such as Moses, Jacob and Daniel became a "new fictive kin" which "opened common ground on which whites and blacks could share religious experience," Sobel writes.[99] I will return to this theme regarding the use of a "Mosaic" persona by Frederick Douglass and Bob Marley.

An Afropean culture: "blackening" of the Watts hymns

The new styles of worship that emerged from eighteenth-century revivals, including hybrid forms of singing and inclusive readings of the Bible, are part of a sociocultural context in which a shared culture was being forged, at the same time that certain differences were being reinforced. The forms of singing that emerged from interracial interactions are particularly suggestive of the Afropean roots of American culture. By Afropean, I mean products of a "collision between parallel discursive universes," as Henry Louis Gates says, that exhibit both African and European antecedents.[100]

The hymns of Isaac Watts played an important part in this process. Watts, an English hymnist, from 1707 to 1719 published a collection of church songs that later became the most popular and widely distributed form of Protestant music in the eighteenth century. These hymns were multi-denominational, used by Anglicans, Baptists, Congregationalists, Methodists, and Presbyterians. The melodies were part of the popular culture of the day.

Sobel notes that "Along with Bibles, Watts hymnals were among the first books given to blacks. Both blacks and whites quickly came to know his songs as though they were old folk-songs, and they became an important part of a growing 'common' heritage." This common ground was literally English/"white" in origin but increasingly "black" in adaptation. Slaves took the Watts hymnals, and as they had done with the Bible, made it "their own." They "blackened" the music, not only in style but in their focus on hymns that assisted in their thematic "appropriation of the history of Israel and its heroes."[101]

This hybrid music greatly influenced many whites. In his 1756 journal Samuel Davies wrote: "Sundry [Negroes] have lodged all night in my kitchen; and, sometimes, when I have awakened ... in the morning, a torrent of sacred harmony poured into my chamber, and carried my mind away to Heaven. In this seraphic exercise, some of them spend almost the whole night." Davies later expressed his belief that "the *Negroes* above all the human species that ever I knew, have an ear for Music, and a kind of extatic [*sic*] delight in Psalmody."[102]

The presence of blacks and their impact on worship styles was noted by many preachers during a wave of religious fervor coinciding with the American Revolutionary era. In July 1776 Thomas Rankin preached on Ezekiel's vision of dry bones to a congregation of 500 at White's Chapel, Virginia. There was "great shaking" which Rankin says he tried to control, but could not. Hundreds of Negroes were present, tears streaming down their faces. Rankin clearly linked excitement with a black presence.[103]

A Methodist named James Meacham who was preaching in Virginia in 1789 recorded going among "the dear black bretheren" in their cottages to join them in prayer and song. Once in the middle of the night "I awakened in raptures of Heaven by the sweet Echo of Singing in the Kitchen among the dear Black people (who my Soul loves). I scarcely ever heard anything to equal it upon earth. *I rose up and strove to join them.*"[104]

These passages feature some interracial dynamics present during the Revolutionary era, before racial divisions hardened. Some whites felt free to go among the cottages of blacks to engage in acts of worship. Blacks were close enough to white preachers to spend the night in their kitchen and to "take over" their worship services. Some whites were put off by the "blackening" process, but others "rose up and strove to join them."

The call-and-response format of revival services shaped the conversion experience of both blacks and whites: preaching became less monologic and more interactive. This widespread interracial interaction in religious contexts also had a significant impact on a broader, secular culture. West African precursors, in particular call-and-response, inform many of the cultural forms employed, often unconsciously, by all Americans, as Robert Farris Thompson emphasizes. Multiracial religious revivals give us a glimpse of the deep roots of this cultural interraciality. They give us evidence of the use of call-and-response as a forum for democratic experimentation at an early, indeed foundational stage.[105]

Elites did eventually succeed in popularizing an ideology of white superiority, but the evidence suggests that this battle had not been won by the time of the American Revolution. A principal site of opposition to this ideology was the evangelical movement, and music played a central role in this process. Hybridized "black" music, in forms both secular and sacred, has continued to play an important role throughout American history. Even in colonial days, it exhibited the "dual function" theorized by Nancy Fraser of counter-publics: it served simultaneously as a site of "resistance" and "cooptation." Afro-Americans used this biracial "black" music both to voice and popularize their resistance to racial oppression, and as a mask to entertain or distance themselves from white "intruders." Whites used the same music in a variety of ways as well: by turns as a form of solidarity, as a path to self-transformation, to explore cultural difference, and to reinforce their racial stereotypes.[106]

White, black, and multiracial public spheres

During the 1790s, two distinct public spheres emerged that were "differentially empowered" in an increasingly unbalanced way. I will focus here on one archetypal instance of a "black public sphere" – Richard Allen's somewhat mythologized role as "founder of the black church." His story is symptomatic of the pressures which produced a growing trend towards segregation and establishment of "parallel" institutions.

Albert Raboteau calls a "gallery incident" that led to the creation of the African Methodist church "the most famous event in Afro-American religious history."[107] One Sunday in 1792, the black parishioners of St. George's Methodist church in Philadelphia were informed that they could no longer sit in the pews they were accustomed to using. From now on, they were told, they would have to sit in a recently constructed gallery at the rear of the church. Most black members complied with the order, even though they had contributed, along with whites, to the remodeling of the church. But a respected black parishioner named Absalom Jones remained in his pew. When a white trustee urged Jones to move, Jones asked him to wait until the prayer ended. But two white trustees lifted Jones by his knees and removed him. As soon as the prayer was over, the black worshipers stood and walked out *en masse*, soon to form their own separate black church.

This incident dramatized for black parishioners how quickly the interracial climate was changing. During the 1780s Methodist leaders had pressured politicians to incorporate blacks as full citizens into the new republic. In 1784 Methodists had put into place a policy refusing communion to slaveholders. But by the early 1790s egalitarian sentiment seemed to be fading, and prejudice was becoming entrenched. Even so, Albert Raboteau thinks historians have tended to "overemphasize white racism as the reason for the development of the black church." "Black religious independence arose from black initiative and not simply in reaction to white discrimination," Raboteau argues.[108] Still, the "black initiative" towards separation and the growth of a white supremacist ideology must be seen as mutually constituting. And even the growth of "independent" churches such as the African Methodist Episcopal (AME) and "black" movements such as the Free African Society cannot be understood outside of a multiracial context.

When the Free African Society (of which Allen and Jones were founders) began searching for a permanent meeting house in 1791, they turned to Benjamin Rush, a well-known white physician and philanthropist in Philadelphia. Rush drafted the church's articles of faith, and with Robert Ralston, a wealthy white merchant, called on friends in high places. Benjamin Franklin, Thomas Jefferson, and President George Washington all promised economic and moral assistance for constructing the black church.[109]

Both Baptist and Methodist "black" churches in the early years of the republic usually remained under the nominal control of "white" church leaders. But there were many contradictions in this "white" control. Even though the trend towards segregation and increased conflict became more pronounced in the nineteenth century, there were many nuances that make it hard to draw clear lines between black and white "spheres." The original charter of the Bethel African church in Philadelphia, Richard Allen's "flagship" black church, subjected this offspring to supervision and discipline by the "parent" church. This led to a long, often antagonistic struggle with white elders, who eventually sued in 1807 to try and retain control of the black congregation. But Pennsylvania's Supreme Court ruled in favor of Bethel after a long, expensive battle. Thus we see during an era of ascendant white supremacism, a legal sanction of a black counter-sphere.[110]

In political terms, the American public sphere was originally predominantly Euro-American, although informed by the presence of blacks (and to a diminishing degree, in North America, by Native Americans). A "black" public sphere emerged, sometimes in opposition to, and sometimes more as a parallel to, its "white" counterpart. All of these black institutions – churches, masonic lodges, newspapers, schools, and abolitionist organizations – emerged out of close interactions with white

Americans. In almost every case – from Richard Allen's first independent black Methodist church, to Frederick Douglass' first national "black" paper – these organs of a black public sphere relied heavily on economic and moral support from whites. This had two main effects. One, it led among some to a drive for black self-sufficiency, for a "black" sphere independent of "white" interference. But this was not the only effect: there emerged a significant area of black and white interaction that I choose to view in procreative terms: as the biracial child of black and white parents. One can say that a multiracial public sphere emerged out of what was at first a contact zone, and later became an expanding frontier.[111]

Despite the trend towards religious segregation in the early nineteenth century, there continued to be significant areas of overlap between black and white congregations. There was still a market, as it were, for speakers who could be persuasive with black, white, and mixed congregations. Even though institutional segregation was encouraged by many religious leaders, both black and white, not all of the multiracial traditions of the early revivals disappeared. These revivals endured as a liminal arena between black and white institutions throughout the nineteenth century, most notably in the camp meetings observed by Douglass and others. Even when revivals began to initiate separate seating assigned by race and gender, the tradition of a "union ceremony" was maintained as a climax. Barriers which had separated black and white worshipers during the week were pulled down on the last day. Union ceremonies were epiphanies in which the mixed audience could ritually experience, however briefly, their cohabitation in a multiracial "imagined community."[112]

Maria Stewart in context: multiple discursive strategies

The rhetorical strategies employed by abolitionists from the 1830s on drew on over a century of experience, among black and white speakers, in addressing mixed audiences. Some speakers had only religious goals in mind. But over time, religious and political aims merged, for the stream of egalitarian thought that flows from the Great Awakening into abolitionism. Speakers in this secular church had to employ multiple discursive strategies. They fused scripture and natural rights philosophy. And they developed distinctive strategies to address black and white members of their audience, as well as a multiracial "imagined community." In this interface between religious and political discourse addressed to multiracial audiences, a "common rhetorical culture" developed, as Celeste Condit and John Louis Lucaites write. In their fascinating book *Crafting Equality: America's Anglo-African Word*, Condit and Lucaites argue that in fact our very understanding of the concept of equality has evolved "*only*

through the public rhetorical interaction of blacks and whites." In this concluding section, I want to give readers a glimpse of some of the challenges
faced historically by speakers addressing multiracial audiences, and then
examine a few of the rhetorical strategies that Maria Stewart devised to
meet this challenge in the early 1830s.[113]

The preachers responsible for bringing Christianity to blacks in the
1700s faced great obstacles in achieving effective interracial communication, notably language and style differences. This can be seen in a report
of the Society for Propagating the Gospel (1701), which noted of a
missionary to New York slaves that he was "labouring earnestly to ac-
commodate his Discourse to their Capacities." Not all white preachers
were able or willing to cross that linguistic and cultural divide; sometimes
blacks showed passive resistance by snoring loudly or otherwise tuning
out their guests. But the more emotional preachers who tried to employ a
language and delivery familiar to blacks encountered an enthusiastic
response. This enthusiasm educated and "acculturated" the white
preachers, sometimes fundamentally altering both their worldview and
the style of communication they employed.[114]

As black preachers began addressing mixed and white audiences, they
too underwent linguistic and cultural changes, and in the process assisted
in the process of co-creating a new communicative culture. "Many of the
leading black preachers, as well as the whites who preached to blacks,
tried to serve both communities," Sobel points out. "The interrelationship that was worked out affected the character of both sides."[115]

Three discursive strategies were evident in early multiracial churches.
Sometimes speakers delivered different messages to different "racial"
audiences in the same language. Sometimes they preached the same
message in different languages. And at times they encoded different
messages in different languages. These varied discourses indicate that
there were several emerging and interconnected language styles, loosely
typed as black, white, and interracial. Readers can find many examples
of the varieties of these discursive styles in the ground-breaking work of
Mechal Sobel. I want to mention in passing here that a noisy style of
worship, which was closely tied to a black presence, was an issue
of central importance for much of the eighteenth and nineteenth centuries. Many early white preachers engaged in "hollering and stamping" in
an effort to reach the black members of their congregation. Since this was
a very controversial style, they took care to justify such demonstrative
preaching by citing scriptures such as Ezekiel 6:11 and II Samuel 6:14–
15. In the early nineteenth century, during an era in which churches were
increasingly divided by race, a wide number of black, white, and biracial
preachers tried to "stamp out" noisy worship. Some of the very preachers

who had led the "black exodus" to independent churches led this crusade. "Music itself became suspect," Sobel notes, a concern that has
carried over into contemporary churches. When "decorous music" was
brought into the AME church during the 1840s, many older "sanctified"
members jumped ship.[116]

• • •

After the Revolutionary era, and in the wake of the Haitian revolution,
black churches came under increasing suspicion. This turned into out-
right oppression after a series of real or rumoured slave revolts in the
South which, as in the Caribbean, were led by charismatic men with close
ties to black churches.[117] As a result, antislavery activism moved out of the
churches, and after 1830, into the abolitionist movement. Abolitionist
meetings often took on the tenor of the "union ceremonies" which had
been characteristic of multiracial gatherings during the Great Awakening.
This is evident in the speeches delivered by Maria Stewart in the early
1830s. More than any other American before Douglass, Stewart showed
an ability to balance the distinct needs of two different "racial" communities, while simultaneously envisioning a multiracial or transracial "third
space."

Stewart was born in Hartford, Connecticut, in 1803, orphaned at age
five, and raised in a white clergyman's family. She married James Stewart
in 1826 and was widowed in 1829. Her husband had a shop in Boston
where he outfitted sailors. He was apparently involved in distributing
David Walker's *Appeal to the Coloured Citizens of the World*, first published
in 1829. Since Walker died shortly after a second edition of this pamphlet
appeared in 1830, there has been speculation that both were killed as a
result of their antislavery activism. Only two months after Nat Turner's
revolt, Maria Stewart introduced herself to William Lloyd Garrison and
convinced him to print an essay she had written: "Religion and the Pure
Principles of Morality: The Sure Foundation on Which We Must Build."
Garrison had in fact already published Walker's jeremaic broadside.
Maria Stewart would have studied Walker's essay closely, and known
about Turner's bloody slave uprising.

These two events, and her husband's death, clearly had a major influence on her. While Turner and Walker had used the Bible to advocate
violence, Maria Stewart took a very different approach. She argued "for a
revival of Christian morality and for social advancement through education." Furthermore, while Turner largely ignored whites, Stewart's message "was obviously intended for a mixed audience," emphasizes Frances
Foster. In her speeches and writings to "promiscuous audiences" –
integrated across class, race, and gender – "Stewart frequently addressed

particular remarks to particular segments of that audience."[118]

To black women in particular ("ye daughters of Africa") Stewart demanded: "What have you done to immortalize your names beyond the grave?" To black people in general, she sometimes urged them to "plead our cause before the whites," but at other times advised: "It is useless for us any longer to sit with our hands folded, reproaching the whites; for that will never elevate us."[119]

Stewart sometimes chastised white women: "fairer sisters, whose hands are never soiled, whose nerves and muscles are never strained, go learn by experience!" To white people in general, she used a variety of strategies, including warnings of the black prophets who would "shortly arise" to "spread horror and devastation around" if their rights were refused; but also reassurance, promising to whites: "nor will we attempt to rise above you: we will presume to be called your equals only."[120]

During the process of pleading and cajoling with whites and exhorting blacks, Stewart also consistently pointed out the commonality between white and black people. In a lecture in Boston in 1832, Stewart proclaimed: "I am a true born American; your blood flows in my veins, and *your spirit fires my breast.*" Elsewhere she emphasizes that "Our souls are fired with the same love of liberty and independence with which your souls are fired ... too much of *your blood flows in our veins*, and too much of your color in our skins, for us not to possess your spirits."[121]

In Stewart's writing and speeches, an emphasis upon black pride coexists with a portrayal of a multiracial imagined community in which miscegenation is an irrevocable fact of life. Sometimes she deals literally with that miscegenation: "your blood flows in our veins." But more often she is concerned about varieties of cultural, political, and religious miscegenation. Thus in her attempts to imagine a multiracial society and a nonracial concept of redemption, Stewart told her mixed audience: "God hath raised you up a Walker and a Garrison." The leaders she chose as icons for a multiracial movement were a black prophet of liberation and a white abolitionist. Garrison was seen by many blacks as "the Moses raised up by God, to deliver this modern Israel from bondage," as Douglass later wrote. And Walker, of course, presented himself as, and was perceived by many blacks as, a messianic figure.[122] These attitudes were shared by some whites in the abolitionist movement.

From within the semi-secular forums of the incipient abolitionist movement, Stewart called on Americans to recognize that both the Bible and the Constitution legitimated her equal rights. "[God] hath made you but a little lower than the angels; and, according to the Constitution of these United States, he hath made all men free and equal ... It is not the color of the skin that makes the man, but it is the principles formed within the soul." On this Biblical and Constitutional foundation, she argued passionately that she too had the ability and the desire to "sing America."[123] The way in which Stewart used both the Constitution and the Bible echoed eighteenth-century egalitarians and foreshadowed the strategy taken by Douglass. Indeed, we see here the opening of a path that leads directly to Martin Luther King, Jr. and the Civil Rights movement. It is also a cousin to other strategies developed in the "secular church" of black liberation, such as the Bible-inflected music of Bob Marley.

2   Frederick Douglass as integrative ancestor: the consequences of interracial co-creation

> I ventured to take my stand at a sort of half-way place between the blacks and whites.
>   Douglass, *My Bondage and My Freedom*, (194)

"A SORT OF HALF-WAY PLACE": DOUGLASS AS BIRACIAL "BLACK CULTURE HERO"

Introduction

In this chapter I call on Frederick Douglass, as a biracial "black culture hero," to serve as a human symbol of interracial co-creation. He provides a window on the racial ambiguity present at the foundation of the American republic, and also prefigures many of the themes of interraciality which I will discuss in twentieth-century literature and music.

Douglass was a nineteenth-century abolitionist journalist, orator, and editor, and later a Republican Party loyalist and a diplomat to the Caribbean. His charismatic power as a public speaker was such that for several decades, Douglass enjoyed a status something like that of a pop star. He held enormous, multiracial audiences spellbound on both sides of the Atlantic, and his speeches were widely reprinted in major newspapers of the day, and distributed as pamphlets.[1]

Douglass' life spanned almost the entire century, from 1818 to 1895, and his legacy has continued to reverberate throughout the twentieth century. In the 1990s, Douglass is still making waves. These repercussions range from the rap star KRS-One's dismissal of Douglass as a "house nigger" and a "sellout," to political theorist Michael Lind's view of Douglass as "the greatest American" and as a "standard-bearer" for a transracial "fourth American revolution."[2] Public figures with competing agendas, from Booker T. Washington and W. E. B. Du Bois at the beginning of the twentieth century to Supreme Court Justice Clarence Thomas at the end, have all claimed to be following Douglass' example.

Douglass has sometimes been seen as a sort of "black Ben Franklin" – a "self-made man" whose memoirs are part of a larger genre that transcends "race."[3] More often, public perceptions of Douglass have been skewed by the polarized racial filters which have become an ingrained part of American culture and collective memory. The most pervasive misreading of Douglass has been to characterize him as a hero or icon of "black history" and then to ghettoize him within a "black studies" box, where he can be conveniently ignored by those studying the "mainstream" of American history and political theory.

Yet Douglass described himself as "something of an Irishman as well as a Negro." He also sometimes acknowledged that he was "part Indian." His biraciality, or hybridity, was not only biological, but also cultural and political. A dominant feature of Douglass' public career spanning six decades was the crafting of strategies to mediate between "white" and "black" publics. Acting as an interracial mediator, Douglass in fact came to speak for and embody an interracial "third space." Douglass' roots were in abolitionism, an antislavery movement, but from an early period, he defined his position more broadly as antiracialism, which took the form of a sustained attack on racial categories themselves. His determined transraciality is in abundant evidence from his earliest journalism to his late interracial marriage.[4]

In this chapter, I will illustrate the strategies Douglass devised to communicate effectively with different parts of his multiracial audience. I will also examine the ways in which Douglass chose to occupy an interracial and potentially transracial "third space," through symbolic acts which include, but are not limited to, his interracial marriage. As a means of laying the groundwork for an analysis that reads Douglass' life, writing, and oratory as a form of symbolic interaction with his multiracial audience, I will draw attention to the interracial contexts of Douglass' abolitionist career. I will argue that Douglass' personal biraciality and his cultural hybridity were cornerstones in the emergence of his rhetorical style and political philosophy. These themes are interesting and underappreciated in their own right, but in my view, an effort to understand Douglass in a multiracial context is also great practice for citizens of a would-be multiracial democracy. With this horizon in view, I want to suggest that Douglass can serve as an integrative ancestor for those trying to build a multiracial society, or what Nelson Mandela has called a "nonracial democracy."

As previously indicated, I view the concept of a multiracial public as an acceptable transition on the way to eventually freeing ourselves of the

1   The Douglass years: daguerrotype of Douglass at age twenty-five,
before writing the *Narrative*, when he was a Garrisonian agent.

"mental slavery" of racial mythology. But we have to come to terms with
interraciality, and the variants of biraciality that this has produced, in
order to move in that direction. Such a perspective may appear "utterly
impossible," as Douglass admitted to readers while laying out his vision
of an eventually mixed-race America. But it is also historically grounded,
as Douglass always insisted.[5]

If North America's "moral center" in the 1950s and 1960s can be
located in the Civil Rights movement, then Taylor Branch is correct to call
this era "the King years." Civil Rights had many leaders and fault lines, but
Martin Luther King's role as global spokesman for this crisis means that he

has come to embody the movement. Likewise, the antislavery struggle was America's "moral center" during the nineteenth century. Frederick Douglass articulated most clearly, on an international stage, what was at stake in the abolitionist movement(s). Therefore, I believe that it would also be fitting to refer to this era as "the Douglass years."

Another glance in the contemporary rear-view mirror

Trying to (re)claim a positive interpretation of cultural and personal hybridity can be a fiercely contested move, in an era of "ethnic cheerleading" and "oppression studies."[6] I am conscious of entering a field of debate in which "commonality" and "difference" are often seen as opposing concepts. Critics who want to "do the right thing" often react *against* a history of *imposed Eurocentric commonality* by then emphasizing an *essentialized difference*.[7] In my view this is a historically necessary, but still shortsighted step. The decentering of cultural history is an ongoing process I endorse heartily. And yet as Gayatri Spivak points out, perpetual opposition to a presumed Eurocenter merely reifies that center, and confines one to an "accusing position." One runs the risk of getting stuck in oppositional poses that are "merely gestural."[8]

This is a debate which has begun to percolate in cultural studies, but if my experience on California campuses is a fair barometer, it has made little impact on most students moving through the system.[9] They are strongly attracted to a racial romanticism in which dual allegiances are likely to be seen as evidence of "cooptation," rather than as a valuable resource – at least if it involves a European component.[10] Trying to argue that commonality and difference can coexist is a hard sell in this environment. A "hermeneutics of suspicion" is wielded as a weapon, and anyone so naive as to assert that diversity includes elements of a shared heritage will be asked, in so many words, whose side they stand on.[11]

The suspicion of claims of cultural kinship derives from an assumption that commonality exists *only* because Eurocentric norms have been imposed. The conventional wisdom of Cultural Puritans is that the Right Thing is to focus on difference, on heroic resistance, on a history of oppression presumed to be the prime cause of this *resistant* difference.[12] "History" is wielded as a weapon to discipline those who would be so naive as to claim the existence of a shared heritage or a contemporary common ground.

My exposure to cultural forms and forums with multiracial audiences led me to suspect that this vision of history as mere oppression, racial or otherwise, was as one-sided as the earlier histories which uncritically glorified European colonization, or conquest of the Western frontier. As I studied the history of interactions between black, brown, and white people, I posed the somewhat rhetorical question: must the ideal of a multiracial public sphere remain a utopia which is marginalized from the actually existing "center" of political culture? The answer coming out of my research was that both nonfictional and artistic forms of communication concerned with multiracial community and citizenship have a very long history. Indeed, "interraciality" is embedded within the very core of American political and communicative culture, from colonial days to the present.

Yet all I have to do is put my finger to the wind to know that this interracial heritage is all but invisible: as real as Ellison's invisible man, but off the collective radar screen.[13] *Vibe*, a "black" magazine founded by Quincy Jones, ran an interview of rapper KRS-One in which KRS dismissed Frederick Douglass as a "house nigger" and "a fuckin' sellout." To me this reflected how pervasive a sort of reactive oppositionality has become in the culture, as well as the academy. It also offered more disheartening evidence of the degree to which many urban youths are self-perpetuating racial stereotypes. KRS had led rap music's move in the late 1980s and early 1990s towards a "sampling" of black history.[14] His allusions to Malcolm X prefigured the resurgence of interest in Malcolm as a cultural icon. KRS pioneered what he called "Edutainment" to impart cultural history to young people who were disdainful of public education. As an acronym, his stage name signified "Knowledge Reigns Supreme." Under the moniker of "The Teacher," KRS lectured widely on college campuses. Yet in the mid-1990s KRS had retreated into gangsterism, both in word and deed. This was a transparent effort to win back his "hardcore" audience, in which being a "real nigger" – i.e., not a sellout – was often equated with the antisocial attitudes of the "thug life."[15] Now KRS admitted that he had quit reading. He felt that books only represented "other people's opinions."

This interview with KRS came to my attention while I was researching Douglass and the abolitionist movement.[16] I had just finished reading Douglass' famous "July 5 Speech" of 1852, in which he thundered that "for revolting barbarity and shameless hypocrisy, America reigns without a rival." If KRS ever read Douglass, he would know that Douglass was something far more complex than an assimilationist.[17] Yet KRS' attack was probably an inevitable result of his uncritical use of Malcolm X's binary view of American history. In Malcolm's typology, blacks are divided between two camps: "house niggers" and "field niggers." *House niggers* loved the white man. *Field niggers* hated the white man. *House niggers* "sold out" to the white man's oppressive system. *Field niggers* resisted against that system by any means necessary. Malcolm believed that the same division applied in his own day: Martin Luther King, the integrationist, was a "house nigger," and Malcolm, the black nationalist, was a "field nigger." Malcolm, of course, did not invent this racial typology. As Wilson Jeremiah Moses has illustrated, the roots of this racial mythology can be found in two binary archetypal black figures of the nineteenth century: Nat Turner as a revolutionary black messiah, and Uncle Tom as the passive, long-suffering "house nigger."[18]

In this Us vs. Them binary mythology: one is not really "black" unless one is unalterably opposed to all things "white." By this definition, then, Douglass was insufficiently oppositional and therefore a "sellout." Rather than reading the evidence for himself, KRS had "read" him through Malcolm, and consigned Douglass to the "lie-bury" – the place where books, as useless lies, are buried.[19]

Why should I worry about what a rapper says about Frederick Douglass? Because the young people who buy this music constitute my ideal audience, even though I am using a language that would be tuned out by most of this audience.[20] I see the enormous gap between the world that KRS and his audience inhabit, and the world of academic research, as a symptom of a cultural crisis. KRS speaks for a generation who mostly have contempt for the life of scholarly inquiry, whether as practiced by Frederick Douglass or by present-day academics. And the academy, if it does not have contempt for "post-literate" urban cultures, is certainly not usually capable of speaking in a language that would enable these youths to take advantage of its resources. I write in part out of a desire to build bridges between those two worlds, to mediate between them in some way, even as I suspect that for the most part such mediation is not presently possible. And I am writing out of the conviction that KRS is very wrong about Frederick Douglass, and that the binary racial filters worn both by him and by too many cultural critics are a form of willful blindness that has dangerous consequences.

Douglass contradicts the division of nineteenth-century history and culture into two camps, black and white. Douglass resided on the racial frontier his entire life, engaging in what Ralph Ellison would call "antagonistic cooperation" with both black and white Americans. One could only affirm that he was an integrationist if that word was qualified as signifying "inclusion, *not* assimilation," in Ellison's words.[21] That sense of integration is largely absent from the public discourse of the present era. Oppositional intellectuals now even dismiss the ideal of inclusion, arguing that it masks attempts to force-fit "minorities" into a Eurocentric, patriarchal norm.[22] The question of "inclusion into what?" is a valid one. Yet even a brief study of Douglass' life and writings, and the political and religious currents from which he emerged, will discourage a simplistic answer. As Ellison's definition indicates, inclusion need not mean a loss of cultural identity or critical consciousness, although Douglass' life does illustrate that this is a danger.

Frederick Douglass as biracial "black culture hero"

Although Frederick Douglass is widely viewed as a "black culture hero," an icon of nineteenth-century Afro-American history, Douglass himself referred often to his biraciality in both a biological and cultural sense. Using his own life and words as a guide, we can say that Douglass represents biraciality as much as "blackness" – at least, he is a voice for both "racial" and transracial communities.

Douglass sometimes referred to himself as an Anglo-African, and throughout his life, Douglass used his biraciality to subvert "race prejudice." In his *Narrative* Douglass commented that his biraciality undermined the so-called "curse of Ham" myth, which white racists claimed offered Biblical legitimation of black inferiority. On the way to a Cleveland convention in 1848, Douglass encountered a slaveholder who refused to speak to a "nigger." Unruffled, Douglass told the man that if it would make him feel more comfortable he could speak to the half of him that was white. Late in life Douglass often referred to an "intermediate race of a million" as proof that Negroes were not so "repulsive" as many pretended. And he responded to criticism of his interracial marriage by observing, with tongue in cheek, that he was closer to the color of his white wife, Helen Pitts, than he had been to his black wife Anna.[23]

Nor were Douglass' claims on his mixed blood merely a matter of black and white. His family, the Baileys, passed on a belief that Frederick's grandmother, a free woman named Betsy Bailey, was of Indian ancestry. Dickson Preston, whose research into Douglass' Maryland years has revolutionized Douglass studies, believes that there is "a substantial body of evidence" to support this claim. Douglass recalled that his master, and possibly his father, Aaron Anthony, used to call him his "little Indian boy." His appearance often caused people to ask "whether I was not part Indian as well as African and Caucasian?" Douglass was apparently willing to answer this question in the affirmative. He once told the student body at the Carlisle Indian Institute that "I have been known as a Negro, but I wish to be known here and now as an Indian."[24]

Douglass persistently claimed a social identity as a Negro, it is true. But in practice this was a strategy of claiming to represent blacks before a primarily white audience. For although Douglass continued to play the role of interracial mediator, his social relations were almost all with white people. Yet at the same time, even though Douglass' adult cultural tastes were largely European, he had been indelibly shaped by a slave culture. In truth, he "merge[d] two traditions," as Gregory Lampe writes, arguing that it was the fusion of oral slave culture with European traditions that made his oratory such a "potent combination." In keeping with this perspective (neither black nor white yet both) I interpret Douglass as a "biracial black culture hero" whose discursive and personal space cannot be seen as "just black." This outlook requires an understanding of Douglass' cultural and biological biraciality, as well as the multiracial contexts of his communication. Positioning himself between black and white communities, Douglass engaged in "antagonistic cooperation" with both black and white abolitionists, and tried to do the same with supporters of slavery. As an interracial mediator, he drew on both Enlightenment and Biblical egalitarian traditions in order to construct a multiracial "imagined community."[25] This public career was firmly rooted in a private context.

In 1833, when Frederick Douglass was fifteen years of age, he persuaded his master Thomas Auld to attend a "camp meeting" on Maryland's Eastern Shore. The youth then named Frederick Bailey had invited Auld hoping that "If he has got religion ... he will emancipate his slaves."[26] Camp meetings were one of the few public arenas in the early nineteenth century which sanctioned a degree of social interaction between blacks and whites. This was far from an egalitarian arrangement: blacks stood in a fenced-off area behind the preacher, who occasionally spoke to them over his left shoulder. Whites were seated in front of the altar. Between blacks and whites was a straw-filled "pen" in which white "mourners" could prostrate themselves while experiencing conversion. It was only while on their knees before a greater power, that blacks and whites could experience a momentary, partial equality. Douglass recalled that "I ventured ... to take my stand at *a sort of half-way place between the blacks and whites.*"[27] He hoped that once he and Auld were both believers, they could stand on common ground.

This image of Douglass taking up a stance at a "half-way place between blacks and whites" foreshadows a course he would pursue the rest of his life. His inclination to seek a middle ground that was neither black nor white was in some ways rooted in his own biraciality. He was driven by a lifelong desire to understand the "mystery" of his birth to a white man and a black woman, neither of whom were around to assist in his upbringing.[28] On another level, Douglass' impulse to mediate between blacks and whites was a result of a cultural and ideological biraciality, in which he imagined his identity and his role as an American citizen through the "deep texts" of the Bible and Enlightenment philosophy.

If one read Douglass' account of the camp meeting incident in isolation, it would be easy to imagine that he was only interested in the impact he could have on white people, or the benefits he could derive from white people. However, his inclination to take a stand at "a sort of half-way place" on the Racial Divide was clearly driven by an urge to change the balance of power on both sides. That "half-way place" would later become a place of residence in its own right, but in the beginning, Douglass used it to engage in strategies aimed at two different racial communities. This is evident in the same section of *My Bondage and My Freedom* when Douglass/ Bailey recalls his efforts during the fall of 1833 to not only "redeem" his master, but to teach literacy to other black children. Inspired by a Methodist minister, George Cookman, who had preached against slavery, and by the example of a local man who followed Cookman's advice and freed his slaves, the young Bailey organized his own Sabbath school. However, at the second meeting of these budding liberation theologists, a delegation from the regulation Methodist Sabbath school, which included Thomas Auld, broke up Frederick's school by force, asking Bailey if he "wanted to be another Nat Turner."[29]

Douglass' biracial view of the "half-way place" he occupied was deeply rooted in the interracial context within which he achieved literacy, according to biographer William McFeely. And the texts through which he learned to read, speak, and write were, tellingly, both religious and political: the Bible, and *The Columbian Orator*.

As Willard Gatewood's study *Aristocrats of Color* indicates, the mulatto sons of white slaveholders often had privileges beyond the reach of most slaves, and young Frederick's experiences were not uncommon in this regard. When Frederick was eight he was sent to live in Baltimore with Hugh Auld's family, brother of his master Thomas. While on the plantation he had been treated as an animal or *thing*, in the Baltimore home he was "treated as a *child*." Hugh's wife Sophia Auld drew Frederick to her side as she read Bible stories to her two-year-old son Tommy. Frederick asked her to teach him to read. Soon he had committed pages of the Bible to memory. But Hugh was displeased: "if you teach that nigger . . . how to read," he predicted, "he'll be running away with himself."[30] Hugh directed Sophia to terminate her lessons. But the seed had been planted. Frederick began studying *Webster's Spelling Book*, which Tommy brought home from school. He persuaded and sometimes bribed his white playmates to repeat the lessons they had learned at school. And one day when he was twelve, after hearing a white friend recite a speech from a schoolbook, *The Columbian Orator*, Frederick took fifty cents he had saved from shining shoes and bought a copy of this book from a local bookshop.

"Seldom has a single book more profoundly shaped the life of a writer and orator," McFeely writes. First published in 1797, this schoolbook was "committed to the proposition that American boys, as the inheritors of a tradition of great oratory, were destined to speak the virtues of the new republic." As a "book of liberties," *The Orator* was a product of the revolutionary era, and as such, included several pieces critical of slavery. The young Frederick was first exposed to John Locke here. He memorized these speeches, reciting them over and over in a kind of rehearsal for his future vocation.[31]

The patriotic speeches and rhetoric of equal rights in *The Columbian Orator* provided the youth who would become Frederick Douglass with a roadmap for constructing a personal and political identity. Douglass had been since boyhood intensely curious about social and political worlds from which he was excluded. But he always viewed this exclusion as a challenge to be overcome rather than as an insurmountable obstacle.[32] The pieces of Enlightenment-era "natural rights" philosophy he encountered in *The Orator* provided him with evidence that inclusion was his *right*. This was a conviction he would never lose, a conviction that was the cornerstone of his urge to position himself at a "half-way place" from which he could mediate between black and white Americans.

The persona of *Frederick Douglass*, forged through speeches, writings, and a "symbolic life," was interpreted by much of his audience as a symbol for something that could not then be fully articulated. Part of Douglass' symbolic value derived from his status as a "self-made man"; a part of the symbol he embodied expressed his country's unfulfilled democratic potential, and on yet another level he was seen by some of his contemporaries, notably white women, as a sex symbol. To many black Americans he was a hero and a role model. In all of these components, Frederick Douglass served a mediating function: between blacks and whites, between men and women, between classes, between literacy and illiteracy, between America and other nations.

My portrayal of Douglass as a biracial black culture hero contains elements of all the symbolic functions noted above. I want to begin defining this term by taking yet another look back in the contemporary rear-view mirror. A sense of the meaning of "black culture hero" can be obtained by observing a T-shirt that was popular among black youth in the early 1990s, "The Five Ms." This T-shirt read: "**M**arcus, **M**alcolm, **M**artin, **M**arley, **M**andela, and **M**e." The faces of each of these five men appeared on the T-shirt: Marcus Garvey, Malcolm X, Martin Luther King, Bob Marley, and Nelson Mandela. Each of these five men is seen as a "race man," a prophetic figure involved in the uplift of black people. The "Me" signifies that this prophetic tradition is being forwarded in the present generation. The essence of this "racial uplift" is the use of "black culture" in order to help black people achieve their destiny. As Wilson Jeremiah Moses has observed, such "culture heroes" are often seen as messianic figures who appear in order to "redeem" black people, or to prod them into a higher consciousness of their status as a "chosen people."[33]

The disparaging comments of KRS-One notwithstanding, many black intellectuals would place Douglass within this group of "black culture heroes."[34] Indeed, Douglass can be seen in many ways as a forerunner to these "Five Ms." As with so many "black" icons, one is confonted with the issue of the borders of "the race." Bob Marley was the son of a white man and Malcolm was the grandson of a white man. Marley's mother, Cedella, has asserted that he was born out of love. Bruce Perry's biography has cast doubt on Malcolm's claim that his biracial mother was conceived through rape. Indeed, many of Malcolm's stories about violent conflict with white people – such as the confrontation with Klansmen and the supposed murder of his Garveyite father – appear to have been invented, because they lent dramatic support to the binary racial mythology that Malcolm had acquired from the Nation of Islam.[35]

Those used to looking at "black culture heroes" without racial ambiguity may react to such claims with indignation – such as the character in *White Men Can't Jump* exhibits when confronted with evidence that Jimi Hendrix's rhythm section was white. Others who would be willing to concede that the "white blood" in Marley and Malcolm was introduced consensually would still respond with a "so what?" – claiming that miscegenation has nothing to do with the form or function of "black culture."

I do not want to base my argument on the "slippery slope" of *mixed blood*, but rather to interpret personal biraciality as a symbol for cultural *mestizaje* or hybridity. Certainly, the knowledge that their absent fathers were white had a huge psychological impact upon both Douglass and Marley. But more importantly, both used personal biraciality as a foundation from which to articulate a vision which, although focused upon the theme of "black liberation," insisted that black freedom could only be achieved through the more inclusive project of multiracial democracy or multiracial redemption.

Without in any way discounting the importance of Douglass' and Marley's function as "black culture heroes," I want to make the point, by adding the qualifier *biracial* black culture heroes, that they cannot be "owned" by a "black" racial collective. Douglass and Marley also speak to other collectives. They can also be looked upon as "culture heroes" by white people, as well as people of mixed "race" who decline to choose sides. Douglass' willingness to acknowledge Indian ancestry, and his critiques of American imperialism in Latin America and the Caribbean, also point towards his iconic status in a larger, hemispheric "*nuestra America*."

The personal and cultural biraciality of Douglass and Marley invests their symbolic value, as cultural icons, with a transracial element and a mediatory capacity. Their lives and work point to the extremely fluid nature of many of the cultural symbols with which racial mythologies have been constructed. The terminology I employ is an effort to move beyond or at least *see through* the language of racial mythology. It may be helpful here to review how I intend for these terms to be seen as part of a process. Interraciality produces biraciality. "Biracial" is one of many identities possible in a multiracial public. We must go through biraciality and multiraciality in order to get to transracial language and identities. These are transitional moments in the movement from racial mythology to postracial possibilities.

Racial signs and transracial symbols

A fuller understanding of the way in which I am using the concept *biracial black culture hero*, as a tool with which to interpret Douglass and others as cultural symbols, requires some discussion of the word "symbol." One of the roots of the word which points to the mediating function I want to emphasize is *symballein* – "to throw together."[36] Symbols are a product of a collision, of different worlds being thrown together, and being synthesized into a collage which is fundamentally hybrid. Carl Jung distinguished between symbols, which have multiple meanings, and semiotic signs, whose intended meaning is singular. There is always something adhoc about a symbol, something unplanned and not fully conscious.[37]

In racial mythology, the tragic mulatto is a sign which signifies a pathology resulting from miscegenation. The tragic mulatto is "torn between two worlds," and is unable to bridge or synthesize these worlds. Therefore, the sign of the tragic mulatto is *"more a symptom than a symbol."* In Jung's terms, the tragic mulatto is "the symptom of a repressed antithesis." That is, since the "dominant culture's" thesis is that the racial divide is unbridgeable, then the threat that biracial people pose to that racial ideology must be repressed. They must be pathologized.[38]

I want to explore a notion of biraciality as a polyvocal symbol, which emerges when two people/cultures are "thrown together" and produce an offspring. Gates speaks of the "two-toned" character of Afro-American discourse resulting from "a collision between parallel discursive universes."[39] Douglass is a *two-toned symbol* of the collision between black and white worlds. He was something more than the sum of his parts. He represented a new type of American which the signs of racial mythology could not encompass. The sign of tragic mulatto did not fit him.

2   Cazenovia Fugitive Slave Law Convention (1850). Douglass at age thirty-two, with friend and patron Gerrit Smith at his right shoulder, at a typically multiracial gathering

Douglass was a biracial man who became a black culture hero. Douglass, like Marley, generally described himself as a "black" man, but like Marley, he was also quite conscious of, and publicly articulate about, his biraciality. He sometimes referred to himself as an "Anglo-African," and described himself as "something of an Irishman as well as a negro."[40]

As a human biracial "mediatory symbol," Douglass cannot be accurately "typed" according to the field nigger/house nigger myth, either. Douglass had lived in the "Big House," but he had also worked under the whip in the field. Both of these experiences shaped his worldview, but so did his study of the Bible and equal rights rhetoric. The nineteenth-century binary typology of Nat Turner / Uncle Tom does not contain him, either. Douglass transcended these binaries – the symptomatic signs of reductive racial mythologies. He was in some ways a synthesis of these types, fusing elements of both Nat Turner and Uncle Tom. But in other ways he represented a new type rooted in much deeper cultural traditions, which cannot always be engaged through racial terminology.

To illustrate how Douglass functioned as a biracial mediatory symbol, I will take three approaches. First, in the remainder of this section, I summarize how Douglass decentered the white-led abolitionist movement, primarily through the establishment of a quasi-independent black press, which in fact functioned as a third space or contact zone between black and white abolitionists. In the second section, I will interpret Douglass' July 5, 1852 Speech as an illustration of how Douglass, even at his most oppositional, founded his critique of racialism upon Biblical and Enlightenment traditions which enabled him to maintain a sort of antagonistic cooperation with the political and religious mainstream. And in the concluding section, I will interpret Douglass' later interracial marriage (in 1884) as a symbolic act which formally publicized his allegiance to two "racial" communities, as well as his residency in a third "interracial" community which he had helped to co-create.

Multiracial abolitionism: "a sort of half-way place"

Although there is a tradition among Afro-American historians of attention to black abolitionists, even as late as the 1970s, most histories of abolitionism tended to treat it as a monolithic movement, focusing on white activists such as William Lloyd Garrison or the Grimke sisters.[41] Douglass himself described abolitionism as a movement with multiple centers,[42] and recently historians have begun to follow his lead. Jane and William Pease point out in their study of black abolitionists that there were "two overlapping movements," one white and one black.[43] This area of overlap was in fact a "contact zone" in which the two "wings" parented a third, multiracial abolitionism.[44] Douglass spearheaded the growth of the black wing, but he also later positioned himself in a third space which was "at a sort of half-way place between the blacks and whites."[45] In the process of mediating between black and white activists he came to embody an multiracial abolitionism.

Douglass' paper the *North Star* represents the difficulty of defining which part of this multiracial public sphere was "black" and which part was really "multiracial." Douglass founded the paper in 1847 as a declaration of independence from Garrison and the white-led "mainstream" abolition movement. Historians view his paper as the first national black press. Martin Delany was briefly his coeditor, and for the first time, black writers had an impact on national political debate. Yet 80 percent of Douglass' subscribers were white. He mostly relied on white women to manage the day-to-day affairs of editing and production. Its very existence was originally made possible through funds raised by English women. Throughout the 1850s, Douglass' major underwriter was Gerrit Smith, a wealthy white New York philanthropist who was elected to Congress on an abolitionist platform.[46]

Special attention should be paid to Julia Griffiths' enormous role. Douglass met Griffiths, who had family ties to the British abolitionist Wilberforce, in 1847 while in England. They became close friends, and Griffiths raised funds to help launch Douglass' paper. In early 1848, when Douglass' fledgling *North Star* was on the brink of collapse, he wrote Griffiths an emergency appeal. She quickly relocated to Rochester to take over the management of Douglass' finances. She served as publisher and de facto coeditor of his paper. Douglass had not had a day of schooling when he began his editorial career, and Griffiths "taught him the rules of grammar . . . and used her blue-pencil mercilessly to perfect his writing."[47] She wrote most of Douglass' book reviews, organized endless fund-raising and publishing ventures, and seems to have had a close hand in the editing of *My Bondage and My Freedom*.

Griffiths also booked Douglass' lectures, corrected his speeches, and arranged to have them published in pamphlet form, as well as serving as Douglass' "constant companion" in Underground Railroad work. In 1854 Douglass acknowledged that his journalistic career was "indebted to none more than to . . . Julia Griffiths."[48] She returned to Great Britain in 1855, where she engaged in extensive fund-raising activities for Douglass, organized many antislavery societies, and contributed many articles to *Douglass' Monthly*. Douglass and Griffiths remained close friends for almost fifty years. In 1892 Douglass paid tribute to Griffiths' "inexhaustible" resources and management, which had ensured the survival of his antebellum editorial activism. Griffiths was merely the most prominent of a large group of British, German, and American white women who played major roles in Douglass' career. "The role of Euro-American women in the history of Afro-American ad-vancement is a major episode in American cultural history waiting to be written," as Orlando Patterson notes. Griffiths' relationship with Douglass certainly deserves a book-length study. Because of her fundamental contributions, and those of a very large group of white supporters on both sides of the Atlantic, Douglass' papers can be seen, in a sense, as interracial co-creations.[49]

Positioning Douglass is not so simple as listing white and black influences, without acknowledging their interpenetration. For instance, one of his closest advisors was James McCune Smith, a black man who earned MA and MD degrees from Scotland's University of Glasgow. And one of the keys to Douglass' move away from Garrisonian "moral suasion" (a branch of abolitionism often thought of as "white") and towards recogni-

3 Frontpiece for "Autographs for Freedom" edited by Julia Griffiths, 1854. Douglass at about age thirty-five. His only piece of fiction, "The Heroic Slave," appeared in this collection.

tion of the need for violent resistance (a supposedly "black" perspective) – was the enormous influence of John Brown. This was a "white" man who thought like a "black" man, one might say. Douglass met Brown in 1847, and afterwards, Douglass recalled, "my utterances became more and more tinged by *the color of this man's strong impressions*." What color were these impressions, we might ask? The color of the freedom struggle was becoming an intersubjective, interracial arena.[50]

Douglass in fact embodied and articulated a "third space" in American culture and politics, an emerging "multiracial public sphere" with deep historical roots. Douglass fused oppositional and integrationist impulses: he fiercely criticized Americans for failing to live up to their democratic and Christian ideals, yet reaffirmed that natural rights philosophy and Judeo-Christian scripture were "redeemable" tools capable of helping build a multiracial democracy.[51]

In its editorial stance the *North Star* came to stake out a middle ground between the "white" wing, and a group of black abolitionists, many with their own papers, who often adapted separatist or emigrationist stances.[52] And it was from this middle ground that Douglass counselled President Lincoln, and in a real sense defined the Civil War's focus – while Garrisonians and separatist black abolitionists shrank in size and impact.[53]

Both black and white abolitionists puzzled in different ways over how to envision and build a multiracial society. A debate emerged over whether or not a *biracial republic*, or a *multiracial society*, could be built on existing foundations. The Constitution, as a contested cornerstone of the American republic, was a primary bone of contention. Douglass' mentor Garrison called it a "covenant with Death and an agreement with hell" which should be abolished. But as Douglass emerged as the first (inter)national voice of black abolitionism after his 1845–57 English sojourn, he came to question this view. Douglass grew to believe that the Constitution and the Declaration of Independence "gives us *a platform broad enough*" on which to build a multiracial democracy, "*without regard to color*, class, or clime." This belief was a heresy to Garrisonians, and led to his break with Garrison. But it also came to define "the generative center" of abolitionist thought. Douglass pulled the mainstream of abolitionist thought to his position, and eventually a main *stream* of American legal theory and political practice followed.[54]

Douglass' life dramatizes the importance of factoring into our analysis of black leaders their almost inevitable European sojourns and their rootedness in European philosophy and cultural traditions (as Paul Gilroy suggests). Douglass' view of the Constitution grew out of an independence he achieved through three interracial, international processes. First, he wrote an autobiography which introduced him to a broader audience of white elites. Second, he lived and spoke publicly in England and Ireland for two years, coming into contact with other movements with which abolitionism could be allied. Third, he founded his own newspaper, with funds raised in Great Britain, which allowed him to work out his emerging philosophy for an audience that transcended race, class, and gender. This illustrates how "black" history and culture in fact occur within a transnational, transracial space, what Gilroy calls the *Black Atlantic*, and what I conceive of as a racial frontier.[55]

Abolitionism as a "secular church"

Abolitionism, it has been noted, "became a kind of religious congregation," an American "civil religion."[56] Douglass' reactions were typical in this regard: when he read the *Liberator* for the first time in 1839, the paper "took a place in my heart second only to the Bible," he records. After first hearing Garrison speak in 1841, Douglass imagined him as "the Moses raised up by God, to deliver His modern Israel from bondage." Garrison served, in a sense, as an ideal substitute for Douglass' own unknown white father. We can say about Douglass, as Jung once confessed to Freud, that he had something of a "religious crush" on Garrison. As we shall see in the analysis of Douglass' "July 5 Speech," this father complex took Douglass almost two decades to resolve.[57]

For Douglass, "abolitionism quickly assumed the status of a religion, drawing upon the best Christian ideals: love, morality, and justice," writes Waldo Martin. Like many other abolitionists, he added Enlightenment philosophy to a Judeo-Christian foundation, and even when he abandoned formal ties to the church, the moral language remained. He described abolitionism as a "combination of moral, religious, and political forces."[58] Significantly, Douglass described *moral* forces as something that could be separate from politics or religion, although he certainly did not believe that religion and politics *had* to be morally bankrupt.

This union of moral language with political vision and religious conviction enabled abolitionism, as a semi-secular church, to inspire many societal changes. Before the Civil War, abolitionism "was about the only area in which white women and black women came into contact on anything near a level of equality," Frances Foster points out. It also spawned an alliance of abolitionism and women's suffrage movements, a fusion that Douglass, as mediator, helped achieve.[59]

Black abolitionists could challenge white stereotypes in print through nationally distributed networks, to a degree not previously possible. These institutional channels created unprecedented space for interracial interpersonal contact, and this "promiscuous" contact, both personal and political, cleared space for the use of a "shareable language." As that audience learned to "sing America" together, in sometimes clashing but sometimes harmonizing style and substance, they began to use more of what was becoming a *mutually created language*. Douglass embodied and gave voice to this process, opening a channel within a multiracial public sphere through which black and interracial discourse "slowly infiltrated the mainstream public vocabulary."[60]

Abolitionists were an oppositional community and a unruly secular church. They shared the goal of ending slavery, but on how to achieve that goal were fiercely divided. Schisms proliferated over the defining of ideological boundaries and over "naming the enemy." Douglass came into conflict with elements of both black and white "wings" over the nature of their opposition. Through "antagonistic cooperation" with both black and white peers, Douglass came to believe it was as important to define what one stood *for* as to condemn what one *opposed*. He began to question condemnations of entire groups and traditions. He outgrew Garrisonian dogma that political action was immoral, and that the Constitution was pro-slavery. And he resisted the tendency of some black abolitionists to write off America, or to perpetuate the same sort of racialism they claimed to oppose. Douglass' emerging philosophy was a deeply reasoned critique of racialism in all its forms. The solutions he proposed were deeply rooted in Judeo-Christian scripture and Constitutional law, read inclusively.

"Redeeming" Christianity and the Constitution

When Douglass determined that the Constitution provided a "broad enough platform" on which to build a nonracial democracy, he was taking up the unfinished business of the American Revolution. The text of the Constitution is indeed a "covenant" with slaveholders, but it also contains language and provisions intended to steer the young republic towards more inclusive employment of its egalitarian ideals. The Constitution is a product of the immediate political concerns of the founders, but it also offers a window on deeper egalitarian currents, of both religious and political character. These shaped the worldview of the founders and flowed into the foundational documents which they devised for their experimental republic.

This was the *platform on which Douglass proposed to build*: deeply rooted in the past, and cautiously geared towards the future. The moral and political practice Douglass envisioned was not black nationalism or racial Christianity – two paths chosen by most nineteenth-century black intellectuals. Nor was it assimilation, as we define that word now. Douglass' vision was of multiracial democracy as "inclusion, *not* assimilation," as Ralph Ellison put it.[61] Douglass held this notion up as a horizon to the American public for the rest of his life, no matter how far it appeared from the "actually existing" American practice.

Douglass' vision was rooted in two "religions." Christianity provided his first moral language and his first glimpse of a forum in which he could link personal redemption and political freedom. And abolitionism was the *secular church* of the nineteenth century, as we have seen. Even abolitionists who renounced Christianity continued to use an evangelical style in their appeals to conscience. Douglass himself discovered that "he could not marry the two religions, Christianity and antislavery, though one led to the other," McFeely writes. Douglass had served as a lay preacher in New Bedford's AME Zion chapel just before launching his career as an abolitionist speaker. This training "helped to prepare me for the wider sphere of usefulness which I have since occupied," Douglass wrote. "It was from this Zion church that I went forth to the work of delivering my brethren from bondage."[62]

In his blending of religious and political egalitarianism, Douglass echoed eighteenth-century revivalists, and foreshadowed twentieth-century Civil Rights leaders. Like Anthony Benezet and other eighteenth-century Christian abolitionists, and like Martin Luther King, Douglass believed that both Enlightenment ideals of "equal rights" and Christian ideals of "one blood" were "redeemable ideals."[63] What is original about Douglass, and the tradition in which he was based, is that he foresaw what we might call the "conditions of redemption" in a multiracial context. That is, both Christian and Enlightenment ideals were only capable of being redeemed if they were enacted in an inclusive, multiracial context. Only when the standards of inclusion were based on something beyond "race prejudice," as Douglass called it, could participants in the American experiment experience "the true meaning of our creed," or redemption in both its political and spiritual sense.

The black convention movement: Douglass as a "colored man" reborn

A further theme that needs to be explored in order to better understand Douglass' relationship with his multiracial publics is the "constructed" nature of Douglass' blackness, and later, his biracial identity. This formation of racial and then transracial identities was a gradual process. The most important factors of this evolution were his involvement in the "black convention movement" of the late 1840s and early 1850s, and his estrangement from William Lloyd Garrison as a father figure, which was made possible through being introduced to a new circle of friends, both black and white, who were more broad-minded than Garrison.

It is important to realize that only from 1838–41 did Douglass operate within a predominantly black context, among black churches and abolitionists in New Bedford. After signing on as an "agent" with Garrison's Anti-Slavery Society in 1841, Douglass spoke to and wrote for a predominantly white audience. His status among blacks "depended in large measure upon his status among powerful whites and his resulting facility

at orchestrating among them support for tangible black advances,"
Waldo Martin notes.[64]

And appeal to whites he did, in unprecedented ways. Douglass was
"an extremely popular calling card" for Garrisonians. He brought a new
eloquence in an attractive new package which made him a valuable
commodity. Douglass was marketed in several ways. At first he was
something of a curiosity as an ex-slave who spoke flawless English. He
was also a model of a positive outcome to social and sexual miscegenation – a model which still made many progressive white abolitionists
uncomfortable. Their discomfort was obvious as Douglass became an
antebellum sex symbol. Early photos show a very handsome man, and
both black and white women "unquestionably found Douglass irresis-
tibly charming," Martin writes. But his broad appeal to women was not
merely sexual. Women flocked to Douglass because his "quest for liberation urged them on in their repressed quest for their own," McFeely
argues.[65]

As compliments regarding Douglass' charm and eloquence grew, so
did suspicions that he was not really an ex-slave. White backers worried
about their "calling card." They advised him to keep "a little of the
plantation speech." Douglass rejected this advice because he wanted to
become "a principal, and not an agent." To put doubts about his authenticity to rest, in 1844–45 Douglass wrote his *Narrative*. The book was
a critical and commercial success, selling out nine English editions by
1848 and appearing in French and German translations. One reviewer
noted his "talent for melody" and "ready skill at imitation," revealing
common racial preconceptions. Another reviewer took a transracial
point of view, remarking that Douglass' talent "would widen the fame of
Bunyan or De Foe."[66] The book led to his sojourn in England: Douglass
was legal property and had published evidence which could lead to his
recapture.

The ground for Douglass' "almost legendary popularity" in Ireland,
Scotland, and England had been prepared over the previous fifteen years
by many Afro-American abolitionists, as R. J. M. Blackett chronicles in
*Building an Antislavery Wall: Black Americans in the Atlantic Abolitionist
Movement, 1830–1860*. England had outlawed slavery in her colonies in
1833. Thereafter, black abolitionists such as Nathaniel Paul, Charles
Lenox Remond, Moses Roper, and James McCune Smith found an
audience in Great Britain eager to support their efforts to build and
maintain a "moral cordon" around America. In fact, black abolitionists
became "so much in vogue that white women and men sometimes
colored their faces and hands," notes Blackett. A London *Times* correspondent remarked on the "demand for the 'article' of Ethiopian lions in

the London Market." Richard Webb, who "chaperoned" Douglass, observed that Edinburgh's elite were competing for Douglass' attention and treating him as "quite a lion." Most of those lionizing Douglass were women: Webb wondered "how he will be able to bear the sight of his wife after all the patting he gets from beautiful, elegrant and accomplished women." Douglass himself was not without a sense of humor regarding British demand for "article" black men. "It is quite an advantage to be a nigger here," he told one American friend. "I find I am hardly black enough for British taste, but by keeping my hair as woolly as possible I [can] pass . . . for half a Negro at any rate." Racial authenticity and sexual attraction aside, the apparent absence of "color-phobia" made Douglass feel reborn. Writing Garrison from Belfast on January 1, 1846, after four months in Ireland, Douglass reflected: "I seem to have undergone a transformation. I live a new life." His *Narrative* sold as fast as it could be printed, and his lectures throughout Great Britain were attended by fervent overflow audiences of all classes. Newspaper reports were effusive, songwriters and poets quoted him, and the lower classes chanted his slogans and wrote lines from his speeches on church walls.[67] By his return to America in 1847, after British friends had purchased his freedom, Douglass was a celebrity. He could not be contained by the Garrisonians.

Aside from new self-confidence, Douglass also brought back from England the funds to start his own newspaper. Garrisonians tried to discourage Douglass from publishing the *North Star*. Then Garrison and his lieutenants, both black and white, tried to sabotage Douglass' credibility. Their attacks sharpened when Douglass moved towards political abolitionism around 1849, and turned personal when Garrison printed rumors that Douglass was having an affair with Julia Griffiths, his white assistant. But in 1852 Douglass could still write to an associate, explaining why he felt reluctant to respond to Garrison's attacks: "I stand in relation to him something like that of a child to a parent."[68]

Douglass' close ties to Garrisonians "tended to set him apart from . . . black abolitionism," Martin notes. During most of the 1840s, his primary contacts with black Americans were developed through the black convention movement. The Buffalo convention of 1843 was dominated by a clash between Douglass and Henry Highland Garnet. Garnet delivered a "savage indictment" of slavery, which he afterwards reprinted along with David Walker's incendiary *Appeal*.[69] Douglass objected to Garnet's call for an uprising, reflecting his allegiance to Garrisonian principles of moral suasion and nonresistance. After several days of debate, the convention voted against Garnet's measure by one vote.

At the 1847 convention in Troy, Douglass and Garnet clashed again.

Still voicing Garrison's position, Douglass urged blacks "to come out from their pro-slavery churches," arguing that "they were not the places for colored men."[70] Since Douglass seemed to think at this point that all churches were pro-slavery by association, his opposition offended black ministers like Garnet, pastor of a Presbyterian congregation. Douglass also disappointed delegates by opposing a national Negro press. This seemed to reflect his desire to maintain control of his own forthcoming paper, the *North Star*.

Douglass dominated the 1848 black convention in Cleveland. He was chosen convention president, and the *North Star* was declared to be the "voice of black abolitionists." Press coverage of Douglass was widespread and polarized – with papers sympathetic to abolitionists lavishing praise on Douglass, and pro-slavery papers demonizing him. Douglass' thinking was in transition at this point, and is sometimes inconsistent. In March 1848 he published a column arguing against separate black churches and schools. Such separation would perpetuate segregation in other institutions, he argued: "The axe must be laid at the root of the tree. The whole system of things is false." Douglass situated himself "upon grounds vastly higher and broader than any founded upon race or color," and this postracialism brought him into conflict with incipient black nationalists who demanded complete separation.[71]

Yet in 1849, disturbed by the factionalism he had seen in black conventions, Douglass began a campaign to establish a National League of Colored People. He hoped that building a united front would give Negroes more political leverage. White supporters praised the idea, but it was largely ignored by the black press. Garnet attacked Douglass on supposedly religious grounds, accusing him of having denied "the inspiration of the Bible." Garnet's attack helped turn Negro clergymen against Douglass' League. This in turn helped motivate, in concert with Julia Griffiths' counsel, Douglass' willingness to interpret Judeo-Christian scripture as a potentially powerful tool in changing racist attitudes.[72]

Douglass "differed quite strikingly from other black leaders of the period, particularly clergymen, whose liberatory rhetoric was at all times interwoven with appeals to Providence and divine intervention," write Shelley Fishkin and Carla Peterson. In early speeches Douglass said that he had "prayed often for freedom," but that he did not obtain freedom "until I prayed with my legs." In 1849, when there was intense debate about giving slaves the Bible, Douglass said: "Give them freedom first, and they will find the Bible for themselves." But in this same year, we see evidence of Douglass' willingness to use the Bible to change racist attitudes. Reviewing *A Tribute for the Negro*, Douglass wrote: "'I am black, but comely,' is as true now as it was in the days of Solomon."[73]

As editor of the foremost abolitionist paper Douglass was able to develop positive contacts with numerous free blacks. Among prominent blacks who regularly contributed to the *North Star* were Henry Bibb, Martin Delany, Samuel Ward, and James McCune Smith. In 1849 Douglass engaged in a spirited but friendly debate with Ward over whether or not the Constitution was antislavery. Douglass was still arguing against the Constitution at this point, but he was willing to concede that someone "in his sober senses" could interpret it as an antislavery document, or pro-slavery, or as some combination of the two, because of its studied ambiguity.[74]

A hint of Douglass' ambiguous racial identity, and the irony with which some black peers viewed his role as "race leader," comes through in an 1848 letter his colleague James McCune Smith wrote to Gerrit Smith. "Only since his Editorial career has he seen to become a colored man!" he remarked. In other words, the increased dialogue with other black leaders made possible by Douglass' journalism was removing some of the "whitewash" he had acquired under Garrison's tutelage. Smith insinuated, writes Martin, that "Douglass was becoming more comfortable with the black half of his mulatto identity; his white patrimony, then, was diminishing in psychological and practical significance."[75]

Douglass was also discussing the Constitution with Gerrit Smith, his closest white ally. And Julia Griffiths was helping moderate his criticisms of Christianity. Both Smith and Griffiths were free of the condescension Douglass had found among many Garrisonians. The interracial social circles he entered through them apparently influenced him as much as their philosophy. Douglass' thinking was becoming "blacker," in a sense, but he was increasingly operating from within an interracial context.

Douglass was at first reluctant to accompany the wealthy Gerrit Smith to social functions. But Smith told him: "you must go Douglass; it is your mission to break down the walls of separation between the two races." Douglass later recalled this as a defining moment. As interracial mediator, Douglass saw establishing a "black voice" as coexistent with creating a multiracial sphere. The *North Star*'s statement of purpose revealed this blend of black independence and interracial interdependence. In the first issue, Douglass explained the role of the "black press" this way: "It is evident we must be our own representatives and advocates . . . not distinct from, but in connection with our white friends."[76]

In 1851 Douglass changed the name of his paper from the *North Star* to *Frederick Douglass' Paper*. Garrison criticized the change as an example of Douglass' egotism, but it actually had more to do with Douglass' desire to emphasize his editorial independence after a Gerrit Smith-funded merger. Douglass often used the paper to support Smith's Liberty Party causes. He campaigned relentlessly for Smith in 1852, when Smith won a congressional seat. Douglass was worried about the perception that he was now publishing a mere party organ. One of his gestures of independence was that at the same time he was generally (but not always) endorsing Smith's ideas, he was also crusading for "race pride." Some of his writing at the time sounds much like Malcolm X's criticism of blacks who tried to look or act white. And some comments have a 1990s ring: in 1852 Douglass wrote that "there are some things which ought to be said to colored people . . . that can be said more effectively among themselves, without the presence of white persons. We are the oppressed, the whites are the oppressors, and the language I would address to the one is not always suited to the other." This appeared in a paper whose readership was 80 percent white. Martin concedes that despite these rhetorical gestures, "Douglass shared few thoughts with blacks . . . that he did not share with whites as well."[77]

With the preceding survey of Douglass' "antagonistic cooperation" with black and white abolitionists behind us, we are prepared to turn now to a close reading of the most famous of Douglass' speeches, the "July 5 Speech" of 1852. Douglass' personal and professional life in the years preceding this speech were characterized by a "reborn" sense of political blackness, which coexisted with a growing sense of comfort in cultural environments which were interracial, but predominantly white. One of Douglass' principal claims of this speech, that blacks have a "claim to ownership" in American political institutions and cultural traditions, is premised upon Douglass' sense of belonging in both black and white worlds.

Douglass faced the challenge of demonstrating solidarity with "his people," while also trying "to make their cause at one with that of the nation," David Blight observes. In this way, "a chosen people and a suffering people might find common ground through a compelling myth and a shared sense of peril."[78] Douglass had to articulate this myth so that "his people" could be seen in both racial and transracial aspects. His strategy was to utilize Biblical and natural rights egalitarian thought as mediating tools, capable of critiquing the failures of the republic, but also calling it to redemption. These tools demonstrated both the peril, and the hypocrisy, of the failure of this "Christian republic" to accept Douglass and his people into their community. In Douglass' hands, they also pointed towards a synthesis of the white/black binary in a multiracial imagined community.

"ANTAGONISTIC COOPERATION" AND "REDEEMABLE IDEALS" IN DOUGLASS' JULY 5 SPEECH

On July 5, 1852, Frederick Douglass gave an address entitled "What to the Slave is the 4th of July?", often called the "July 5 Speech" because Douglass attacked the hypocrisy of Independence Day celebrations in a slaveholding republic. William McFeely calls it "the greatest antislavery oration ever given."[79] David Chesebrough similarly believes it is "the best antislavery speech in history." I would agree with these assessments, and add that it is also a text with deep poetic resonance and moral vision. I will examine here some rhetorical strategies Douglass employed in order to effectively communicate with the different constituents of his multiracial audience. Since many of these strategies were derived from Bible stories and "natural rights" philosophy, I will pay particular attention to the streams of Christian and political egalitarianism which fed Douglass' vision.

I have three main goals:

(1) to give contemporary readers a sense of Douglass' stature in his own time;
(2) to indicate the deep religious and philosophical roots of Douglass' moral and political and worldview;
(3) to illustrate the continuing timeliness of Douglass' critique of American racialism.

Until recently, there has been a paucity of scholarship on Douglass' oratorical style and heritage. Gerald Fulkerson noted in 1972 that Douglass had been "largely ignored by rhetorical critics." However, two book-length studies of Douglass' oratory published in 1998 by Gregory Lampe and David Chesebrough indicate a "rediscovery" of Douglass as public speaker.[80] The relative absence of studies of Douglass as orator, for most of the twentieth century, does not seem to be for want of testimonies of Douglass' enormous talents as a speaker, either in our era or in Douglass' day. He is often cited as the greatest Negro abolitionist speaker, or even as the most effective orator in all of antebellum America.[81] During Douglass' career one observer wrote that his voice "rivalled Webster's in its richness and in the depth and sonorousness of its cadences." The author of a letter to William Garrison's *Liberator* simply declared that "It is impossible to do justice to the power and eloquence of Mr. Frederick Douglass." Reporters who did try to describe the electric appeal of Douglass often indulged "in embarrassingly florid prose."[82]

Not only did Douglass speak to ecstatic, overflow multiracial audiences, newspapers of his day took his influence far beyond abolitionist circles.

Papers such as the *New York Tribune* and the *Chicago Tribune* printed full-length stenographic accounts of Douglass' lengthy speeches during the 1850s, and many other papers such as the *New York Times* printed summaries. His speeches were distributed widely in the US and Great Britain as pamphlets.[83]

Such was Douglass' reputation that Stephen Douglas, who ran against Lincoln for president, once feigned sickness to avoid having to share a stage with the famous abolitionist.[84] Douglass' unprecedented package of skills as a handsome and charismatic speaker, editor, author, and political strategist translated into a real political power, which included but was not limited to advising political candidates and even presidents.

Douglass in context, now and then

Douglass' autobiographies have become part of the canon in English departments, and to a lesser degree, for historians. What then accounts for the paucity of studies of Douglass' oratory? There are certainly several answers to this question. It may be that Douglass' idealism and use of the Bible make us uncomfortable. And certainly Douglass has been hurt by a tendency to "ghettoize" him in a "black studies" box, and a parallel Eurocentric bias towards abolitionism, as I have argued. It would seem that our racialized "binary filters" cause us to turn blind eyes and deaf ears to social actors who define themselves and communicate in terms at least partially transcending "race."

Another factor is that Douglass' careers as public speaker and editor have played second fiddle in scholarly studies to his autobiographies, which provide well-defined windows for textual or psychological analysis. Most textual studies have focused on Douglass' first *Narrative*, which only hints at his career as public servant. At least superficially, this text seems to support our ingrained habit of separating white and black actors into separate cultural and moral universes, with whites taking the role of "oppressors" and "people of color" as the "oppressed." Yet the *Narrative* is "a composite text mediated by white editors," as Russ Castronovo notes. If it is true, as Peter Walker writes, that Douglass "found his tongue while speaking to white men," then the *Narrative*, for all its apparent oppositionality, gives a picture of Douglass at a time when he had not yet begun to speak specifically to a black audience, much less to mediate between black and white listeners.[85]

My Bondage and My Freedom, which is arguably Douglass' best piece of sustained writing, has received only a fraction of the attention accorded to the *Narrative*, either as an object of critical study, or as a required classroom text.[86] Yet this book presents the more fully expressive voice of a "newly formed" colored man. Douglass in the 1850s is both far more deeply engaged with his black peer group, and far more critical of white leadership, than the better-known, but more one-dimensional self-portrait of 1845. *My Bondage and My Freedom*, which includes the July 5 Speech as an appendix, pays far more attention to interracial themes. The tone is still heroic, but the hero is more explicitly located in a multiracial context. So perhaps it is not surprising that neither those with a preference for images of heroic (and oppressed) black rebels, nor those who pay "obsessive attention to Douglass' attraction to white leaders and culture," have seen fit to grapple with the complex Douglass of this transitional period from 1852 to 1855.[87]

Since I am reading the July 5 Speech as a literary text, as well as a psychological and social document, it may be helpful to situate Douglass' work at this moment in time in relation to some other literary and political texts of this period. This is of course something of a high-water mark in American literary history. I want to list four of the best-known novels published within a year of Douglass' speech, and characterize them in a way that illustrates how the central themes of these novels reflect concerns that also appear in Douglass' work.

Hawthorne's *The House of Seven Gables* (a family haunted by a curse for an ancestral crime) and Melville's *Moby Dick* (a self-destructive obsessive quest with a multiracial cast) both appeared in 1851. Hawthorne's *Blithedale Romance* (a utopian community gone awry) and Stowe's *Uncle Tom's Cabin* (the immorality of slavery, and blacks as suffering saints) appeared in 1852. I do not claim that the first three of these novels had any direct influence on Douglass, but of *Uncle Tom's Cabin* there is no doubt. Douglass' journalism and private letters are filled with enthusiastic references to Ms. Stowe's novel, and with reports on correspondence with and meetings with Stowe herself.

The first mention of *Uncle Tom's Cabin* in *Frederick Douglass' Paper* was a review on April 8, 1852, probably written by Julia Griffiths, Douglass' managing editor and best friend. His own writings on the book in subsequent months, which include the period in which he composed and delivered the July 5 Speech, "reveal Douglass as a creatively appropriative reader of Stowe's novel," writes Robert Levine.[88]

Among the things Douglass was "appropriating" from Stowe were models of how to reclaim Judeo-Christian scripture as a potentially liberatory tool, and how to most effectively engage in antislavery agitation within a political domain. It was only a year before the publication of *Uncle Tom's Cabin* that Douglass had made his final break with Garrison, publicly announcing his commitment to political abolitionism, and his antislavery reading of the Constitution. Three of his most important allies in this shift were two white women – Stowe and Griffiths – and a white man, his patron Gerrit Smith. Yet this should not be seen as a matter of one-way influence: as Levine notes, a dominant theme in "Douglass' interactions with Stowe is his working assumption that he could shape her politics and action."[89]

Just as Douglass had a white peer group among whom he found both allies, and anti-models against which to define himself, so a similar process of antagonistic cooperation was taking place between Douglass and his black peer group. William Andrews has placed Douglass' work in the early to mid-1850s within the context of "the first Afro-American Literary Renaissance." The dominant model of black writing up until this time had been the fugitive-slave narrative, of which Douglass' *Narrative* was the main prototype. But this genre was becoming formulaic. Many white readers and a growing group of literate black readers grew dissatis-fied with its constraints. These narratives had been mostly mediated through abolitionist transcribers or editors, but now there was a move towards black self-expression. This led to "a period of generic experimen-tation." Douglass again served as a dominant prototype. In his July 5 Speech, for instance, he "signified" on two genres in a creative fusion: both the "Jeremiad," which was a common form of oratory in a broader American context, and a specific form of Afro-American oratory based on anti-holiday or counter-holiday speeches.[90]

But there were other free blacks, some far more educated than Dou-glass, who also "aspired to be literary spokesmen." William Wells Brown published *Three Years in Europe* in 1852, the first travel book by a black American writer, and *Clotel; or, The President's Daughter*, the first Afro-American novel, in 1853. Both of these books presented images with which Douglass was in sympathy: the first, of a cosmopolitan black whose concerns were not limited by abolitionism, and the second, a story about the rumored mixed-race offspring of Thomas Jefferson which critiqued both Christianity and the unredeemed ideals of the democratic republic. This was a form of "revisionistic myth making," notes Andrews, which illustrated that "the black writer of the 1850s had begun to render American reality not only according to objective facts but also in accord-ance with his subjective interpretation of the country's myths and sym-bols."[91]

There were other black writers during this same 1851–53 time period against which Douglass found himself in opposition. One of those was Martin Delany, his former coeditor. Delany published his *Condition, Elevation, Emigration, and Destiny of the Colored People of the United States* one month after *Uncle Tom's Cabin* was published in 1852. Whereas Stowe had revealed her sympathy for African colonization, Delany presented voluntary emigration as an alternative modeled on the Biblical Exodus. And he looked not to Africa but to "a third place that was within the Americas but not a part of the United States – Central and South America and the Caribbean," Levine points out. What seems remarkable, in hindsight, is Delany's "appropriation" of Manifest Destiny rhetoric. Delany presents Afro-Americans as being destined by "the finger of God" to be leaders of their fellow blacks in Latin America. Yet he never examined his assumption that these Latin Americans would want to be governed by North American blacks. While Douglass presented race as secondary to national citizenship, Delany believed that race trumped national boundaries. Since Delany presented himself as an alternative and pure-blood "representative black leader," in competition with Douglass' mixed-blood model, Levine believes that much of Douglass' writing and speeches during this period should be read, in part, as an indirect response to Delany.[92]

Douglass and Delany clashed over their divergent views of *Uncle Tom's Cabin*. Delany harshly criticized Stowe, both for her presumption in claiming to understand blacks and her sympathy for colonization ventures. Douglass printed some of Delany's attacks on Stowe, yet consistently defended her. Douglass believed Stowe's shortcomings could be changed through dialogue. His stance can be summed up in James McCune Smith's comment about *Uncle Tom's Cabin* that Douglass printed on May 27, 1852: "I am thankful for the sunlight without finding fault with its spots." Both Stowe and Douglass publicly declared their intention to "modify" each others' views, while Delany seemed more interested in castigation. Delany's attacks on Stowe eventually led Douglass to respond: "To scornfully reject all aid from our white friends, and to denounce them as unworthy of our confidence, looks high and mighty enough on paper; but . . . of what use is such display?"[93]

Douglass' complex positionality in this realm may further illustrate why scholars have been less inclined to engage his oratory and journalism, which are created in and addressed to multiracial contexts. In fact, Douglass' speeches and short writings take place in such a fluid, intersubjective public space that it is better not to treat these period pieces as the work of *only* an individual. These efforts at public persuasion emerge through interaction – both hand-to-hand combat *and* cooperation – with several audiences that partially intersect.

"Black and white reasons"

Douglass' July 5 Speech reflects his links with two audiences largely inaccessible during his years as a Garrisonian agent. These are the networks of black abolitionists which he developed through the black convention movement and his journalism, and a growing comfort in "white worlds" beyond the apolitical Garrisonians. His white contacts now included a range of European supporters, local and national political representatives, feminists, and wealthy philanthropists. Douglass' work as editor and orator functioned as a meeting ground for these two "wings" of abolitionism.

In his proclaimed work of "abolitionizing the public mind," Douglass quite explicitly divided this public sphere into white and black components. "I am willing to accept a judgment against slavery, whether supported by white or black reasons – though I would much rather have it supported by both," he proclaimed. His definition of coalition is remarkably inclusive: "He that is not against us, is on our part."[94]

As we will see as we turn to a reading of the July 5 Speech, Douglass was becoming quite self-conscious in his role of representing black Americans to audiences composed mostly of white Northerners. Often this required emphasizing differences, before Douglass went on to partially resolve these differences by rhetorically constructing a multiracial imagined community. Before a meeting of the American and Foreign Anti-Slavery Society (anti-Garrisonians), Douglass felt compelled to remark upon "the peculiar relation subsisting between me and the audience I am to address. Sir, I am a colored man, and this is a white audience." In this speech, Douglass explicitly addressed a controversy which was implicit in the July 5 Speech: who was or was not "a colored man," and who did or did not have the right to speak for black Americans. It is worth repeating that this very issue of the right to representation – and of the racial ambiguity which might undermine this right – was the driving force behind the composition of Douglass' *Narrative*. And it continued to be an obsession of Douglass' during the 1850s.

Thus, Douglass felt compelled to underline his race, or it would be more accurate to say, his representative identity:

as a colored man I do speak; as a colored man I was invited here to speak; and as a colored man there are peculiar reasons for my speaking . . . I would place myself – nay, I am placed among the victims of American oppression. I view this subject from their stand-point, and scan the moral and political horizon of the country with their hopes, their fears, and their intense solicitude.

Yet despite the fact that Douglass claims unity with "colored people" who are "becoming a nation, in the midst of a nation which disowns them," his very posture of scanning "the political and moral horizon" reveals his dual strategies, dual loyalties. Douglass is in fact employing moral and political "horizons" constructed primarily by Semitic and

European peoples in order to offer a prescription for the crisis in the relationship between the emerging "black nation" and a larger "American people." Asserting his membership in both collectives, he also insists that these moral and political guideposts must inevitably serve as foundations on which black and white Americans can unite in a multiracial structure. As David Blight writes, "He must be at one with his people and at the same time strive to make their cause at one with that of the nation." By uniting both peoples in "a compelling myth and a shared sense of peril," the boundaries of inclusion of a "chosen people" in this self-willed "redeemer nation" could expand.[95]

The re-visioning of a "chosen people mythology" is a central rhetorical strategy of Douglass' July 5 Speech, delivered at Rochester's Corinthian Hall, a home base in Douglass' labor to "abolitionize the public mind." Douglass shows himself to be keenly aware of the North American tendency to envision their republic as a "redeemer" nation destined to carry out a divine destiny through political, indeed imperial, means.[96] And he is in fact deeply invested in this millennial worldview. Yet Douglass marshalls political, economic, cultural, and Biblical evidence to argue that Afro-Americans are God's new chosen people, and the truer sons of the revolution, by virtue of their suffering. In this sense, Douglass lends partial support to Stowe's cultural mythology, but aligns himself against Delany: the people are chosen not to colonize other lands and peoples, but to redeem the land of their birth. In Douglass' view, recognizing the distinctiveness of Afro-Americans is a prelude to allowing their commonality to leaven the whole. Claiming a deeper moral foundation which legitimates them as political agents, black Americans will correct the larger America's myopia (its inability to imagine a multiracial society), and enable this multiracial society to fulfill its creed.

"Your fathers": rhetorical distancing as "antagonistic cooperation"

Douglass' remark in 1852 that he stood "in relation as child to father" towards Garrison seems to indicate that he was still working through a powerful father complex. We know that Douglass became conscious of this, because in his 1855 autobiography, when he confesses that he had seen Garrison as a modern-day Moses, he is self-critical. His "hero worship" was something of a "slavish adoration," he admits. There seems to have been a messianic projection involved. In Jung's terms, we can say that he found a way to "recall" that projection. The July 5 Speech reveals that Douglass was learning to resolve his father complex through a critical reappraisal of both political and religious patriarchs.[97]

The July 5 Speech indicates that Douglass meant his comment about having a "child to father" relation to Garrison in the sense of being personally indebted, rather than psychologically dependent. Early in the speech he honors Garrison by quoting a line from the first issue of the *Liberator*: "I will not equivocate; I will not excuse." And he closes the speech with a direct tribute to Garrison. In private he could write that he had outgrown the Garrisonian school because it was "*too* narrow in its philosophy and too bigoted in spirit to do justice to any who venture to differ from it."[98] But in public Garrison retained his honored place in Douglass' pantheon of abolitionist heroes.

Garrison was still in the house, but Douglass' horizons had lifted to a new set of fathers, both American "founders," and Biblical patriarchs. These mythic fathers now provided Douglass with a baseline for his identity – fathers against whom and with whom Douglass could redefine his roles as son and citizen.

The July 5 Speech ruminates upon a series of opposites, all deriving from the July 4/July 5 double with which Douglass began his oration. "This Fourth of July is *yours*, not *mine*. *You* may rejoice, *I* must mourn," he told his primarily white audience in Rochester, New York. The contrast between July 4 and not-July 4 initiated a radical critique of American citizenship, symbolized by a series of seemingly irreconcilable doubles: white and black, American and not American, free and not free, celebration and mourning. Many anthologies only extract the first part of this speech in which these binaries appear unresolvable.[99]

However, in the full speech, Douglass also utilized a series of "mediatory symbols" from the Bible and Enlightenment philosophy that signify his vision of a "third space" capable of synthesizing these binaries.[100] Douglass' July 5 Speech was the product of a long process of personal and intellectual maturation in which he achieved a measure of independence from his abolitionist mentors. Douglass' resolution of Constitutional doubleness gave him one of the "mediatory symbols" with which he depolarized the series of binary doubles in his speech. The speech also shows Douglass moderating his earlier critique of Christianity in order to recover the Bible as a liberatory document.

This speech is in fact permeated with the theme of ambiguous paternity. As Douglass recounts the origins of the Declaration of Independence, and comments on the contemporary context of July 4 celebrations, he distances himself from his white audience by repeatedly employing the adjective "your": "your nation," "your freedom," "your fathers." These "yours" are piled on and on through eight pages of text until Douglass has used "your," by my count, forty-five times, of which seventeen are references to "your fathers." Russ Castronovo remarks that Douglass is "invoking the fathers even as he refuses to discuss them," but it would be more accurate to say that he is refusing to idolize them. The terms of the discussion are not so much the sins of the fathers themselves as the uses to which their political grandchildren have put them. As Priscilla Ward notes, this ambiguity towards founding fathers was "a prominent characteristic of antebellum political culture." Abraham Lincoln himself would use a similar ambiguity later in the 1850s, to dramatize "the conflict between being at once good, obedient sons and worthy competitors of heroic fathers." This may also be another instance of Douglass' having been influenced by black abolitionists: in an 1850 speech, Martin Delany had declared that "Whatever ideas of liberty I may have, have been received from reading the lives of *your* revolutionary fathers." Douglass is not as explicit about his debt, but the result is the same: this distancing serves the dual function of marking black abolitionists as the truer sons, or as the only political descendants of these fathers who are putting their revolutionary ideas into practice.[101]

One one level, Douglass is engaged here in a Jeremiad: like Jeremiah and other prophets, chastizing the "chosen people" for failing to uphold their covenant, and warning of destruction if they continue their lawlessness. In a study of *The American Jeremiad*, Sacvan Bercovitch notes that the classic writers in this tradition "tended to uphold [Republican] ideals even when they most bitterly assailed their society." Douglass is clearly a classic exponent of this tradition. Yet Douglass and other ex-slaves "repeat with a difference," as Castronovo observes: by invoking the national narrative of the founders, they "produced a hybrid narrative in which black rebels resemble white patriots even as they differ from them." Castronovo calls this strategy "discursive passing": not so much that Douglass and others who invoke the national fathers are trying to pass for white, but that the ex-slave "'passes' as revolutionary patriarch."[102] Yet Douglass is not a typical Jeremiah, or a typical Moses. He is advocating no Exodus here, unless it would be a journey away from the practice of the "actually existing American republic," and toward the redemptive horizon of equal rights.

Douglass hints at the strategy he will employ at the start of this string of "yours" when he observes that to his audience, July 4 represents "what the Passover was to the emancipated people of God." The linking of American freedom with Biblical emancipation drops out of the mix for the rest of Douglass' distancing, except for a brief comparison of the Revolutionary-era British to Pharaoh. Otherwise Douglass does not signal his coming reversal. He is full of praise for the founders, even as they are designated as "your fathers." There is a hint that Douglass is aiming to reclaim their project when he notes that the founders "preferred revolution to peaceful submission to bondage," and "did not shrink from agitating against oppression." Douglass even seems to hold out the hope of common ground when he admits, somewhat begrudgingly, that these were men who were "great enough to give frame to a great age," and that he is willing to "unite with you to honor their memory."

But fulsome praise in itself should arouse suspicion, since "men seldom eulogize the wisdom and virtues of their fathers, but to excuse some folly or wickedness of their own." Douglass' examples are both Biblical and American. The children of Jacob were prone to boast about having Abraham as "our father," Douglass observes, "when they had long lost Abraham's faith and spirit." And now slave-traders had the gall to call George Washington "*our father*," even though Washington at least had the decency to emancipate his own slaves before he died.[103]

Douglass then turns the tables, asking his audience directly why they have asked him to speak on this day, and what "those I represent" have to do with this holiday. The aforementioned quote ("This Fourth of July is *yours*, not *mine*") concludes the long sequence of distancing "yours," and completes the transition from irony to accusation. "Do you mean, citizens, to mock me, by asking me to speak to-day?" he asks. This is in a sense "merely" a rhetorical question. Douglass would certainly have not appeared if he felt he was being mocked, and his audience in Rochester knew enough about him not to expect an oration of patriotic platitudes. After all, Douglass had taught a course on slavery "every Sunday during an entire winter" in Corinthian Hall.[104]

There seems to be a psychological subtext at work here. One can read Douglass' struggle with white paternity in this speech as a commentary on Douglass' own racial ambiguity. Peter Walker surely overstates the case when he argues that Douglass, during the Garrisonian years, "supposed himself free of his blackness." Yet Douglass left many clues that he desired to integrate his "white side." Douglass had grown up fatherless, although his master, and possible biological father, Aaron Anthony, who had also grown up fatherless, served as "Frederick's first father image." His professed hero worship of Garrison was certainly in part a projection of a father-substitute. Then there is his adapted last name, which was taken from Sir Walter Scott's *Lady of the Lake*, in which a character known as "black Douglas" has his paternity restored to him. During his 1845–47 English sojourn, Douglass spent a great deal of time in Scotland, where he learned to sing and play on his violin many Scottish ballads. A letter to Garrison at this time records his fascination with the "black Douglas" and remarks on "a great change in me!" During the subsequent years as a "coloured man reborn," leading up to his final break with Garrison in 1851, there must been great pain and resentment that his father figure had turned on him. There is certain "won't get fooled again" tone to the rhetorical distancing during the July 5 Speech, as if Douglass wants to let his audience know how much the balance of power had changed since that night in Nantucket, over a decade earlier, when "he had found his tongue while speaking to white men."[105]

But the deeper purpose of this accusatory question – "Do you mean to mock me?" – is to make the audience think historically, and to claim an unassailable legitimacy for his critique. To accomplish this, Douglass turns to the Bible, aligning black Americans with the children of Israel. His strategy is once again a form of interracial "antagonist cooperation." The distancing is antagonistic and critical, but the use of the Bible and Constitution shows hope of cooperation. And Afro-Americans hold the key to a potential collective redemption.

"By the rivers of Babylon": the redemptive power of suffering

An archetypal feature of Afro-American/Caribbean religious expression is Biblical typology, which "links biblical types or figures to postbiblical persons, places, and events." Blacks in the diaspora often contrast a Biblical "type" with a post-Biblical "antitype" which is "understood to represent a fulfillment of prophecy," Theophus Smith writes.[106] I would describe it as recreations of archetypal figures: Moses reappears continuously in Afro-American music, literature, and political discourse, as well as in the art of other ethnic groups.[107] In any case, the intent of this rhetorical strategy is to claim a status for post-Biblical people or events as "prophecy fulfilled." Douglass' representation of Afro-Americans as "virtual Jews" clearly is a part of this tradition of Biblical archetypology.

Douglass' equation of the enslavement of Africans in America with the enslavement of the ancient Jews is made most explicit in his following (unattributed) quotation from Psalms 137:

By the rivers of Babylon, there we sat down. Yea! we wept when we remembered Zion... For there, they that carried us away captive, required of us a song ... saying, Sing us one of the songs of Zion. How can we sing the Lord's song in a strange land? If I forget thee, O Jerusalem, let my ... tongue cleave to the roof of my mouth.

Those in Douglass' audience who knew their Biblical history would have recognized that this Psalm was written in Babylonian exile, after Jerusalem was sacked in 587 BC. Those in my audience with some knowledge of the Harlem Renaissance, or of Afro-American history in the 1920s, may recall that Marcus Garvey made use of this scripture in his "Back to Africa" movement. And fans of reggae music would recognize this passage as having been adapted by Rastafarian groups such as the Melodians in 1973 and Steel Pulse in 1980.[108] Douglass, Garvey, and the Rastafarians were all using Psalms 137 as a tool for similar purposes: to describe a sense of being outsiders, and to claim parallels between people of the African diaspora and diasporic Jews, as God's "chosen people." Suffering endows a people with "redemptive power," as Martin Luther King, Jr., would later claim for Afro-Americans.

In this manner, Douglass dramatically claimed moral authority and illustrated why he could not share the spirit of celebration. Echoing the Psalm again, he said his own tongue should "cleave to the roof of my mouth" if he should forget the millions of slaves who could not reap the benefits of the American Revolution. Therefore, "I shall see this day and its popular characteristics from the slave's point of view." And from this perspective, where "the name of the constitution and the Bible ... are disregarded and trampled upon," Douglass could unequivocally proclaim: "this nation never looked blacker to me than on this 4th of July!"

"Black" here seems to signify "without hope." But in context, it also carries an ironic resonance, a double meaning. Because Douglass follows this declaration with a laundry list of all the work which black people were doing for America while some white citizens were still debating their humanity. This work included "ploughing, planting, and reaping, using all kinds of mechanical tools, erecting houses ... digging gold in California, capturing the whale in the Pacific." Again, Douglass piles on the evidence until its sheer weight gives one the clear sense that the very foundations of the American republic have been built, and are being maintained, by black people. Without credit. The intent of this rhetorical strategy, as Robert Levine writes in his study of Douglass' relationship with Delany, is to show that "Western culture and the economic systems driving and perpetuating it are not so white after all."[109]

What Douglass has accomplished through these rhetorical maneuvers is to position himself "*outside* the American dream but *within* the circle of the post-Revolutionary generation's rhetoric," writes Eric Sundquist. He argues that Douglass was "the truer 'son', the truer inheritor of the flawed yet *redeemable ideals* of the Revolutionary generation." Douglass employs three legitimation strategies to claim this status as "truer son." First, his reference to the founding fathers as men who "did not shrink from agitating against oppression" makes it clear that it is black freedom fighters (and their white supporters) who are continuing this heroic tradition. Hence, he is "passing" as one of the "real revolutionaries." Douglass has "recast the Revolution as an arrested struggle for general emancipation," Maggie Montesinos Sale writes, with abolitionists in the heroic role of redeeming or fulfilling the emancipatory ideals of the

Revolution. Second, he portrays black Americans as a double of the Children of Israel. And third, he describes black people as having built the nation through their "invisible" work.[110]

The idea of "redeemable ideals" is a key to this speech, and to Douglass' philosophy. He argues that both the ideals of America's founders and the emancipatory visions of Biblical patriarchs are worth "redeeming," or reclaiming. This was a form of self-fathering on Douglass' part, Sundquist argues. Douglass is looking beyond his biological father and beyond Garrison to a much deeper paternity. He finds his deepest legitimating roots by drawing a parallel between the situation in which he finds himself, as a "coloured" man asked to speak before whites, and the ancient Children of Israel, who had also been asked to "perform" by the people who kept them in bondage.[111]

"Ethiopia's hands": "blackening" the Bible

Douglass is engaged in a "blackening" of the Bible, of American democracy, and to some degree, of himself. He puts an exclamation point to this "blackening" by ending the speech with a quote from Psalms 68:31: "Ethiopia shall stretch out her hand unto God." Albert Raboteau calls this "the most quoted verse in black religious history."[112] Douglass actually names the first man to use Psalms 68:31 to argue for black equality, white Boston judge Samuel Sewall in 1700. Many black leaders such as Richard Allen had made use of this and other Ethiopian references in the Bible. By Douglass' time Psalms 68:31 was saturated with millennial associations, including the belief that black people had been chosen by God to teach Americans "the true meaning of their creed," as Martin Luther King later said. So Douglass' use of this verse signifies upon a very specific subcultural context, but at the same time, it also is a part of and a commentary on the "mainstream" belief in America as a "redeemer nation."[113] Like Psalms 137, this passage also later reappears in the speeches of Marcus Garvey and in the music of Rastafarians.

The extent of Douglass' Biblical references, and his use of Psalms 68:31 in particular, is not typical. It is hard to imagine Douglass citing it after 1860, as this verse came to be associated with colonization ventures which replicated the worst of American racialism and Christian imperialism. Furthermore, the adult Douglass, although he went to church as an example, often commented that he had "prayed with his feet." He once remarked that it was only through the acts of conscious men and women that he "could get a glimpse of God anywhere."[114] So why did Douglass use a reference to Ethiopianism, an Afro-Christian millennialism, at this moment? The answer may lie in Douglass' "antagonist cooperation" with black abolitionists, as we have seen. Douglass most likely used this verse as a legitimating device, and because of its evocative power on his audience, without himself believing in a literal interpretation.

Garrisonians were inclined to attribute Douglass' changes – the outreach to Christians, political activism, and interpretation of the Constitution as antislavery – to the "heretical" influence of his publisher Julia Griffiths, and Gerrit Smith, a radical abolitionist who was elected to Congress in 1852. These two white friends did have a large influence. But the view of Douglass as having been infected by the "apostasies" of anti-Garrisonians was, of course, extremely patronizing. It shortchanged Douglass' independent frame of mind, his ability to listen to a diversity of viewpoints and then to formulate his own position. And it did not take into account Douglass' relationships with other free blacks. As I have suggested, the "blackening" of American democracy and the Bible that one sees in the 1852 speech seems to reflect the impact on Douglass of the black conventions he had attended, as well as his editorial alliance with black writers.

"Christian liberty" and "one blood"

At age thirty-four, Douglass adopted a familiar position in relation to his predominantly white audience at Corinthian Hall – a spokesman of blacks pleading their case to whites. But his comments on Christianity and the Constitution also reveal a more complicated positionality which was emerging through call-and-response with his mixed publics: emphasizing great differences but also stressing deep common roots.

After recounting the vast range of black labor, Douglass asked the rhetorical question of the speech's title: "What, to the American slave, is your 4th of July?" This day revealed to the slave above all America's "gross injustice." "To him, your celebration is a sham." The "shocking and bloody" practices of Americans were so widespread, argued Douglass, that one could travel the world and document all the abuses of other nations and still come to the conclusion that "for revolting barbarity and shameless hypocrisy, America reigns without a rival."

Douglass then "dramatized" the inhumanities of the slave trade in great detail, as he had been doing for over a decade. Lest his audience imagine that these barbarities were a thing of the past, Douglass drew attention to the 1850 Fugitive Slave Bill, which had "nationalized" slavery. Worst of all, this "vile" and "abominable"[115] law had been supported by by "the chosen men of American theology," said Douglass, naming names. These "champions of oppressors" had "deliberately taught us, against the example of the Hebrews, and against the remonstrance of the Apostles, *that we ought to obey man's law before the law of God.*[116] Such a Christianity "makes God a respecter of persons," despite Peter's remark in Acts 10:34 that "God has no favorites." Douglass again turns to scripture to ground his critique. Quoting Isaiah and Psalms 68, he reads: "Your hands are full of blood." This passage exhorts those who have abandoned the "higher law": "cease to do evil ... relieve the oppressed; judge for the fatherless; plead for the widow."[117]

Thereafter, Douglass proceeds to moderate his critique. He wants it to be "distinctly understood" that "there are exceptions." Again he names names. He also calls attention to Christian participation in British abolitionism. "The anti-slavery movement there was not an antichurch movement, for the reason that the church took its full share in prosecuting that movement." Douglass points out that abolitionism in America will "cease to be an anti-church movement" when Christians as a "great mass" throw their weight behind the principles of what Douglass calls "Christian Liberty."

Douglass' stance towards Christianity here is a cautious and partial rapprochement. He thinks that the tendency of some abolitionists to be anti-church is understandable. But he has also come to see the church as a "redeemable" institution which, should it interpret its own scriptures properly, could still be a powerful tool in the struggle for equal rights. This reflects Douglass' view of the historical currents in which he was situated. Abolitionism was "a byproduct of the upsurge of revivalism" known as the Second Great Awakening, John McKivigan notes, and has even deeper roots in the First Great Awakening (chapter 1). But Garrisonians abandoned the church as unsalvageable and developed "an extreme brand of perfectionist philosophy."[118]

When Douglass joined the Garrisonians, their "come out of the church" dogma made sense to him. After all, Covey the slave-breaker was also a preacher. In the 1840s only the Quakers still held a strong anti-slavery position. It took time for Douglass to become aware of the deeper antiracist roots of evangelicals. And it may have taken the charges by black abolitionists that he was anti-Bible, as well as the proddings of Julia Griffiths, for him to revisit the scriptures that once enthused him in his youth, before he found in Garrison a "new Moses."[119]

It is significant that Douglass uses the term "Christian Liberty" as representing the antithesis of the Fugitive Slave Law. As the "truer son" of the Revolution, Douglass has chosen to take his stand at the crossroads where Christian principles intersect with natural rights philosophy – the same fusion of ideals which had brought abolitionism into the mainstream of public sphere discourse during the Revolutionary years. That Douglass understands this doubling to have an emancipatory potential is made clear, near the end of the speech, when he pairs quotes from both of these interrelated traditions. He reminds his audience, as citizens of a would-be democracy, of the natural rights philosophy enshrined in the Declaration of Independence: "all men are created equal."[120]

Douglass also quotes the famous passage in Acts 17:26 that "of one blood, God made all nations of men to dwell on the face of the earth." This scripture also has historical resonances that reach far back and far forward. Foreshadowed again by Samuel Sewall in 1700, both black and white writers and preachers employed the "one blood" motif to argue for multiracial equal rights throughout the late eighteenth and early nineteenth centuries. Douglass' contemporary Harriett Beecher Stowe used it in *Uncle Tom's Cabin*, and the piece continued to echo through Afro-American and Carribean cultures, as well as other ethnic literatures. In a recent manifestation "One Blood" reappeared as a reggae anthem sung by Junior Reid in the 1990s.

The Biblical precept of "one blood" established in America "a sacred textual basis for the spiritual unity of a secularly divided people," writes Werner Sollors. Like most texts used by mixed audiences, it conveyed multiple meanings. Different speakers used it inclusively and exclusively, to pursue both consensus and conflict. But the end result was to "establish a common language within which dissent can take place."[121]

Douglass' approach, as a form of "antagonistic cooperation," allowed for both cooperation and conflict. Douglass read into the concept of "one blood" a legitimation of his own mixed heritage. His attitudes towards miscegenation, eventually formalized in an interracial marriage, reflect his belief that hybridity, as a "composite" identity, was the invisible "deep roots" of America, and its inescapable future.[122]

DOUGLASS' INTERRACIAL MARRIAGE AS "MEDIATORY SYMBOL"

In 1979, Douglass' great-granddaughter, Anne Weaver Teabeau, re-marked that his marriage to a white woman seemed to be the only thing most of "his people" knew about him.[123] This is somewhat of an exaggeration which may reflect a cultural climate, at the end of an era of resurgent black nationalism, in which "Black Power" advocates like Malcolm X and Julius Lester had been deriding Douglass as insufficiently radical. Blacks opposed to interracialism viewed Douglass' marriage to Helen Pitts as a "serious, if not unforgiveable, error."[124] Wilson Moses agrees that the marriage "contributed to the opinion that he was anti-nationalist." At the same time, Moses notes that Frantz Fanon, Kwame Nkrumah, Father Divine, and Richard Wright, among others, also married white women without hurting their credentials as "race men." So it is unclear why Douglass should be held to a different standard, unless this was a product of his having been more open, or "unrepentant," about his marriage.[125] August Meier surmises that most of Douglass' Negro contemporaries opposed the marriage. He also repeats the view, first voiced in Booker T. Washington's ghostwritten biography of Douglass, that the marriage led to the "decline of his position as leader." However, recent surveys of scholarship on Douglass make it clear that most Afro-American scholars continue to express a largely positive evaluation of Douglass, and are only occasionally concerned with his interracial marriage.[126]

Teabeau's remark may reflect a sort of "folk perception" that contributes to the milieu in which a KRS-One will dismiss Douglass as a "sellout." I cannot speak for KRS, but I do know that interracial romances remain an explosive topic for many Afro-Americans, as reflected in Spike Lee's *Jungle Fever*. I also know that the primary opposition to the creation of a "biracial" census category in the 1990s has come from Afro-Americans. Boundary maintenance of the racial community remains a very sensitive issue. Some of the fiercest opposition to the concept of biraciality has come from mixed-race people themselves, as evident in commentary by Lenny Kravitz, Lisa Jones, and Itabari Njeri.[127]

Like all interactions on racial frontiers, Douglass' marriage is open to multiple interpretations. Some people from Douglass' day to the present have reacted to it as a "polarizing sign." Others have viewed his marriage as a "mediatory symbol" – an action which symbolized Douglass' commitment to building a multiracial society. Despite his protestations that he did not mean for this marriage to serve as a model, Douglass himself clearly viewed his second marriage as both a personal and a symbolic act, which in its public dimension continued his lifelong dedication to interracial mediation. This comes through above all in Douglass' tendency to defuse criticism of the marriage by calling attention to his own biraciality – both biological and cultural.

Terms like "biraciality" are not a long-term solution to the problem of the language of race, in my view. But both of the principal alternatives of which I am aware seem less attractive, or currently impossible: to retain a binary conception of race, into which everyone must fit into one box or another, or to "transcend" race by subsuming it within a more inclusive humanism. As Wilson Moses notes, Douglass struggled with this problem throughout his life. His paradox was that he became ever more deeply embedded in the language of race in an effort to transcend racialized thinking.[128] I bring up this contemporary context now for the same reason that I previously quoted KRS: to illustrate why our binary "racial" filters make it hard for us to see clearly those persons or those cultural traditions that do not fit clearly within one "racial" box or another.

Many historians think Douglass "lost touch" in the years after the 1877 Southern Compromise. Waldo Martin believes that "his alliance with the Republican party dulled the critical edge of his political insight." This assessment needs to be qualified, I would argue. Douglass had already himself concluded by 1880 that "our reconstruction measures were radically defective." It would be futile to argue against the claim that "in crucial ways he increasingly lost touch with the ordinary Negro,"[129] but I do not think it is unreasonable to ask why Douglass should be expected to make the "ordinary Negro" the touchstone of his entire life. After all, he was not an "ordinary Negro," whatever that term means. There is something to be said for the importance of even "symbolic inclusion" in mainstream politics for "ordinary Negroes," which is the role Douglass often played with Republicans.

Furthermore, one can see in comments about Douglass being a "sell-out" or "betraying his race" hints of a projected desire for a self-sacrificing Black Messiah – a persistent undercurrent in much writing about Afro-American history, as Moses has richly documented.[130] The assumption is often that a black culture hero who is in touch with his people must give up his life at an early age – as we see in a series of figures on to whom messianic hopes have been projected, such as David Walker, Malcolm X, Martin Luther King, and Bob Marley. Douglass problematizes these assumptions: although he was a believer in a form of self-sacrifice (work and discipline), he was certainly not the kind of man who was caught up in the mythology of sacrificial prophets. And he was not the kind of "culture hero" who was prone to define the "ordinary Negro" by the lowest common denominator. So in response to declarations that Douglass "lost touch" with "his people," the question must arise as to who "his people" really were. To answer that question with a binary definition of a racial community is to contradict the answers that Douglass himself often gave.

The racialist reading of the perception that Douglass "lost his way" during the post-Reconstruction years would be to view his 1884 inter-racial marriage as the most visible evidence of his having "sold out." This view would interpret his "redemption" as originating in 1892 with the beginning of his collaboration in Ida B. Wells-Barnett's anti-lynching campaign. I want to problematize that in two ways. The first is to note that Douglass had long been involved in battling the virulent expressions of white supremacy which were ascendant in the late nineteenth century. He had written against the "lynch law" from 1871 on. And he continually tried to keep the legacy of slavery in the nation's vision. The critical and commercial failure of his last autobiography, *Life and Times*, was not merely due to his repeating himself, or his irrelevance. It was also due to Douglass' insistence on trying to use this book – which first appeared in 1881 – as a means of reminding his nation that it could not yet wash its hands of slavery.[131]

The second principal way I want to problematize the notion of the later Douglass as a prodigal son of the black community is to place his inter-racial marriage within the context of his lifelong opposition to racialism. I am in agreement with Wilson Moses' view that it is more accurate to say that Douglass' "long-standing distaste for racial chauvinism" allowed him to develop the relationship with Pitts that led to their marriage, rather than to infer, as Waldo Martin and August Meier do, that the marriage caused him to de-emphasize "race pride."[132] Douglass' interracial mar-riage was an outgrowth of his radical critique of the racialism which had prevented the Revolutionary generation from developing a vision of a "multiracial society." This racialism had led to the growth of white supremacist politics, the entrenchment of slavery, and the Civil War. If racialism was wrong for whites, then how could it be right for blacks? Or for biracial people and "other" Americans?

The trend towards interracialism in Douglass' thinking that led eventu-ally to his interracial marriage was very much in evidence during the antebellum period. I want to contextualize this section about Douglass' interracial marriage by noting the themes present in Douglass' "opposi-tional" stance of 1852 that provide a direct link to his "integrationist" marriage of 1884.

The diversity of black labor which Douglass had detailed in 1852 dramatized his view that "colored" people, along with the founding fathers, shared responsibility for laying "the corner-stone of the national super-structure." His message was always: "we are *here to stay*." In the year of his interracial marriage, Douglass published an essay in the prestigious *North American Review* which made the same case. After asking rhetorically if the "colored people of the United States" would emigrate, Douglass answered emphatically: "No! Individuals may, but the masses will not. Dust will fly, but the earth will remain." And the American soil was inalterably multiracial. "Drive out the Negro you drive out Christ, the Bible, and American liberty with him," Douglass insisted.[133] This perspec-tive foreshadows the work of black theologian James Cone in the 1960s, who defined blacks as embodying true Christianity in America.

The 1852 speech spoke of nations as rivers, which gave Douglass hope. His "consolation" was that America was still young, and that "Great streams are not easily turned from channels, worn deep in the course of

ages." Presumably he found this metaphor encouraging because these
deep channels were themselves hybrid, which would eventually force
America to abandon its artificial racial separation. In the same 1884
article which attempted to envision the future of "colored people" in the
US, Douglass again returned to this theme of nations, and "races," as
rivers. With typical irony he noted that "It was once degredation intensified for a Norman to associate with a Saxon; but time and events have
swept down the barriers between them, and Norman and Saxon have
become Englishmen."[134] Douglass viewed at least partial synthesis as
inevitable for both nations and "races." This shows the continuity of his
thought between the period in which he was most oppositional, and the
era a third of a century later when his philosophy was apparently most
integrationist.

Another continuity between 1852 and 1884 is the intense public criticism Douglass received for his associations with white women. Julia
Griffiths, whom Douglass had met during his English sojourn, lived
in-house with Douglass 1848–1852, managing his financial affairs and
often acting as de facto editor. This inspired gossip among white abolitionists who could not bear the thought of a black man with a white
woman. The public and private accusations and insinuations by Garrisonians against Griffiths and Douglass became so vicious that Griffiths
moved out of Douglass' offices in 1852 to another Rochester home. Even
this did not satisfy their one-time allies. "By 1855, the criticism had
become so shrill that the two could no longer withstand its pressures,"
McFeely writes.[135] Griffiths returned to England, married, organized
twenty new antislavery societies, raised funds for Douglass, and contributed a regular column to *Douglass' Monthly.* They remained in correspondence the rest of their lives and died within three months of each other in
1895.

In the midst of this rancor, Douglass' colleague James McCune Smith
remembered the 1830s as an interracial "honeymoon" among abolitionists. There was some truth to this, but there had always been tensions
over race-mixing among abolitionists. Some of this can be attributed to
the hypersensitivity abolitionists developed as a result of the constant
accusations that they supported amalgamation. Arthur and Lewis Tap-
pan, for instance, were so frightened by anti-abolitionist mob violence in
New York City in 1834 that they felt compelled to publicly assure Mayor
Cornelius Lawrence that they had no intention of "encouraging intermarriages." The truth was complex – many local antislavery societies did
campaign against anti-miscegenation laws, but many other abolitionists
who supported political equality did not support interracial social intercourse, much less sexual.[136]

Douglass was exposed to both sides of this divided mind among abolitionists early on. In 1842 he visited two utopian communities in Massachusetts, Hopedale and Florence, where interracial unions were common.[137] There he met Lydia Maria Child, who had published a novel about interracial marriage, *Hobomok*, in 1824. Child had scandalized the literary world in 1833 by publishing *An Appeal in Favor of That Class of Americans Called Africans*, which called for the abolishment of all discriminatory laws, including anti-miscegenation statutes.[138] Child and Douglass became lifelong friends, and she was one of an ever-growing circle of progressive white women who encouraged Douglass' belief in his right to occupy an interracial "third space." This conviction blossomed during Douglass' stay in England and Ireland from 1845 to 1847, when Douglass' writings reveal his elation at the relative lack of "color-phobia." After Douglass returned he and white women formed something of a mutual admiration society. Letters between white abolitionist women remarked routinely upon his good looks. Douglass seems to have enjoyed shocking social norms almost as much as he enjoyed the company of these women, as comes through in his 1849 article, "On Being Seen Walking with Two White Women."[139]

For perhaps the first time in American history, here was a mixed-race public figure who was not only at home in both of his "parent cultures," but recombined elements of both of those worlds within a new "third space" he occupied, which he then succeeded in replicating in his life and work. His third space became a multiracial community: most notably, a space in which black abolitionists and white women working for women's suffrage found common cause. In fact, Douglass' relationships with white women can be seen as having been essential to his identity formation and intellectual growth throughout his life, from the time he was a boy until old age. Douglass' marriage to Pitts had been foreshadowed by his relationship with Julia Griffiths, but it also recapitulated in some ways his relationship with Sophia Auld, Moses believes.[140]

It must be borne in mind here that Douglass' wife, Anna, was illiterate, and did not feel at home in the interracial circles her husband increasingly frequented. There is no evidence that Douglass actually had an affair with Griffiths, but there is no doubt that she and other white women provided the sort of intellectual stimulation that he could not find with his wife. Many of Douglass' white women fans continued to see him as something of a sex symbol well into his middle age. Celia Logan, a white woman who worked as an editor of the *Capital*, wrote of her meeting with Douglass in 1874: "the play of his fine features made a little thrill run through me. The dignity of his attitude, the majesty of his stature made Frederick Douglass look every inch a man."[141] Douglass had grown accustomed to

4   Helen Pitts Douglas, at about age forty-five. Pitts was the daughter
of abolitionists who lived near Rochester. "How good it is to have a wife
who can read and write, and who can cover one in all his range,"
Douglass wrote Elizabeth Cadey Stanton in 1884.

both intellectual companionship and sexual attraction with white women
long before he met Helen Pitts.

Significantly, the means through which they came together were both
ideological and class-related. Helen's parents were both abolitionists. Her

5   Douglass with two white feminists in 1884. His wife Helen is at the right.

father Gideon had met Douglass during the 1840s. Helen, born in 1838, grew up within forty miles of Rochester and probably had childhood memories of Douglass. She graduated from Mount Holyoke Seminary in 1859 and then taught at Hampton Institute, a black college, during the 1860s. Her family background and professional training gave her common ground with Douglass. But the immediate means by which Pitts and Douglass were brought together was more a matter of socioeconomic status and incidental geography. In 1880 Pitts had come to live with her uncle Hiram, whose residence was adjacent to Douglass' Cedar Hill home. Both of them shared a commitment to abolitionist and feminist causes, and both were upwardly mobile. In the year Douglass' wife Anna died, 1882, Douglass hired Pitts as a clerk in his "Recorder of Deeds" office. She managed the office during his many absences. The professional relationship blossomed into romance in 1883, when Douglass was recovering from an apparent depression related to his wife's death.[142]

Equally noteworthy was who Douglass chose to perform the ceremony. Vows were exchanged in the interracial home of Francis and Charlotte Forten Grimke. Francis Grimke was "the minister of perhaps the nation's

6   Douglass and Helen Pitts at Niagara Falls, 1884. They later toured Europe and Egypt and visited Julia Griffiths in England.

most distinguished African American church, but also the acknowledged product of the best-known and most honored interracial union in the land," writes McFeely. Like Douglass, Grimke was born to a slave mother and a plantation owner. However, the white side of his family was no "mystery," as with Douglass. Grimke received the assistance of his white abolitionist aunts Angelina and Sarah Grimke when he came north during the war. He was trained for the ministry at the elite Princeton Theological Seminary.[143]

The criticism Douglass and Pitts received came quickly, in both private and public. Helen's father Gideon essentially disowned her, as did Hiram Pitts, Douglass' neighbor. Her sisters and nieces remained loyal, however, and her mother later came to live with Frederick and Helen at Cedar Hill. Douglass' children felt that their father had repudiated them, despite his long and intimate relationships with white people. Similar feelings of betrayal were expressed publicly in much of the black press. However, some of Douglass' longtime black associates such as Thomas Fortune came to his defense, and most of his white friends were fully supportive.

Douglass sometimes refused to respond to the criticism, and sometimes merely remarked that marriage was a private matter. When he did engage in something like self-defense, he typically used his biraciality to place himself in a "third space." He sometimes remarked humorously that the color contrast had been greater with his first wife than it was with Helen Pitts. He also denounced, in a more bitter mood, the "false friends of both colors" who reproached him. At the same time, after the dust had settled, he confided in a friend that he and Helen were very happy together, and that their marriage had not reduced the number of social invitations he once received. This observation seems significant. Helen Pitts and Frederick Douglass were part of an interracial social network. They and their friends lived in a third space, a racial frontier of their own choosing and their own co-creation. The howls of protest on both sides of the Racial Divide, during an era of rising racial hostilities, could not dislodge them from this space, or deter them from claiming a right of residence within this multiracial community.[144]

Along with his ties to white women, another lifelong consistency of Douglass' was repeated comments about how his biraciality subverted racialist mythologies. In the *Narrative* Douglass had commented that his mulatto-ness undermined the so-called "curse of Ham" myth, which white racists claimed offered Biblical legitimation of black inferiority. In 1848, when his daughter Rosetta was excluded from a white private school, Douglass wrote the principal: "We differ in color, it is true (and not much in that respect), but who is to decide which color is most pleasing to God?" On the way to the Cleveland Convention in 1848, Douglass encountered a slaveholder who refused to speak to a "nigger." Unruffled, Douglass told the man that if it would make him feel more comfortable he could speak to the half of him that was white. Such encounters often made a lasting impression. In an 1883 cover story on Douglass in *Harper's Weekly*, Isaiah Rynders recalled a Garrisonian meeting four decades earlier in which Douglass was cited as proof of the equality of the races. "That won't do; he's half white, and that accounts for him," claimed Rynders. Retorted Douglass: "Oh, then I am only your half-brother," which Rynders remembered "as good a shot as ever I got in my life."[145]

Direct expressions of biraciality by Douglass diminished during the repressive 1850s. However, in 1859 Douglass voiced his opposition to chauvinists on both sides of the racial divide, during a debate with Garnet over the African Civilization Society's emigration schemes. He believed mulattos had little to gain by aligning themselves with people of any color who believed in "pure race." He sometimes referred to himself as an

Anglo-African, and during Reconstruction remarked that he was "something of an Irishman as well as a Negro." And in an essay written the year of his marriage to Pitts, and intended for a primarily white audience, Douglass sarcastically observed that as "ignorant, degraded, and repulsive" as "the Negro" was during slavery, "he was sufficiently attractive to make possible an intermediate race of a million, more or less." Shades of "attraction and repulsion," once again![146]

Regarding how Douglass understood the symbolic value of his interracial marriage, his comments on biraciality (or transraciality), are again crucial. Douglass' remark that he was closer to his second wife's color than to his first wife indicates that Douglass believed that a mulatto's marriage to a black spouse could be considered "interracial" just as easily as a marriage to a white spouse. During the height of the controversy over his marriage to Pitts, he denied that he was trying to be a role model for black. "If I have advocated the cause of the colored people it is not because I am a Negro, but because I am a man," he stated the day after his marriage. "I conceive that there is no division of races." He also denied that he considered amalgamation as a "solution" to the race problem, telling a reporter who asked him this that the question itself "has its motives and mainspring in a vulgar prejudice of race." Yet at the same times, he told the reporter from the *Washington Post*: "I adopt the theory that in time the varieties of race will be blended into one." These denials and qualifiers did not keep many people from seeing him as a black role model, nor some idealists from viewing his marriage as a mediatory symbol. One correspondent wrote him immediately after his marriage that "your act . . . will do more to harmonize the 'races' than all constitutional amendments, civil rights laws and judicial decisions." Yet if Douglass was unwilling to politicize his marriage, he was even more willing to recognize his own iconic status and to insist on a multiracial or transracial reading of his image. In 1886 Douglass told an audience:

A painter was painting me today and insisted on showing my full face, for that is Ethiopian. Take my side face, said I, for that is Caucasian; though you try my quarter face you would find it Indian. I don't known that any race can claim me, but, being identified with slaves as I am, I think I know the meaning of the inquiry.[147]

This consistent use of biraciality, as a tool or weapon to point out the illogic of racialism, provides the context necessary to understand that Douglass' comments about race-mixing during the 1880s were not merely a by-product of his own marriage. These commentaries provide hints on how Douglass intended for his own marriage, as a cultural symbol, to be read.

In an 1886 article on "The Future of the Colored Race," Douglass gave a clear endorsement of the need to recognize biraciality. One day Americans would not "pervert . . . the verity of language as they now do by calling a man of mixed blood, a Negro; they will tell the truth," he predicted. It was mixed-blood people themselves, having internalized the "One Drop" ideology, who "more noisily opposed" biraciality than anyone else, Douglass noted. His endorsement of a biracial identity came after predicting that in the long run, the Negro would be "absorbed." This lends itself to the criticism that Douglass assumed the Anglo would absorb the Negro. But the historical examples he uses do not support such an interpretation, despite Douglass' use of the word "assimilated." He sees that future American as looking something like the descendants of the Phoenicians – a "blended race"; hence, "people of color."[148] The model of blending he has in mind is of a composite. Like the current residents of the Mediterranean, this composite will include many traces of its origins. Some of these traces may remain in conflict: as with the Jews and the Palestinians, Semitic cousins who claim separate origins, but whose biggest differences are competing mythologies rather than appearance.

Douglass concedes that this vision of America as a "blended race" may appear "utterly impossible" to many readers. But he asks them to think about their own ancestors. "Two hundred years ago there were two distinct and separate streams of human life running through this country: all black on the one side, all white on the other. Now, between these two extremes, an intermediate race has arisen, which is neither white nor black, neither Caucasian nor Ethiopian, and this intermediate race is constantly increasing." Douglass claims he is not advocating this process, and pointedly says that such a future postraciality "*will not arise out of any theory* of the wisdom of such blending of the two races."[149]

Martin believes this "alleged neutrality" is "ironic and misleading," given his own marriage. It cannot be denied that Douglass is *theorizing* biraciality (or interracialism). But I am inclined to take Douglass at his word when he distinguishes between advocacy and prophecy: "I am not a propagandist, but a prophet. I do not say that what I say *should* come to pass, but what I think is likely to come to pass, and what is inevitable. While I would not be understood as advocating the desirability of such a result, I would not be understood as deprecating it."[150] Douglass spoke from the long view, almost from the vantage of what Wallerstein has called the "right time," when one age transforms into the next, through adaptation of a new paradigm or "ruling archetype."[151] Douglass was comfortable with his historical and contemporary involvement in race-mixing, since he knew that he was part of a widening stream that would some day become the mainstream. But he insisted that this postracial destination could not be reached through "any hurried or forced process." The process he was describing was more like continental drift.

In our era, Douglass' "prophecy" may seem absurd. Reporters routinely refer to distinct entities called "white America" and "black America." But let us keep in mind that Douglass was comparing his day, when there were around a million biracial people, to the almost total separation of two centuries earlier. We who live a century after Douglass have tens of millions of "mixed-race" people. When we factor in Latinos, as we must, it becomes evident that we are indeed moving towards a "postracial" society. Or at least a thoroughly multiethnic society, which has not yet found an acceptable postracial language in which commonality and difference can coexist. What will this society look like two centuries after Douglass? Only time will tell.[152] But the language of race inherited from the nineteenth century will be painfully inadequate to describe that society, as Douglass was acutely aware, and was trying to forewarn us.

. . .

Douglass' view of America as facing a hybrid future was reinforced by an 1887 visit to Egypt, a nation bred on a crossroads where the peoples of Africa, Asia, and Europe engaged in continuous penetration and interpenetration. Douglass saw in Egypt a people who looked much like himself. His response was entirely consistent: he saw them as both black and biracial. He claimed them as the African founders of civilization. But if Egyptians were fundamentally African, they were also indelibly hybrid. In describing them as looking like mulattos, he took care to make the distinction that this was an "American description." The system of racial binaries that led to mulattos would not necessarily hold up in other countries. He was aware of the different varieties of racial classification emerging in Latin America, and conscious of the insularity of North America's own racial obsessions.[153]

If one foresees an inevitable future, one does not necessarily try to rush its arrival, but neither does one waste energy trying to fight it off. One prepares for it. Reading between the lines, Douglass clearly thought that people on racial frontiers would tend to be better prepared for a hybrid future. But he never argued that miscege-*nation* was the only way to create, or prepare for, this "mixed nation." Indeed, he was more interested in cultural exchange, with interchange taking place through shared languages, such as the Bible and the Constitution, which still allowed some room for difference, as we have seen in Douglass' "blackening" of the Bible.

7   Wood engraving of Douglass, *Harper's Weekly*, Nov. 24, (1883), shortly before Douglass married Helen Pitts. This issue contained a typical story of how Douglass, now an icon in "mainstream" American cutlure, had used his biraciality to disarm a racist.

Du Bois' definition of Douglass may come in handy here. Du Bois objected when Booker T. Washington tried to claim Douglass for his model of assimilation. (All three men were biracial.) Contrary to Washington's view of assimilation as accommodation, Du Bois wrote, Douglass believed in "ultimate assimilation *through* self-assertion, and on no other terms."[154] Which should remind us that our definitions of integration and assimilation are impoverished now. In the binary, either/ or model, self-assertion can be enacted *only* through opposition. Yet given our interconnected history, can we envision a both/and democracy in which these concepts coexist: assimilation into a model that retains inclusion of difference?

Douglass did not frame the issue in exactly those terms, but he remained centrally concerned with the nature of inclusion to the end of his life. He also remained critical of the ways that the "American dilemma" was being framed by both blacks and whites. In one of his last major addresses, an 1889 speech on "The Nation's Problem," his "doubled" form of antagonistic cooperation had evolved to a new level. This speech finds Douglass in perhaps his most critical mood since the 1852 speech. He is again speaking on the occasion of a ritual celebration, in this case the anniversary of the abolition of slavery in the District of Columbia. Again, he pays respects to forefathers – white abolitionists – and then remarks that his honest assessment of the state of union precludes a celebratory mood. Douglass confesses that he has a "buoyant disposition" and is inclined to "look upon the bright and hopeful side of affairs," but even so, he believes that the "character of the Negro" has never been discussed in such unfavorable terms as at present. The principal difference here is the increased agency with which Douglass invests black people, and his insistence on assigning equal responsibility to both black and white people for "the nation's problem."[155]

This speech is best known for an often-quoted excerpt in which Douglass declaims: "There is no Negro problem. The problem is whether the American people have loyalty enough, honor enough, patriotism enough, to live up to their own constitution."[156] This is not essentially different from 1852: Douglass is still calling on his countrymen to live up to the Revolutionary-era egalitarian creed.

However, his most extended critique here is of racialism among black people, "a sentiment which we are pleased to call race pride." He prefaces his critique by asserting that no other group of people are "less tolerant of criticism than ourselves, especially from one of our own number. We have been so long in the habit of tracing our failures and misfortunes to the views and acts of others that we seem ... to have lost the talent and disposition of seeing our own faults."

Douglass finds that a reactive "race pride" is omnipresent in contemporary black discourse. As in his prewar battles with black abolitionists, his disagreement concerns the nature of opposition being voiced in the black community. Douglass does not contest the need to fight white supremacy, which he agrees is in ascendancy. But he disagrees vehemently over using "the master's tools" – i.e., racialized language, in an effort to destroy the house of race prejudice.

I see no benefit to be derived from this everlasting exhortation by speakers and writers among us to the cultivation of race pride. On the contrary, I see in it a positive evil. It is building on a false foundation. Besides, *what is the thing we are fighting against, and what are we fighting for in this country*? ... What is it, but American race pride; an assumption of superiority upon the ground of race and color? [my emphasis]

I want to draw attention to two aspects of this passage. First, Douglass is asking the black portion of his audience to think clearly both about what they are *opposing*, and what they *support*. If they *oppose* privilege based on skin color, then how can they also be *in favor* of perpetuating this "false foundation"? Secondly, there is an interesting, probably unintended doubleness in his use of the term "positive evil." Douglass seems to mean this in the sense of positively, or beyond the shadow of a doubt. But the term carries another meaning which prefigures late twentieth-century discussions of "strategic essentialism": that is, the argument that even though racialism is an *evil*, it may have a *positive* value when used by "people of color" in search of social equality.

Douglass himself is clearer here about what he opposes than what he supports. He stands against "our noisy assertion of equality with the Caucasian race." He alludes to Jeremiah 13:23, which says that, as a leopard cannot change his spots, so the Ethiopian cannot change his skin.[157] Since skin color is "not of our own choosing," people "should neither be proud of it nor ashamed of it." To dramatize his point he refers to "the poorest and meanest white man," who, having nothing else to brag about, can always proclaim: "I am a white man, I am." Douglass sees in many assertions of black pride a parroting of this white racialism. Again, he draws on the Bible: "God has made of one blood all nations of men to dwell on all the face of the earth." When compared to 1852, we can see that Douglass has completely reversed his usage of Acts 17:26. In the July 5 Speech, Douglass had utilized this scripture to argue against white racism. Now he uses the same passage to argue against black racialism.

Aside from urging intellectual and moral consistency, Douglass also emphasizes political expedience. He argues the reverse of the old cliché that "united we stand and divided we fall," calling for a decentered polity, a sort of "unity in diversity." "In quoting these wise sayings, colored men seem to forget that there are exceptions to all general rules, and that our position in this country is an exceptional one." Given that "exceptional" position, black Americans "cannot afford to draw the color line in politics, trade, education, manners, religion, fashion, or civilization," Douglass argues. "When we thus isolate ourselves and say to those around us: 'We have nothing in common with you' . . . the reply of our neighbors is in the same tone and to the same effect; for *when a people care for nobody, nobody will care for them.*" His position here is of course at variance with the vast majority of his contempories. He also offers an effective critique of the sort of "racism is eternal" self-fulfilling prophecies taken up a century later by "critical race theorists."[158]

The alternative Douglass offered during the 1880s was the "composite American." This theme is oblique in 1889. Douglass notes that "I have seen myself charged with a lack of race pride." His first response is to reference his "fifty years of uncompromising devotion to the cause of the colored man." He then adds his customary, but now muted, theme of biraciality as problematizer. "When a colored man is charged with a want of race pride, he may well ask, *What* race? for a large percentage of the colored race are related in some degree to more than one race . . . Let us have done with complexional superiorities or inferiorities, complexional pride or shame."

If Douglass does not repeat his vision of a "mulatto America" here, then neither does he repudiate it. The mood of the day is of a growing racialism, and Douglass feels called upon to attack racialism rather than repeat his postracial utopia. In any case, in none of his speeches during the 1880s did Douglass call attention to his own interracial marriage. He did seek to publicize the broader phenomenon of which his marriage was a part. He sought recognition of a foundational interrelatedness which, if fully understood, would make intermarriage no more than a by-product of a much broader stream of intercultural exchange. Returning to the nations-as-rivers concept he had used in 1852, Douglass offered this vision of historically mandated inclusiveness: "We are surrounded by a civilization which is the accumulation of ages . . . It belongs to no people or nation exclusively. It does not belong to the white man. It does not belong to the black man."[159]

Given his focus on this shared heritage, I think it is accurate to say that Douglass did largely think of his marriage as a private affair. But he also provided a historically grounded subtext which allowed those who were so inclined to read this marriage – and the interracial community of a million people within which it was situated – as a symbol signifying a path leading away from America's racialized hall of mirrors.

Conclusion: Douglass as integrative ancestor, reconsidered

The binary filters we have internalized often prevent us from understanding Douglass' relevance to contemporary Americans of all colors. Throughout his mature years, he held up as a horizon the vision of what historian David Hollinger has called a *Postethnic America*, an equivalent, in nineteenth-century terms, of what Nelson Mandela calls a "nonracial democracy." Constructing a multiracial, or, in time, a nonracial, democracy requires at least a partial "fusion of horizons" or merging of worldviews.[160]

Douglass can serve as an "integrative ancestor" who aids this partial fusing of horizons. By sharing the same ancestor, and acknowledging ourselves as both co-creators and inheritors of his legacy, we can move away from "zero-sum" worldviews and towards positive-sum solutions, in which the transracial whole is greater than the sum of its parts. Douglass is the human embodiment and symbolic representative of that transracial "whole."[161] He represents a history which cannot be "owned" by one racial collective. His life and work must be seen in some sense as an interracial co-creation, whose significance must be continuously redefined by his multiracial legacy. Because he cannot be ghettoized in a "black studies" box, he challenges us to "reintegrate" our versions of history.[162]

Douglass always spoke of America as "our country," even when he was being most critical of the country's citizens for failing to live up to the egalitarian ideals they espoused.[163] It was a country both black and white people had created, Douglass believed, and it was a country to which people of all colors could lay claim. To do so, he came to believe, would require the development of a political and moral language that transcended race. Douglass "functioned as a race leader to help realize a nation where race was insignificant," Waldo Martin writes. This paradox underlay everything Douglass said and did. He was a pioneer in building black institutions, yet he saw these "racial" institutions as a short-term stage, leading to the construction of color-blind institutions. As we have seen, he decried the "everlasting . . . cultivation of race," whether for "black reasons" or "white reasons," as a "false foundation" which could not support a multiracial democracy.[164]

Claiming Douglass as a transracial icon is not an effort to diminish "black history." To the contrary, it acknowledges that black and biracial historical subjects, when fully accounted for, must fundamentally alter the framework and the tenor of a larger historical and cultural narrative, as Nathan Huggins and many other scholars have insisted.[165]

"Harriet Tubman and Ida B. Wells should inspire all students, not simply African-American females," Gary Nash insists.[166] This relevance beyond ghettoized "racial" boxes is especially true of Douglass: his cultural/ biological biraciality means that people of all colors can claim him as an icon. Douglass' embrace of religious and political egalitarianism was an effort to refute the idea that there is a "mainstream" which can be defined as "white," and "tributaries" to this stream which can be defined as "black" or "brown." Rather, our cultural and political history is an intersubjective arena which should properly be viewed as an inter"racial" co-creation – as Ralph Ellison would repeatedly emphasize. Douglass embodies the interpenetration of African and European elements in the American experience. Black and white cultural spheres in effect "parented" a biracial sphere, and this biraciality, although it has been actively repressed, is part of the very foundation of our cultural, political, and religious traditions.

• • •

Roy P. Basler, writing about the mythologization of Abraham Lincoln, observed that "when a figure becomes symbolic, [he] is no longer simply historical."[167] In this chapter my aim has been to recognize how the historical and the symbolic/mythological shape each other. I have treated Frederick Douglass as a human symbol, a "biracial black culture hero," but I have also sought to ground this analysis in his own words, in sociocultural and political contexts in which he lived, and in the historical currents in which he was rooted.

In closing this assessment of Douglass' role as an integrative ancestor, I want to reflect more broadly on Douglass' significance as both a symbolic and historical figure on the racial frontier. Just as Afro-Americans have revisioned the Bible, "blackening" it, so I want to reclaim Turner's frontier as the Racial Frontier. Turner wrote that "Thomas Jefferson was the John the Baptist of democracy, not its Moses."[168] If so, then who then was democracy's Moses? When Douglass described himself as a "prophet," did he have a *Mosaic* model in mind?

If we see Douglass as someone who led "his people" to the threshold of the promised land, who *redeemed* the rhetoric of justice, as someone who more fully envisoned a multiracial society, then yes, Douglass could be seen as a Moses-type. Of course, there are many Moseses. Walt Whitman has been claimed by many American writers as a Moses of democracy. This archetype does not fully contain Douglass. But he did employ the motif as part of a very old tradition of seeing America as a "New Canaan." Douglass observed that for slaves, "The North was our Canaan." One could argue that Douglass "crossed over," as Moses did not. And yet he did not cross over into a Promised Land of "racial redemption." Instead, he stopped at that "half-way place" where he struggled to find a way beyond the language of race.[169]

Douglass "prayed with his feet," and this was an avenue open to all. He did not try to "own" or "inhabit" political and religious symbols such as Moses. These were rhetorical devices to be used as liberatory tools. McFeely believes that Douglass' private myth "was that each person should be his or her own Moses and confront Pharaoh on equal terms." He called Harriett Tubman a "Moses of her people," and the general tenor of his thought does seem to indicate that he believed anyone was capable of playing such a role.[170]

At the same time, Douglass was uniquely suited to playing the role, or "inhabiting the type," of a racially ambiguous Moses. This was an undercurrent in both European and Afro-American culture that would find direct expression in 1939 books by both Sigmund Freud and Zora Neal Hurston.[171] It is interesting that the word Moses shares the same root as the word mosaic. To play on the previously discussed concept of symbols acquiring polyvocality through having been "thrown together," we could say that Douglass was less of a Moses type than a Mosaic figure. That is, someone in the tradition of Moses, as an archetypal figure leading an exodus to a "promised land," could be referred to as *Mosaic*. But Douglass did not lead a *crossing over* to a new land so much as a co-creating of this promised land in the contact zone where the two "races" are thrown together.

Sundquist refers to the doubleness in Douglass as being a "symbol of an identity crisis" in America, an incarnation of Lincoln's "house divided."[172] In a sense, Douglass' inclination to interpret his doubleness as having a "mediatory" capacity represents the path not taken in North American history. It stands, in some sense, in stark contrast to Du Bois' view of doubleness as constituted by racially divided "warring selves." As outlined in chapter 1, American literature was thoroughly saturated with the theme of racial ambiguity in the late nineteenth and early twentieth centuries. But it was not until the appearance of Ralph Ellison's *Invisible Man* in 1952 that another major writer and thinker would pursue the concept of biraciality as having a mediatory and even redemptive potential, to the extent that Douglass did.[173] As we will see, Ellison picks up on many of Douglass' central obsessions, most notably a feeling of being constrained by racialized writing, and a historically informed awareness of the limits of oppositional thinking.

3   Invisible community: Ralph Ellison's vision of a multiracial "ideal democracy"

> with your black and white eyes upon me, I feel ... I am a new citizen of
> the country of your vision   (Ellison, *Invisible Man*, 345–6)

Introduction: Oklahoma roots and father substitutes

Although many writers over the last half century have called Ralph
Ellison's *Invisible Man* a classic, few, it seems, have been able to resist the
temptation to put it in a "black box." Typical is the claim by R. W. B.
Lewis that *Invisible Man* is not only "the greatest American novel in the
second half of the twentieth century," but also "the classic representation
of American black experience." I would be inclined to endorse the first
half of that claim. But in this chapter I will contest the view that this novel
is merely about the "black experience." There is an undeniable element
of truth here, yet this interpretation has tended to obscure the novel's
multiracial message, structure, and origins. Almost all of the novel takes
place within interracial contact zones – on racial frontiers. Much of
Invisible Man is in fact about the search for a multiracial community, I
argue. The nameless hero of *Invisible Man*, although clearly located
within, and in part loyal to, an Afro-American community, cannot be
thought of as "just black." He serves as something of a Hermes archetype
who carries messages back and forth between "white" and "black"
worlds. He also acts as a trickster who undermines the assumptions of
both of these "racial" groups.[1]

I do not claim this as the "correct" reading, but Ellison's essays and
interviews do point to this as a "preferred" reading. Ellison's pride in his
"Negro" heritage, and his claim to roots in a transracial cultural tradition,
coexist. As with Frederick Douglass, Ellison's determination to resist
"the deadly and hypnotic temptation to interpret the world and all its
devices in terms of race" arises from close encounters with "breaks" in
the Racial Divide. These breaks allow Ellison "to leave the uneasy sanctuary of race," and to lay claim to a history for which the language of race is

114

inadequate.[2] And in a manner similar to Douglass and Bob Marley, the absence of his own father shaped Ellison's search for cultural "legitimating fathers" – ancestors who would endow him with the vision necessary to address a multiethnic, international audience.

"One cannot overestimate the extent to which [Ellison] derives his point of view from the experience of growing up in Oklahoma," insists John Callahan, his literary executor. Oklahoma was admitted as the forty-sixth state in 1907, seven years before Ellison's birth. Oklahoma was a racial frontier: prior to joining the United States, it was known as "Indian Territory." Many Southeastern tribes, such as the Cherokee, had been forcibly resettled there. And for many years before Oklahoma became a state, "the Territory had been a sanctuary for runaway slaves who sought there the protection of the Five Great Indian Nations," as Ellison noted. There was another large emigration to Oklahoma by Afro-Americans after the collapse of the Reconstruction. Many of these emigrants conceived of it as, and lobbied for it to be, a "black state." This notion of a westward exodus to Indian territory as a land of freedom found expression in popular culture, Ellison pointed out, as when Bessie Smith sang about "Goin' to the Nation, Going to the Terr'tor'."[3]

Euro-American settlers came relatively late in this process. In the first years of statehood they did not have the same degree of political and economic dominance as was typical of other Southern states. Segregation laws were imported from neighboring Texas and Arkansas a decade after statehood, but in Ellison's childhood, race relations were in a state of flux. Recalling the interracial friendships which he and his family had during that time, Ellison remarked: "I guess it's the breaks in the pattern of segregation which count." This liminal period of *breaks* in Oklahoma's Racial Divide has been captured in Edna Ferber's *Cimarron*. Domination by white elites was increasing, and there was racist violence, as in the Tulsa riots. But there were also numerous black and Indian millionaires. The segregation laws being passed were not uniformly enforced, in the state's early years.[4]

Ralph's father Lewis Ellison was from South Carolina; his mother Ida Milsap from Georgia. They emigrated to Oklahoma from Chattanooga, Tennessee, determined to start a family in the relative freedom of a frontier state. Like most of the "Brown Americans" discussed in chapter 1, the Ellisons had a "mixed heritage." Ellison's description of the Invisible Man as "ginger-colored" is probably also a self-description. Lewis Ellison was a book-lover, and named his son after Ralph Waldo Emerson, the nineteenth-century Transcendentalist, and occasional abolitionist. Lewis died when Ralph was three, but the literary hopes that he projected on to his son via this name seems to have worked as an unconscious force, and later as a conscious influence, in Ralph's life.[5]

Both Lewis and Ida Emerson moved in interracial circles. Of his childhood in Oklahoma City, Ellison recalled that they lived in a "white middle-class neighborhood," and that "there was never a time that we didn't have white friends." His father "had many white friends who came to the house when I was quite small, so that any feelings of distrust I was to develop towards whites later on were modified by those with whom I had warm relations."[6]

But it was hardly a privileged childhood, or a predominantly white cultural mileu. After Lewis Ellison died, the family was quite poor. Ralph attended a segregated school. His immediate cultural referents were largely Afro-American. Oklahoma may have been a frontier state, but Oklahoma City was a modern urban center, and in fact a hotbed of jazz music. Ralph grew up knowing black dramatists and black newspapermen who were nationally respected. His mother was active in anti-segregation struggles. Somehow, in this frontier environment which was both provincial and culturally vibrant, Ralph and a group of "Negro boys" grew up thinking of themselves as potential "Renaissance Men."[7]

Ellison remembered his circle of friends as "members of a wild, free, outlaw tribe which transcended the category of race." "Some of us were fatherless," he recalled. Their need for "father and mother substitutes," as he wrote, was an important factor in their perpetual search for, and fabrication of, "heroes and ideals" on which to model themselves. Where they got the ideal of being "Renaissance Men," he was not sure: from a book, from someone whose shoes he had shined, or perhaps it was just "in the air" during this transitional period of Oklahoma history. At any rate, the models for these budding "Renaissance Men" were a mixed lot: jazz musicians, scientists, gamblers, scholars, stunt men, figures from Italian literature, etc. "We were seeking examples, patterns to live by," Ellison recalled. "We were projecting archetypes, re-creating folk figures, legendary heroes, monsters even, most of which violated all ... accepted conceptions of the hero handed down by cultural, religious and racist tradition."[8]

This youthful ideal of a transracial "Renaissance Man" is of crucial importance for understanding what Ellison had in mind when he wrote *Invisible Man*. As he himself admits, he carried this "boyish ideal" with him during his three years at the Tuskegee Institute in Alabama, and brought it with him to New York, where it served to "caution" him during his early interest in the Communist Party. This ideal then guided Ellison when he made the transition from aspiring composer to budding novelist.[9]

Ellison remembered the archetypal figures which he and his often fatherless childhood friends were imagining as "wildly improvisionary projections, figures neither white nor black, Christian nor Jewish." One of the most important models for Ellison, an archetypal figure capable of containing both black pride and transracial Renaissance ambitions, seems to have been Frederick Douglass. There were direct reminders in his life of Douglass. As Ellison later recalled, "the only public school I ever attended was named after Frederick Douglass."[10] And there were other reminders of Douglass' legacy in Ellison's cultural milieu, which found their way into his essays, and his novel.

Ellison knew something of a modern Douglass, as a boy, in the person of black editor Roscoe Dunjee. Dunjee was a NAACP official in Oklahoma and battled segregation through his paper, *The Black Dispatch*. Ellison points out that Dunjee, like Douglass, knew the Constitution well and used it to argue for a nonracial justice. Ellison sold this paper from when he "was fresh out of diapers" up into his teens. In a 1972 tribute to Dunjee, Ellison observed several parallels between Dunjee's newspaper career and that of Douglass. First, the support networks for such papers invariably seemed to be interracial: some white citizens of Oklahoma City helped support Dunjee's paper, "just as a black sailmaker ... kept William Lloyd Garrison's paper, *The Liberator* going in the name of Abolition," and just as "whites kept Frederick Douglass' paper going." Also, the dual function of *The Black Dispatch* was similar to the diverse rhetorical strategies employed by Douglass: both reported on the affairs of black Americans, but both were also intent on "defining the American reality" in multiracial or transracial terms. And Dunjee understood that "America moves through myth," cultural myths which are always in a state of flux and transformation, Ellison wrote. Therefore, "the problem is to keep up with the metamorphosis and find out who Frederick Douglass is today." Because despite generational change, "the patterns of society demand again and again repetition of that same heroism with a new body and a new face."[11]

If the best-known hero for a prior generation was Frederick Douglass, who would it be for youth in the post-depression years? Ellison looked at this question through the lens of writings on the "New Negro." While he was at Tuskegee, he heard a lecture by Alain Locke, editor of the 1925 volume *The New Negro*. "Dr. Locke saw the importance of trying to define us," Ellison reflected, in the transitional moment "when we were far enough away from the traumas of Reconstruction to begin to think of leadership on a very broad scale, in that moment when we realized whatever the new leadership, there would not be another Frederick Douglass ... There would be a metamorphosis of [his] ideas and styles."[12]

If the heroes of the past, such as Douglass, were repeatedly called up by a pattern of societal demand, within "a new body and a new face," and if their ideas reappeared only in metamorphosized form, then what would a "new heroism" look like? In what style and in what format would the new generation project their archetypal ideas? Around 1935 (the year in which Frederick Douglas Patterson became Tuskegee's third president), Ellison began to formulate his own artistic answer to these questions, in what was a fusion of the "Renaissance Man" and "New Negro" ideals. In typical fashion, he chose both black and white models. His first literary hero was T. S. Eliot. The rhythms of *The Wasteland* seemed kin to the jazz he had heard in Oklahoma. But more importantly, the poem's classic sources, which served as a study guide for young Ellison, enabled him to see the mythic dimension of his own experiences (as a Negro American) for the first time. Locke was also a role model because "He stood for a . . . conscious assessment of the pluralistic condition of the United States." Ellison reread Locke many times. His theory of the "New Negro" (or the "Newer Negro," some said in the 1930s) pointed Ellison towards the realization that "black culture" was so central to the American experience that "everyone who is touched by it becomes a little bit Afro-American."[13]

Before moving on to briefly consider Ellison's critical reception, and then to my textual analysis, I want to draw some conclusions about the role that his Oklahoma background, and specifically the loss of his father, played in his search for role models. It was the richness of Afro-American folk culture in Oklahoma which most consistently fired Ellison's imagination, yet it was cultural traditions from outside the black community which often gave him the "lense" through which to see the uniqueness of this specifically "Negro" culture. "I was taken very early with a passion to *link together* all I loved within the Negro community and all those things I felt in the world which lay beyond," Ellison writes in *Shadow and Act*. It was this "passion to link together" his pride in a specifically "Negro community," and his hopes for the redeemable elements of a larger multiracial community, which led him to spend his life dramatizing "the true inter-relatedness of blackness and whiteness." And very often, it was an Oklahoma context, in which the interpenetration of black and white cultures was abundantly evident even during segregation, which gave Ellison the grounding, even in the face of rabid attacks, to go on criticizing "the insidious confusion between race and culture which haunts this society."[14]

Ellison's linking of the racial with the transracial (via interracial exchange) is a dominant feature of his thought – what Mark Busby calls Ellison's "integrative imagination." In a tribute to Locke, Ellison asserted: "There is no specifically American vernacular and language which has not been touched by us and our style." "I don't recognize any white culture," he emphasized in a widely cited interview, with James Alan McPherson. "I recognize no American culture which is not the partial creation of black people. I recognize no American style in literature, in dance, in music, even in assembly-line processes, which does not bear the mark of the American Negro." One hears in these comments an echo of Douglass' "blackening" of American labor, and of Marley's refrain: "I & I build the cabin / I & I plant the corn."[15]

But if there is an assertion of "black pride" in Ellison's comments on American culture, there is also a claim of fundamental hybridity. There is no "pure stream" at the source of either "black" or Euro-American culture, Ellison insists. His models of cultural change are of interpenetration, of archetypal re-creation, and of interracial call-and-response. "Culture is exchange . . . It's a dialectical process," he explained to Hollie West in 1973. "You look at 'John Henry' – that seems absolutely black. But you look a little closer and you remember the tales of Hercules, you recognize the modification. I'm not saying it's not ours. But I'm saying it was not created out of the empty air but out of the long tradition of storytelling, out of myth."[16]

If Oklahoma played a crucial role in the origins of Ellison's dialectical view of interracial culture, the early death of his father, and his search for "substitute fathers" during young manhood, surely shaped the further evolution of this worldview. It is certain that his perspective was complicated by the continuing attempts of his associates to cast certain mentors in the role of "intellectual fathers." Richard Wright had befriended Ellison soon after he moved to New York in 1936, at the tender age of twenty-two. For much of his life, Ellison seemed to be resisting, and attempting to revise, interpretations of this as a father–son relationship. Since Ellison downplayed Wright's influence, and tended to pay more tribute to white writers, his denial was often "racialized." In response, Ellison insisted even more strongly on the transracial character of his "literary ancestors."

In their 1976 interview with Ellison, Robert Stepto and Michael Harper introduced a Freudian note into their questions about his relationship with Wright, "of sons wanting to slay the fathers." Ellison's answers are revealing. First, he observed that "writers as artists are sons of many fathers." He asserts that he was quite independent minded and well read at a young age, which sounds rather egotistical, but has been attested to by numerous people who knew Ellison at Tuskegee and during the early years in New York. When Stepto pursued this line of questioning, Ellison remarked: "If we stick to the father–son metaphor I'd say that,

given a reasonable degree of psychological independence on the part of
the younger man, it would be difficult to decide who at any given moment
is in the position of 'father,' who of 'son'."[17]

"Still the father/son metaphor persists," Stepto continued. Whereupon Ellison recounted a story of having been "outraged" when a Tuskegee teacher wrote him, applying the father–son metaphor to a famous
artist Ellison had befriended. He was piqued because this artist "hadn't
begun to read the books that I had read, even before entering college."
This youthful arrogance (or hypersensitivity) also came into play in his
relationship with Wright. Wright condescended by assuming his younger
friend "hadn't read many books with which I was, in fact, quite familiar,"
Ellison said. After naming these authors, and explaining his determination to "learn even when I disagreed" rather than "casting him in the role
of misunderstanding 'father'," Ellison interjected:

Speaking of fathers: I lost my own at the age of three, lost a step-father when I was
about ten, and had another at the time I met Wright. I was quite touchy about
those who'd inherited my father's position as head of my family and I had no
desire, or need, to cast Wright or anyone else, even symbolically, in such a role.[18]

This is a rather rare moment of self-revelation for Ellison. We get a
glimpse of a man who, despite a tendency to idealize his youth, had
actually experienced considerable instability. Not only had his father,
Lewis, died when Ralph was three, but he seems to have grown close to,
and then lost touch with, the man who became his mother's partner after
Lewis' death. Not only did he have yet a third stepfather when he met
Wright in 1936, but his mother died in 1937, when Ralph was twenty-
three. So it would be understandable if such a young man, of artistic
sensibility and fierce independence, were cautious about forming close
attachments with father substitutes. It would be natural if he were to
determine not to put all his eggs in one basket, to insist that he could have
"many fathers." This tendency seems to have been strengthened by the
"father-knows-best" authoritarianism he encountered in the Communist
Party. And his "touchiness" about Wright as a presumed father figure
was reinforced when many black writers treated his denials of Wright's
centrality as an artistic influence as evidence – proof that he was trying to
"pass," artistically, as white.[19]

During an interview with three Afro-American writers in 1977, Ellison
took offense when Ishmael Reed accused him of "always mention[ing]
Hemingway as an influence" and never mentioning Wright. "I find the
assumption that no Negro can do anything unless another *Negro* has done
so before him rather simple-minded, and as far as I'm concerned, it's an
inverted form of racism," he declared. In what has become perhaps his

8   Ralph Ellison with his wife Fanny

most famous statement about artistic ifluence, he added: "An artist can't
do a damn thing about his relatives, but he can sure as hell choose his
artistic ancestors. I had read Mark Twain and Hemingway, among
others, long before I even heard of Wright."[20]

Ellison's touchiness about matters of "substitute fathers" and artistic
influence seems to be a result of the confluence of three factors: personal
biography, artistic sensibility, and moral conviction. His loss of a series of
parental figures made him suspicious of projecting "father-images." His
omnivorous and eclectic reading habits, as well as his deep rootedness in
folk culture, made it impossible for him to conceive of any one author,
tradition, or genre as a sole *stream* of influence. And a long history of
interracial alliances, as well as his love for world literature, made it seem
morally just, and worth defending, that his "artistic ancestors" should be
both black and white. When Ellison came to write *Invisible Man*, he would

have the "Vet" advise his young alter ego, still prone to hero worship: "Be your own father." This is a form of "self-fathering," as we have seen with Douglass, and as we will see with Marley.[21] And in Ellison's case, this self-fathering was determinedly biracial.

Literature of borderlands and racial frontiers

Critical assessments of Ellison have been rather polarized. A tendency to treat Ellison as a "sacred icon" has produced a vast body of "celebratory" work, Jerry Watts notes. On the other hand, some black nationalist and Marxist critics have attacked Ellison as a race traitor or as insufficiently oppositional. I can only footnote some broad outlines of Ellison's relationship with his critics.[22] But I do want to sketch Ellison's conflict with "Black Aesthetic" critics, as it relates to my claim that Ellison can be situated as a writer of border cultures or racial frontiers.

Wilson Jeremiah Moses, who has written about Ellison in his studies of black nationalism, is not an racial essentialist, and in fact pays considerable attention to interracial networks. But he wants to pay respect where respect is due to Afro-American antecedents. In this context, Moses observes that it is "remarkable" that, after Ellison's "repudiation of his ties to all black literary traditions," he still "somehow [managed] to produce something that was quite distinctly black."[23]

Charges that Ellison "repudiated" his debts to black culture ignore his repeated references to "Negro culture," and also the contexts in which Ellison claimed European models. The context was often one in which critics tried to fit him into a Procrustean "black box," or asserted an innate form of black culture. A good example is Ellison's oft-quoted assertion: "I use folklore in my work not because I am Negro, but because writers like Eliot and Joyce made me conscious of the literary value of my folk inheritance." This comes from an essay titled "Change the Joke and Slip the Yoke." As George Kent points out, Ellison "usually gave greater emphasis to folk traditions," but was trying here to correct Stanley Edgar Hyman's "attempt to create archetypes of blackness." The title itself comes from Afro-American folk culture. It illustrates the interrelationship between subcultures and the mainstream, even when subcultures try to be oppositional. In Ellison's hands, the "yoke" which the subculture is trying to "slip" is imposed racial categories – the whole idea of racial, rather than cultural, inheritance.[24] This depends on a trickster-like ability to "change the joke" – to alter the terms of debate or transform the frame of reference.

What Ellison objects to in Hyman's "archetype-hunting" is not the use of a theory of archetypes, but the assertion that there are archetypal features within black literature which have "racial" origins. He notes that the trickster, "Hyman's favorite archetypical figure," appears in all cultures. Even if "the figure in blackface" is "an archetypical trickster figure originating in Africa," which Ellison doubts, "its adjustment to the contours of 'white' symbolic needs is far more intriguing than its alleged origins," he argues. It is in this context that Ellison declares "the true inter-relatedness of blackness and whiteness." And then asserts that his understanding of the literary value of his own Negro "folk inheritance" was made possible only by using European writers such as Eliot and Joyce as points of reference.[25]

Ellison's attitudes about archetypes illustrate his thinking on the difference between race and culture. His objection is to *racialized* archetypes, presented as inborn. Ellison emphasizes, as he did in writing about his Oklahoma boyhood, that archetypes are projected out of materials found in the culture at hand – materials which are always mixed, hybrid. Between archetypes and literature, Ellison reminds us, "there must needs be the living human being in a specific texture of time, place and circumstance." Therefore, archetypal images are always constructed, and not inherited. They can act as "equipment for living," in Kenneth Burke's metaphor which Ellison often quoted – tools for communication with communities beyond the boundaries of imagined racial groups.[26]

It was Ellison's continuing insistence on the impossibility of locating pure racial symbols, or identity, which seems to have most infuriated proponents of a "Black Aesthetic." Some of the most vitriolic attacks on Ellison appeared in a 1970 edition of *Black World*. While Ellison deplored "those who tried to reduce literary discussion to the level of the dirty dozens," he was also humorously defiant. In a 1976 interview with Robert Stepto and Michael Harper, he expressed "amusement" at the "hateful straw man whom they'd labeled 'Ellison'." He then declared: "But for all their attacks I'm still here trying – while if I'm asked where is *Black World* today my answer is: Gone with the snows of yester-year/ down the pissoir – Da-daa, Da-daaa – and good riddance!" (I am reminded here of Carlos Fuentes' comment that he "eats his critics for breakfast"!) In a more serious vein, he concluded:

The "Black Aesthetic" crowd buys the idea of total cultural separation between blacks and whites, suggesting that we've been left out of the mainstream. But when we examine American music and literature in terms of its themes, symbolism, rhythms, tonalities, idioms and images it is obvious that those rejected "Neegroes" have been a vital part of the mainstream and were from the beginning.[27]

There are racial and transracial voices here. He again points to a "mulatto mainstream" which makes the categories of "black culture" and "white culture" arbitrary. Yet there is an undercurrent of "racial pride." In sketching yet again the many ways in which Afro-Americans have shaped this mainstream, he suggests, as Bob Marley would sing (quoting the Bible), that black people have been "the stone that the builder refused," which culturally speaking, have become "the head cornerstone."

$\bullet \bullet \bullet$

To read *Invisible Man* and its reception merely as a chapter of black intellectual history is to largely miss the point of what Ellison is up to. As a classic of American literature, *Invisible Man* can neither be fully understood without a knowledge of Afro-American culture, nor its achievement fully recognized if it is "racially" ghettoized. I mean to show how this text's double-voiced symbols dramatize our interracial foundations. This is Ellison's "preferred reading," I have argued, because for almost half a century he rejected "glib talk of a 'white culture' and a 'black culture' in the United States." As in his 1979 tribute to Oklahoma educator Inman Page, Ellison stressed that "between the two racial groups there has always been a constant exchange of cultural and stylistic elements." This point of view is "easy to trace historically and to document empirically," as Watts concedes, but is "at times difficult to defend politically." But if we are serious about acting on the implications of the socially constructed nature of "race," then Ellison's text may have more to tell us about this interracial domain than it does about a Procrustean "black box."[28]

Given Ellison's canonical status, and his insistence on the hybrid interrelationship of the "mainstream" and its subcultures, it would surely be fruitless to treat *Invisible Man* as a species of minority discourse.[29] One route beyond minor/major or black/white binaries has been sketched by ethnographers of border cultures. Renato Rosaldo, a "Chicano" who is mixed Anglo/Latino by birth, defines border discourses as a "creative space of resistance" and most often "a site of bilingual speech."[30] Guillermo Gomez-Peña has used the concept of border cultures to describe an emerging majority of people who have "multicentric" identities, and who cannot accurately be described with black/white, majority/minority binaries. The reference points used by "border culture" writers are most often Latin American notions of "mestizo" identity, or *mestizaje*, which translates roughly as "mixed." Border culture scholars often define *mestizaje* as a hybrid "third space" that transcends "racial" markers.[31] This clearly shares many commonalities to the references by Ellison and his peers to a "mulatto mainstream."[32]

In my view, an analysis of texts produced on cultural borders or racial frontiers cannot imagine that these texts are merely "the product of damage," as JanMohamed and Lloyd argue.[33] The historical practice of interracial communication has produced forms of discourse on the expanding borders between "races" that cannot accurately be designated as either black or white. They constitute a *mutually created language*, an "Anglo-African Word."[34]

Call-and-response as a communication paradigm is a concept central to my study of Ellison's novel. "Call-and-response is a distinctively African and African American form of discourse," writes Ellison scholar John Callahan, but "it is also especially well suited to the vernacular culture of an experimental democratic society." The utility of call-and-response in a multiethnic context is that it lets speakers "turn to their advantage dissenting as well as assenting voices in the audience."[35]

One can see clearly in American literature, as it has been articulated by black writers addressing mixed audiences, and by white writers responding to the concerns of black speakers, an illustration of the multiracial utilization of the call-and-response process within an "experimental democratic society." This is particularly evident in the long and sustained call-and-response between white Americans and black Americans over the proper interpretation and application of Biblical morality and Constitutional guarantees.[36] These forms of interracial interaction are probably the closest we have come to a more inclusive "ideal speech community" – a concept which remains a "necessary fiction," or what Vaclav Havel calls a "horizon" towards which democracies must orient themselves.[37]

Ellison himself articulated a vision of an "ideal democracy" in which the "new culture" created on racial frontiers was our best hope of curing our racial neurosis. He believed that "the culture of the United States has always been more 'democratic' and 'American' than the social and political institutions in which it was emerging." Therefore it was this "new culture" towards which we should look as an orienting horizon, rather than expecting our political institutions to create a democratic culture.[38]

Ellison and the "black protest novel"

There has been a tendency to peg *Invisible Man* – against Ellison's expressed wishes – as a "black protest novel." To the degree that Ellison used this fiction to dramatize aspects of America's racial neurosis, it is understandable why so many readers would think of *Invisible Man* as "black protest." Yet the adjectives "black" and "protest" have limited applicability here – both within *Invisible Man* and in Ellison's nonfiction.[39]

Writing for a 1981 reissue of the novel, Ellison recalled that when he began *Invisible Man*, he was struggling with a dilemma. While in part he wanted to dramatize racial injustice, he did not want to be chained to a "black protest novel." He was "trying to avoid writing what might turn out to be nothing more than another novel of racial protest instead of the dramatic study in comparative humanity which I felt any worthwhile novel should be."[40]

An obsession with racial victimization reduced the wildly complex music of the black experience in America to a one-chord blues – an approach that is potentially addictive yet also reductive and monotonous. Ellison, who was trained as a symphonic composer, had a more complex music in mind. So while the narrative voice that cornered Ellison's attention was concerned with Afro-American life "since the abandonment of the Reconstruction," he was also trying to cast a much wider net. He wanted to capture what he felt was the previously ignored reality of a black character with "intellectual depth," and show that character's place within the context of the larger "study in comparative humanity." Ellison compares his narrator with that of the narrator of Dostoevsky's *Notes From the Underground*. He makes it a point to locate his black narrator within "the pluralistic literary tradition from which I spring." As we have seen, James Joyce was a primary model through which he approached his own folk culture.[41]

Ellison saw racial identity as a subset to something larger, a "literary tradition" which should, he felt, help us to envision an "ideal democracy." Ellison's writings indicate that he would have agreed with Habermas that this ideal is a "necessary fiction."[42] In his 1981 Introduction, Ellison argues that

> If the ideal of achieving a true political equality eludes us in reality . . . there is still that fictional *vision* of an ideal democracy [which] gives us representations of a state of things in which the . . . black and the white, . . . the native-born and the immigrant are combined to tell us of transcendent truths and possibilities such as those discovered when Mark Twain set Huck and Jim afloat on the raft. (xx)

The fictional tradition with which Ellison most closely identified was that of nineteenth-century American literature. It was during this period that he believed American writers mostly clearly articulated the moral dilemma of slavery. "During Melville's time and Twain's, it was an implicit aspect of their major themes," Ellison wrote in *Shadow and Act*. But "by the Twentieth Century and after the discouraging and traumatic effect of the Civil War and the Reconstruction, it had . . . become *understated*." Ellison saw his task as one in which he would counter this understatement by going back to the tradition of Melville and Twain, where he found assumptions he could share – about the centrality of black people in American democracy, a centrality that had been marginalized and rendered largely invisible in American fiction after Melville and

Twain.[43] The act of writing *Invisible Man* was for Ellison a form of "communicative action" in which he engaged in call-and-response with an American tradition that he viewed as multiracial, but which had later been covered with whitewash.

In retrospect, *Invisible Man* is something of a hybrid between the "dramatic study in comparative humanity" that Ellison wanted to write and the "novel of racial protest" to which he feared it might be reduced. *Invisible Man*'s hybridity results not only from Ellison's competing fictional visions, but from the way in which he combined Afro-American voices and European influences. In this sense *Invisible Man* is clearly a "dialogic" novel, or a "two-toned" text.[44] I want to approach Ellison's text by searching for evidence of the ways in which he portrays the search for a "black and white fraternity," focusing on the ways in which double-voiced symbols signify on both the potential for this multiracial "ideal democracy," yet also on the enormous obstacles preventing realization of that ideal.

Both Ellison and his narrator express a sense of racial allegiance; an obligation to help "uplift the race." But Ellison refuses to choose sides. His criticisms of black nationalism and black assimilationists are just as fierce as his criticisms of explicit and implicit white racism. His narrator, while struggling to find commonality between "black" and "white" communities, is guided by the hope of finding a space in which he can live out that interracial "fraternity," even as he apparently comes to the conclusion that current social conditions prevent its realization.

A new citizen of the country of your vision

The centerpiece of my analysis is a moment when the nameless hero of *The Invisible Man* (IM) is speaking in a labor auditorium. Having been recruited as a spokesman for the Brotherhood (modeled on the Communist Party), and facing a large multiracial audience for the first time, he loses his way in his speech. He then "confesses" that he is experiencing "something strange and miraculous and transforming" (345). "With your black and white eyes upon me, I feel…" he says, that "after a long and desperate and uncommonly blind journey, I have come home… Home! With your eyes upon me I feel that I've found my true family! My true people! My true country! I am *a new citizen of the country of your vision*, a native of your fraternal land" (345–46, my emphasis).

In this moment, we are witnessing a dramatic but all-too-brief illustration of Ellison's "fictional vision of an ideal democracy." IM will be shown the underbelly of that vision soon enough. But I want to first focus on the theme of a rebirth that occurs after an "uncommonly blind journey" when the sojourner encounters a sea of "black and white eyes" and feels that he has found "My true people! My true country!" This new country which enables him to be reborn is not a geographic entity or a racial configuration but rather "the country of your vision": an "imagined community" that transcends race.[45] IM is standing before this large multiracial audience, but with the spotlight blinding him, he cannot see their faces. He can only hear their encouraging responses. It is the inability to distinguish between black and white eyes that makes him feel, for the first time, like a "new citizen." After his "long blind journey," during which he has been taught to perceive white people as both enemy and benefactor, as an either superhuman or subhuman force which must be both placated and resisted, he is suddenly faced with a multiracial audience which is responding to his call for solidarity with what seems like one voice.

Recently arrived from the South, chased out of a black college by a black man for revealing too much blackness to a white man, IM encounters a group of whites who seem to regard him as an equal. The day before, he made an impromptu speech to a group of black tenants who were being evicted. That speech had happened during a confrontation between black tenants and white authority figures. His usual conflicted feelings about whites intensified when he saw the black crowd gather to rush some white policemen. He "both wanted it and feared the consequences" (275). He veered between a wild urge to provoke this clash, and a feeling of obligation to defuse the situation, to talk the blacks and whites into talking to each other. At this point he still perceived whites as a likely enemy. When he witnessed a few whites taking the side of the black tenants in the confrontation, he felt "uneasy about their presence and disappointed when they all joined the crowd" (282).

Yet clearly he had not encountered these types of whites before. He noticed a protester who was "A white man but someone else altogether" (282). While escaping, he encountered a "white girl" who complimented him on his speech, called him "Brother," and advised him on avoiding the police. After a mad dash across the rooftops, he was invited into a coffee shop by a white man, Jack, who talked in conspiratorial terms about arousing "the people" to action. IM was suspicious and resentful of this white man presuming to call him "brother." Yet he was intrigued.

During the eviction, it was the sight of an old black couple and the tattered remnants of their lives that had inspired his speech. The couple aroused "a warm, dark, rising whirlpool of emotion which I feared" (270). The fear had to do with the shared memory of black folk and the racial solidarity this memory imposed. Among the bricabrac of the old couple that had been thrown out on the dirty snowy street, IM saw many objects which evoked that racial memory: "a small Ethiopian flag . . . .a yellowing newspaper portrait of a huge black man with the caption: MARCUS GARVEY DEPORTED, and an ex-slave's 'free papers' in 1859" (271–72).

In a scene that foreshadows changes in IM's sense of racial solidarity, Jack asked him during their first encounter about this old couple. Jack had just offered IM a job with his organization as a speaker "who can articulate the grievances of the people." IM declined the offer and was about to walk out, declaring that "I'm not interested in anyone's grievances but my own."

"But you were concerned with that old couple," he said with narrowed eyes. "Are they relatives of yours?"
"Sure, we're both black," I said, beginning to laugh . . .
"Seriously, are they your relatives?"
"Sure, we were burned in the same oven," I said.
The effect was electric. "Why do you fellows always talk in terms of race!" he snapped, his eyes blazing.
"What other terms do you know?" I said, puzzled. "You think I would have been around there if they had been white?" (292)

IM was still speaking in racial terms because he had no other language to describe the rigidly segregated world in which he was raised and the racism that he still saw in New York. It is Jack that will expose him to a new, apparently transracial terminology.

IM fled back to his apartment, which had been provided to him free of charge by Mary, a black woman who took him in off the streets and "asked for nothing . . . except that I make something of myself that she called a 'race leader'." But the smell of the cabbage she is cooking reminded him of her poverty and made him realize that he could not refuse Jack's offer of a job. He rushed back out, called Jack, and was taken that very night to an interracial party of the Brotherhood, where "Brother Jack and the others talked in terms of 'we,' but it was a different, bigger 'we'" (316). This new multiracial community required a black spokesman to take its message to the masses.

The messianic undertones in IM's "racial uplift" education at a black Southern college and the utopian Marxism of the Brotherhood found common ground in their belief in the necessity of a "black culture hero." When IM made the speech to the black Harlemites being evicted, he seemed to step into this messianic role. Trying to stop the black crowd from self-destructive violence, he yelled: "Let's follow a leader, let's organize . . . We need someone like that wise leader, you read about him, down in Alabama. He was strong enough to choose to do the wise thing in spite of what he felt himself . . ." (276). IM could not shake the belief that "doing the right thing" involved compromise and cooperation with whites.

That night, at the Brotherhood party, Jack asked him, "How would you like to be the new Booker T. Washington?" (305). IM feigned disbelief, but was intrigued as Jack explained his vision of the necessity of a multiracial movement. "Destruction lies ahead unless things are changed ... by the people," said Jack. "Because, Brother, the enemies of man are dispossessing the world!" (307).

IM was "greatly impressed" at this vision of opposition to an enemy that is defined in terms of class, not race. Just a few hours earlier, he had listened to "the people" defining the enemy in very different terms, when an old black woman declared that "These white folks [are] all against us. Every stinking low-down one of them" (270). He heard a Caribbean woman urging racial vengeance: "Strike him, our fine black men. Protect your black women! Repay the arrogant creature to the third and fourth generations!" (281). (This echoes Biblical themes of cross-generational vengeance, as in Exodus 17:16 or Deuteronomy 23.)

But now he began to believe in a very different struggle as Jack insisted on his inevitable destiny: "So it isn't a matter of whether you *wish* to be the new Booker T. Washington, my friend... This morning you answered the people's appeal and we want you to be the true interpreter of the people. You shall be the new Booker T. Washington, but even greater than he" (307). Ellison here echoes Matthew 3:11, where John the Baptist says, in reference to Jesus: "the one who comes after me is greater than I."

When IM entered the spotlight the next evening in front of the large multiracial audience, he would be playing a new role in which the messianic urges implicit in his training at the black Southern college and the messianic projections of the Brotherhood converged. The only requirement, Jack told him, is that "you must put aside your past" and take on a "new name" and a "new identity" (309). With this new persona, he would be ready to begin learning the "new terms" necessary for communicating with and mobilizing the multiracial "bigger we."

One-eyed brothers

As tools for his new identity, the Brotherhood gives IM a new name, a new apartment, and a stack of their books and pamphlets, which he looks over before his debut speech. But when he hits the stage, he "can't remember the correct words and phrases from the pamphlets." He has to "fall back upon tradition" (342). He describes his style as a political technique he had heard at home, a sort of "I'm mad as hell and I won't take it any more" approach – drawing not only from Southern politics but also on the oratory of the black church. As such, the dominant feature of his speech is its reliance on the call-and-response format.

IM uses a technique of inverting metaphors which have negative connotations of isolation and powerlessness into positive images of collectivity and self-determination. He turns the description of his audience as "common people" into a rumination about their uncommon capabilities. He transforms their "one-eyed blindness" into a metaphor of their potentially collective vision: "They think we're blind – un-commonly blind. And I don't wonder. Think about it, they've dispossessed us each of one eye from the day we're born. So now we can only see in straight white lines. We're a nation of one-eyed mice" (343).

I will return to the image of a "straight white line," a sign for the racial divide and interracial dependency. But I want first to note how IM, facing his first multiracial audience, converts the image of their collective part-blindness into a vision of a brotherhood in which they work better together than apart.

Did you ever notice, my dumb one-eyed brothers, how two . . . blind men can get together and help one another along? They stumble . . . but they avoid dangers too . . . Let's get together, uncommon people. With both our eyes we may see . . . *who* makes us so uncommon! Up to now we've been like a couple of one-eyed men walking down opposite sides of the street. Someone starts throwing bricks and we start blaming each other and fighting among ourselves. But we're mistaken! Because there's a third party present. (344)

Incorporating a sports metaphor supplied by his audience, IM suggests an "alliance" based on their teamwork, pitching and catching, call-and-response. Encouraged by the audience cries that they have caught his pitch, he shouts: "Let's take back our pillaged eyes! Let's reclaim our sight; let's combine and spread our vision . . . Look down the avenue, there's only one enemy. Can't you see his face?" (ibid.). It is here that IM pauses and gropes for "new terms," before confessing that the "black and white eyes" make him feel like "a new citizen of the country of your vision."

This is, in my view, the only moment in the novel in which IM is able to fully envision a multiracial community. Within moments, the "theoretical Nijinskys" of the Brotherhood will be admonishing him for his "politically irresponsible" speech. Soon he will be faced with the constraints placed upon realization of a multiracial ideal democracy, not only by the rigidly "scientific" worldview of the Brotherhood, but also by the rigidly oppositional view of black nationalists. But in that brief epiphanic moment, he has a vision so powerful that he will never be able to relinquish it.

Having come to understand the existence of an enemy that cannot be defined by color, he will never again be able to tolerate either whites or blacks who define their enemy along color lines.

This is a vision that is, in some ways, diametrically opposed to the lessons he learned during his upbringing in the South. But it is a vision that could not have arrived without his conflicted relationship to the Southern/black culture into which he was born.

IM is haunted by the deathbed advice of his grandfather. Just before dying, he called in his son and confessed:

our life is a war and I have been a traitor all my born days, a spy in the enemy's country ever since I give up my gun back in the Reconstruction ... I want you to overcome 'em with yeses, undermine 'em with grins, agree 'em to death and destruction, let 'em swoller you till they vomit or bust wide open. (16)

IM's parents were "alarmed" by these words. "I was warned emphatically to forget what he had said." Yet those words "had a tremendous effect on me ... whenever things went well for me I remembered my grandfather and felt guilty and uncomfortable. It was as though I was carrying out his advice in spite of myself" (ibid.).

His family's reaction to his grandfather's dying words reveals that they were what used to be called "good Negroes" who aspired to assimilation. IM, a "ginger-colored" (22) honor student, "was praised by the most lily-white men of the town" (16) for being "an example of desirable conduct" (17). His guilt arose from the fact that the very behavior that won him acceptance from whites had been defined by his grandfather as traitorous. Yet his grandfather had also said that this same yes-sirring behavior could be used as a form of subterfuge, an invisible opposition to white oppression. This led to considerable confusion on IM's part as to what his proper attitude towards whites should be.

IM's social identity centered on trying to satisfy the desires of white folks, even though their desires could in truth no more be fathomed than his own real motivations for trying to appease or influence them. On the one hand, IM envisioned himself "as a potential Booker T. Washington" (18), a missionary of racial uplift. On the other hand, he seems to care less about racial uplift than with impressing white authority figures. Even when white businessmen in his hometown degrade him in the "battle royal" and set him to fighting other young black men, he is still focused upon using his words to impress whites. "I wanted to deliver my speech more than anything else in the world, because I felt that only these men could judge truly my ability" (25).

With a scholarship awarded by these white men, IM enters the Negro state college. When the white benefactor Mr. Norton visits, IM acts as his

chauffeur. He treats Norton with a reverential deference. A tragi-comedy
ensues when Mr. Norton asks to be taken for a ride away from the
campus. They end up at the cabin of a black man named Jim Trueblood
who has been banished from the realm of "Good Negroes" after impreg-
nating his own daughter. Mr. Norton finds Trueblood's tale so absorbing
that he gives him a $100 bill, much to IM's disgust. Mr. Norton, overex-
cited, asks IM to stop for a drink. This leads to another farce in which Mr.
Norton is brought into a black whorehouse called the Golden Day.

After IM is booted out of school, he realizes that his duty was not to
show a powerful white man the underside of the black world, but to keep
black and white worlds separate. Only if they were quarantined would the
proper order be maintained, in which white benefactors could maintain
the illusions that assured their money flow. When these worlds were
brought into contact, the balance of power would be upset. The money
flow might either stop or else be redirected into the hands of "unscrupu-
lous Negroes" who did not have the best interests of the "race" in mind.

The volatile nature of the line separating the white and black communities is illustrated by Ellison through numerous "two-toned" symbols.
They often seem to signify on the rigidity of the "Racial Divide." But
Ellison also structures them to double as an indicator of an American
cultural reality in which "black" and "white" folks engage in a type of
call-and-response with each other, and thus erode the line between them.
I want to focus on three symbols which contain within themselves a
seeming contradiction: both utopian and dystopian readings, having both
"black" and "white" antecedents.

"A straight white line"

The phrase "straight white line" pops up in IM's labor hall speech as an
image of partial blindness or tunnel vision – a metaphor for a situation in
which a white and a black eye have been separated at birth and made to
work at cross purposes. The image is introduced early in the book, during
the ill-fated journey of IM and Mr. Norton to a black-owned whorehouse
called the Golden Day.

The pink-faced, white-haired Mr. Norton is a philanthropist who
smokes cigars and tells polite "Negro stories" as part of his duty as
"bearer of the white man's burden" (37). The straight white line image
first occurs as IM drives Norton away from the Negro college, and the
Bostonian tells IM about his role as co-founder of the campus. IM listens
"with fascination, my eyes glued to the white line dividing the highway as
my thoughts attempted to sweep back to the times of which he spoke"
(38–39).

The white line serves here as a reminder of the very different sociocultural realities separating the white philanthropist from his black beneficiaries – a chasm of which Norton seems oblivious. Immediately after this image, Norton recalls that the founding of the state Negro college occurred as a collaboration between him and his friend, the "great Founder," a man modeled (in part) on Booker T. Washington. At the time, he says, neither white nor black people knew which way to turn. "But your great Founder did. He was my friend and I believed in his vision. So much so, that sometimes I don't know whether it was his vision or mine . . ." (39). This line seems to signify on both the cooptation and co-creation of which the Founder (Booker T.) is an embodiment. Whites sometimes want to take credit for the visions of black/biracial people, and sometimes deny responsibility.

Norton has an almost religious conviction that his destiny is closely tied to the fate of black people, a sense that "what happened to you was connected with what would happen to me" (41). Swept up in the nostalgic emotion of the moment, he personalizes this conviction: "Yes, you are my fate, young man . . . whatever you become, and even if you fail, you are my fate. And you must write me and tell me the outcome" (43–44).

IM's feelings are mixed: "Was he talking to me like someone in a book just to see how I would take it? . . . How could I tell him his fate? He raised his head and our eyes met for an instant in the glass, then I lowered mine to the blazing white line that divided the highway" (44). IM does not know if this white man is crazy or not, and is not ready for the possibility that their fate could in fact be closely linked. So he focuses on the white line, the symbol of the Racial Divide. "Half-consciously I followed the white line as I drove, thinking about what he had said" (46).

After their stop on the "wrong" side of the Racial Divide to hear Jim Trueblood's twisted saga, they encounter a group of black veterans shuffling down the highway, headed for the Golden Day. The effete Mr. Norton, gasping for air, begs for "a little stimulant." IM is forced to stop at the Golden Day. Since the vets are "blocking the way from the white line to the frazzled weeds" (71) that bordered the Golden Day, IM has to cross the white line and approach this flophouse from the wrong side of the road.

To understand fully the double-voiced way in which the straight white line and the Golden Day are being used, Ellison's text must be situated historically as a commentary upon Lewis Mumford's book, *The Golden Day*. This book, which argued for a Golden Age of American Literature from 1830 to 1860, drew attention to texts that were hardly being read at the time – Emerson, Thoreau, Whitman, Hawthorne, and Melville. Mumford cast the Civil War as a watershed marking the end of the age of heroic individualism, and the subsequent decline of American literature. But Mumford's romanticized take on American literature virtually ignores the impact that the debate over slavery had on these writings. In his nonfiction writing, Ellison criticized the elision of racial oppression in American letters – "that tradition of intellectual evasion for which Thoreau criticized Emerson in regard to the Fugitive Slave Law, and which had been growing swiftly since the failure of the ideals in whose name the Civil War was fought."[46]

When Ellison places Norton in the Golden Day, he is making us revisit a site that has been whitewashed and abandoned. The Golden Day is a dismal building with peeling paint. Originally a church and a bank, it has now gone to seed and services crippled or half-crazed black vets looking for carnal pleasure. The bartender will not sell IM a drink-to-go, saying "we don't Jim Crow nobody" (76). The flophouse is in chaos and IM can find no help. He runs back and forth between the car and the bordello, trying to meet Norton's wishes, yet also to keep him separated from the reality inside. But fate will not let him keep black and white realities apart.

The Golden Day into which Norton is brought would be, even under "normal" circumstances, what Bakhtin calls a "carnivalesque" realm in which normative values are turned upside-down. Things are especially topsy-turvy this time, since "Supercargo, the white-uniformed attendant who usually kept the men quiet, was nowhere to be seen" (76). The inmates are rioting, and in their abandon, they signify repeatedly upon the incongruities of Norton's presence in a way that serves to counter the whitewashing of both Mumford's Golden Day and the illusion of white supremacy which continued to be maintained by the "dominant" American culture of that day.

Norton is dragged in upside-down, his "white hair dragging in the dust," symbolizing the inversion of perspective that will dominate inside this Golden Day. One patron calls Norton "Thomas Jefferson" and another responds that he has always wanted to "discourse" with Mr. Jefferson. After Norton is revived with a shot of whiskey, a riot ensues, with the "inmates" throwing bottles and attacking their returning resident authority figure, Supercargo. In this chaos, IM is pushed into "a mass of whiteness" he recognizes as Mr. Norton. He reacts with "a shudder of nameless horror," as he "had never been so close to a white person before." Norton takes on the appearance of "a formless white death" (86). Perhaps this death is meant to refer to the carnage visited upon black soldiers in the defense of the "white" American system of economic apartheid that has made Norton's wealth possible.

Here, on the wrong side of the white line, in the madness of the Golden Day, voices which have previously been silenced try to rid both IM and

Norton of their illusions. "He's only a man. Remember that. He's only a man!" someone shouts in IM's ear. IM resists this assessment, thinking that "Mr. Norton was much more than that, that he was a rich white man and in my charge" (86).

When a former doctor known as "the vet" looks into Norton's face without the proper subservient mask, IM rushes to intervene since "Men like us did not look at a man like Mr. Norton in that manner" (90). Freed from his reserve by drink and the carnival atmosphere, the vet tells Norton that his black peers see him as a "lyncher of souls." He expresses his desire for vengeance. IM muses that "the vet was acting toward the white man with a freedom which could only bring on trouble," yet admits: "I received a fearful satisfaction from hearing him talk as he had to a white man" (93).

When Norton again voices his belief "that your people are in some important manner tied to my destiny," the vet ridicules him. He scaldingly critiques the way in which IM and the vet are blinded by their projections on to each other: "Poor stumblers, neither of you can see the other. To you he is a mark on the scorecard of your achievement . . . And you, for all your power, are not a man to him but a God . . . He believes in that great false wisdom taught slaves and pragmatists alike, that white is right" (95).

Norton is suddenly angered by the unflattering reflection held before him. His young charge has been pleading with him to leave all this time, just as he pleaded with him to leave during Jim Trueblood's tale. But Norton has been spellbound by his close encounter with black history; now, having drawn too close for comfort once again, he exits on threat of bodily harm.

Back in the car, IM "followed the white line of the highway" (98), back on the "right" side, the "white is right" side, as the vet had said. Although for a moment he had been thrilled to hear black men talk back to a powerful white man, he can think now only of duty and submission to this white man. He wants to confess to Norton that he was "far from being like any of the people we had seen," that in fact he "*hated*" those kinds of undisciplined black folks (99). But he senses that his unwitting bringing together of white authority and black history has destroyed his chance to become a successful "race man" on this campus, where a sort of "pretend blackness" depends on keeping "living blackness" at bay, on keeping white people insulated from the "unordered blackness" that rages beneath the whitewashed surface. Sensing the price he will pay for linking of black and white worlds, IM's eyes fill with tears. The campus of the black college "froze for a moment in mist, glittering as in winter when rain froze on the grass and foliage and turned the campus into a world of whiteness" (100).

The image of "a world of whiteness" that blankets a black college foreshadows IM's incipient sense that black realities often have white surfaces; that white realities often have black roots. To outgrow his white-identified "one-eyed blindness" he will have to enter that world of whiteness, and better negotiate the line that both separates and joins blackness and whiteness.

He will also have to outgrow his father complex. As he boards the bus to depart the South the next morning, IM encounters the vet once more. His parting "fatherly advice" is: "Be your own father, young man" (156).

"A bath of whiteness"

Ellison uses the "straight white line" to comment on highly stratified black–white relations in the South. It symbolizes just how clearly defined is the Racial Divide in the South. It also signifies on just how ludicrous the maintenance of that artificial Racial Divide is, since just out of view on the "wrong side" of the white line is a turbulent "black world" without which the reigning mythology of the "white world" could not have been constructed and defended. The black vets have always been around, but out of sight and out of mind from white eyes.

After IM flees to New York, Ellison uses more ambiguous symbols that indicate the continuing power imbalances between black and white worlds, and the volatile nature of efforts to mix them. Yet they also signify on the erosion of boundaries between the black and white worlds. This transitional ambiguity is dramatized during IM's brief tenure as a Liberty Paints employee.

IM was referred to Liberty Paints by the "young Emerson," son of a white trustee of the black college, who sees his relationship with black men as a "Jim and Huck" affair. This can be seen as the beginnings of IM's awareness that there exist relationships between blacks and whites – as articulated in Twain's novel – that move beyond blind hate, blind power, or blind subservience.

Signs outside the factory read "KEEP AMERICA PURE WITH LIBERTY PAINTS" (196), and "If It's Optic White, It's the Right White" (217). IM's assigned job is to put ten drops of "black dope" into each bucket of Optic White paint and "stir it 'til it disappears." It is the "glistening black drops" which give the Optic White its glossy surface – "as white as George Washington's Sunday-go-to-meetin' wig," IM's supervisor brags (200–02). The paint he is given the task of mixing is being taken to a national monument.

On the surface we see a symbol of the whitewashing of America. The founding fathers and latter-day monuments erected in their memory require repeated coats of white paint in order to represent the official American history. We can also think of the ten drops of black dope as representing, on an obvious level, the cooptation of "black culture" into a historically white supremacist system.

Ellison encourages this literal interpretation, in part. He has IM reminisce, as he stirs a "special mix" of Optic White, about the brightly painted white buildings on the black college from which he has been banished – buildings whose whiteness and the power that this whiteness signifies are made even more pronounced by contrast with nearby cabins, where the elements had worn off the paint. IM seems here to still be partly in denial, longing for the sureties he had once felt in the structured world of the black college, yet also seeming to accept the logic of the fate that carried him to New York. In the rhythm of the falling black drops upon the white paint he imagines some sort of dream in which he might be able to interpret the meaning of his life.

We can read this chapter as a symbolic dream sequence, but Ellison complicates any attempt to locate a "pure" latent meaning. IM's duties as a driver for Norton involved complete submission to the "white line" with an imperative of total separation of black and white realities, except for the dream-like psychological projections in which black and white actors can imagine themselves to be tied by fate. But now in the paint factory, IM is assigned an explicit duty of mixing black and white together. This is a delicate balancing act, for it is a very precise amount of "black dope" that must be mixed into this "Optic White" – ten drops – and a very specific type of blackness, as well.

IM is sent to serve as an assistant to Lucius Brockway, an old black man who works in the bowels of the factory. His duty is to mix the raw materials that make the factory's Optic White paint so famous. "Right down here is where the real paint is made. Without what I do they couldn't do nothing" he brags (214). He is very proud of the company's product, claiming that "Our white is so white you can paint a chunka coal and you'd have to crack it open with a sledge hammer to prove it wasn't white clear through" (217).

Frederick Douglass' words have come to pass: rejecting schemes to resettle blacks in Africa, Douglass scoffed, "The only tolerable substitute for such colonization would be plenty of *whitewash*."[47] This symbol signifies on the whitewashing of America, complicity of blacks in this act, and conditions of underpaid and underrecognized servitude under which blacks perform their role in this whitewash. We find that Brockway "actually functioned as an engineer though he drew a janitor's pay" (211). But Ellison's symbol also points to a more complex, reciprocal relation between blackness and whiteness. Brockway notes that the white owners are helpless without him. "They got all this machinery, but that ain't everything; we the machines inside the machine" (217). He claims "Liberty Paints wouldn't be worth a plugged nickel if they didn't have me here to see that it got a good strong base" (215).

One can read in these lines a critique of capitalism and racism that goes beyond mere exploitation and victimization. Here is a picture of Afro-Americans as the soul inside the machine; even as a black base to a "white" superstructure. There is potential power in this hidden arrangement, if its true intersubjectivity were to be recognized and its constituents organized.

But this power is unrealized, for reasons that include but are not primarily caused by racial oppression. The workers, both black and white, who might join together are consumed with internal bickering and paranoia. The mixed-race labor union at first persecutes IM as a spy and then belligerently recruits him. As for Mr. Brockway, the solitary black man in the basement of the white paint factory, his hatred of unions is pathological. His only ally is his knowledge of his importance to the production of the paint, and he is prepared to fight by all means necessary against any one, black or white, who might interfere with the primacy of his own position at the lonely base of this superstructure. So when he learns that IM has "run into" a union meeting, he threatens to kill him. The two black men are soon at each other's throats, in yet another rerun of the battle royal. The wily old man sets up IM to cause an explosion that blasts him "into a wet blast of black emptiness that was somehow a bath of whiteness" (230). Once again, IM will have to start from scratch in his search for a less volatile, more constructive space in which black and white can mix.

Biracial culture heroes

To understand why IM seems so compelled to search for an elusive multiracial community in a fictive ideal democracy, we must take into account not only IM's conflicted view of white folks, rooted in his grandfather's deathbed words, but also the presence in his imagination and life of a series of "black culture heroes" who are, in fact, biracial. These biracial culture heroes are more two-toned symbols that signify for IM the impossibility of rooting himself in a community that is "just black."

On his last night at the black Southern college, IM heard a speech by a blind black man, Homer Barbee, which dramatized the historical circumstances in which the *Founder* (the virtual Booker T. Washington) made his mark upon history. Barbee describes a post-Emancipation landscape with "clouds of darkness all over the land, black and white folk full of fear and hate, wanting to go forward, but each fearful of the other" (119). "And into this land came a humble prophet, lowly like the humble carpenter of Nazareth . . . knowing only his mother" (118).

Later this "black Aristotle" travels across a "black sea of prejudice," preaching the gospel of emancipation. And "during his journey he was stopped by the strange figure of a man whose pitted features revealed no inkling of whether he was black or white . . . Some say he was a Greek. Some a Mongolian. Others a mulatto – and others still, a simple white man of God" (120–21). This biracial ally appears as "an emissary direct from above" in order to aide the Founder in "the black art of escape" (121–22). Other allies appear to assist his passage. "Mostly it was our own who aided," but he was "passed from black hand to black hand and some white hands," including "the white blacksmith who held no hatred – surprising contradictions of the underground" (122–23).

The *surprising contradictions of the underground* center upon how "black emancipation" is constructed as a venture that could not succeed without multiracial cooperation. A "black Aristotle" only seems like a contradiction until we have learned to read the two-toned history of the Greeks.[48] During the days in which "the Founder was building the dream," he learns that he has not only dual allies but also "enemies of both complexions" (124). Ellison may have Douglass in mind here, who had denounced "false friends of both colors" for criticizing his interracial marriage. Even the Founder's death calls forth multiracial symbols, with the image of "a black man and a white man of the South, both crying" (129).

The Founder is a biracial leader who is the novel's first archetype of blackness, and IM's principal role model for the first third of the novel. IM's speech to the white men at the smoker borrows heavily from Washington's 1895 Atlanta Exposition Address. Washington has often been dismissed as a tool of the white racist power structure. Yet Washington's self-help message also had much in common with the self-reliance later espoused by black nationalists, including Marcus Garvey. IM stressed Washington's call for "responsibility" on the part of blacks at the expense of his parallel insistence that the larger society must develop "a determination to administer absolute justice."[49] Yet his reading of Washington had at least as much to do with his racial blindness at the time, as with the limitations of Washington's pragmatism.

Later, after IM is named spokesman of the Brotherhood's Harlem office, an old black member, Tarp, gives him a portrait of Frederick Douglass. "Douglass belongs to all of us," Tarp says (378). Douglass is the novel's second biracial hero and role model. Douglass was culturally as well as "genetically" biracial. He had feet planted firmly in both black and white worlds and had begun to clear space for a new multiracial community in between the two. Thus he is not only a Hermes figure, as I have described Ellison's Invisible Man, but also an interracial trickster, according to Lewis Hyde.[50]

But how are we to interpret Tarp's comment that "Douglass belongs to all of us"? We can get a sense of what Tarp meant by "all of us" from his gift to IM of a metal link that he sawed off his leg during his escape to freedom. Tarp cannot articulate the meaning of this gift, but probably intends to remind IM of where he came from, of the debt he owes to black folk who paid the price with their bodies to enable him to ascend to his position of multiracial leadership. But the gift is also Tarp's response to IM's request for advice on his receipt of an anonymous note that warns him "*do not go too fast.*" The note reminds him: "You are from the South and you know that this is a *white man's world*" (383). Tarp, like the portrait of Douglass, brings out "echoes of my grandfather's voice" – echoes he simultaneously remembers and refuses to hear (379). Tarp calls his attention to "a symbolic poster of a group of heroic figures" near his desk. It pictured: "An American Indian couple, representing the dispossessed past; a blond brother (in overalls) and a leading Irish sister, representing the dispossessed present; and Brother Tod Clifton and a young white couple . . . surrounded by a group of children of mixed races, representing the future" (385).

The poster, "After the Struggle: The Rainbow of America's Future," was conceived by IM. Tarp notes that while some black Brotherhood members resisted this multiracial poster at first, now they were "tacking 'em to their walls 'long with 'God Bless Our Home' and the Lord's Prayer" (386). At this point Tarp gives IM the leg iron, to help him "remember what we're really fighting against" (388). IM interprets Tarp's actions to mean that "whoever sent the message is trying to confuse me; . . . to halt our progress by destroying my faith through touching upon my old southern distrust, our fear of white betrayal" (390–91). His belief in the righteousness of building a multiracial brotherhood is confirmed.

He finds images of a multiracial community in his co-workers, particularly the youth organizer, Tod Clifton, who is the novel's third archetypal biracial hero. Clifton's "head of Persian lamb's wool had never known a straightener" (366), and in this sense he is "blacker" than many of his black peers at the time. Yet the "Afro-Anglo-Saxon contour of his cheek" reveals his origin "in southern towns in which the white offspring of house children and the black offspring of yard children bear names, features and character traits as identical as the rifling of bullets fired from a common barrel" (363).

Watching the Brotherhood members talk, IM observes: "They seemed absorbed with the cause and in complete agreement, blacks and whites. But when I tried to place them as to type I got nowhere." A large black woman spoke "in abstract, ideological terms." And Tod Clifton looked like a "hipster." "I could place none of them. They seemed familiar but were just as different as Brother Jack and the other whites were from all the white men I had known. They were all transformed, like familiar people seen in a dream" (366). They constitute an incipient multiracial community.

When Clifton comes into IM's office, he immediately reveals his dual allegiances. He talks about "our people" in racial terms, believing that their work in Harlem would be "bigger than anything since Garvey." Yet he also believes in the "scientific plan" laid out by the brotherhood's Marxists (367). In Clifton's clashes with the black nationalist Ras the Exhorter, we witness the principal fault line in this incipient multiracial community, a line that will eventually destroy Clifton and send IM into exile, removed from the black, white, and multiracial communities alike.

Ras' "hoodlums would attack and denounce the white meat of a roasted chicken," says a Brotherhood woman. "He goes wild when he sees black people and white people together." Clifton responds, "We'll take care of that," touching his "Afro-Anglo" cheek (365). Yet when Clifton and Ras cross paths, their antagonism is far from one-dimensional. Ras seems to see Clifton as a special case, and pulls out all stops in his efforts to reclaim and redeem Clifton for a racial solidarity. And Clifton's enraged reactions signal that he is simultaneously attracted to and repelled by Ras' racial romanticism.

In one part of his consciousness, in his "racial self," Clifton is tempted by Ras' portrayal of him as "the real black mahn" and "a black king." (It is historically resonant that a mixed-race "marginal man" is often called upon to embody "real blackness" and lead black nationalist or anticolonial movements, as Frazier and others noted.) Clifton derides Ras as someone who would would "say something about 'Ethiopia stretching forth her wings'" (376). This passage from Psalms 68:31, which had such an evocative power in Douglass' day, had become a racial parody for educated blacks by mid-century. Yet it clearly still had great appeal for the masses. One of the "inmates" at the Golden Day had cited Psalms 68:31 (81), and in the "real world" backdrop of the novel, this was a favorite passage of Garvey's – a prototype for Ras. Clifton's troubled response ("I don't know ... I don't know") makes it clear that Ras is tugging on a repressed part of his consciousness. The attraction of this biracial character to Ethiopianism, an ancient form of racial romanticism, previews the path taken by Bob Marley.

But whereas Marley would find no reason to resist his attraction to the mythology of black kings, Clifton is appalled by the narrowness of a worldview in which the enemy's face is painted white. Yet he also seems to be increasingly unable to deny that there is some truth in Ras' critique of the Brotherhood. His only response is blind rage. His inability to bridge those two worlds eventually leads him to "plunge outside history," to reject the ideological straightjackets of both the Brotherhood and black nationalists. IM will also reject both options, but while Clifton descends into self-hate and parody, IM retreats into a hibernation-like isolation.

Clifton represents the tragedy of those who try to bridge the gap between the masses and elites, blacks and whites, without institutional support (or cultural role models). In this sense, although he is portrayed as a potential "biracial culture hero," Ellison writes Clifton in a manner closer to the "tragic mulatto" tradition. IM and Clifton have both trusted the "scientific" worldview of the Brotherhood over Ras' emotional call to a race-based brotherhood. But Clifton realizes much sooner than IM that the Brotherhood's rules for membership in a transracial community are in fundamental conflict with a "home base" in a racial group.

Conclusion: "diversity is the word"

The conflicting definitions of community between "racial" allegiance and the Brotherhood are based on opposing concepts of authority and communication. The Marxist brotherhood believes in a monologic model of communication, in which there is only "one truth" and "one history" which must be imparted by a vanguard to the masses. This would-be universal truth is of course that of class solidarity. In the Marxist worldview, class "trumps" race. The theoretical elite of a supposedly proletariat-led revolution attempts to silence or marginalize race as a form of "false consciousness." By contrast, call-and-response, as an African-rooted form of communication, privileges interactive modes in which authority truly must be granted *from the people*. To be successful, the speaker must adjust to the responses of the audience. Truth can only be *arrived at* (not imparted) through a continual process of (ritual) interaction. The call-and-response format is incompatible with the Brotherhood's worldview, a vanguard elitism posing as populism. This is why several Brotherhood members, after IM's first public address, denounce his style as "unscientific" and "incorrect."

The Brotherhood's ideology is not explicitly racist, but it has no room for difference within its commonality. And its condescension becomes implicitly racist in application. It cannot see blackness and whiteness, only enemies and allies, defined by class. The leaders of the Brotherhood even presume to define blackness – either through their "scientific" framework, or in the case of Tobitt, simply because he is married to "a fine, intelligent Negro girl" (468).

During a final argument, IM understands that he is, after all, just a hired hand. "Things have been so brotherly I had forgotten my place. But what if I wish to express an idea?" IM asks Jack. The Brotherhood's leader reveals his hand: "We furnish all ideas ... The committee makes your decisions ... We do not shape our policies to the mistaken and infantile notions of the man in the street. Our job is not to ask them what they think but to tell them!" (470–73).[51]

IM realizes that Jack is acting like another "great white father" (473). He has by now (perhaps like Ellison, his creator) come to accept the vet's advice to "be your own father." The limitations of Jack's vision are symbolized when, in a fit of rage, his glass eye "erupts" from his face (474). He is revealed as yet another of the "one-eyed mice," doubly blind because he takes his blindness as authority rather than as a sign that he needs assistance. IM realizes that no society that the Brotherhood can imagine will allow them to see him for who he is: both black *and* a prospective member of a multiracial partnership.

But his experience on Harlem's streets convinces him that the black community is also unwilling to allow dual allegiances. "With Ras calling for the destruction of everything white in Harlem" (485), he knows that blacks who have formed alliances with whites will be targets. He longs for "allies with whom we could join as equals" (510). But a final confrontation with Ras convinces him that he can no longer claim racial solidarity. Falling through a manhole, he has a vision of the multiracial face of oppression, with Jack, old Emerson, Bledsoe, Norton and Ras all "demanding that I return to them and ... annoyed with my refusal" (569). But he realizes that return is impossible. He would have to wait underground, hoping for a day in which allies could be equals.

IM's burning of the papers given to him by white and black authority figures signifies his rejection of both "black" and "white" versions of exclusive identity and community. Some critics found this conclusion unsatisfying. Addison Gayle attacked Ellison for choosing "individualism instead of racial unity," and Irving Howe questioned Ellison's racial loyalty.[52] Which reminds me of the woman in *Invisible Man* who wonders whether IM is "black enough" to serve as spokesman, or Frederick Douglass' wry remark that he was *not black enough* for some of his British friends. Ellison, however, always insisted on the impossibility of choosing "racial unity" as a long-term solution to our racial neurosis.

Ellison has observed that "my problem is to *affirm while resisting*":[53] to both affirm his American-ness while resisting the continuing oppression that a part of the American system represents. Ellison, who often wrote with the forms and styles of musical composition in mind, once noted that "true jazz is an art of individual *assertion within and against the group.*" This seems to also serve as a metaphor for Ellison's relationship with "mainstream" society – a process of *"antagonistic cooperation"* which he sees as the only attitude possible if one is to carve out a niche in which commonality and difference can coexist.[54]

After the labor hall speech, IM envisioned a multiracial coalition.

> For the first time . . . I could glimpse the possibility of being more than a member of a race [and of following] a way not limited by black and white. As a Brotherhood spokesman I would represent not only my own group but one that was much larger. *The audience was mixed*, their claims broader than race. I would do whatever was necessary to serve them well.

Perhaps, he reflects, "this was what was meant by being 'dedicated and set aside'" (353, my emphasis). Here, he takes a saying from the black church and tries to apply it to a destiny as servant to a multiracial community. And although IM was not able to find an institution that would allow him to play that role as an equal, he continues to hold that vision of an "ideal democracy" during his time underground.

In trying to imagine the "next phase" of race relations, IM comes to the conclusion that "men are different and that all life is divided and that only in division is there true health" (576). He has come to distrust all totalizing definitions of commonality: "Whence all this passion toward conformity anyway? – *diversity* is the word. Let man keep his many parts and you'll have no tyrant states . . . America is woven of many strands . . . Our fate is to become one, and yet many – This is not prophecy, but description" (577).

Only by trying to balance diversity and unity can we approach the horizon of a multiethnic "ideal democracy," Ellison suggests. And only by seeing "the true interrelatedness of blackness and whiteness" can we understand that all parts of American culture are part of "the expressive heritage of a biracial culture," and that we are all "co-workers in the kingdom of culture."[55] Thus, for Ellison's hero, the projected solution to his invisibility is not a declaration of racial allegiance. Rather, he ends where he began, in a "border area" (5), the only space, apparently, in which commonality and difference can coexist. And if this space cannot be found in the social world, Ellison insists, then it must be continuously re-created in the imagination.

I have sought to draw attention to the ways in which Ellison's classic functions as a "border discourse," or a text situated on a "racial frontier." As racial frontiers expand, they take on the characteristics of a new culture with their own distinct linguistic practices. One can see the beginnings of this process in *Invisible Man*, when Norton comments, "I am no longer sure whether it was his vision or mine," or in IM's ongoing uncertainty as to whether he should be engaged in racial uplift, outreach to whites, or the building of structures that could house multiracial audiences.

Writing at mid-century, Ellison had to try to imagine his "ideal democracy" within a context in which the actually existing democracy in the US was far from hospitable to multiracial enterprises. They tended to take place within semi-outlaw groups, such the Marxists of the "Brotherhood," or among jazz musicians. In Ellison's post-*Invisible Man* writing, he described several strategies toward the fate "to become one, and yet many." As we have seen, these centered on "an art of individual assertion within and against the group," a process of "antagonistic cooperation" in which people "affirm while resisting."[56]

This double-voiced strategy implies that the larger group within which one's sub-group is located contains both desirable and undesirable elements. To "affirm while resisting" means to remain open to beneficial and mutually defined alliances, while remaining opposed to relationships constructed through "constraints of domination," in Habermas' words. To engage in "antagonistic cooperation" means to accept that the line between coercion and persuasion will not always be clear. This concept also acknowledges the existence of multiple public spheres in the US which are based on sometimes conflicting, sometimes overlapping interests. Historically, if one takes Frederick Douglass as an example worth emulating (as both Ellison and I have done),[57] that has meant saying yes to the constitution, but no to reductive interpretations of that document; yes to the message of redemption in the Judeo-Christian tradition, but no to attempts to use the Bible to justify oppressive practices.

In *Invisible Man*, Ellison affirmed "counter-publics" such as that of the Marxists as a contact zone, in which blacks and whites could share some goals, yet remained "differentially empowered." He also resisted the ways in which black nationalism and Marxism employed "metanarratives" claiming a historically transcendent truth, based on race or class.[58] This is their form of limited empowerment, and their ultimate manner of self-marginalization: by setting themselves merely in opposition to reified categories like "white racism" or "capital," they ensure that in some form they will mirror the totalizing tendencies of those categories.

"Counter-publics" like black nationalism, Marxism, or religious groups are able to offer, through their construction of "spaces of withdrawal and regroupment," as Nancy Fraser writes, new spheres of public discourse. These alternative or oppositional public spaces can play an important role in "housing" new forms of identity and political alliances, and in critiquing the exclusionary practices of a larger public sphere. But the public bases which they construct in an effort at outreach cannot maintain purity – ideological, racial or otherwise. They are "invadable" or "co-optable," if you prefer that sort of framework. I prefer to think these "margins of the margins" as the multiple centers of our imagined mainstream. The "antagonistic cooperation" which Ellison reveals as characteristic of racial frontiers is a "potentially emancipatory" process that may be as close as we can get to an inclusive form of "discursive redemption" in multicultural nation-states.[59]

• • •

Let us return, in closing, to Ellison's reflections on the reappearance (the reconstruction) of archetypal hero-figures in each generation. Ellison observed that cultural myths define national character. Since these myths were in a constant state of evolution, the challenge was "to keep up with the metamorphosis and find out who Frederick Douglass is today." But of course the heroes of each new generation would appear "with a new body and a new face." If the legacy of a culture hero like Douglass survived and was made current, it could only be through "a metamorphosis of [his] ideas and styles," Ellison insisted.

In the next chapter, we will look at Bob Marley as the return of a "biracial black culture hero" – another offspring of our repressed interraciality, of which Douglass was an archetypal example, and to which Ellison pointed throughout his writing. It might be more accurate to say that Marley was a reinvention or a restructuring of this type, because of the complex levels on which his public persona was constructed. Within the purposes of this book, I will begin by thinking about Marley as the reappearance of Douglass in a "new face" and a "new body" – as the Mosaic leader of a self-proclaimed "revolutionary posse." The oppositional space to which Marley gave voice has truly "gone international." The trajectory of Marley's career raises serious questions, often wrestled with by Ellison, about the meaning of "black liberation," and of what constitutes being a "real revolutionary" in the postcolonial "new world border."[60]

4   Bob Marley's Zion: a trans-racial "Blackman Redemption"

> My father was a white and my mother black, you know. Them call me half-caste, or whatever. Well, me don't dip on nobody's side. Me don't dip on the black man's side nor the white man's side. Me dip on God's side, the one who create me and cause me to come from black and white, who give me this talent.
> (Bob Marley, 1975)

ROOTS

Overview: "come we a chant down babylon one more time"

Bob Marley is probably the most enduringly influential popular song-writer of the twentieth century, worldwide. He is also one of the most beloved songwriters among mass audiences: two decades after his death, demand for Marley as a *product* in all shapes and forms is accelerating. There are hundreds of millions of copies of his albums in circulation around the world. And Marley's face has taken on an iconic status not unlike a Buddha or the Virgin Mary. Travelers sight Marley's name and image in the most remote corners of the earth, on everything from stained glass to shoelaces, "from Peru to Poland, Tokyo to Timbuktu, the top of the Himalayas to the bottom of the Grand Canyon," as Roger Steffens writes.[1]

The distance between Marley's Jamaican roots and his global reception is vast. This chapter is about the movement from the roots to the fruits, as it were. Marley's music is deeply embedded in Jamaican cultural traditions and political movements, and cannot be fully understood apart from that context. Yet I want to emphasize Marley as a cultural phenomenon who transcended "racial" and national boundaries. Marley lived for extended periods of time in the United States and Europe, toured "every shore," as he put it, and viewed himself as both Jamaican *and* a world citizen. He was a missionary for a form of personal and collective identity he called *Rasta* – a word that both signified on a history of racial oppression, and yet pointed to a definition of community beyond the language of race.

We can glimpse how far Marley traveled from his roots by comparing his "One Love" ideal to the character "Ras the Exhorter" in Ralph Ellison's *Invisible Man*. Ellison's portrayal of Ras as a leader of a group of racialists who hate white people so intensely they would "denounce the white meat of a roasted chicken," is a parody of Caribbean-born, Marcus Garvey-style black nationalists. Yet it is also a fair approximation of the attitudes of many early Rastafarians – the group or movement in which Marley was based. The Rastas were and are rooted in Garvey's black nationalism, and in an older tradition of "Africanized" Christianity known as Ethiopianism. This tradition often acted as "a voice in the wilderness" calling for, or warning of, a "racial armageddon."[2] When in Ellison's novel "Ras the *Exhorter*" metamorphosizes into "Ras the *Destroyer*," we are witnessing a transformation from the "racialized Christianity" of Ethiopianism to the anticolonial resistance Marley would popularize.

Early Rastas adapted the battle cry of anticolonial rebels in Kenya: "Death to the white oppressor." By 1960 this had evolved to "death to black and white oppressors," but a certain binary racialism has persisted in Rastafarian thought. In opposition to a white supremacist thesis, Rastas voiced a "black supremacy" antithesis. It is only to a limited degree that many Jamaican Rastas have moved beyond this binary mindset.[3] One could say that the Rasta belief in a black deity is closely tied to a mythologized "white oppressor," much as Afro-American thought has centered on a despised/chosen coupling. The proof of being chosen is in the persistence of being despised, and the perfect black father is the ultimate refutation of an oppressive white "other" (or imperfect white father, in Marley's case).

Given the similarity of certain strains of Rastafarian thought to the "white man is the devil" racial mythology of Black Muslims, there is a paradox in Marley's role as spokesman for the "One Love" variant of Rastafarianism. I wish to explore some ironies of Marley's role as a corporate-sponsored "biracial black culture hero" who popularized a symbolic *African Zion*. Marley revisioned Judeo-Christian scripture (especially the Exodus story) in order to balance the concerns of black liberation and multiracial redemption, within the context of his international audience. The resulting synthesis voiced a moral philosophy interpreted by much of Marley's audience as a sort of multiracial secular church.

As a means of examining Marley's role as a co-creator of the transracial new culture which I am mapping in this book, I want to think about

Marley's relationship to his audience in several ways. What is the relationship between the messianic mindset of Jamaicans, which many observers have noted, and the international consumption of Marley as the voice of this messianic/millennial tradition? What do we make of the significance of Marley's "Exodus," for a global culture? Can we draw any conclusions about the expectations that this audience projected on to Marley himself?[4]

Trying to talk about Bob Marley is "like trying to take a sip from the ocean," an Ethiopian Orthodox archbishop said at his funeral in 1981. Marley is such a protean character, both as a songwriter, and as a global icon widely seen as a prophetic figure, that I am conscious of the need to be cautious about exploring a part of that "ocean," and claiming that what I have encountered is representative of the whole.[5]

One obstacle for a writer seeking to get a handle on Marley is the sheer immensity of his songbook, "an embarrassment of riches," as one critic put it. These songs "embarrass" by their scope, variety, creativity, and social vision. Critical assessments of artistic merit are notoriously subjective, but Roger Steffens' statement that Marley "had a sense of melody that is unmatched in the history of modern music" is a common perception.[6]

A different obstacle is the extent to which Marley's skills as a songwriter are linked with a perceived status as a prophet. Many assessments of Marley's stature as an artist are inseparable from his parallel reputation as a visionary. Steffens, curator of the Bob Marley archives in Los Angeles, calls Marley's corpus "a legacy of songs unsurpassed in modern music history, the true 'new' psalms." Carlos Santana makes the claim for Marley that "as we enter the new millennium, his songs will be hymns and anthems that people can use to build a new world."[7] I will later discuss what it means to claim for Marley's songs a status as "hymns" or "new psalms." For now I want to merely note that a wide range of people project quasi-messianic qualities on to Marley, much as they have done for Martin Luther King and other "black culture heroes."

There is also the problem of a lack of scholarly precedents. A torrent of books and articles about Marley and the Rastafarians flew off the presses in the years just before and after his death. But although numerous books on Rastafarianism have appeared which try to place Marley within broader social, religious, and historical currents, little of the work on Marley himself has been of a critical nature. Through the 1980s, most writing on Marley has been either adulatory myth-making, or impressionistic popular journalism. However, a wealth of new source material has appeared in connection with the fiftieth anniversary of Marley's birth on February 6, 1995.[8] And academic scholars have begun to historicize Marley and to subject his work to critical analysis. Recent works by scholars such as Barry Chevannes, Carolyn Cooper, Richard D. E. Burton, John Homiak, Carole Yawney, Jack Johnson-Hill, and the many authors in the ground-breaking anthology *Chanting Down Babylon* have integrated studies of Rastafarianism, Marley, and Jamaican popular culture into anthropology, literary studies, social ethics, and religious studies.[9]

In describing the *movement* of Marley and his music, *from* Jamaica and *toward* a global audience, I have relied on several forms of ethnographic research. My first two visits to Jamaica in 1987 and 1988 helped me to *see* Marley's cultural roots. Since then, friends who are radio DJs have supplied me with hundreds of tapes, often filled with singles they brought back from Jamaica. This has allowed me to listen in on contemporary "reggae dancehall" – and not least, to Marley's still pervasive influence in this domain. I have also listened to Jamaican radio shows in which various Rasta "sects" debate their theological differences, compare their attitudes towards Marley, and ponder the mystery of reggae's predominantly nonblack audience. My understanding of reggae's American audience has benefited from the experience of managing a group during the 1980s which sometimes performed on the bill with touring reggae bands. I have since engaged in research on reggae's global audience through the Internet discussion group rec.music.reggae (RMR). This "chat room" has hundreds of participants from around the world, most of them musicians, DJs, and promoters. The "reasonings" on this group have provided many insights into the tensions that still exist over "racial" and transracial interpretations of Marley's vision, in particular, and Rasta-influenced reggae, in general.

This chapter grew out of a longer project in which I trace the uses of references to Ethiopia in the Bible as a strategy for racial equality, from 1700 to the present. Marley is the end point of my study of Ethiopianism. Here, more than elsewhere in this book, I am engaging cultural traditions that have developed a parallel form of "critical theory" which is largely outside of, and overtly hostile to, European critical traditions. My effort has been, as far as possible, to try to engage this postcolonial, Afro-Christian critique in a way that takes seriously its own internal logic.

I have chosen a line from Marley's song "Chant Down Babylon" as a subtitle to this section, to give readers who may have little or no familiarity with Rastafarianism, a glimpse of the "internal logic" of this worldview. Jack Johnson-Hill has defined *Babylon*, in the sense used by Rastas, as "*an artificial affluent society of self-absorbed individuals who worship idols and live decadent life-styles at the expense of the poor.*"[10] At the core of the Rastafarian worldview, as popularized by Marley, is both a critique of the "Babylon System," and the articulation of a replacement worldview. I would point to three main features in the Rasta alternative to the decadence of Babylonian life-styles:

(1) a sustainable life-style (living within the earth's limits);
(2) a postwhite supremacy worldview;
(3) "I and I" consciousness (commonly, I & I). This concept differentiates between an external deity and a "God within."

Those who have experienced "I-sight" reject a human/divine binary. Thus, "I & I" connotes not only a unity between human beings and their "God within," but also a unity with other human beings who have awakened to their "higher consciousness." This is not a merely spiritual notion which leads Rastas to wait for divine intervention, however. The implications of "I & I" thinking are that each individual is responsible for contributing to collective social transformation: "every man to his works," as Michael Rose sings (in "Seeing Blind" [1997]).

In the line from Marley's song, "Come we a chant down Babylon one more time," we see several indications of this unity consciousness. First, the singer designates "come we" – it is a collective endeavor. Second, the act of "Chanting Down Babylon" is a ritual act engaged in by this collective, through the use of what Rastas conceive of as "Word/Sound/ Power." The roots of this concept are in the Old Testament story of Israelites using a ritual blowing of horns, and a great shout, to bring down the walls of Jericho, while conquering the Promised Land. Third, the line "one more time" indicates a *process*. Chanting down the "walls of Babylon," or overcoming "mental slavery," in Marley's words, is an ongoing process. It may not be finished in our lifetime, but participants seek to forward the momentum to the next generation. It is the collective, cross-generational participation in this ritual which lends it strength and momentum, and the hope of fulfillment. The collective comes together one more time to "Chant Down Babylon" because they believe that their actions have a cumulative impact. (In fact there have been hundreds of songs released with similar titles, or variations on the theme of "Chant Down Babylon.") And in this worldview articulated by Marley and the Rastas, it is music which provides the baseline to this collective Word/ Sound/Power. "Music is the key" to chanting down Babylon, Marley sings, and elsewhere: "We free the people with music." (I would encourage readers to listen to Marley's music as they read this chapter, especially the album *Survival*. His vision cannot be understood in full by merely quoting his lyrics, as I do in these pages.)

My overall goal is to sketch how the deep currents which fed Marley's artistic and political vision, such as Judeo-Christian scripture, and post-colonialism, were reformulated by Marley, and flowed back to an international audience in the form of a symbolic African "Zion" which was open to both racialized and transracial readings. The cornerstone of my analysis will be a study of how Marley used the Bible in his masterpiece, *Survival*, to articulate his vision of an imagined community in which "black liberation" and "multiracial redemption" could coexist.

A personal note on the study of religious expression

I could not write an honest assessment of Marley's use of Biblical themes without offering some personal comment on my relation to Biblical study, and the resistances this subject matter is likely to arouse among many in my audience. The reasons for and consequences of this hostility towards or condescension regarding religious expression in public discourse have been made clear by scholars such as Stephen Carter and Jenny Franchot.[11] While I find much of their critique compelling, I must also say that I fully understand the suspicion of many of my peers towards anything associated with Christianity, as I have long shared those suspicions of fundamentalisms.

I was raised in a fundamentalist home, and attended the Church of Christ for my first eighteen years. After leaving home, I quit going to church. I had read the Bible often as a youth, but now I put the Bible aside and rarely looked at it for the next fifteen years. Christianity carried the baggage of all that I disliked about American political/religious culture: a certain self-righteous insularity, and, too often, a spirit of intolerance. The church in which I was raised forbade musical instruments and dance. It prayed to a "God above" but was suspicious of the "God within."[12] The branch of this tradition to which I was exposed seemed Eurocentric, ahistorical, uncritical of its textual foundations, and disconnected from the body.

By the late 1970s, I had been exposed to enough alternative traditions to know that my own experience was not necessarily normative. I had traveled in Mexico, witnessed Native American forms of spirituality in the American Southwest, and studied under Vine DeLoria, Jr., author of *God is Red*. I became aware that the Bible (and more generally sacred scriptures of several varieties) could be used to support social justice within multiethnic contexts, as with Latin American "liberation theology." But it was only after my work in the music business had brought me to Jamaica in 1987 and 1988 that I renewed my interest in Judeo-Christian scriptural traditions. Here I encountered Rastafarian-influenced reggae singers and street folk who quoted the Bible incessantly.[13] Indeed, Rastafarian culture had a distinctly Old Testament feel to me, triggering many associations with the Bible stories of my youth. But the Bible was being used by these dissenters in a very different way than the tradition I had known. They used the Bible to argue for political freedom; with an explicitly black and secondarily multiracial emphasis. Ethiopia was their Zion, and their God was "a living man," and a black or brown man, at that – which they treated as a numinous "God within."[14]

Furthermore, the spiritual concerns of these Jamaicans and their worldwide fans coexisted with a very explicit sexuality. This package of Biblical lyrics, political protest, sensual riddims (bass-centered Afro-Caribbean rhythms), and sexuality engaged me. As I continued to listen to Bible-influenced reggae music, I began to look up the scriptural references that I constantly heard. The Rastafarian dogma that Haile Selassie, late emperor of Ethiopia, was the contemporary reincarnation of Christ seemed irrational to me. But then, it didn't seem any more illogical than Christian beliefs in the historical Jesus as the perfect son of God. Both of these belief systems were speculative projections, from a psycho-historical perspective. But both religious mythologies also expressed psychological and cultural "truths" about transformation and redemption that could not be contained in rational language.[15]

In a sense, it was the black man who took me back to church: not to an institution, but to study of the scriptural cornerstone of Judeo-Christian culture. Black people sang my roots back to me in a new voice, using the same scriptures, but applying a radically different interpretation. The Rastafarian variant of Christianity had roots in an Ethiopian church which had maintained almost 2,000 years of independence from "Western" forms of Christianity. Rasta believed Biblical assertions that prophecy was an ongoing process. Rasta articulated a critical theory within an artistic vision that applied Enlightenment philosophy to the multiracial realities of the postcolonial world.[16] In the hands of these latter-day prophets, the Bible was converted into a tool for black liberation as well as multiracial redemption.

It was only this "black" and music-based reading of the Bible that inspired me to use the tools I had acquired in academia to investigate scriptural traditions. The further I explored this domain, the more I became convinced that religious expression is truly "the stone that the builder rejected" when it comes to understanding interracial communication in a historical context.

Marcus Garvey as Rasta's patron saint: ironic contradictions

During the second decade of the twentieth century, Marcus Garvey was already quoting Psalms 68:31 – "Ethiopia will soon stretch forth her hands unto God" – in the service of his "back to Africa" movement. Garvey's call for people of the African diaspora to look at God "through the eyes of Ethiopia" referenced a thoroughly invented Ethiopia, just as the Amharas, the ruling class of Ethiopia, had invented a mythology of Solomonic descent in order to justify their imperial ambitions.[17] Garvey's blend of Ethiopianism and black nationalism would become an ideological cornerstone of the Rastafarians, who would in turn spread this vision worldwide through reggae music.

"Jamaica's reggae music exhibits an amazing fixation with the memory of Garvey," observes Robert Hill. According to Leonard Barrett, "in the pantheon of Rastafarians, Marcus Garvey is second only to Haile Selassie."[18] The importance of Marcus Garvey as an ideological father to Rastafarians is evident in many ways, from the music of Burning Spear to the iconic images of Garvey at many reggae concerts. On Bob Marley's 1979 masterpiece *Survival,* the album jacket featured a drawing of the interior of a slave ship, its human cargo packed like so many sardines. The accompanying quote from Garvey reads: "A people without the knowledge of their past history, origin and culture is like a tree without roots."

Marley's use of this quote (and reggae's Garvey fixation) is ironic, given Garvey's ahistorical view of Africa. I want to give an overview of Garvey's thought that illustrates why he is a paradoxical choice as patron saint for Marley-era Rastafarian reggae. I will focus in particular on two of his attitudes that are relevant for my treatment of Marley as a "biracial black culture hero": first, his conflicted attitudes towards Ethiopia, beginning with an uncritical romanticization and ending with contempt for Haile Selassie; and second, his pathological hatred of mulattos and race-mixing.

Garvey has been characterized as a fascist or proto-fascist by scholars such as Wilson Jeremiah Moses, Clarence Walker, and C. L. R. James. Garvey himself told J. A. Rogers that "We were the first Fascists ... Mussolini copied our Fascism." I point this out because I want to stress that my own criticisms of Garvey are not driven by an ideological agenda, or by an urge to "tear down" an icon of "black liberation." However, one does not have to dig far into the historical record to realize that the revival of interest in Garvey, both among Rastafarians and during the "black power" phase of the Civil Rights movement, has been "characterized by a blindness to his personal faults and ideological shortcomings," as Moses writes.[19] These shortcomings include persistent anti-Semitism, a pathological hatred of race-mixing, and a dictatorial and culturally Eurocentric worldview.

I feel reluctant to criticize this icon, because I have seen the veneration many Jamaicans feel for Garvey. In Jamaica Garvey is both a folk hero and official "National Hero."[20] When I visited for the first time in August 1987, Jamaica was celebrating its twenty-fifth year of independence and the hundredth anniversary of Garvey's birth. Garvey was everywhere: from the face of Jamaica's 50 cent coin to a thirty-foot portrait that was a backdrop to the stage at Sunsplash – Jamaica's international reggae festival. The edge of the stage had been designed to resemble one of Garvey's "Black Star Line" ships. In the spirit of cross-cultural exploration, I acquired a T-shirt with Garvey's image. This inspired a great deal of positive feedback from the locals, who expressed their joy that someone from "foreign," and especially a white man, would show a gesture of respect for their national hero.

It was not until several years later, while reading scholars of Caribbean culture such as James and historians of black nationalism such as Moses, that it became evident how selective was the collective memory of Garvey among Pan-Africanists in general and Rastafarians in particular. Most of those invoking his name seemed to have very little idea of what Garvey actually stood for, and what he fought against.

On the plus side, respect is due to Garvey for raising the self-esteem of millions in the African diaspora. Garvey can be credited with forging unprecedented links among the international black intelligentsia, not only in North America and the Caribbean but also in Latin America, England, and West Africa. The efforts of Garvey and his cohorts led to a new interest in "African foundations," which has found expression above all within forums of artistic expression. Garvey has also been an impetus behind various schools of Pan-African scholarship and quasi-scholarship, including (but not limited to) Afrocentrism.[21]

On the down side, Garvey popularized a "race pride" that was xenophobic, anti-Semitic, and dismissive of the "lessons of history" other than a need for self-mythologization. Walker calls Garvey a "charlatan." Aside from his "reactionary" ideology and messianic delusions, his business ventures alone justify this charge. Garvey's Black Star Line, his "Achilles heel," has ironically remained "one of the most enduring symbols of Garveyism, both in Jamaica and West Africa," Derek Bishton writes.[22] The Black Star Line, which was supposed to transport blacks "back to Africa," was a boondoggle, yet the concept had such an appeal that Kwame Nkrumah named Ghana's state shipping line after it. Like many "Back to Africa" confidence men who preceded him, Garvey never set foot in Africa. But he did raise millions of dollars from poor black people who bought his dream of a black promised land. Their money sank: none of the ships Garvey bought, beginning with the *Frederick Douglass* in 1920, was ever sea-worthy. The Black Star Line symbolized the unbridgeable gap between the ideals and the practice of Ethiopianism in this era.

9 Marcus Garvey, the "patron saint" of Rastafarians, in full Victorian regalia.

In one area, at least, Garvey's success is undebatable: he was a stupendously successful publicist and speaker. His public posture lacked racial ambiguity, and this seems to have been "giving the people what they want." Like Alexander Crummell (who was also Du Bois' early mentor), Garvey was "conservative on every conceivable issue, save equal rights for black[s]." Although the embrace of Garvey by later black nationalists and Rastafarians has saddled him with a reputation as a radical, his conservatism was in fact so extreme that the Klan found in him "an answer to their prayers," as Clarence Walker puts it.[23]

Many writers have accepted much of Garvey's myth-making at face value. For instance, contemporary writers still often repeat the legend that Garvey was a hero of poor black people who rose up from the bottom of Jamaican society to become an international statesman. Yet Garvey was the "son of a fairly prosperous stonemason," Wilson Moses points out, had extensive contact with whites in his youth, and benefited from a privilege unavailable to most Jamaicans.[24] The myth has Garvey as a "black culture hero," but the reality was that Garvey was staunchly Victorian – including an emulation of the mores of British imperialism. Despite living in New York during the Harlem Renaissance, Garvey bad-mouthed Afro-American cultural expressions such as jazz. The music heard during Garveyite gatherings at Liberty Hall was light classical music. The models of literacy Garvey held up to blacks were usually British. Indeed, Robert Hill makes the case that Garvey's slogan "One God, One Aim, One Destiny" was a paraphrase of a patriotic line written by Tennyson on the occasion of Queen Victoria's opening of the Indian and Colonial Exhibition:

> Sons, be welded each and all,
> Into one imperial whole,
> One with Britain, heart and soul
> One life, one flag, one fleet, one Throne[25]

Garvey had no interest in sub-Saharan Africa: he looked to the northeast Africa of the Pharaohs. Even the images of Ethiopia he employed were filtered through a Victorian lense.[26]

Since my discussion of Garvey is meant to provide context for Bob Marley's role in the evolution of an interracial culture, I want to focus on Garvey's efforts to "repress" interraciality. Indeed, one could say that Garvey "perfected" the repression of interraciality in diasporic African culture, and that Marley represents a "return of the repressed." The pervasiveness of interracial themes in Marley's life and work is proportionate to the zeal with which Garvey and like-minded "Black Zionists" repressed the interraciality in which they were embedded.

Garvey's method regarding the recovery of black history, and the repression of interraciality, is consistent: he employs rumor as a form of semiotic warfare. This is evident in his advice on how to deal with threats to a "racial community." Garvey's general advice is as follows: "Insist on a campaign of race purity . . . and close ranks against all other races. It is . . . a disgrace to mix up your race with other races." For those who disobey this strategy, Garvey's advice is more specific: Negroes who marry outside the race, especially those who marry below their socioeconomic status, are to be excommunicated.

Teach the people to abhor such Negroes, and have nothing to do with them so long as they continue in that relationship. This must be done [out of] the hearing of the white race. For safety, let the advice take the [form] of a whisper campaign . . . [W]hisper it right through the neighborhood and never stop until the burden of your campaign is felt by the individuals, so as to learn them a good lesson that others may not do the same thing with impunity.[27]

Garvey urged the same "whispering campaign" against Jews. "Never trust a Jew," he advised.

He plays with loaded dice, his card is marked, you can never win against him. Make this a secret whispering propaganda in every community where you go into a Negro home. Whisper all the time that the Jew is bad . . . he believes he is the

chosen of God and as such all other men must pay tribute to him. This is false ...
Jewish propaganda, ignore it and let him pay tribute to you if tribute must be paid.

If necessary, "let them know that they were once your slaves in Egypt."[28]

Garvey often employs the same tactics he has condemned in whites, or in Jews. In the above passage he condemns "Jewish propaganda" as "false and fictitious." But in the interests of constructing a positive black history, Garvey sanctions a "fictitious" form of "black propaganda." Reading material should be scanned "to see what you can pick out for the good of the race," Garvey said. "Search all history and all literature and the Bible and find facts to support this argument" that blacks are superior. "*Things that may not be true can be made if you repeat them long and often enough.* Therefore, always repeat statements that will give your race a status and an advantage. That is how the white man has built up his system of superiority."[29]

In each of these three examples, Garvey achieves an imagined "racial purity" and a heroic "black community" through a repression of the multiethnic interconnectedness in which he is embedded. The artificiality of his construction of a "black history" which used models from imperial Britain, and which ignores all but "fulsome praise," should already be evident. It brings to mind Cabral's warning against the uncritical use of "indiscriminate compliments."[30] I want now to comment briefly on Garvey's repression of interraciality in his own life.

Garvey recalled his father as being someone who "always acted as if he did not belong among the villagers." Young Marcus' first playmates were white children, notably four children of a Wesleyan (Methodist) minister, and five children of another white man whose property adjoined the Garveys. Marcus was particularly close to a daughter of the minister. They played together like "two innocent fools who never dreamed of a race feeling and problem." This continued until Marcus turned fourteen, whereupon the minister shipped the girl off to Edinburgh, Scotland, and told his daughter not to try to get in touch with Marcus as he was a "nigger." Wilson Moses argues that "his life-long obsession with intermarriage would seem to indicate that this experience, coming as it did at the age of sexual awakening, was a very traumatic one."[31]

Garvey would later call mixed-race people "degenerates" and "monstrosities." He posited the same sort of "mulattos are trying to control us" conspiracy theories earlier favored by Edward Blyden, Alexander Crummell, and other "mulatto-hating Ethiopian millennialists." Garvey's vitriolic attacks against Du Bois were part of an effort "to read 'light-skinned negroes' out of the black race," believes Jervis Anderson.[32] This was a somewhat inconsistent attitude as there were high-ranking mulattos in Garvey's United Negro Improvement Association, such as T. Thomas Fortune, who had been around long enough to join Crummell's American Negro Academy in the 1890s, and to defend Douglass' interracial marriage in the 1880s.[33]

A key to what made Garvey "tick" – what drove him to embrace and mythologize his particular breed of messianic Ethiopianism – is visible in his account of reading Booker T. Washington's autobiography in London. Garvey asked himself where was the black man's "king and kingdom." Realizing that he could not find them, he vowed: "*I will help to make them.*" And this is exactly what he did: Garvey *created* an imagined African kingdom based at first on a Biblical model of Ethiopia, and later on the most tenuous of references to a "real" Ethiopia which was itself an invented tradition with quasi-Biblical roots.[34] Again, the seed sown by Garvey would bear fruit in the mythology of an Ethiopian Zion, carried to the four corners of the earth by Bob Marley.

Bernard Lewis argues that the reinvention of history – as in Garvey's advice to repeat positive versions of black history until accepted as "fact" – is typical of formerly enslaved or colonized peoples. They try "to rewrite the past" – first, to reveal the concealed villainy of the imperialists, and second, "to restore the true image of the pre-imperialist past which the imperialists themselves had defaced and hidden."[35] This model accurately describes Garvey's quest to recover a pre-imperial Ethiopia as a mythological cornerstone for his own would-be "black kingdom."

My view of the "inventedness" of Garvey's "black history" is rooted in an awareness that *all* nations and religious traditions are invented. I am only insisting that the roots of Rastafarianism must be subjected to the same critical examination, for instance, as the racial assumptions (and psychological projections) that caused Euro-Americans to imagine a white Jesus – or the assumptions that led the "founding fathers" to imagine a "democracy" limited to white male landowners. Furthermore, just because we say something is *invented* does not make it any less *real*, as Werner Sollors notes. We must look closely at the "psychological reality" of the people who invented traditions, in order to understand their internal logic. With Garvey, we must understand his "psychological structure," in order to understand what compelled him to project messianic aspirations on to Ethiopia.[36]

Garvey's quest to "help make" an African kingdom, and to recreate himself as its king-in-waiting, became a secular religion. Garvey's movement has been described as a religion by E. Franklin Frazier, Randall Burkett, and Garvey himself. Garvey wrote that "The masses of the race absorb the doctrines of the UNIA with the same eagerness with which the masses in the days of . . . imperial Rome accepted Christianity. The people seem to regard the movement in the light of a new religion."[37] Garvey called his new religion "African Fundamentalism," with the subtitle: "A racial heirarchy and empire for Negroes." It was formulated during a fundamentalist revival that swept the United States after World War I. As with any fundamentalism, "religious truth," not historical accuracy, was the primary concern. Garvey's "truth" was centered on the notion of "race pride" and required the articulation of a "race catechism." This catechism was explicitly founded upon the mythology of a pre-imperialist, divinely sanctioned Ethiopia. Garvey's African Fundamentalism, which emphasized a "Black God," had its roots in nineteenth-century Ethiopianism. Henry McNeal Turner had written in 1898: "We do not believe that there is any hope for a race of people who do not believe that they look like God." Garvey's logic was similar: "since the white people have seen their God through white spectacles, we have only now started out . . . to see our God through our own spectacles," he reasoned. "We Negroes believe in . . . the one God of all ages . . . but we shall worship him through the spectacles of Ethiopia."[38]

Garvey's references to Ethiopia were at first generic and depoliticized.[39] He told the 1924 United Negro Improvement Association (UNIA) convention in Madison Square Garden: "Our desire is . . . to lay down our burden . . . by the banks of the Niger and sing our songs and chant our hymns to the God of Ethiopia." This conflation of West Africa and Ethiopia illustrates that Garvey's Africa is essentially fictional. A geopolitical Ethiopia gradually impacted Garvey's depiction of a mythological "black kingdom." By 1930 he declared: "We have great hopes in Abyssinia in the East – the country that has kept her traditions even back to the days of Solomon." Garvey expressed the confidence that Abyssinia would "rise . . . to *repossess the Imperial Authority* that is promised by God himself in the inspiration: Princes coming out of Egypt and Ethiopia stretching forth her hands."[40] But if Garvey's "lense" through which he viewed Selassie was Biblical, his hopes were political, argues Rupert Lewis: "for a reign based on modernity within the framework of Pan-African solidarity." His view of Selassie as the head of a geopolitical empire, rather than as a deity, would bring him into conflict with the early Rastas.

Rastafarians attribute to Garvey the prophecy "Look to the East for the coming of an African King." Such sentiments had been in circulation for some time – for instance, in Pauline Hopkins' 1903 magazine novel, *Of One Blood*. The source of this oracular utterance may have been James Morris Webb, a clergyman who published a book in 1919 entitled *A Black Man Will Be the Coming Universal King, Proven by Biblical History*. Webb, an associate of Garvey's, apparently spoke these words at the 1924

UNIA convention.[41] At any rate, after Garvey was deported by the United States, he staged a play in Kingston in 1929 called "The Coronation of the King and Queen of Africa." Some synchronicity seemed to be at work here, since early Rastas interpreted the play as a rehearsal for Selassie's coronation on November 2, 1930.[42]

Garvey expressed scorn for the Rastas he saw in Jamaica before departing for permanent exile in London. Garvey's followers had marched through Harlem in 1931 carrying posters of Garvey and Selassie. But in 1933 Garvey refused to allow early Rasta leader Leonard Howell to distribute pictures of Selassie at his Kingston headquarters. The *Jamaica Times* reported that in Garvey's address to the 1934 UNIA convention he "referred to the Ras Tafari cult . . . with contempt." This contempt was aroused by at least two factors. There was probably a sense of class difference involved. The early Rastafarian movement arose entirely among lower-class Jamaicans. As we have seen, Garvey's father "acted as if he did not belong" among the villagers. Garvey saw the Rastas as a threat to social order. He grouped the Rastas with "the large number of revivalist cults which are driving our people crazy" – which supports the argument by Chevannes that Rastafarianism was essentially an offshoot of Revivalism for its first quarter century of existence. In addition, Howell's followers had very early begun treating him as a Christ-figure, and this would have evoked a sense of competition or resentment from Garvey, who had a messianic self-concept. Garvey had no tolerance for those who declared Selassie's divinity. After Selassie fled Ethiopia following Italy's invasion, Garvey's public comments about Selassie became vicious.[43]

Regarding Garvey's acknowledged affinity with Mussolini's fascism, we might ask: what were the similarities between the ways that Mussolini and Garvey treated Ethiopia? Mussolini invaded Ethiopia militarily, because he wanted it as a material anchor to an Italian empire. Garvey "invaded" Ethiopia rhetorically, because he wanted it to serve as a cornerstone of his imagined "black kingdom." I do not suggest that these two "invasions" can be placed on the same (im)moral plane. But I do think that the parallels between physical and rhetorical "colonialism" reflect a similar imperialistic worldview: a belief in the *right* to colonize, and to fulfill imperial ambitions. Many Rastas inherited Garvey's view of Africa. They did not usually replicate Garvey's fascism, although the messianic projections (or aspirations) so visible in Garvey's life, and Ethiopianism, did remain prominent.

Whether or not Garvey actually uttered the words "Look to the East for the coming of an African King" is less important than that Rastafarians *believed* he had said this. So they set about looking for the "higher one" of

Garvey's prophecy, real or imagined. By the late 1930s a series of events pointed to Ethiopia as the most likely place where "prophecy fulfill."[44]

In June 1931 *National Geographic* published a pictorial of Selassie's coronation, which was passed among Rastas already looking for a black king. The photos of Selassie in his full regalia, and the wording of his official title ("King of Kings, Lord of Lords, Conquering Lion of the Tribe of Judah") made a big impression on black Jamaicans. In the midst of an upsurge in Revivalism, they were accustomed to hearing the Salvation Army sing "The Lion of Judah shall break every chain" – a traditional song later recorded by Marley. And so "Marcus Garvey's words come to pass" – the Rastas searched their Bibles and found references in Revelations 19:15–16 and 17:14 to the "King of Kings and Lord of Lords" who had hair like wool. Revelations 5 described this Messiah as "the Lion from the tribe of Judah, the shoot growing from David's stock," before whom the elders "were singing a new song." Several preachers "from foreign" appeared on the island, bearing pictures of Selassie and proclaiming: "Look 'pon this man and see if him don't favor the same white Jesus, only thing him black!" These pictures were widely seen as indisputable truth from a world outside Jamaica, where the truth was not suppressed, that the black Jesus had arrived.[45]

The Rastafarians' name comes from Selassie's pre-coronation name: Ras Tafari Makonnen. Ras translates from Amharic literally as "head," and is the equivalent of "Duke." As Bob Marley would later repeat in countless interviews, the Rastas believe since Tafari means "creator," Rastafari is then the "head creator." Both names signified on the Rastafarian belief in a "God within": Rastafari is often rendered as Rasta Far-Eye, or the all-seeing-eye, as in the Masonic symbol on the dollar bill. Selassie-I (power of the trinity) is pronounced Selassie-Eye.

Three international events 1935–37 had a formative influence on Rastafarianism. First was the 1935 reprint of an article titled "Secret Society to Destroy Whites" in the *Jamaica Times*. This piece had first appeared in Europe, and was "almost certainly the work of a proto-Italian lobby," writes Bishton.[46] The article warned of a "black peril which darkened the European horizon." It claimed a secret warrior society called "NYA-BINGHI" had been formed, which meant "Death to the Whites." The author wrote that this movement was now headquartered in Ethiopia, where "Haile Selassie is regarded as a veritable Messiah, a saviour of the coloured people, the Emperor of the Negro Kingdom."

This article represents a strange confluence of Amhara religious mythology, racist Italian propaganda, fragments of reportage of anticolonial resistance in East Africa, and an uncanny expression of the unconscious projections of black Jamaicans. The article was "intended to scare the whites into preemptive action," Chevannes writes. But it had an entirely unintended effect in Jamaica, where Rastas found the article to be inspirational evidence of a literal "league of black people against the whites, headed by Haile Selassie." Rastas took the name Nyabinghi for themselves as a sort of "rootsman" alter ego. And so Rastas constructed a self-image as anticolonial warriors and a new chosen people, with whatever they had at hand – a *National Geographic* article, a seond-hand piece of fascist propaganda, and a picture of Jomo Kenyatta with a field general whose hair was worn in "dreadlocks."[47]

In 1936 Italy invaded Ethiopia, bringing Selassie to international attention. The Rastas' hero was suddenly also a hero to many other Westerners. In 1937 the Ethiopian World Federation (EWF) was founded in New York. EWF branches were quickly established throughout the Caribbean. The EWF put out a newspaper called the *Voice of Ethiopia*, whose slogan was "One God, One Brotherhood." Many of the Rastas' beliefs can be traced to this paper.[48]

The international cross-currents typical of Garveyism were in effect from the beginning, as can be seen in two of the early Rastafarian "prophets" who adapted Garvey's message. Joseph N. Hibbert (b. 1894) had emigrated from Jamaica to Costa Rica at age seventeen. In Central America, where there was a large contingent of emigrant Jamaicans, he became a member of the Ancient Order of Ethiopia, a Masonic Lodge. Hibbert returned to Jamaica in 1931 to preach the divinity of Haile Selassie. Like several early Rasta preachers, Hibbert was an Ethiopianist Christian, with roots in the Ethiopian Baptist Church founded by George Liele (Lisle). Liele emigrated to Jamaica in 1784 from South Carolina, where he was baptized by a convert of George Whitefield, the legendary barn-storming preacher of the First Great Awakening (sketched in chapter 1).[49]

The best-known Rasta leader, Leonard Howell (1898–1981), was a soldier in Panama and a cook in the US Army Transport Service, by which means he came to New York. Garveyites remembered Howell as a con man. When Howell returned to Jamaica in 1932 he sold thousands of photos of Selassie, passing them off as a "passport" to Ethiopia. An older Rasta interviewed by Derek Bishton remembered Howell appearing on the scene holding a storm lantern, claiming to be an ambassador from Ethiopia sent to do the work of "my father," and identifying himself as "the same Jesus Christ that was crucified." Howell's numerous followers referred to him as "Gong" – which later became Bob Marley's best-known nickname.[50]

Howell developed a sizable following willing to publicly validate his messianic self-concept. He taught that white supremacy represented evil and black supremacy represented good, with the black good destined to overcome white evil. This view of an immanent racial Armageddon echoed both Garvey and the view of turn-of-the century Jamaican Ethiopianist Alexander Bedward. As with so many Jamaican leaders, Bedward also had spent time in Central America. These folk prophets invariably got much of their prestige from having returned from "foreign" – which in Jamaican context was widely interpreted as a parallel to the sojourns of Moses and Jesus in the wilderness. We will see this archetypal pattern again with Marley. Bedward preached a millennial scenario in which a "black wall" rose up against a "white wall." "The white wall has oppressed us for years; now we must knock the white wall down," he told his followers in the 1890s. Like Burning Spear and other reggae singers would do in the late twentieth century, Bedward called on his listeners to "remember the Morant War," the uprising of 1865 whose black martyr, Paul Bogle, is now a national hero.

The myth of black supremacy replacing white supremacy through an uprising led by a black or brown messiah has been a persistent feature of Jamaican culture for two centuries, weaving in and out of the island's folk culture like the disappearing and reappearing themes of dub music. Garvey, the link between Bedward and Howell, was telling audiences in 1919 that "there will be no democracy in the world until the Negro rules." But Garvey ostracized Howell. This helped marginalize Rastas "from mainstream political thinking in Jamaica for the next quarter century," Bishton thinks. Many Rastas donned sackcloth and other symbols of their rejection of "mainstream" society, and retreated to the hills – the repressed theme disappearing for a while. When police destroyed Howell's Pinnacle Compound in 1955, a large group of these millennialist Rastafarians descended into Kingston. Their growing presence in Kingston slums corresponds with Bob Marley's teenage years, and the years leading up to Jamaican independence in 1962.[51]

In his ethnographic research among older Rastas, Barry Chevannes found four types of myths about Garvey. One was of Garvey as a Moses figure, with Bedward often seen as the Aaron, or high priest, of the movement. The other three myths were of Garvey as John the Baptist, as himself divine, and as a prophet – the latter group being the most numerous. Garvey's middle name is Mosiah – a cross between Moses and Messiah. But most Rastas have come to feel that Garvey's movement was "only a rehearsal" for what was to come. And this seems to be the view of Garvey that Marley had – as a "culture hero" who combined Moses and "John the Baptist" roles.[52]

Marley often asserted that Garvey's prophecies were still being fulfilled. And he used "flag" portraits of both Garvey and Selassie as stage backdrops. On his first Island album, *Catch a Fire*, this verse appears in "Kinky Reggae":

> I went down to Picadilly Circus, there I saw Marcus
> He had a tan guitar all over his chocolate bar
> Think I might join the fun, but I had to hit and run
> I just can't settle down in the kinky part of town.

The mood here is somewhat inscrutable, a seeming commentary on the "Swinging London" scene of the late 1960s and early 1970s that Marley encountered. (There's a sexual riff going on – the line written as "tan guitar" may have been "candy tart.") Marley seems to be attracted to the "psychedelic" version of Marcus, but decides that he cannot sink his roots in this subculture.

There are numerous direct and indirect references to Garvey in Marley's songbook. Marley's song "So Much Things to Say" (*Exodus*, 1977) invokes Garvey, along with Jesus and Paul Bogle, as martyrs who serve to remind the people of "who you are and where you stand in the struggle." Marley's 1979 album *Survival* opens with the exhortation: "Rise ye mighty people." This invokes Garvey's rhetorical flourish "Up ye mighty race: you can accomplish what you will." And Marley's famous line from "Redemption Song," "emancipate yourselves from mental slavery" – also signifies on Garvey.[53]

• • •

Just as many young black Americans look back through the field nigger/ house nigger racial mythology of Malcolm X, so Rastas often looked back to Ethiopia through Marcus Garvey's distorted mirror. If Malcolm's point of view is misleading, as seen in KRS-One's dismissal of Frederick Douglass, then Garvey's blinders would seem to be pernicious, leading to a willful blindness that often ends up supporting the repressive political ideologies that it claims to oppose.

Yet Rastas altered Garvey as much as Garvey reinvented Ethiopia. They followed the "black first" philosophy to its logical conclusion: if Africa was the mother of all races, then "The Whole World is Africa," as Black Uhuru would sing. Quoting the Bible, Marley sang of black people: "the stone that the builder refused shall be the head cornerstone." Yet the edifice itself, clearly, was multiracial, for those who chose to read the Bible, and history, inclusively. Far more so than Garvey or earlier Ethiopianists, the Rastas grew to think inclusively. Their Zion was most immediately for black people, but ultimately it was "a house of prayer for all people."[54] A "One Love" shift was underway before Marley began recording, but he personified and extended this inclusive tendency. Marley's biraciality must be seen as a key to this shift.

STRUCTURE

Anti-mulatto prejudice in Jamaican history and Marley's life

Bob Marley was born to a white father and black mother in 1945, at a time in Jamaica when there was a huge gulf between black and white worlds. In an interview included in the video *Time Will Tell*, Marley was asked if he was prejudiced against whites, or whose side he was on. "I don't have prejudice against myself," Marley reasoned. "My father was a white and my mother black. Them call me half-caste, or whatever. Well, me don't dip on nobody's side. Me don't dip on the black man's side nor the white man's side. Me dip on God's side, the one who create me and cause me to come from black and white."[55]

Marley here expresses both a memory of the hostility he encountered because of his biraciality, and the transracial philosophy he evolved in order to unite "racial" differences within a greater whole. The "anti-mulatto" prejudice Marley experienced marked him deeply, as his family has affirmed. His insistence on combining black liberation with multi-racial redemption represents, in the light of his personal and cultural history, a remarkable synthesizing effort (and one, it must be emphasized, firmly rooted in Judeo-Christian precedent).

Marley's father was not around to help raise him. Bob (or Nesta, as his mother called him) only saw him a few times before the older man died. Bob came of age in Kingston's shanty towns and absorbed a grassroots anticolonial religious culture that worshiped (or looked for inspiration to) a great African Father in Ethiopia. Bob would reinvent this African Father, at first for himself, for all Rastas, and finally for an international audience. The journey is a long one, a cultural, political, and spiritual "exodus" that I can only sketch in broad strokes here. The story begins in a history of "fundamental ambivalence towards Jamaicans of Mixed race," as Richard Burton writes – an ambivalence whose one extreme was a sometimes rabid anti-"brown" prejudice in Jamaican history, and whose other extreme was a tendency to project messianic qualities on to mixed-race leaders.[56]

At the time of independence in 1962, Jamaica was 77 percent black, 20 percent brown, 1 percent white, and 2 percent Asian. A "brown stratum" had been a firmly established intermediate class since the early colonial days. In contrast to North America's "peculiar institution," West Indian slaveholders usually recognized their biracial offspring and often arranged for their education in Europe. Horace Campbell remarks that many slave revolts were betrayed by "mulattoes who were the eyes and ears of the masters." The tendency of browns to distance themselves from blacks was evident to nineteenth-century observers. An Englishman who toured Jamaica in the 1820s, Cynric Williams, noted that "the mulattos kept aloof, as if they disdained to mingle with the negroes." An American visitor in the 1840s, John Bigelow, wrote that the browns shunned all contact with "negroes or Africans" and "can experience no more unpardonable insult than to be classified with them in any way."[57]

There were significant exceptions: most notably, a rich mulatto named George William Gordon who left the Anglican church of his white father in order to adopt the religion of his mother, and of most black Jamaicans, the Baptists. Gordon converted Paul Bogle, who led the 1865 Morant Bay Rebellion, and provided political support for the uprising, calling on his "black flock" to rise up and protest. Gordon was hanged, which increased the distance between browns and whites without, for the most part, ameliorating the tension between browns and blacks. Yet the Morant Bay Rebellion bequeathed a gallery of archetypal figures: the black martyr (Paul Bogle); the colored/brown redeemer (George Gordon), and the white ogre (John Eyre – the governor responsible for brutally squashing the rebellion); and the far-off benevolent King or Queen. The archetypal figure of the King or Queen was sometimes interchangeable with the myth of the "Good White Man" – a Caribbean-wide figure who supported emancipation, even when local rulers did not.[58]

By the 1940s, the decade in which Bob Marley was born, browns had developed into a large middle class which "eagerly accept the white man's badges of imperial conformity," according to Paul Blanshard. With few exceptions, wrote Blanshard, "the general practice of the successful brown men in the Caribbean is to disassociate themselves as completely as possible from the lowly blacks." But again, there were significant exceptions, notably "brown redeemers" such as Alexander Bustamante in the late 1930s and 1940s, and Michael Manley in the 1970s. Both Bustamante and Manley were "manifestations of the savior figure so deeply embedded in [the] Jamaican political psyche," Burton writes.[59]

Black Jamaicans were still suspicious of "browns" in Marley's youth. The *Report on the Rastafari Movement* (1960) noted that Rastas viewed Fidel Castro favorably: he was seen as preferable to "white and brown Babylonians." The first Rasta to run for public office, Ras Brown, wrote in his campaign literature: "To white supremacy has been added Brownman supremacy and the mongrel children of the Black woman came to think and behave contemptuously of Black people." In 1962 C. L. R. James decried a "Brown" cover-up: as he saw it as a Labour Party conspiracy to whitewash the real state of race relations in Jamaica with the slogan "Out of Many One People." This idealism was still seen as a sort of "premature integration," at least when voiced by white and brown politicians.[60]

Bob's mother Cedella began a romance with Captain Norval Marley, a colonial supervisor, when he was fifty and she was seventeen. Norval married Cedella after she became pregnant, but his family disowned him. He was in ill health, so he left rural Nine Miles in St. Anne's parish to return to Kingston. When Bob was five, Norval persuaded Cedella and her family that Bob should be educated in Kingston. Bob was shipped to Kingston by bus. According to Cedella, Norval placed him in an unknown home, then disappeared. Bob's whereabouts were unknown to his mother for the next year, until he was rediscovered. Cedella took him back to the country until 1952, when they returned to Kingston. Bob was not to see his father again until 1955, a few months before he died. In the absence of a father, his role models came from the shantytowns of Kingston. (In the section titled "Fruits" [pp. 187–91] I will examine in more detail Cedella's relationship with Norval, Bob's conflicted attitude toward his biological father, and his early "substitute fathers".)

Rita Marley, his wife, recalls that Kingston toughs often taunted Bob on account of his absent white father. "Having come through this white father caused such difficulties that he'd want to kill himself," she says. She describes him as being "lost in that: not being able to have anyone to say it's not your fault, or that there's nothing wrong in being like you are." What Rita describes is essentially a struggle to escape from the "Tragic Mulatto" syndrome: "Bob had to put up with a lot of resistance. If he wasn't that strong in himself he wouldn't be what he became today. He would be down-trodden and seen as another half-caste who would never make it."[61]

In 1962, the year of Jamaican independence, and the year in which Bob released his first single, "Judge Not," he had an affair with a girl in a Trenchtown "yard" or government project. But "them style him a white man," one friend remembers, and the girl's older brother forbade her to carry on the relationship, explaining to Cedella that he didn't want "no white man screwing up our bloodlines." The authors of *Songs of Freedom* write: "Considered a white boy, his complexion would often bring out the worst in people: after all, why was this boy from 'country' living down in the ghetto and not uptown with all the other lightskin people?" Clearly, Bob did not fit the preconceptions of black Jamaicans: he had neither the anti-black racism nor the economic privilege that they had come to expect from browns.[62]

Benjamin Foot, Bob's first tour manager in Great Britain in 1973, picked up on a lingering racial ambiguity. "I felt that Bob wasn't secure in himself at this time," he recalled. "I think he was perturbed that one of his parents was white, and he wanted to prove himself very much as being a black Rasta." Behind the screwface persona Foot glimpsed a certain doubleness: "Bob's particular problem, I always felt, was that he was an up-and-coming black star, based on this entire Rasta philosophy; and he didn't quite feel the part."[63]

Peter Tosh later made the bitter accusation that Bob had only achieved stardom because of his "white blood." Rita Marley argues that the opposite was true: "the sacrifices Bob had to make in his teenage years for being half-white allowed him to become famous or successful." Such a question is not resolvable, but while I would affirm that Bob Marley's biracial look contributed to his stardom, his vision grew out of a struggle resulting from that biraciality, not an accompanying privilege. Bob repeatedly went against type: he was a Jamaican "brown" who was black-identified. He was a Pan-Africanist, yet shed most if not all of the anti-white prejudices of early Rastas. His attitude was consistent: as he told Dennis Morris on an early tour of England, "It's the system we're against – it's not a black and white thing."[64]

In interviews, Bob was free to talk at length about the transracial implications of his black liberation philosophy. But Bob was carried along by a movement that was primarily focused upon the black part of the equation. Naturally, we might expect that, within his public art, Marley's feelings about biraciality were repressed. However, Marley was a master at employing double-voiced lyrics, and some of these lyrics take on new shades of meaning when read through his biraciality. I will give just one example, from "Sun is Shining," an impressionistic song Bob wrote in the late 1960s, and then later rerecorded for *Kaya* (1978).

> When the morning gathers the rainbow
> Want you to know I'm a rainbow too
> To the rescue here I am
> Want you to know, just if you can, where I stand

Bob presents himself here in his pre-tragic "natural mystic" mode, gathering all the colors of the rainbow about him and claiming all these colors as his own. The key here is in the qualifier "just if you can," which Bob also uses to set up the "gathers the rainbow" line. If the audience can understand where he stands, then Bob wants to be seen as like the rainbow. And in his multiracial mood, he offers to come "to the rescue" of those who understand.

The Island connection: marketing Marley for a multiracial audience

The Bob Marley best known internationally is the one recorded by Island Records from 1972 to 1980, and marketed by Island both during this period and after Marley's death in 1981. Marley had several other careers before signing with Island chief Chris Blackwell, beginning with his first single "Judge Not" in 1962 and progressing through a long string of different producers and labels. But no one else with whom Marley collaborated had succeeded in taking his music beyond the Caribbean and West Indians in Great Britain. Marley's subsequent emergence as international icon must be seen as a co-creation between the Island production and marketing team, and Marley and his "massive."[65]

Blackwell, a wealthy white Jamaican, founded Island in 1962, drawing the name from Alec Waugh's novel *Island in the Sun*.[66] Initially the label imported Jamaican music to West Indians in England. But by the late 1960s, Blackwell was earning most of his money, and devoting most of his attention, to a stable of "progressive rock" groups such as Traffic. It was only with the 1972 release of Perry Henzell's film *The Harder They Come*, starring Jimmy Cliff, that reggae reached a "mainstream" audience. The soundtrack, released through Island, was a best seller, and the film and music made Jimmy Cliff an international star.

The key to the image of Bob Marley that was sold to a global audience is the character played by Cliff in *Harder They Come*, Rhyging, who also appears in Micheal Thelwell's novel of the same name.[67] Rhyging was a a Jamaican folk legend, sort of a cross between Robin Hood and Clyde Barrow who had been gunned down in a shoot-out with police in 1948. The rude boy/gangster image was one of the personas that Marley had worn during the 1960s, and Rhyging, now recirculating in 1972 in cinematic and musical form, supplied the type in which Blackwell cast Marley.

"[Marley] came in right at the time when there was this idea in my head that a rebel-type character could really emerge," Blackwell recalled later. "I was dealing with rock music, which was really rebel music. I felt that would really be the way to break Jamaican music. But you needed somebody to be that image. When Bob walked in, he really was that image, the real one that Jimmy had created in the movie."[68]

Blackwell makes a distinction here between reality and fiction. The two are mutually constituting, of course, but he sees Marley as the "real one," the real-life prototype of the fictional character which Henzell and Cliff had constructed. His marketing strategy played off of this concept, accentuating the rebel in Marley, "fictionalizing" his Rhyging persona, as it were, so that it became his dominant image.

Previously, reggae had been sold only as singles, with no attention given to long-term marketing strategies. In contrast, Bob Marley and the Wailers' *Catch a Fire* was marketed as the first reggae concept album. Rock-style keyboards and guitars were overdubbed. Great attention was paid to packaging – playing up both the revolutionary image, and the association with marijuana consumption, of Marley and the Wailers.

The only whites who had previously paid much attention to reggae were skinheads, but *Catch a Fire* was marketed to the elite of England's progressive rock establishment. The strategy worked: the album drew rave reviews, although it only sold moderately at first. When the Wailers toured England for the first time in 1973, their thirty-one concerts revealed dual target audiences: fifteen dates were at reggae clubs, the rest at rock-style clubs. Their four shows at the fashionable Speakeasy were "the hippest event that London had experienced that year," attended by Bianca Jagger, Bryan Ferry, Brian Eno, and Traffic.[69] The result of this marketing strategy and the resultant "buzz" was that for most of Marley's Island career, his biggest audience was white. Marley became the biggest live draw in Europe before black radio in the US consented to play him: black DJs considered reggae "jungle music." The irony of this militantly "black" music finding its first mass audience among whites elicited considerable commentary from Marley, and drove many of his later career moves.

To keep a manageable focus, I will primarily focus on Marley's 1979 album *Survival* as a capstone of his career. To contextualize this album I will show how in the work preceding *Survival* Marley refashioned his image as a Rhyging-type rebel in a form that spoke more directly to the Pan-African elements within his multiracial but predominantly white audience. Then I will analyze the use of Biblical themes in *Survival*, as part of Marley's effort to recreate an ideal African Father who would replace the inadequate white father he had never known.

Marley recorded hundreds of songs from 1962 to 1972, which run the gamut from syrupy love songs to Biblical aphorisms to political commentary to covers of current hits by American and English pop, rock, and soul acts. The variety is astonishing, but several recurring styles emerge. One way to approach this "embarrassment of riches" is to group them according to a variety of personas that Marley wore. I would suggest five somewhat distinct but overlapping personas that Marley adapted in his music, dictated by his philosophical convictions, marketing needs, and current artistic and political trends:

(1) Biblical philosopher/prophet;
(2) Rude Boy champion;
(3) lover;
(4) Natural Mystic;
(5) mediator/peacemaker.

As Marley interacted with a growing international audience, these merged into three dominant personas during the Island years:

(1) Rhyging (1962–75)
(2) Moses (1976–78)
(3) Messianic (1979–)

Marley's boyhood was divided between his birthplace in rural St. Anne's parish, and Kingston's slums. In Nine Miles Bob was remembered as a charming, well-mannered boy with a clairvoyant bent. In Kingston he developed a reputation as a tough kid. Like many teenagers, he was exposed to, and was perhaps attracted to, the gangster-like wildness of what were called "rude boys," and to the "spiritual alternative," the Rastafarians, who in this time were viewed as an antisocial menace by most parents. But Jamaican youth liked to mimick their behavior, much as suburban teens now mimic the behavior of rap stars. According to biographer Timothy White, Bob's mother Cedella chastised him once around 1961 by remarking: "Nesta, why yuh keep company wit dem bad bwai?... People judge yuh by company ya keep, and dem lot is *rhyging!*"[70]

The name Rhyging itself carries the connotation of *raging* – as in out of control. As a hero or anti-hero, Rhyging was still a fresh collective memory, exerting a dangerous attraction for Jamaican youth, and representing a negative type to be avoided at all costs for their parents. Bob is said to have reassured his mother that the tough boys with whom he hung out could not make him engage in unlawful activity. But gangsters and gunmen would remain intimate with Marley throughout his life. His first hit record, "Simmer Down," was an admonition to "rude boys" to "control your temper." However, at a time when most other singers were condemning rudie violence, Bob Marley and the Wailers emerged as rude boy champions, singing that these reckless youth were "gonna rule this land."[71]

Marley's first single, "Judge Not," reflects another persona, that of Biblical folk poet/philosopher. The song is an adaptation of the Gospel injunction to "judge not that you be not judged." (Marley perpetually recycled his lyrics, and the lines about "someone else is judging you" reappeared in his late single "Could You Be Loved.") As postcolonial Rastafarian currents entered Marley's thinking in the late 1960s and early 1970s, this philosopher-poet persona evolved into that of a bonafide prophet.

The accusations that Marley had "sold out" or "gone soft" on *Kaya* (1978) ignored the fact that Bob had recorded ballads throughout his career, and had always enjoyed playing the role of a "ladies' man."

Throughout the 1960s, both original ballads and cover tunes were an essential part of his repertoire. Among the songs Marley covered were "And I Love Her" by the Beatles, "What's New Pussycat?" by Tom Jones, and "Ten Commandments of Love," originally by the Moonglows, and later covered by Aaron Neville. Marley articulated his own rationale as to why it was important to continue doing love songs, even when his audience expected him to strike only revolutionary postures, as we will see.

Another consistent persona was that of "Natural Mystic," as in the song of that title, which led off the *Exodus* album.

> There's a natural mystic blowing through the air
> If you listen carefully you will hear
> This could be the first trumpet, might as well be the last
> Many more will have to suffer, many more will have to die
> Don't ask me why. Things are not the way they used to be

The Natural Mystic persona is also evident in two previously discussed songs, which were both written "a foreign," as Jamaicans say of the world outside their island. "Kinky Reggae" takes a mystical view of the so-called "psychedelic Sixties." "Sun is Shining," later included on *Kaya*, was first written in 1966 while Bob was working the "Night Shift" at a Chrysler plant while living with his mother in Wilmington, Delaware. The Natural Mystic persona of Bob includes elements of other personas, such as Rastafarian philosopher, but also signifies on an older folk tradition, what Zora Neale Hurston called the "natchul man."[72]

Marley referred to his music as an "earth force, a rhythm of people working, people moving." This rhythm was forwarded by the Rastas, but rooted in a deeper tradition, which is why Marley also referred to his art as a "Pocomania type of music." This is a clear expression of Rasta's affiliation with Revival, as Barry Chevannes' ethnographic work has made clear. It was this sense of embeddedness in deep roots, and not sheer ego, that allowed Marley to make the claim in 1975 that "my music will go on forever."[73]

Finally, Marley adapted a peacemaker/mediator persona early on in his career. Elements of this are visible in Marley's Rude Boy tunes, which, although sympathetic to unruly youth, also try to encourage more constructive models of behavior. Marley's best-known songs in the mediator mode are, first, "One Love," which ponders the possibility of common ground between the oppressed and their oppressor:

> Is there a place for the hopeless sinner
> Who has hurt all mankind just to save his own
> One Love, One Heart, let's get together and feel alright

Second, at the end of his life, "Redemption Song," like so many Marley compositions, holds out music as the key to collective redemption:

> Won't you help to sing these songs of freedom
> All I ever had, Redemption Songs

A review of shifts in Marley's image helps historicize his music, and problematize assumptions that Marley's career was either corporately imposed, or entirely self-determined. Like most Jamaican singers of the 1960s, Marley's primary musical influences were American soul artists. The favorite artists of the early Wailers were slick groups like the Moonglows and the Impressions. Marley particularly admired the latter group. For much of the 1960s, the poses he struck were often an "impression of the Impressions."[74] A 1964 photo of the Wailers shows the group in gold lamé stage costumes. In 1965 the group wore formal suits and black leather shoes with pointed toes. In the late 1960s, Marley increasingly mirrored the fashions associated with the "Black Power" movement in the US. A 1969 photo shows Bob in a very stylized "black pride" mode, wearing glasses identical to those favored by then-popular Curtis Mayfield, a former Impression.

Marley's metamorphoses during the late 1960s and early 1970s supports the view that Bob's Rastafarian persona was something he grew into. His Rasta beliefs took root during the 1968–72 period, before he had "gone international," but he only gave public voice to these beliefs, and crafted a mature Rasta persona, in the context of interacting with a multiracial public from 1973 to 1980.

The Rasta persona never encompassed his entire worldview. Biographer Stephen Davis notes that Bob listened to a lot of Jimi Hendrix and Sly and the Family Stone around 1970. He cut off his budding dreads, and wore an Afro for the next several years. The record store Bob and Rita ran around 1969–70 was called the "Soul Shack." In 1969 the Wailers released ten songs produced by Leslie Kong, then Jamaica's hottest producer, and these sessions reveal the pervasive influence of rock and soul. Marley employs James Brown mannerisms, and songs like "Soul Shakedown Party" are a blatant attempt to cash in on a commercial dance market. Two albums subsequently recorded for Lee "Scratch" Perry, *Soul Rebels* and *Soul Revolution*, reflect a slower, rootsier modulation of this new soul/Rasta fusion.[75]

While Marley tried to renew the Wailers, he was also trying to make it as a solo act outside of Jamaica. Marley signed a publishing deal with CBS records and Johnny Nash, a black American singer whose pop-style music sold almost exclusively to whites. Nash felt that Marley could help him reach a black soul audience, and he later had a hit with Marley's "Stir It

Up." In turn, Marley hoped that Nash could open doors to the pop market. A medley of acoustic songs included on the *Songs of Freedom* box set shows Marley teaching Nash primarily love songs. Marley's publisher Danny Sims recalls that "There was no 'Jah' in the music Bob was making back then."[76] Marley even went to Sweden to work on a film score for Nash in 1971. Presumably, he was willing to follow the "soul train" to the "top of the pops," rather than the "Zion Train" he eventually boarded.

Two other musical and cultural sources during the late 1960s would shape Marley's attitude towards his career and his eventual mixed audiences. From 1967–1970, when not in Kingston, Marley was a farmer in Nine Miles, working the property of his grandfather Omeriah, who had died while Bob was in Delaware. Marley would later often say that he was really "just a farmer" and could always survive on the land. Although the rural context in which Marley was raised was almost entirely black, this background seems to have helped him connect with a multiracial and international audience. He had a perspective that was not available to those who could not imagine a world beyond the "Concrete Jungle" of Kingston.

"Scratch" Perry, later a favorite with punk-rockers, retooled the Wailers' sound into the form that took them to Island.[77] Perry supplied Marley with his rhythm section, drummer Carlton Barrett and his brother Aston, a bassist who became Marley's musical alter ego. Marley and the Barretts formed the musical foundation of the large, fluid extended family known as the Wailers, in which musical compositions were inevitably a collaborative process. Over the years Perry helped provide Marley with specific strategies to reach both white and black elements of his audience.

Island's marketing strategy, as Blackwell's comments make clear, was to play off of Bob Marley's rebel image within a rock'n'roll iconography. Marley was a sometimes willing, sometimes reluctant participant in this process. Producing and packaging Marley as an icon accessible to an international public required a partial, though not complete, de-racialization of the Wailers. After all, it was in part the group's "Third World" origins that appealed to white audiences who were hungry for some of the rebellious edge that rock had lost in the 1970s. Blackwell was convinced, however, that blackness should not be overplayed. This strategy showed up in both direct and indirect ways. A blatant example is the album *Survival*, which was originally titled *Black Survival*. "Black" was dropped from the title in a nod to Bob's white fans, although one look at the African flags or the slave ship on the cover, or a listen to the songs, would have made its Pan-African focus abundantly clear. So Island's "erasure" of raciality was often more cosmetic than substantial.

Some of Island's marketing strategies had a long-term impact on Marley's self-identity as well as the general self-concept and vocabulary of Rastafarians and Rasta-influenced reggae music, as a genre. A telling example is the retitling of the 1975 album *Natty Dread*, the lead single of which was first released in Jamaica as "Knotty Dread." This minor change represented a significant alteration of Marley's meaning, within a Jamaican context. The word "natty," Bob explained, described some Johnny-come-lately Rasta in an expensive suit with manicured dreadlocks. For Bob, "knotty" carried the connotation of the ropy locks of the street and back-country Rastas. As John Homiak and Barry Chevannes observe, these Rastas wore their "knotty" dreads as a sort of "Dread Warrior" persona which advertised their rejection of, and insured their exclusion from, upscale Jamaican society. A *knotty* dread implied "a cultural agent provocateur, spreading psychic terror through Jamaican society, even capturing its young," writes Stephen Davis. The term *natty* dread relocated Rasta uptown.[78]

Although Island clearly intended for Bob to *be* Natty Dread, this did not detract from the radical quality of the music inside. Here was Marley calling for "Revolution," and declaring on "Talking Blues": "I feel like bombing a church / Now that I know the preacher is lying." These revolutionary lyrics had become bolder since Michael Manley was elected in a 1972 campaign in which Rastafarian music and symbolism played a prominent role.[79] Although Marley's music positioned Rastas as outsiders, the cultural revolution Marley embodied was in fact becoming the (contested) face of the new Jamaica. Marley and Manley, two "brown" Jamaicans, were the two dominant faces of the new Jamaica. In some senses, they co-created, or were the mutual beneficiaries of, the millennial expectations of the 1970s.

Island's effort to "move Rasta uptown" was an example of art and life imitating each other. In fact, Marley *had* moved uptown: in 1975 he bought Blackwell's Hope Road residence. The Island House became an uptown Rasta encampment. It was located just a stone's throw from the prime minister's residence, and Manley was a frequent visitor at Marley's new digs during this period. As much as Marley may have initially objected to Island's Natty Dread makeover, he soon embraced this persona. After introducing the band on the 1975 tour, Bob would conclude by announcing dramatically: "And I . . . I am Natty Dread." As the ideological and cultural revolution embodied by Marley became commodified, there was a sense in which Natty Dread inspired what I have elsewhere called "Fashion Dread," although those who considered themselves "real" Dreads would of course deny that fashion had anything to do with the life-style or image they adopted.[80]

"Natty Dread" became a unifying persona for Marley. It fused several facets of his "performative personality": Biblical prophet, lover, rude boy, etc.[81] This persona was *fabricated* within the context of an international audience, yet was also *organic* to Marley's life and the politico-cultural currents in which he was situated. After his exile following an assassination attempt in 1976, Marley would increasingly try to deflect attention from himself, as messenger, to his message, which he portrayed as being the "work of my father," i.e., Haile Selassie as a mythologized "black deity."[82] But before discussing this reinvented African Father, I want to review three themes that emerged in 1975 which "prestructured" the relationship Marley would try to forge between his multiracial audience and his "African Father." These are the reciprocity between Marley's international reception and the flowering of the Rastafarian movement in Jamaica; the formal articulation of a philosophy concerning the whites in his mixed audience; and the death of Haile Selassie.

When Marley moved "uptown" in 1975, Rastafarianism was in a state of flux. The movement had been visible in Jamaica for forty years, but was only beginning to shed its antisocial reputation. In early 1975, most Jamaicans still looked upon the Rastas as an undesirable underclass, but in this year middle-class Jamaican youth began to flock to Rasta. The quantum leap in the *Jamaican* popularity of Rasta is directly related to Marley's reception abroad. Much as American jazz musicians had to achieve success in Europe before they could gain a measure of "mainstream" respect in the United States,[83] it was not until European audiences, and "white" rock and soul acts like Eric Clapton and Stevie Wonder embraced Marley, that most Jamaicans took him seriously.

Prior to 1975, British West Indians had not paid as much attention to Marley as rock fans. But Marley's 1975 concerts at London's Lyceum were powerful enough to "convert" the West Indians in attendance. Dennis Morris, a Jamaican-born British photographer, remembers that "every person who was there decided they were a Rasta, and it snowballed. The whole movement just spread."[84] In Jamaica, in late 1975, the Wailers performed with Stevie Wonder at Jamaica's National Stadium. When Wonder joined Marley on stage to jam on "Superstition" and "I Shot the Sheriff," middle- and upper-class Jamaicans suddenly discovered that Marley had arrived. Sylvan Morris, an engineer with whom the Wailers worked, recalls that it was during the recording of *Rastaman Vibration* in late 1975 when Rasta consciousness "blossomed" in Jamaica.[85] This blossoming was closely tied to the power brought by the political, cultural, and economic capital earned through Marley's international reception. The Jamaican movement and the international mythology-in-the-making fed off each other.

Marley's multiracial audience was becoming more evident. The first American tour was seen mostly by whites, but in 1975 West Indians and a few Afro-Americans began to show up. The 1973 English gigs had been divided between rock and reggae clubs, but in 1975 blacks and whites came to the same shows. There was some tension regarding the "blackness" of Bob's music: on this tour, manager Don Taylor would stand in front of Lee Jaffe during his harmonica solo – to hide Jaffe's whiteness.[86] Some blacks began to assert an "ownership" of Marley. West Indians, seeing in Bob a black culture hero, were prone to read Rasta as a black power philosophy. But Bob himself always resisted this interpretation.[87]

Rastafarianism underwent several significant changes in 1975. What had always been a decentered "community of prophets" began a degree of "routinization." In this year Marley endorsed the Twelve Tribes of Israel, a Rasta sect which was making significant inroads among middle-class Jamaicans. The "Twelve Tribes" were more heirarchical and closer to Protestant Christianity than most Rasta groups. They allowed relative equality between the sexes. They also liked to advertise the fact that they had white members – probably as a way of distancing themselves from the "black superiority" roots of Rastafarianism. And of course Marley's sanction gave this version considerable clout.[88]

Most importantly, Rastas of all stripes faced a crisis in August 1975 when Haile Selassie died. Selassie, who had been deposed in a 1974 Marxist coup, was seen by Rastas as a "living God" who could never die, just as Christians do not believe in the death of Jesus. His death presented "a moment of doubt in faith" for many Rastas. Marley responded by recording "Jah Live" in September 1975. It is a measure of how far Marley had come in Jamaica that "Jah Live" received extensive airplay in his homeland, whereas a few months earlier some of his Trenchtown rudies had to rough up DJs to get any airplay for *Natty Dread*.[89]

Marley told a reporter that the message of "Jah Live" was that "ya cyaan kill God." Whether he meant that literally or figuratively – "you can't kill faith" – is an open question. Some "progressive" Christians, for instance, do not believe in the literal resurrection of Jesus, but they do believe his spirit is ever-living. Some of Marley's statements seem to support this stance, while at other times he talked as if he believed his "living God" could not physically die.

By 1976, Marley had outgrown Jamaica. His political alliances and gangster associations led to an assassination attempt in late 1976. Marley fled Jamaica and spent little time in his homeland for the rest of his life. Artistically, he would transform his self-doubt about "Running Away" into an "Exodus" to a mythical African fatherland. The *Exodus* album (1977) situated Marley in a long line of "black culture heroes" who reconfigured the Biblical Exodus story – from Frederick Douglass to Marcus Garvey to Martin Luther King.

In *Conjuring Culture: Biblical Formations of Black America*, Theophus Smith takes note of a tradition of Biblical typology "that links biblical types or figures to postbiblical persons, places, and events." It is the pairing of a Biblical "type" with a contemporary "antitype" that gives this tradition its legitimating power as a manifestation (to believers) of prophecy/fulfillment. Smith links this tradition to Werner Sollors' discussion of an archetypal pattern in which Americans from the Puritans to contemporary ethnic groups have redefined themselves as a new "chosen people" to whom God has given a "promised land."[90] Marley's use of the Exodus story falls within this pattern, although I think it would be more accurate to speak of the *reinvention* of a type, or the "inhabiting of a type." One can also interpret this process as variations on archetypal patterns. The important thing to recognize is that people in this tradition do not go *against* Biblical types so much as *reshape* these types to their own needs.

Marley was quite clearly reshaping Biblical mythology through a Pan-African sensibility much earlier in his career, but it took the assassination attempt and exile for this tendency to be foregrounded. And it would take the onset of cancer – first diagnosed in 1977 – for Marley's embrace of a Moses-like role to take on an obsessive, fatalistic quality.

"My trip is to gather the children, you know you hear dem say gather de flock?" Marley reflected in a Jamaican Broadcasting Company interview. "Me no wan say it's a big 'ting, like is Moses or something like dat. But all me do is beg Jah for give me work to do." This attitude would be typical of the last three years of his career: he denies he is trying to live a Moses-like role, yet he affirms that he is doing the "work of my father."[91]

Part of the "children" Marley tried to gather were punks. This alliance came through his "black roots" connection, Lee Perry, during the *Exodus* sessions. Marley had initially been disgusted by the appearance of punks. But groups like the Clash were recording Jamaican songs, and black Brits like Don Letts were pushing Bob to think twice. After reasoning with Perry, Marley recorded "Punky Reggae Party" with Aswad as a backing band. This tune, which was released as a single and appeared on *Babylon By Bus*, "paved the way for punk's close alliance with reggae, the outcast youth of two races banding together for solace and support," as Stephen Davis writes.[92]

Marley recorded enough during the *Exodus* sessions (just after the shooting) to fill two albums. He injured his toe at the start of the *Exodus* tour, and had to cancel an American tour when melanoma cancer was detected. After surgery, Marley recuperated and did not record for Island Records during a two-year stretch. The out-takes from the *Exodus* session were released in 1978 as *Kaya*, Marley's most commercial album, content-wise.

While the militant album that followed, *Survival* (1979), was clearly aimed at blacks, it is not commonly understood that *Kaya*, which was roundly cited as evidence that Bob had "sold out," was also, in large part, aimed at blacks. It was his reaction to the "slickness" of American R&B. Neville Garrick noted that black disc jockeys had been discounting reggae as "jungle music," or claiming it did not fit their format. He describes *Kaya* as an attempt to reach Afro-Americans: "Is like you fishing and the fish kinda pick up the little sweet bait and you just jerk him in." This approach had already been prefigured on the second half of *Exodus*.[93]

Marley had already faced criticism for "going soft" before. Some critics did not like the upbeat tunes and the rock influences on *Rastaman Vibration*. The crisp sound and Junior Marvin's rock-style guitar on *Exodus* were criticized. Marley generally claimed that he did not care what critics said, but faced with persistent attacks on *Kaya*, he offered a number of revealing self-defenses. "How long must I protest the same thing?" he asked rhetorically. "So I must still sing 'Get Up, Stand Up'? I am not going to sing the same song again. *I do not want to be a prisoner*." He also explained *Kaya* as a "cooling off" album dictated by violence in Jamaica, suggesting that if he had made a political album at that point, it might have cost him his life.[94]

Like other people surveyed in this book – eighteenth-century evangelists, Maria Stewart, Frederick Douglass, and Ralph Ellison – Marley employed multiple strategies to reach different elements of his multiracial audience. Yet his approach was different from theirs in fundamental ways, because of the scale of his outreach, and the multi-media context in which his words were situated. Operating within an electronically mediated realm, he extended this diversity of approaches to sound and image.[95]

Marley's music and interviews are permeated with references to "my people." The question of who Marley saw as "his people" might appear simple at first: he seemed to be reaching out to people of the African diaspora, especially to those some Rastas referred to as "careless Ethiopians," who were unaware of their African heritage.[96] Yet Marley's active agency in the creation and marketing of a product designed for a multiracial audience suggests that his view was more complex than this. This is borne out in many interviews.

After a performance in Santa Barbara on July 23, 1978 (Selassie's birthday), a reporter asked Bob what he made of the fact that white people in America were following a black man. "Is God who mek everybody, and him mek a way for the black man that the white man have to follow, because out of the black man came the white man, all men," he responded.[97] Marley had carried an Afrocentric paradigm through to its logical conclusion: if Africa was the mother of all races, and if the forerunners of modern humans did first appear in Ethiopia, then all "races" were related. Black and white people were cousins, and even Europeans were "Ethiopians," in an ancestral sense.

The manner in which Marley tried to sell this concept to black people was true to his roots, yet kept a more inclusive horizon within view. "What we black people cannot deal with in America is color prejudice," he advised. "You mustn't bow to the white man. You must be *superior* to him. That means you cannot be prejudice, because if you are superior, how can you be prejudice?"[98] When we read these comments through the history of Ethiopianism and Rastafari, we see that Marley was refashioning the concept of "black superiority" in which Rasta was rooted. The true "superiority," in his view, had to be radical equality, transracial in character. This transracial horizon needs to be borne in mind as we look at Bob's "last will and testament" to black people on *Survival*.

FRUITS

Marley's reinvention of an African Father

"Put an [archetypal] idea into the heads of small people and they become big and tremendously efficient," Carl Jung once said. "The archetypes are sources of energy," and when "small people" catch hold of the energy of a big idea, they can ride it to unexpected heights. Bob Marley's archetypal idea was of a "perfect" African Father as "earth's rightful ruler." Although this cultural myth was a fiction, its energy carried Marley to international superstardom. Marley was in some sense the fulfillment of Malcolm X's late advice that the "back to Africa" movement which Garvey and others had advocated should be read and enacted as a cultural turn, rather than a physical return. Marley was the voice and the embodiment of that cultural reorientation, on a scale Malcolm probably could not have imagined. Yet Marley never ceased portraying Africa as a literal destination. However, after he visited Ethiopia in late 1978, he did begin to concede that his "African Zion" might have to be located somewhere other than Ethiopia.[99]

Marley's cultural "turn" (or Exodus) to Africa was a cultural and religious move rather than a geopolitical movement. The Africa which Marley popularized, in commodified form, was a thoroughly "invented" space – a "Zion" of *faith*, just as the Jerusalem imagined by most Jews and Christians is a "Zion" rooted more in religious mythology than political reality. This *Zion* was the imagined resolution of or redemption from its opposite: *Babylon*. Babylon was not a specific place or a race but a *system* of "self-absorbed individuals who worship idols and live decadent life-styles at the expense of the poor." Yet Marley felt compelled to portray his African Zion as a literal geographic destination, for two principal reasons. First, Marley's encounter with violence in Jamaica, and the relentless projections of Jamaicans who came to see him as a prophet or a ghetto chief (to be either solicited or destroyed), led him to believe that Jamaica was not "big enough" to house his vision, nor the aspirations of him and his "massive." Secondly, the imperfections and almost total absence of Marley's own biological father, Norval, led to a largely unconscious projection on to Haile Selassie as a "perfect" African Father. Selassie became Marley's absent father, writ large.[100]

In an interview included on *Time Will Tell*, Marley was asked about political boundaries and homelands. "Well I must pick a place on earth where I and I know I must live," he said. "I know I wanna be near my father, and my father live in Ethiopia. So I must live where my father is." Marley also explained the Exodus he was advocating in terms of geographic constraints. "My future is in a green part of the Earth, big enough where we can roam freely," he said.[101] "I don't think Jamaica going to be the right place, because Jamaica likkle bit small ... the only place big enough for us is Africa."

In this quote, Marley exhibits a complete psychological identification with Haile Selassie as a spiritual father who transcends both physical limitations and political boundaries. He also seems to have forwarded without critical examination the imperialist assumptions about Africa that were evident in nineteenth-century colonizationists such as Edward Blyden and twentieth-century Ethiopianists such as Marcus Garvey. He assumes that people of the African continent will welcome New World blacks who want to "roam freely" there. He also assumes the universality of the religious mythology of the Amhara, which Selassie had used to create an imperial Ethiopian empire.[102]

Both of these assumptions echo European colonialists, who presumed the universality of their own interpretation of Judeo-Christian tradition, and took for granted their right to "occupy" and "civilize" Africa.[103] One could write a book on the imperialist assumptions of Ethiopianism and the form of Rastafarianism popularized by Marley. However, my primary concern here is not to single out the seemingly irrational elements of Marley's Ethiopianism, particularly its invention of a "living God," and its emphasis on transcontinental emigration as a solution to the crisis of postcolonialism. Rather, my aim is to illustrate the "psychological reality" of Marley's vision. Bob Marley's art, as a political and religious philosophy, makes "perfect sense," when understood within the context of his own life, and more broadly, when situated within a historical tradition of uses of Judeo-Christian scripture for "liberatory" social movements.

Survival is Marley's fullest artistic vision of a cultural return to an African source, and of the worship of a God "through the spectacles of Ethiopia," as Garvey said.

> Africa Unite, for we're moving right out of Babylon
> and we're going to our father's land

Marley used the Bible as a cornerstone in constructing this vision. In order to glimpse the "psychological reality" within this cultural mythology, I take several steps. First, I situate Marley's use of the Exodus story within a historical context in which many peoples have reimagined Exodus in order to carve out a niche within "world history." In Jamaica it is part of a postcolonial process of collective identity formation. On a psychological level, I reconsider Marley's absent white father, and the series of father figures who tutored him prior to Marley's invention of Selassie as a "perfect" father. And I place *Survival* as a response both to criticisms of Marley's previous commercial efforts, and as a probable outgrowth of Marley's awareness of his own imminent mortality.

"Diasporians" had been been employing the Exodus story as both a cultural metaphor and political organizing tool for two centuries before Marley. Frederick Douglass had criticized those who took the Exodus story as a literal model. He opposed antebellum blacks who wanted to colonize West Africa. In the 1870s he was critical of black leaders who used the Exodus myth to encourage Southern blacks to migrate to western states such as Kansas and Oklahoma. The Western frontier was being portrayed as a new "promised land" during this time, when racial repression was epidemic in the South. However, Douglass came to understand that the Exodus myth also had a potentially pragmatic value. In a speech to the American Social Science Association in 1879 (a century before *Survival* was released), Douglass argued that black laborers could exact better terms for their work by "wisely using the Exodus example." In a very suggestive metaphor, Douglass said: "*Exodus is medicine*, not food."[104]

The speech in which this quote appears discourages Exodus movements. Yet Douglass recognized that the "right and power to leave" could help those utilizing this myth to restructure power relations at home. So Exodus can serve as a *historically necessary corrective*. Douglass also suggests that the Exodus story has a *healing* capacity: it helps "sufferers" imagine a better future by holding up a horizon, a map to a better world. This is what Jung called a "healing fiction."[105]

But Douglass' use of culinary and medicinal metaphors also functions as critique. Douglass believes that although Exodus can heal by moving to correct unjust historical imbalances, it is not a *sustainable* strategy. Douglass is suggesting that the Exodus story is a short-term corrective "medicine," but that it cannot feed our children. "Dust will fly, but the earth will remain," as he would say in 1884.[106]

Both Douglass and Marley participated in a tradition of "blackening" the Bible – emphasizing an African presence in Judeo-Christian scriptures in order to legitimate their *historical agency,* and to reimagine their *contemporary identity.* People from many different cultures have used the Bible in similar ways. They often come to recognize that Bible stories have an ideological agenda within a specific historical context: to universalize the Hebrews' self-concept as God's "chosen people." So they have to re-envision their relationship to the Biblical world, in order to "feel ourselves to be elements in the structure of universal history," as Erich Auerbach writes."[107] Marley portrayed his *Exodus* to an "African Father" as a path to cultural survival for black people, and more broadly for all people who suffered in "a world that forces life-long insecurity," as he sang on the song "Survival." In Marley's vision the return to Africa represented not a quest for racial purity, but a return to a more humane philosophy. Africa was Marley's utopian horizon: a place to escape from the "atomic misphilosophy" of the Babylon system and a model of a sustainable way of life structured upon "earth rhythms."

If we follow Douglass' view of "Exodus as medicine," we can see Marley's Exodus as a strategy to restructure postcolonial power relations. The aim of this process is to be "a principal, and not just an agent," as Douglass said: to become a subject, and not just an object, within the "structure of universal history." This restructuring process begins, in Marley's music, with a critique of received religion, as a means of reordering Eurocentric representations of history. This is, as previously observed, resistance to "symbol imperialism."

On "Crazy Baldhead," Marley observes: "We build your penitentiaries / We build your school / Brainwash education / To make us the fool / Your reward for our love / Is telling us of your God above." Slaves and their descendants in the colonial system have built the very schools which portray them as inferior, and are expected to worship an inaccessible "God above." The Rasta that Marley represents declares: "We're gonna chase them crazy baldheads out of town." (More echoes of a "racial Armageddon.")[108] The *God above* will be replaced by a *God within.* Brainwash education is to be replaced by self-representation, achieved through music. "Music gonna teach them a lesson," Marley declares on an earlier song that asks why the youth couldn't learn about "one of them great Africans" instead of Marco Polo and Christopher Columbus. On one of Marley's last songs, "Trenchtown," he sums up the Rasta model of liberation through Word/Sound/Power: "We free the people with music."[109]

In 1903 Du Bois wrote: "Few men ever *worshipped Freedom* with half such unquestioning faith as did the American Negro for two centuries."[110] For Jamaicans (as part of "nuestra America") this "worship of freedom" is especially explicit. The ability to "Chant Down Babylon" through music and speech is an article of faith among Rastas. Their belief in the cumulative power of the ritual repetition of "drums and bass and conscious lyrics"[111] is modeled on the story of the Children of Israel employing the ritual use of trumpets to bring down the walls of Jericho, during the conquest of the "promised land." This "article of faith" functions as a political strategy of colonizing or occupying space. It also serves as a manner of worship, and as such is an essential component of the *contemporary identity* of Rastas. 1990s reggae dance hall is filled with references to the sacred mission and magical power of music, sometimes linked to the Exodus myth, as in this lyric by the late Garnet Silk:

> Music is the Rod and we are Moses
> Leading God's children to the Promised Land
> Music is the voice of his brother Aaron
> Preaching and comforting at the father's command[112]

In Marley's music, Exodus as a quest for freedom is not always distinguished from Exodus as an act of worship. This search for freedom is done "at the father's command." Thus, seeking freedom shows respect to the father, and defines the identity of the son. Marley often speaks of the "the work of my father" in a language that echoes the Gospels. The search for freedom, or *the worship of the search for freedom*, begins in Jamaica with a "rebellion" against churches perceived to be unconcerned with "equal rights and justice." Jean Comaroff has called this strategy an effort to "snatch the Christian message from the messenger." For instance, "Get Up, Stand Up" denounces Christianity's "Ism schism game / Die and go to heaven in a Jesus name" and affirms: "Our mighty God is a living man." On "Talking Blues" Marley feels ... "like bombing a church / Now that I know the preacher is lying." But he also sings that "revelation reveals the truth." The Revelation here refers both to the last book of the New Testament, which Rastas believe describes a black Messiah, and to the revelation of prophetic inspiration: an "inner light" or "God within."[113]

In his study of black "appropriations" of the Bible, Theophus Smith writes: "To designate a deity ... means also to *imagine a self*."[114] Rastas designate a deity constructed in their own image: he is black/Semitic, or biracial. He is involved in a reciprocal relation with his people through the "I" or God within – signified by rendering Rastafari as Rasta Far-Eye. And he reveals his purpose both through revelation and revolution: the act of prophetic inspiration, and the process of revolutionary restructuring, are assumed to be intertwined. (This pairing of revelation/revolution is explicit on Bob's 1974 song "Revolution.") Since the Rastas' God is located in Ethiopia, Ethiopia can be said to be "in the house" – Ethiopia, as a representative of Africa, the mother of all races, has been reclaimed as "the head cornerstone" in the "structure of universal history." "Rastafari transposes Africa from the bottom to the top politically, aesthetically, and culturally," Nicholas writes, a reordering that Wilson Moses describes as a "cosmic rotation of elites." Variations on this belief often coexist with expressions of nonracial unity: on "One Love," Marley's quintessenial song of multiracial redemption, the line "as it was in the beginning, so shall it be in the end" echoes Jesus' saying "the first shall be last, and the last shall be first." To listeners *within the culture*, this prophecy has a clear racial subtext.[115]

$$\bullet \;\; \bullet \;\; \bullet$$

Marley's artistic vision of a cultural migration to an African fatherland is also a deeply personal mythology. In the context of his life, it can be read as a quest for pscyhological wholeness. Marley was in essence an "abandoned child," as Stephen Davis notes. This abandonment – the almost complete absence of his white father and the frequent absence of his black mother – had a major impact on his psychology, his artistic sensibility, and eventually on his theology. Being abandoned is of course part of an archetypal pattern in "the birth of the hero." Marley would choose to model himself on a Mosaic variant of this pattern. The Biblical Moses was an abandoned child of low birth who was raised by a royal family. In like manner, Marley would make sense of the painful circumstances of his abandonment by imagining himself to have been "grown" by Ethiopian royalty.[116]

At first glance, the conditions under which Norval Marley and Cedella Malcolm came together, and Norval's later absence from his son, would seem to conform to stereotypical expectations about interracial relations during "the days of slavery" or the colonial era. Captain Marley, a quartermaster in the British West Indian Regiment, impregnated a back-country black teenager, Cedella, then all but disappeared from her life after their offspring was born. Many journalists have interviewed Cedella both during Bob's life and after his death. Predictably they often encouraged Cedella to bad-mouth Bob's long-lost father. Yet Cedella has consistently defended Norval through the years.

"He was a very handsome, loving and sweet gentleman. He told me he loved me, and I believe that he did," Cedella told Stephen Davis. "He told me that he was the black sheep of his family, because the Marleys did not like black people, but Norval liked them very much." In her 1996 memoir, Cedella's account of Norval is more complex. We learn that Norval had lived in Nine Miles, where Cedella grew up, since she was a girl; was a close friend of Cedella's father, Omeriah Malcolm, and in fact courted Cedella for several years. The economic differences between the white and black sides of this union were not as great as one might expect. Although the Marleys were upper-middle-class traders in Kingston, Cedella describes Norval as "poor." Omeriah owned several properties in rural St. Anne's parish, and as the local "custos" or magistrate, was the most respected citizen of Nine Miles. Cedella's account is also revealing about the source of some of Bob's troublesome attitudes towards women. Omeriah had "twenty or thirty" children by numerous women outside of his marriage. Omeriah also had what seems to be a typical Jamaican attitude about the rights of men to whip their women into line. He encouraged Norval to use a horsewhip on Cedella, after Norval's lover had "caught religion" and refused to continue sleeping with him.[117]

The biggest difference between Bob's parents, aside from "race," was their age: when Bob was born, Cedella was only eighteen, while Norval was at least fifty. They had a passionate love affair, according to Cedella, and when she became pregnant, he agreed to marry her. Norval soon developed health problems, however. Because of a hernia he had to give up his job in the saddle for a new position in Kingston. Norval left Cedella the day after their wedding, just as his son Bob would later do.

During Norval's infrequent visits, he told Cedella that his family disowned him because of the marriage. Norval sent money often, but under pressure from his mother, the visits thinned out. When Bob turned five, Norval arranged for him to go to school in Kingston. But with familial relations strained, Cedella lost track of Bob, who Norval had placed with an old relative, a Mrs. Grey.

In later years, Cedella felt that Norval's behavior had been caused by his ill health, and by having been cut off from the family purse-strings. When Cedella finally found Bob, this Mrs. Grey told her that Norval wanted her to raise Bob as a son and heir. "Norval did this, I believe, because he did not have anything himself to give to Bob," Cedella conjectured. In her memoir Cedella recalls that after a last visit in 1955, when Norval was dying (quite possibly from cancer), he pressed two copper pennies into Bob's hand and wept.[118]

• • •

Bob Marley carried a chip on his shoulder during his teenage years in part because he was angry at his father. One time he told Cedella: "I think my father was a bad man," because he felt Norval had mistreated him and his mother. Cedella told him, "No, your father was a good man, a very good man. But because of society, he couldn't do better." This question still haunted him as he lay dying in Germany. After Bob's death Cedella remembered Norval as "a wonderful person in his way," although she has been more critical in her memoir.[119]

No matter how one rationalized Norval's absence, Bob had to look elsewhere for male role models. One of the first was his grandpa Omeriah, who supervised Bob for several years while his mom was in Kingston. He passed on much of the "folk wisdom" that would later appear in Bob's songs (along with a tradition of siring numerous children out of wedlock, apparently). Bob was also mentored by another relative, Clarence Martin, who had been a well-known guitarist in the 1940s Jamaican dance halls, and let the young boy try to play his guitar. "So began a pattern of older wise men taking a mentor-like role in the life of the essentially fatherless Nesta Robert Marley," writes Chris Salewicz.[120]

Bob lived with his mother only briefly in Kingston. In late 1962 Cedella emigrated to Wilmington, Delaware, where she married an elderly Afro-American man, Edward Booker. Bob chose to stay behind and sing. By early 1963, at age eighteen, he was homeless. This young man, whose "nature was always stubborn," Cedella recalled, passed through most of his teenage years without a family. Late in life Bob would recall that "Me grow stubborn . . . Me just grow inna the ghetto with the youth [and] nuh obey no one."[121]

Selah.[122]

One of Marley's most important father figures was Clement "Sir Coxsone" Dodd, the famed Studio One head. He took Bob in off the streets, letting him sleep in a back-yard shed. He released Bob's first hit, "Simmer Down," and let Bob coach developing talent, which was how he met his wife Rita. Dodd remembers the relationship as a de facto adoption.

Marley's first mentor in Kingston was Joe Higgs, who served as his vocal coach. Higgs was the first Rasta to have hit records, and he had enormous prestige among Trenchtown youth, who gathered in his yard for harmonizing and reasonings that lasted far into the night. Higgs singled Bob out for private lessons. Alvin Patterson, later called "Seeco" as the Wailers' percussionist 1975–80, was also a resident Rastafarian "wise head" in Bob's teens. He taught Bob and his buddies the heartbeat "burru" rhythms that were the foundation of traditional Rasta reggae.[123]

Bob married Alpharita Anderson on February 10, 1966. Like his father before him, he only stayed with his bride one day after the wedding. Bob flew to Delaware the next day, where he lived with his mother for the better part of a year, trying to save enough money to start his own record label. Bob's own sons would later continue this mode of absentee fatherhood. The Marley family is a microcosm of what one could call an archetypal Jamaican pattern of paternity. One gets a sense of how this absenteeism is embedded in the culture from a scene in *Rockers*. A Rasta musician, briefly visiting the mother of his children, rejects her plea for help with the comment: "the culture will raise him." If "the culture" is expected to supply patterns of behavior, the women are most often left to do the hands-on parenting.[124]

While Bob was working in Wilmington, he had a dream about his father that his mother believed had enormous symbolic significance. He dreamed he saw a short man wearing a military uniform and a battered fedora hat. This man entered through the front door and stood beside Bob as he napped. He took a ring from his pocket, a gold ring with a tiny diamond set in onyx. Taking Bob's hand, the man pushed the ring on his finger and told him: "This is all I have to give you."[125]

When Bob told Cedella about the dream, she retrieved a ring that had belonged to Norval, which looked like the ring Bob had described. Cedella told him that the dream "might be a blessin' from ya faddah," and put the ring on his finger. It fit perfectly. "He never give yuh anyt'ing when him alive, suh maybe him want ya ta have a blessin' now," Cedella speculated. Bob wore the ring a few days; then took it off, saying it made him feel uncomfortable. He tried to give it back, but Cedella insisted that he keep it and learn the symbolic meaning of the dream. Marley would later give a very different interpretation to this dream, in regards to another ring that became his personal talisman.[126]

In early 1977, when Marley was living in London after the shooting, he got to know the Ethiopian royal family-in-exile. After a meeting with Selassie's son, Crown Prince Asfa Wossen, the heir apparent to Ethiopia's banished monarchy produced a ring which he said had belonged to the emperor, a gold Lion of Judah set in onyx. He slipped the ring on Marley's finger, telling him: "You are the one who should wear it."

Shortly afterwards, malignant cancer was discovered in Marley's right toe. While he was recuperating from surgery at his mother's Delaware home, he told Cedella that this ring was the one that he had seen in the dream eleven years earlier. Two of Marley's friends in Delaware claim that Bob told them he was going to "die at age 36, just like Christ." This apocryphal story must bear the suspicion of the hero-worship legends that have proliferated after Marley's death. However, this first detection of cancer certainly had a profound impact on him. Cedella remembers his reaction as something of a crisis in faith, with Bob asking: "Why would Jah let me have cancer?" At least in the short term, he seems to have gone into denial, claiming that he did not believe his doctors.[127]

Marley would wear Selassie's ring the rest of his life. He had rejected his biological father's ring: somehow it made him uneasy. But he did come to accept his mother's view that his dream of the ring had great significance. And he believed that the dream-ring was a "blessing." But the only blessing he could accept was the ring from his "true" African Father.

I suspect the ring's personal significance was determined partly by having received it at the same time Bob discovered he had cancer, and as he broke through to international superstardom, with the release of *Exodus*. Everything Marley did thereafter must be read through the lenses of the burden imposed by his cancer, his exile, and the messianic projections of much of his audience. In a sense, he would be compelled to live out the archetype of the self-sacrificing hero. Thus, his answer to the rhetorical question, "How long will they kill our prophets?" was, "we've got to fulfill the book."[128]

The significance of Selassie's ring for Marley was set up by his absent white father's (rejected) ring, by Selassie's death in 1975, and by Marley's (repressed) knowledge of his own imminent mortality. All of these factors must be taken into consideration when we examine the process by which Marley constructed an ideal father, a "perfect" African Father which he projected on to the historical person of Haile Selassie, born Ras Tafari Makonnen.

• • •

Marley had been exposed to the Rasta myth of Selassie as a "living God" in the early 1960s, by father figures, fellow musicians, and Rastas in Trenchtown. He had privately "converted" by 1966, but his public articulation of a personal vision of an African Father was a rather late development. Marley was out of Jamaica, significantly, when Selassie visited on April 21, 1966. Marley was struggling with private conflicts about his biological father in these years. Listening to his music now one senses that he was being "led" by the Rasta "massive." His references to *Jah* prior to 1975 are often mediated through reworkings of traditional Rasta chants and hymns – which are themselves reworked Revival hymns, as Chevannes has noted often. These indirect references are not specifically "Africanized": this Jah is interchangeable with the Jahweh of the Old Testament. But from 1975 on, there is a sense that Marley was leading the Rastafarians: their cultural vision was being mediated through him, internationally. Marley claimed to be a spokesman for "the Rastaman," but he was articulating a vision of a "black" deity which increasingly arose from his own private obsessions.

10   Haile Selassie at the United Nations, October 4, 1963, when he delivered the "What Life Has Taught Me About the Question of Racial Discrimination" speech, which Marley set to music in "War."

In June 1975, on the *Natty Dread* tour, Marley gave an interview in which he described a personal relationship to Selassie, but still expressed in a language accessible to any Christian. "God is my father and him grow me just the way a son suppose to be grown," he said. He referred to Selassie, indirectly, as "The perfect father for me." Marley was then thirty years old. On the verge of stardom, he has not yet begun to write about the "parasites" which would increasingly drain his energy in the last four years of his life. Selassie has not died, Marley has not been shot, and cancer has not appeared. His desire for "Positive Vibrations" is transracial: "You can't come tell me 'bout white and black," he says in this interview. "We fly a color which is red, gold and green . . . Now we're not prejudiced, because we leave our judgement unto Jah. [We] want to cut the negative thing out entirely."[129]

After Marley's "perfect father" died in 1975, there was a transformation in his representation of an African Father. He set out to memorialize Selassie: Neville Garrick painted a mural of Selassie which Marley began using as a stage backdrop in 1976. Marley makes three types of references to Selassie thereafter: (1) as a historical figure; (2) a messianic culture hero; (3) allusions to Biblical traditions which formed the "legitimating foundations" for claims that Selassie was "Earth's rightful ruler."

Marley's attention to the historical Selassie is most evident in his song "War," released in 1976. This song was a direct adaptation of a speech Selassie gave to the United Nations General Assembly, October 4, 1963. Entitled "What Life Has Taught Me About the Question of Racial Discrimination," this speech had been brought to Marley by Allan "Skill" Cole around the time of Selassie's death. Marley put the speech to music as a means of immortalizing Selassie and his antiracist and postcolonial message. I have included the text to this speech in the endnotes, since "War" came to represent a *desideratum*, or creed, for Bob.[130]

After the song was released, Marley told journalists that he had never encountered a wiser philosophy than the one in this speech. He also commented, trying to downplay his fame, that no one would have heard of Rastafarianism, on a global scale, if not for Selassie. This may be true. But conversely, very few people would have heard of Selassie, at least after his death, if not for Marley. One can read this speech as a sort of parallel text to Martin Luther King's "I Have a Dream" speech (also 1963), and affirm it as a statement of great moral vision. One can also see that many of Marley's songs, from this point on, contain variations on themes that Selassie had articulated in this speech.

Marley's depictions of Selassie as a messianic figure are numerous and need not be repeated in detail here. Two examples from *Survival* are the song "One Drop," which contrasts "the teachings of His Majesty" with "devil philosophy," and "Survival," which declares that "the father's time has come." The latter alludes to Marley's millennial belief in a "right time" in which "Babylon," the system of material greed and racist oppression, would fall. Marley believed Rastas were a "third force," an

11   Marley at his Hope Road home in Kingston, 1976, seated under a
poster of Selassie's "What Life Has taught Me" speech, which he set to
music in this year.

alternative to both capitalism and Marxism. As representatives of "Earth's Rightful Ruler," Rastas would enable "righteousness to cover the earth," in the words of Hosea that were also employed by Martin Luther King.[131]

Marley also made many indirect references to Selassie via Biblical passages which Rastas believe legitimate Selassie. For instance, in "Top Rankin'," he sings: "They say the blood runs, and it runs through our lineage / and our hearts, heart of hearts divine / John say them comin' with the truth from an ancient time." This is a reference to Selassie's claim that he was the 225th in a line of divinely mandated kings in Ethiopia, descended from the original union between Solomon and the Queen of Sheba/Makeba, and that his dynasty was thus founded on the "root of David."

• • •

My readers coming from a non-Christian or anti-Christian background may wonder how Marley could "buy into" this religious mythology. In addition to affirming once more the possibility that "irrational" faith and "rational" critique can coexist,[132] I will mention two sociocultural factors that may make the affinity between Rastas and Ethiopians easier to understand. These are the Bible-based nature of Jamaican culture, and their Ethiopian counterparts, and the anti-intellectualism that has been a recurring theme among Rastas, and in Marley's thought.

My first impression of Jamaica in 1987 as having an "Old Testament" feel was an intuitive perception partly rooted in countless hours spent reading illustrated Bible stories as a child. Since my visit coincided with the celebration of Marcus Garvey's 100th birthday, I saw a lot of back-country Rastas who would not normally be in the city. Something about the way they carried themselves struck me as deeply *Jewish*. Their dance movements reminded me of the typical bobbing motion made by Israelis praying at Jerusalem's Western Wall. Rastas see themselves, in fact, as black Hebrews, or as one of the "lost tribes" of Israel. Some of their mannerisms probably derive from the fact that Rastas have for decades studied Ethiopian mythic history, and modeled themselves according to precedents in the Ethiopian Orthodox Church. Rastas have studied photos of Haile Selassie and have copied his gestures. They have also been exposed to reports by their peers who have traveled to Ethiopia. I have seen footage of Ethiopian priests performing a dance which is said to mime the movements made by King David before the Ark of the Covenant, as described in II Samuel 6:14–15. These movements illustrate that Amharas and Rastas are modeling themselves on some of the same sources.[133]

In *The Ethiopian Church* (1968), Ephraim Isaac writes: "if there is any country today where the Biblical life is the way of the people, it is Ethiopia." The seriousness with which Ethiopians have taken their Bible is illustrated in historical legitimation contests between between rival ethnic groups, with Zagwes claiming to be descended from Moses and Amharas claiming descent from Solomon. "Ethiopia alone among the Christian nations has rejected the traditional doctrine of Christianity according to St. Paul that Biblical law lost its binding force at the coming of Christ," notes Isaac.[134] What emerged was a hybrid church that is located "at a sort of half-way place" between the Old and New Testaments. This provides an important clue to the affinity Rastafarians feel for the Ethiopian variant of Christianity.

Rastas, being deeply rooted in Revivalism, are part of a broader stream of North American black religious history. A minister named Higginson who preached to black troops during the civil war observed that they were mostly interested in Moses and Revelation. "All that lay between, even the life of Jesus, they hardly cared to read or to hear," wrote the bewildered Higginson, adding that his black congregation tended to project Mosaic qualities on to the heroes of the American Revolution.[135] This description of nineteenth-century Afro-American religious life comes close to describing the mindset of Rastas. Marley-era Rastas also made the Psalms a part of their "canon," however, and to a lesser degree the prophets and the Gospels. But like their nineteenth-century antecedents, they have an enduring fascination with Revelation, and they also continue to interpret revolutionary figures with a Mosaic lense. Like the Ethiopian Christians, the Rastas occupy "a sort of half-way place" between Old and New Testament worlds.

Jamaican reverence for the Bible is not limited to Rastas and is still evident to the present day, as can be seen in "songs of praise" such as Burru Banton's "Bible Again" (1995) or Macka B's "Bible Reader" (1996). The result has been "a distinctive emphasis on revelatory discourse and poetic biblicism," Theophus Smith writes. Bob Marley's early teachers remember him as a precocious boy who only showed an interest in reading when it was linked to the Bible. He quit school at about age fourteen, and Marley's scanty formal education has led Leonard Barrett to describe him as "not literate." Although he probably did not advance beyond a 6th grade reading level, it would be more accurate to say he was "narrowly literate." This narrowness was both a limitation and a source of strength: his tightly focused vision derived from a "fusion of scribal and oral literary influences," as Carolyn Cooper puts it, "the former, largely derived from the Bible (as interpreted by Rastafari)" and the latter rooted in Jamaican folk philosophy. That fusion gave sustenance to Marley's "highly charged literary sensibility," Cooper writes, an assessment I share.

Marley's mid-1960s associates remember that Bob's Bible was "rarely out of his sight." During the late 1960s when he was a farmer, Bob often read to Rita from the Psalms while they were in the field. Mick Cater, who went on the Wailers' 1973 British tour, remembers that on long drives "The Bibles would come out and the arguments would become very heated." Bible readings continued to be a part of Marley's daily routine for the rest of his life.[136]

Bob's attitude towards the Bible was both spiritual and pragmatic. Asked by an interviewer in 1979 how he spread the Rasta way of thinking, Marley answered, "The Bible, mon. The Bible the whole thing, mon. Everybody have the Bible, regardless of which nation."[137] For Marley the Bible was the "King's highway": there was no other road he could travel that would intersect with a wider audience. It was a tool to build a wider cultural unity shaped by a sustainable life-style and nourished by a shared moral philosophy and practice. The Bible was a transnational and multiracial bassline, a malleable "firm foundation" for Marley's music.

Marley participated in the Rastafarian self-concept of being "a community of prophets." While Bob took his Bible seriously, it cannot be said that he took most of it literally. Rastas believed that the Europeans who edited the Bible had corrupted it; thus their emphasis on the "apocrypha" in the Ethiopian Bible which had not passed through the hands of Catholic or Protestant "censors." For Rastas, Zion did not refer literally to a hill in Jerusalem. "The apparent Middle Eastern milieu of the Bible is part of a European imposture" for traditional Rastas, explains Laurence Breiner. "Zion means Ethiopia, and the notion of Jerusalem as the holy city is another attempt to . . . conceal the truth."[138]

Marley's "narrow literacy" helps explain his acceptance of Selassie's claim to divine kingship. So does his residency on an island just coming out of colonialism. The late Jamaican prime minister Michael Manley made this point in a 1976 *New York Times* article: "Man has a deep need for religious conviction, and Rasta resolves the contradiction of a white man's God in a colonial society." In Manley's view, "the only Jamaican who truly knows who he is has to be the Rasta man."[139]

The Rastas' sense of being a "community of prophets" responsible for midwifing a postcolonial world is also shaped by their anti-intellectualism. Rastas often look at "Babylon" or "the West" as "a nation of intellectuals." One of Tracy Nicholas' informants, Ras Hu-I, commented that "Western man" was crippled by an overreliance on rationality. "They have no . . . divine inspiration. They have no *spiritual diagnosis*," he said.[140] What is meant by "spiritual diagnosis"? Rastas distinguish between three ways of knowing. *Information* and a *"concept of truth"* are seen as "Western" ways of thought. Concepts, which order information, are seen as a sort of half-way step to *"spiritual diagnosis,"* the "third way" of thinking which Rastas believe is necessary for cultural and spiritual regeneration, and, ultimately, survival. Spiritual diagnosis is not merely description, but a strategy for healing and transformation: restructuring in political language, or redemption in spiritual language. This is a perspective which has deep roots, notably an affinity with the concept of "inner light" which was popularized during the Great Awakening, and the belief in a "God within" forwarded by the Gnostics.

Marley's own anti-intellectualism was sometimes blunt: "I don't have education, I have *inspiration.* If I was educated, I would be a damn fool." In a rejoinder to his critics, Marley sang: "Stiff-necked fools / Think you are cool / To deny me for simplicity / But you have got the wrong interpretation / Mixed up with vain imagination." Most often he used indirection, as in "Ride Natty Ride": "Brothers you should *know* and not believe." In this view inner conviction is more important than mere belief. Marley also used the Bible to answer critics who could not understand how he could worship an archaic King in the Horn of Africa. On "Forever Loving Jah," he sang "What is hidden from the wise and the prudent / Shall be *revealed* to the babes and the suckling," quoting Matthew 11:25. The Bible often deflates those who are too smart for their own good, making it a proper foundation for Marley's critique. "Whoever does not receive the kingdom of God like a child shall not enter it," Jesus is recorded as saying. The prophet Isaiah predicted that "a little child shall lead them."[141]

• • •

During most of his career, Marley was rarely seen reading anything besides music magazines or the Bible. That changed on the 1978 *Kaya* tour. Neville Garrick remembers that in May 1978, Bob went into several black bookshops in Chicago and bought "a large quantity of black consciousness literature," including biographies of Malcolm X and Angela Davis. For the rest of the tour Garrick would see Bob reading from these books at every spare moment.[142] This research shows up in the songs he began writing for *Survival* in late 1978.

Several factors influenced Marley's 1978 research. He was responding to critics who said he had sold out. He had a growing sense of international responsibility: in June 1978 the African delegations to the United Nations gave Bob the "Peace Medal" to honor his efforts for "equal rights and justice" for Africans. Bob wanted to live up to people's expectations that he would be a "freedom fighter." Marley was thirty-three and at the height of his creative powers. The reading he was doing and the

12   Marley in San Diego on the 1979 *Survival* tour, aged thirty-four, a year before he collapsed from a brain tumor.

remarkable group of songs inspired by this was evidence of an intellectual maturation.

This widening "literacy" was also probably shaped by the cancer diagnosis. Marley felt his cancer may have been caused by low-level radiation. He began to talk about nuclear power and "atomic mis-philosophy." A partly unconscious knowledge of his own mortality probably helped drive this exploration of black history, as a "last testament" he wanted to leave to "careless Ethiopians." As he said in a 1977 interview after his surgery, "time running out." An awareness of the shortness of time is revealed many times in the lyrics of *Survival*.[143]

"Africa Unite" stresses the urgent need for unity by warning that "it's later than you think." People and nations fight against each other because "they know not the hour," he sings on "Ambush in the Night." This lyric alludes to Jesus' comment in Matthew 25:13 that the disciples "know neither the day nor the hour" in which the old world will be swept away. This sense of millennial crisis is furthered on "Ride Natty Ride," with Bob quoting a dread on the beach telling a politician: "It's too late, fire is burning, man pull your own weight." In "So Much Trouble," Bob feels that the right time, or an apocalypse, is imminent: "We're sitting on a time bomb / Now I know the time has come." The urgency becomes even more acute on the album's closing title song: "We've got to hurry, hurry, hurry, 'cause we've got no time to lose."

I want now to turn now to the use of the Bible in *Survival*, concentrating on how scriptural allusions are used to construct a contemporary "chosen people" mythology – a transnational imagined community in which all African peoples are called to rebellion and regeneration by an African Father.

"Wake Up and Live"

The opening song of *Survival* is a wake-up call to "careless Ethiopians" – people of African descent who are unaware of a great destiny that has been prophesied for them by Marcus Garvey and the Biblical prophets.[144] The opening lines speak to people on a long journey: "Life is one big road with lots of signs / So when you're riding through the ruts, don't you complicate your mind / Flee from hate, mischief, and jealousy / Don't bury your thoughts put your vision to reality." Alluding to Proverbs, Bob represents signs as a detour from reality. To replace the signs, Marley offers a symbolic life: a myth to live by. And what is the "new" myth Marley offers? The next verse reveals this myth to be a variant of "racial celebrity": "Rise ye mighty people / There's work to be done so let's do it little by little / Rise from your sleepless slumber / We're more than sand on the seashore we're more than numbers."

This passage is dense with allusions. The first line is a quote from Marcus Garvey. The third line is adapted from Proverbs 6:9–10, in which a father calls on a son to rise from his slumber, and warns him of men who "plot mischief." The last line is the key to the "chosen people" mythology Marley is reconstructing. Jehovah had promised Abraham, a Chaldean living in West Asia, that if he would go possess a new land, his descendants would be more than the stars in the sky and the sand on the seashore (Genesis 15:5). Paul refers to this promise in his discourse on faith, defined as "the assurance of things hoped for, the conviction of things not seen" (Hebrews 11:1). Paul stresses that Abraham had faith that his God's promise would be fulfilled, even though he was already an old man without children. In a parallel way, Rastas are being asked to have faith in a destiny they cannot see, through the mediation of a God they can see, or at least imagine.

Marley wants his audience to think archetypally – not to clutter their minds with signs while riding through the "ruts" on their long journey. The Bible mythology Marley advocates is offered as a vehicle: a symbol of power to fix their minds on the horizon of their destiny, keeping their "eyes on the prize." By signifying on these scriptures, Marley urges his audience to see themselves as the inheritors of this tradition. Since they are without number, they can become a "mighty race" if only they find a means of unity.

"Africa Unite"

"How good and how pleasant it would be, before God and man, to see the unification of all Africans." This line is adapted from Psalms 133: "How good and how pleasant it is to live together as brothers in unity!" – a "song of the ascents" that also refers to "the mountains of Zion." This verse also calls to mind the admonition: "If a house is divided against itself, that house will not be able to stand" (Mark 3:25).

The chorus continues an Exodus theme: "We're moving right out of Babylon, and we're going to our father's land." Marley describes this Exodus as fulfillment of prophecy: "As it's been said already, so let it be done / We are the children of the higher one." The live versions of this song make explicit to whom Marley refers: "Marcus Garvey said it, so let it be done / I know you know who you are, under the sun / We are the children of the Rastaman / We are the children of the higher man." The Rastaman here serves as a figural "father of all nations," and the "higher man" or "higher one" is of course a reference to Selassie, and, more broadly, to the divinity believed to be present in every Rasta.

The use of the figurative "our father" can be compared to Frederick Douglass' repetitive use of "your fathers." While for Douglass political and genetic paternity was ambiguous, Marley's "perfect" African Father erased ambiguity. At the same time, Marley's use of terms like "Rastaman" and "Africa" is open to multiple readings – a multivoiced-ness Marley himself encouraged, it should be emphasized. In an interview conducted at around the same time *Survival* was being written, Marley remarked: "Sometimes I sing a song and when people explain it to me I am astonished by their interpretation." Yet this is what Carolyn Cooper calls a "permissive astonishment." "You have to play it and get your own inspiration," Marley advised. "For every song have a different meaning to a man."[145]

Like Douglass, Marley is essentially antiracialist, yet stuck with the language of race. His "target audience" was black people, yet Marley chose to see them as also not-black. This is spelled out in a 1977 interview with Afro-American DJ and journalist Greg Broussard, a friend of the Marley family. The taped conversation was conducted in the privacy of his mother's Delaware home, in a one-on-one "reasoning" not intended for a mass audience. In this conversation, Marley spells out his theory that a self-definition of "black" is not an adequate base for spiritual unity. "Rasta" was Marley's effort to define community in a way that recognized historical racial formations, yet did not use racial language.

"When yuh seh 'Rasta,' yuh represent all black people," Marley told Broussard. "Black carry the vibration fe put a wall in front a yuh . . . It have too much different meaning – black. But when you seh 'Rasta,' one vibe you get . . . once yuh know seh yuh Rasta, them cyaan black yuh out again."[146] Marley wants to use "Rasta" because he believes "black" carries too much baggage and is too contested to unify. "Black" is used to "block" people of African descent. Rasta includes all Africans, but it also carries a potential for a multiracial community that is not present in the word "black." Marley mentions Ham, the Biblical father of all Africans, yet Ham had the same father as did Shem, the mythical father of Asians, and Japeth, from who all Europeans supposedly came. *So Rasta is both a short-term means to African unity and a long-term path to multiracial community.*

"One Drop"

The song describes the "bassline" of unity on which Marley hopes to build, a unity based on rhythm – specifically the heartbeat rhythm of reggae music known as the "one drop." This is of course based on the ancient Nyabinghi riddim, which appears in Marley songs such as "Rastaman Chant," "Time Will Tell," and "Babylon System." It continues to inform contemporary Jamaican music, from the computerized "Kette

Drum" riddim of 1997, to the traditional chanting of groups such as the Wingless Angels. Stephen Davis describes the one drop as "a psychic spur that prodded people to higher consciousness."[147] In "One Drop" Marley portrays the consciousness achieved through the rhythm of the heart as one of both resistance and reconstruction. "So feel this drum beat as it beats within / Playing a rhythm resisting against the system / ... fighting against ism and schism." It is this opposition to all divisions that leads Rastas to oppose the use of the word "Rastafarian*ism*" itself. Thus, Marley insists that Rasta is not a religion but a way of life. As this song is about rhythm, it provides an appropriate moment for a disclaimer about the method I have been using: analyzing Marley's lyrics, apart from their musical vehicle. As Cooper emphasizes, "critical evaluation of Bob Marley's song as a literary text" is antithetical in many ways to the spirit of Marley's music and the culture(s) in which it is embedded. Cooper quotes Edward Brathwaite on this point: Marley's music is "based as much on sound as it is on song." Furthermore, "the noise that it makes is part of the meaning, and if you ignore the noise ... then you lose part of the meaning." This is music tailored for people going on a long journey: trodding or stalking music. The Wailers' music – especially the foundation of bassist Aston Garrett and drummer Carlton Barrett – is antithetical to rock in a way. It is more about what is left out than what is put in. Understatement leaves room for addition: responsive improvisation. The main focus is on the bass rather than melody: one could even say that the bass IS the melody in reggae music. Certain inferences arise from this inverted structure which houses a unique music-based philosophy.

Bass-led rhythms or "riddims" are conveyors of cultural traditions in Jamaican culture, and more broadly, in "black Atlantic" cultures, or an Afro-Carribean-influenced cultural community that Linton Kwesi Johnson and others have referred to as "bass culture." In bass culture, the music, the lyrics, and the very way of thinking are *led by the bottom* rather than the top. Priority is given to the unconscious, intuitive mind, rather than the conscious, rational mind. When Rastas say "get conscious," they mean an integration of the whole mind, but one which privileges the bass – revelation. And from revelation comes revolution – not a call for violence but a "burning certain things about our mind, so as to live inna one harmony," as Marley once said in giving the most constructive possible interpretation to "Burnin' and Lootin'."[148]

"Ride Natty Ride"

Having defined the "One Drop" as the basis of African unity, Marley here pictures a heroic "Natty Dread" riding this riddim through "... the mystics of tomorrow / Having no fear, having no sorrow." Yet in Marley's vision the world does not want Natty to "fulfill that mission." This opposition itself is another powerful "psychic spur" to unity, which Marley again explains in Biblical mythology. "The stone that the builder refused / Shall be the head cornerstone," Marley sings (Psalms 118:22). The verse was used by Jesus (Mark 12:10) as a variation on his recurring "the first will be last and the last shall be first" reversal theme (Mark 10:31). The same quote was used elsewhere in the New Testament to present Jesus as a "stone" who had been rejected by his intended audience, the Jews, but would be the "head cornerstone" for a worldwide church open to all peoples (Hebrews 4:11/I Peter 2:7).

"Natty Dread," representative of a new "chosen people" (the Rastas), is seen as having a secret weapon which will allow him to triumph over all the games that "they" try to play: "it's the fire that's burning down everything ... Jah says this judgement could never be with water / No water could put out this fire." In a Biblical context, this alludes to a number of texts. Paul writes that "Our God is a consuming fire" (Hebrews 12:29). John the Baptist contrasted his form of initiation, a baptism with water, to the Messiah who was coming, who would baptise with fire, or the Holy Spirit (Mark 1:8).[149] Rastas, who Marley describes in this song as being guided by "the teachings of his Majesty" rather than "devil philosophy," have a "God within" which is an "inner mounting flame" which no water can douse. In this song, the fire is apocalyptic.

"Ambush in the Night"

As noted earlier, this song opens with an allusion to a "right time" or an immanent "new world," as described in Matthew 25:13. Marley wrote this song as a "moral" to the assassination attempt: since he is "protected by his Majesty," mere political violence cannot bring him down. But he casts a much wider net: the song works as a parable about resilience of people everywhere who are fighting political oppression, or who are simply struggling to emancipate themselves from "mental slavery." Marley presents this moral in a doubled form, however, which makes it clear that tragedy and triumph always coexist. The first verse has a despairing tone in which the "divide and conquer" propaganda of the "Babylon System" is too powerful for the people to resist:

> They say what we know is just what they teach us
> And we're so ignorant every time they can reach us
> Through political strategy they keep us hungry
> When you gonna get some food
> Your brother got to be your enemy

The second verse reverses this relationship to make a heroic declaration of self-determination:

> Well what we know is not what they tell us
> And we're not ignorant, & they just cannot judge us
> Through the power of the most high we keep on surfacing
> Through the power of the most high we keep of surviving

"The power of the most high" is a line which appears in Luke 1:35, spoken by an angel of God to assure Mary that, even though she is unmarried and a virgin, she will bear a son, Jesus, who "will be called the Son of the Most High." "The power of the Most High will overshadow you," she is told. Marley's lyric tries to place Rastas within this same tradition: they have been elected or empowered by the Most High, and this "God within" functions as a guardian spirit. Marley's lyric also signifies on the Rasta belief that the one who undergoes a self-awakening and develops a relationship with Haile Selassie "enters into a divine state of 'sonship'." This belief system has recently been articulated by Tony Rebel in regards to Buju Banton, a former "girls and guns" DJ who underwent a spiritual transformation.[150]

"So Much Trouble in the World"

This tune portrays a world spinning out of control, being destroyed by men without faith who go "sailing on their ego trips" rather than deal with reality. Marley warns against instant solutions which turn out to be illusions. He refers to the "cornerstone" without which survival will not be possible. The line "Blast off on their spaceship / Million miles from reality" has a racial subtext, as Marley in interviews sometimes described white people as thinking too much. In his view, whites often lacked the "symbolic life" and were therefore prone to trying to manipulate their environment.

"Zimbabwe"

This is *Survival*'s only song without Biblical allusions. The opening line restates "Enlightenment" ideals: "Every man got the right to decide his own destiny / And in this judgement their is no partiality." Marley began writing this song during his visit to Ethiopia in late 1978, and it reworks themes from Selassie's "War" speech. Marley's use of this egalitarianism in relation to Africa underscores Paul Gilroy's point that there is no space outside of European or Western philosophy, and that claims of pure opposition are "merely gestural." This song was recorded by numerous African artists after its release. Some claim it helped liberate Zimbabwe.

Marley's line "Soon we'll find out who is the real revolutionary" is ambiguous, given his posture as a "musical rebel" and his statements to the effect that "music is the biggest gun because it save." Given his preference for symbolic battle, what is real? And what is revolutionary?[151]

"Top Ranking"

The refrain "They don't want to see us unite / All they want us to do is keep on killing one another" evidences a "the world is against us" mindset, as in this claim in "Ride Natty Ride": "to see his hurt is their greatest ambition." This can be attributed only in part to Marley's grounding in a Biblical mythology. The sense of oppression is contrasted with the belief that Rastas, via their relationship with Selassie, are descended from the "root of King David." These lyrics have racial undertone: a despised/chosen doubling also pervasive in Afro-American discourse. But Marley's theme of the persecution of Rastas has a uniquely Jamaican tenor. Marley had good reason to view Rastas as a persecuted minority in Jamaica, at least until the mid-1970s. But a persecution complex also resides in this self-fulfilling prophecy. Just as an invented Solomonic ancestry became a "cornerstone" to the collective identity of the Amhara in Ethiopia, a messianic us-against-the-world complex has become crucial to Rasta identity. Some of the persecution complex here may be a tool for unification.[152] Some of it undoubtedly grew out of Marley's increasing sense of being imprisoned in the myth he had helped create.

In any case, Marley left a legacy that is hard to live down: the sense of being persecuted becomes a cornerstone of personal and collective identity. The act (or memory) of persecution feeds one's sense of being "chosen." Rasta-inspired singers continue to be deeply invested in a rhetorical "they" as a permanent oppressor. Sanchez sings: "There are lots of signs, I must confess, yes, that we're a chosen people but we're treated like the rest / But there'll come a day when they'll have to answer" ("Chronic," 1995). The way in which Marley "prestructured" this legacy can be read as a cautionary tale for how those who identify with chosen people mythologies often become invested in "othering" an out-group or enemy. Is mythologizing a collective enemy the only means to achieve unity?

"Babylon System"

The word Babylon is overdetermined to a degree, because of its earlier use by Garvey, the Nation of Islam, and the Black Panthers to refer to a *white* power structure run by *white devils*. Marley has not completely distanced himself from this heritage: he uses terms like "devil philosophy." But in interviews, Marley consistently insisted that the system which he so often criticized should not be interpreted racially. "Babylon System" describes a destructive way of life which replicates itself through institutional structures. Marley's representation of this system has an anti-intellectual and anticlerical cast to it, yet clearly it is the dehumanizing *use* of religious and intellectual institutions to which he is objecting, not the act of worship or intellectual growth:

> Babylon system is the vampire
> Sucking the blood of the sufferers
> Building church and university
> Deceiving the people continually
> Me say them graduating thieves and murderers
> Tell the children the truth . . .

However much Marley insisted that the system was transracial in character, his specific historical referents concern oppression of black people. The opening stanza specifically signifies on issues of black liberation raised by the 1960s Civil Rights and "Black Power" movements:

> We refuse to be what you wanted us to be
> We are what we are, and that's the way it's going to be
> You can't educate I for no equal opportunity
> Talking about my freedom, people freedom and liberty

Certainly much of Marley's black audience has interpreted this song as being directed solely to black people. The fashionably iconoclastic author "bell hooks" has made the claim that white people are incapable of understanding what Marley meant by "we refuse to be what you wanted us to be."[153]

Once more, Marley uses the Bible as a legitimizing and historicizing device. The chorus repeats the refrain:

> We've been trodding on the winepress much too long
> Rebel, rebel
> We've been taken for granted much too long
> We've got to rebel now.

The figure of speech comes from Isaiah 63, where a messianic figure "strides along with mighty power" in response to the lament of the people. "Why are your clothes all red, like the garments of one treading grapes in the winepress?" this redeemer is asked. "I trod the nations in my anger," he says. "I resolved on a day of vengeance; the year for redeeming my own had come." In the nineteenth century this passage appeared in "The Battle Hymn of the Republic," which depicted the conquest of the slaveholding South as a divine mandate for a redeemer nation.[154] Martin

Luther King Jr. made use of this scripture and hymn in some of his most famous civil rights speeches using words that have achieved deep resonance in a progressive and multiracial stream of American culture (as in John Steinbeck's novel *Grapes of Wrath*).

"Survival"

This is a tribute to the resilience of African peoples in the face of inhuman "sufferation." It is surely not by accident that the Biblical precedents to which Marley refers here come from the book of *Daniel* – a prophetic book written during and commenting on the years of Jewish exile in Babylon. "We're the survivors, like Shadrach, Meshach and Abednego, thrown in the fire but never get burned," Marley sings.[155]

Shadrach, Meshach, and Abednego were friends of Daniel, brought to King Nebuchadnezzar to be trained for royal court service. These young men, the nobility of Israeli exiles, were vegetarians (like Rastas), yet healthier than those who ate the king's food. Daniel "had a gift for interpreting visions and dreams of every kind" (1:17). After revealing the meaning of a "big dream" of Nebuchadnezzar, he was given authority over Babylon. At Daniel's request his friends Shadrach, Meshach, and Abednego became administrators of Babylon. But these three ignited the king's fury when they refused to bow before a ninety-foot gold image he had erected. The king had declared that anyone refusing to worship this god-image would be thrown into a fiery furnace. But the author of *Daniel* tells us: "they were willing to submit themselves to the fire rather than to serve or worship any god other than their own God" (3:28). But they escaped from the furnace unharmed, according to this story, whereupon the king "advanced their fortunes."

In another chorus, Marley sings "We're the survivors, like Daniel out of the lion's Den." Daniel's political power ascended as he continued to interpret Nebuchadnezzar's visions, and to "read the writing on the wall" for his son Belshazzar. However, after the Medes and Persians overran Babylon, functionaries who were jealous of Daniel conspired against him. He was thrown into a lion's pit after being caught praying in his house, which had "roof-chambers open to Jerusalem" (6:10).[156] Through divine intervention the mouths of the lions were sealed, and Darius, the Persian king, declared reverence to the "God of Daniel."

The "lion's den" and the "fiery furnace" which concern Bob are "technological inhumanity, scientific atrocity, atomic mis-philosophy, a world that forces life-long insecurity." He sings of "black survival" but these are obviously transracial issues: as Marley sings, rewording the Bible: "the rain don't fall on one man's house." The transracial horizon is present here in the hope "to live as one in the eyes of the Almighty." Marley's last words on *Survival* are: "A good man is never honored in his own country. Nothing change." Jesus had said that "no prophet is acceptable in his own country" (Luke 4:24/ Mark 6:4). This shows that Marley, as a modern Daniel reading the "writing on the wall," is consciously situating himself within a prophetic/messianic tradition.[157]

Survival in relation to Marley's life and songbook

The creation of an African Father was at first liberatory for Marley, but in the end became a prison of sorts. An out-take from the *Survival* sessions, "Mix Up," reflects his weariness with the prophet business: "People waiting for the message that you bring / They're listening to every word that you say / I'm going to break my wheel / I don't care who falls."

Judy Mowatt, Allan Cole, and others believe it was the burden of all the aspirations Marley dragged around, as much as anything, that killed him. As a "Third World Superstar," Marley was often expected to be all things: political chief, spiritual redeemer, and physical provider. Marley's *largesse* was legendary. He would give away from $20,000 to 40,000 some days when he was in Jamaica. Lines of Jamaicans seeking handouts would stretch from his Hope Road residence out into the streets, and Marley would listen to each one's story, usually giving them what they wanted.[158]

In an interview soon after being shot, Marley emphasized: "My life no important to me. Other people life important. My life is only important if me can help plenty people." As usual Marley followed a Biblical model of service: "Whoever would be great among you must be your servant, and whoever would be first among you must be slave of all."[159]

Marley took this model seriously. His closest associates wished they could protect Marley from the hordes of people constantly wanting his attention or his assistance, but they came to accept that this was the way that the Gong wanted it. He thought of himself as a servant or a slave to his people, and he rarely said no. Judy Mowatt, his friend and singer in the I-Threes, believes that he become "saturated" with the needs of others.[160]

Marley's health began to deteriorate in late 1978. While recording *Survival* in 1979, he was distracted and prone to atypical violent outbursts. Some friends attributed this to the anti-cancer medication he was taking. Others felt it was a result of the disintegrating political situation in Jamaica. The truce he had brokered between warring political gunmen at the 1978 "One Love/Peace Concert" had fallen apart. I suspect that the visit to Ethiopia may have had both an inspirational and a disillusioning effect. 1979 interviews reveal his anger over the antipathy to Selassie he had witnessed in Ethiopia. On the 1979 *Survival* tour while riding through northern California, Marley told Donald Kinsey that he was "getting tired of this." He told many people that maybe he should have been a soccer player. He dreamed about other ways of getting out of the rat race. "One of these days I stop play music and I go into Africa and I don't talk to nobody no more nor sing to nobody," he said. "Because this is not a joke."[161]

Marley's late work tapes are permeated with the themes of imprisonment and escape.[162] This was evident in 1978 when he responded to charges he had gone soft by saying he did not want to be a "prisoner" of one style. By what did he feel entrapped? His burden of fame was a particular type of "racial celebrity" characterized by messianic projections. Towards the end, he surrendered to these projections, and they became like a cross or a millstone. His comments about disappearing into Africa, never to perform again, reflect his desire to lay down this cross, as does the lyric "Break my wheel / I don't care who falls."

I also wonder if he desired, perhaps unconsciously, to escape the psychological limitations of having to continue to be the spokesman for this "cult," after Selassie had died, and after Bob got several views of the "real" Africa. He returned saying he was "vexed" with Africa. Was his faith an act of courage sustained because there was nothing else to replace it? Can the *act* of faith be recognized as more important than the *object* of faith, without destroying the faith itself? Marley seems to have been trying to think about this, although his "followers" would hardly let him: in 1979, asked "where is Selassie right now?" he says: "In your consciousness. That where 'im always live – in your consciousness, ya dig?" This is a hint that Bob did see the African Father metaphorically, as a "god within." An interviewer had asked him if his songs should be taken literally or symbolically. "It always wider than that," he said.[163] "I Shot the Sheriff" was not merely about gunplay and "Jah" as "our father" was not just about Selassie.

Marley also understood that people could not "banish the negative" completely: asked whether or not he worried about a "kick from the devil," Marley laughed and said: "You no want to kill the devil – him have him part to play. Him can be a good friend too. If you don't know him, that's the time him can mash you down." This shows an awareness of the interconnection of good and evil – all that is "evil" cannot be projected outward, as a disowned shadow. This included a belief – one that his son Ziggy did not understand – that racial doubleness must also be accepted – the white that lived inside him along with black, "devil" along with living God.[164]

My sense is that Marley was trapped by an all-too-common phenomenon, in which people confuse the message with the messenger. Marley attempted to deflect attention from himself to a deified father, and

13 The 1978 "One Love/Peace Concert": "Rasta between two thieves," as Neville Garrick says: socialist Prime Minister Michael Manley on the left, and soon-to-be conservative Prime Minister Edward Seaga on the right. The peace Marley helped broker was short-lived.

consistently stressed his view that all people had access to a "God within." (In this sense, in Marley's thought, the racial frontier is an inner barrier which must be crossed on the way to emancipating oneself from mental slavery.) But the very process of engaging in deification inevitably trapped him within the messianic obsessions of the Judeo-Christian tradition in which he was firmly rooted. There is of course no direct access to this "God." There is only representation of what we imagine him, her, or it to be. To try to draw closer is to burn in the flame, as prophets throughout the ages have discovered. Many of Marley's fans wanted him to *be* that representation, and in the end their projections were too powerful to escape.

Ultimately, the tragedy and triumph of Marley's life will become less important than his work, and one suspects that his 1975 prediction is true, that his songs will remain. His enduring vision is one of collective work and responsibility, of good overcoming evil. "Emancipate yourselves from mental slavery," perhaps Marley's most famous line, is very close to the attitude that Douglass came to have towards religion: he believed in "praying with his feet." Representations of God and of "God's people" in Marley's work should not be misunderstood as an opiate or an infantile delusion. They are an awakening strategy designed to give the downtrodden enough courage and self-respect to shed demeaning stereotypes, and to reimagine themselves according to a new type that they themselves construct out of the best materials available.

"Jump Nyabinghi," another out-take from *Survival*, was a Marley favorite, and represents the essence of his use of Biblical mythology as political strategy. Looking out at his "massive" dancing, Marley expresses joy at the sight of people "moving to the rhythm" and "dancing from within." From this seemingly innocuous observation, he extrapolates to a much larger vision of music – the One Drop – as a source of collective power and regeneration:

> It remind me of the days in Jericho
> When we trodding down Jericho walls
> These are the days when we trod through Babylon
> We keep on trodding until Babylon falls.

To emphasize that the people, even though poor, have the tools at their disposal, he reminds them: "Davis slew Goliath with a sling and a stone / Samson slew the Philistines with a donkey jaw bone." This lyric comes from "Rastaman Live Up," which was also written along with the *Survival* group, but was specifically targeted at his *roots* audience.[165]

The Jews whose religious mythology forms the "head cornerstone" of Marley's work eventually had to decide, while exiled in Babylon, whether they worshiped a national God or a universal God. The "concept of truth" which emerged from exile was of Judaism as "a house of prayer for all people." The slow move to inclusion eventually resulted in Christianity's attempt at a "spiritual diagnosis," in which the God of the Jews was declared to be an equal opportunity God, "with no respect to nations" and "without regard to race." This same dilemma is still partly unresolved by Rastas, but seemed clear to Bob. His global audience has embraced his view of a "God within," while the worship of Haile Selassie as an Ethiopian God has been for the most part impossible to translate.[166]

LEGACY

Marley as biracial black culture hero

After being shot in December 1976, Marley rarely lived in Jamaica. He spent most of the next four years touring the world or living in Miami and London. Leonard Barrett calls him "the Charles Wesley of Rastafarianism." Chevannes describes Marley's period of global outreach as "the Rasta version of Paul's decision to preach to the Gentiles."[167] If we see Rasta as a postcolonial, religious mythology, this makes sense. The book which recounts Paul's missions, Acts, is in fact a story of a mono-ethnic religious cult's shedding of its "racial superiority" attitudes in order to reach a multinational audience.

Acts is an archetypal model for inclusion of "the Other." The historical Jesus which scholars believe is present in fragments of the Gospels had already made tentative steps towards ministering to non-Jews, as in his encounter with the Syro-Phoenician woman (Mark 7) and the parable of the Good Samaritan (Luke 10). Paul moved from occasional forays among non-Jews to making Gentiles his primary audience. Similarly, the Rastas before Marley made tentative overtures towards whites. Marley took the gospel of black liberation to a predominantly nonblack audience – mainly white at first, and later Asian and indigenous. The result has been the emergence of a form of interracial and international call-and-response that crosses not only racial and national boundaries, but also the barriers of time. In 1980 1 million Irish youth sang "Rivers of Babylon" for Pope John Paul II – a richly ironic event, given the origins of this hymn (Psalms 137) in the Jewish exile in Babylon, and its reformulation by Rastafarians who viewed the Pope as an Antichrist.[168]

Like the Jews in Babylon and Paul among the Gentiles, most Rastas decided that their God was universal. Though they saw him, "through the spectacles of Ethiopia," as black, most understood him to be transracial – at least in reception. This paradox was resolved in the same way that Jews began to internationalize their god: once they admitted that their god had made all nations out of "one blood," then it was only a short step towards the realization that all nations would worship him through their own spectacles.

Marley, the "psalmist of reggae," can be seen and heard in every corner of the planet now.[169] One dramatic story of a Marley "sighting" comes from a Cambridge professor who visited Tibet in 1979 after it had been closed for decades of Chinese occupation. At the Potala lamasert in Lhasa, an aging monk led the visitor through underground catacombs into a room carved out of rock, where a single lightbulb and an old eight-track tape player were plugged into a single electric outlet. In the tape player, a Lebanese bootleg of *Natty Dread* played over and over. Similar stories abound. Chris Blackwell vacationed in Bali in 1989, and as he was exploring the interior of the island, he stopped at a thatched lean-to "in the middle of nowhere." Hanging on the wall was a life-size batik of Marley.[170]

Marley's global audience has adopted him for a wide variety of uses –

most often, political or spiritual, but also as an icon of undetermined meaning – a family uncle or an ancestral spirit. Some Ethiopians see him as a reincarnation of the early Ethiopian church composer the Holy Yahred. In Nepal Marley is seen as a modern incarnation of Vishnu. Havasupai Indians in Arizona claim Bob as a tribal prophet. On the political front, there are reports of the Sandinistas singing "Road Block" while battling the US-funded Contras in Nicaragua in the early 1980s.[171]

On the commercial end of the spectrum, contemporary rappers and dance hall artists recycle Bob. "WASPafarians" (Euro-Americans) have become the biggest consumers and producers of reggae in the United States. The largest reggae label during the 1980s, RAS Records, was run by a Jewish promoter named Gary Himmelfarb who took on the alter ego of Dr. Dread. During a time when Jamaican reggae has been mostly performed by machines, the most reliable sources of full-band reggae, as pioneered by Bob Marley and the Wailers, have been Eastern Europe, Japan, Latin America, and North America.[172]

This is as Bob Marley wanted it. Asked by Greg Broussard in 1977 if he would use specific strategies to move beyond his white audience, Bob responded: "Me no really a sing for white people, me a sing fe all people. Some song, some people can understand it more than some other people. 'Cause everybody suffer when you check it inna certain way, but we the black people suffer more than anyone else." He said he did not worry about the predominance of whites who were coming to hear him because when "the white man tek it, then the black man gwan come. So me never too care, anytime I play a place and see it full up a white people. 'Caw me know seh the word go out."[173]

Marley acknowledged that in the short run, tension would persist between some blacks and whites in his audience. "There should be no more war between white and black," he stressed. "But until white people listen to black with open ears, there must be, well, suspicion." However, Bob always pointed to a horizon which was transracial: as he had said in 1975, "You can't come tell me 'bout white and black . . . We fly a color which is red, gold, and green." After 1979, when he took his black liberation music to Asia, he glimpsed a role for Rasta that moved beyond black and white. In a late interview, a weary Marley reflected: "I don't really have no ambition. I only have one thing fe I would really like to see happen. I'd like to see mankind live together: black, white, china. That's all."[174]

Marley's globalization of the Rasta message was not always supported by his "roots" audience. Many "Nyabinghi elders" were at best "ambivalent about the universalizing trends in the work of Bob Marley," writes Carole Yawney, because "by becoming a global currency, the Rastafari vision has been threatened with dispersion and trivialization."[175] This "trivializing" of Rasta was already in evidence by 1975, with the release of *Natty Dread*, as I have noted. But the "universalizing" of the Rasta vision really dates from 1977, with the *Exodus* album and tour. At this point, Marley had moved beyond mere rebel iconography.

"Exodus functioned as Archetypal event for slaves," wrote Raboteau. Yet Exodus was also an archetype for Puritans and other sects in West Europe, as Werner Sollors and others note.[176] When Marley sings "Send us another brother Moses from across the Red Sea" on *Exodus* and before audiences of up to 100,000 people in Europe, we are witnessing a mutation in the use of Exodus as an archetypal myth of human renewal. Marley's immediate referents are a history of black liberation, but he is being packaged, or "trivialized," by corporate sponsors, and he is being received, or "purchased," by a multiethnic audience with very different sets of cultural references.

What happens to the Exodus myth, as a *archetypal event*, when popularized and commodified in a mass media market? I can only address this question in passing. But I want to note a fundamental racial ambiguity of Moses, as a figure of religious mythologies. As a Mosaic figure, Marley can be placed in a lineage of racially ambiguous Moses types such as Frederick Douglass, and the racially uncertain Moses types fictionalized by Zora Hurston and Freud. What is the nature of the *hegira* Marley was leading?[177]

Before trying to cautiously answer that question, I want to briefly excerpt some research I have done among reggae's audiences over the last two decades, and compare what I have seen to the work of scholars such as Carole Yawney, who have studied reggae's international reception. My own research started informally in the 1980s, when I was a songwriter for a band that played at reggae concerts in the American Southwest. More recently, I have engaged in two forms of ethnographic research. First, I have participated in an electronic discussion group known as RMR (rec.music.reggae), and saved many of these discussions to disc. Second, I have interviewed Marley fans, some of whom I "met" through RMR, and some of whom I came to know through music industry contacts.

My perception is that from the late 1970s through the 1980s, Marley was most often seen by American and European audiences as a political rebel, or a counter-culture icon. Thus the presence of posters of a "spliff-smoking" Bob in dorm rooms, reflecting the success of Island's strategy of marketing Bob though a rock'n'roll iconography. For a typical example of Bob as an icon of political resistance, one can point to the enduring popularity of the Marley/Tosh song, "Get Up, Stand Up," which was a theme song of the early 1990s Amnesty International tour. There is also a more general affinity among an older generation of Marley fans. My old friend Jay Trachtenberg, a long-term reggae DJ in Austin, Texas, likes to quote the line "forget your troubles and dance" (from "Them Belly Full") as an example of what he finds most enduring, and endearing, in Bob's music.

Among younger reggae fans I have interviewed during the 1990s, there seems to be a change in attitude towards Marley. Many young reggae fans came to the music after an early fascination with rap. They often compared what they saw as a negativity in rap music to the "positive vibrations" of reggae, in order to explain their attraction to reggae as something like a "conversion." Many young fans see reggae – and particularly Marley's music – as a moral philosophy, or even a religion. In fact, through my participation in an electronic "imagined community," I have encountered a new generation of Christian reggae fans who are "claiming" Marley. That project is beyond the scope of the present book, but I want to profile two of the Marley fans I have interviewed, who shed light on how younger fans are responding to the spiritual or quasi-religious dimensions of Marley's "Exodus."

In the fall of 1996, Michael DeGraf was a freshman architecture student at the University of Illinois, Champaign-Urbana. At the age of eighteen, he was already one of the most serious Marley fans I have ever encountered – having acquired tapes of some forty to fifty of Marley's concerts from around the globe. His passion for collecting Marley's music seemed to have something of a religious quest about it. When I asked Michael about this, he wrote: "I am pretty sure that Bob has come into my life with the help of the Lord." He saw no contradiction between Bob's Rastafarianism and his own Christianity, because "I don't think God would lead his children astray," and "Bob has also encouraged me to read the Bible more frequently." Like many young fans I talked with, he compared Bob to rap music – in this case, a particular moment in which he was listening to a song by Dr. Dre, which made him realize that "these musics had no fruits." He said he had been troubled by "feelings of hopelessness" before discovering Marley. It seemed to me that Marley had become something of a messianic figure for Michael, as when he commented: "Bob gave his life for everyone, trying to teach God's word."

More typically, young fans feel more ambivalence about their "religious" attraction to the Rastafarianism popularized by Marley. DJ RJ is a reggae drummer and radio disc jockey in Austin, Texas. When I first met him, he was a big rap fan, but over the years, he has become deeply involved in the creation and promotion of reggae music. He has traveled to Jamaica twice, and has interviewed many Rastafarian-influenced reggae artists. Recently I asked him to reflect upon the paradox of a white youth promoting a music that praised a "black God." "I don't feel comfortable calling myself a Christian and at the same time I don't feel comfortable calling myself Rasta either, as I don't worship Rastafari," wrote RJ. "So where does that leave me? I'm still figuring that out. I do feel that I relate more to Rasta as a mindset than I do anything else, and I like Bob's idea that it's a way of life rather than a religion. I prefer Jah as the title most comfortable for me to use to address the Almighty." RJ also described what was essentially a religious experience, of feeling a "power coming down on me – like I was being charged," while he was singing the late Garnet Silk's "Bless Me" on stage.

It should be pointed out that there is a significant strain of reggae music – called dancehall – in which spiritual themes are entirely absent, guns are glorified, and women are degraded – just as in gangster rap, or many forms of rock music. This type of "slackness" was particularly popular in the late 1980s and early 1990s. Yet even during the height of "slackness," "conscious reggae," as the Rastafarian-influenced tradition is called, always had a significant presence in the culture, and kept up a sustained critique of "girls and guns" music – and the antisocial behavior it both reflected and reinforced. One is hard pressed to think of another popular music which has endured for so long, in which political and moral critique are such prominent features. By the celebration of Marley's fiftieth birthday in 1995, "conscious reggae" seemed to be at least on equal footing with "slackness." In fact one of the biggest trends of the 1990s has been former "slackness" artists who grew dreadlocks and began chatting "culture lyrics," such as Buju Banton. It would be hard to overestimate Marley's influence in this process. His lyrics are cited incessantly – like scriptures, to be quoted often by the faithful. DJ RJ and I have done a yearly "Top 20 Conscious Dancehall Reggae" show during the late 1990s, and there would be few tunes on our list that do not either quote Bob directly, allude to his life, or recycle one of his riddims.

• • •

In combining what I have seen of Marley's various audiences, with what other scholars have written about this domain, I would venture a broader claim. Marley's musical vision spoke to two "absences" at the very heart of the social and moral crisis of so-called "late capitalism": the loss of a sense of sacred, and a loss of sense of community. His employment of the Exodus archetype, and his construction of a "perfect" African Father, spoke to both of those absences. Carole Yawney, who studied the international performances of "Rasta elders" after Marley's death, observes that "the range of symbolic ambiguities in Rastafari imagery ... assists in bringing about a consensual community." The consensus is not based on a literal interpretation of "master symbols" such as Selassie. Many people who are attracted to Rastafarian reggae experience its redemptive potential in spite of (or because of) their ambiguity about Rasta's core symbols, Yawney argues. Selassie himself is ambiguous in many ways: racially, in relation to imperialism, as the apex of a rigidly heirarchical monarchy who advocated democracy, etc. He makes an unlikely hero of black liberation in many ways: he was ascetic, aristocratic, with a "racial" identity that was more Semitic than African.[178]

The use of Selassie as the figurehead for *black liberation* and *multiracial redemption* would have been "impenetrable" for global audiences, if not for the fact that Marley spoke "in the metaphors of the Judaic heritage," the closest thing he could find to a universal language. Many in Marley's audience identified with his rejection of a dysfunctional, dehumanizing, and unsustainable "Babylon system." They longed for a simpler way of life. They found a voice for these feelings in Marley's music. The Rasta vision, as voiced by Marley, elicited a sense of moral community, Yawney believes, "*in a situation of symbolic ambiguity.*" The sense of community and moral vision was achieved despite the fact that most of the audience felt "no commitment to the symbols as such," as Yawney writes. Marley's use of the depth symbolism of Judeo-Christian scripture allowed him to achieve a "healing work, even though it uses symbols for which we feel only the echo of allegiance." The Biblical Exodus may be only an echo for many of Bob's listeners, but he is still leading a *hegira*, nevertheless: a flight which means many things to many people, but centers on a "running away" from repressive traditional authority and movement towards a rediscovery of the personal self and of collective identity and responsibility.[179]

In 1852, when Martin Delany spoke of Afro-Americans "singing sweet songs of redemption," he was addressing an audience of a few thousand. When Marley released his "Redemption Songs" in 1980, he sang to hundreds of millions: "Emancipate yourselves from mental slavery / None but ourselves can free our minds." This is a vision of emancipation and redemption firmly rooted in slavery, but it relocates the issue of emancipation and redemption in a transracial context: emancipation from mental slavery cannot take place within a merely racial framework.[180]

But what does it mean to interpret Marley's songs as the "new psalms"? As songs of praise the Psalms have inspired a variety of people for many generations. Marley built on a tradition utilized by black leaders (and sympathetic nonblacks) since the late eighteenth century of using the Psalms and other Biblical passages which could help build black pride or multiracial alliances. Yet he reconstructed this tradition in what we might call a postmodern manner. The essence of postmodernism is its hybridity, achieved through collage, or pastiche. The reliance by Marley and other Rastas on a King James matrix has led Laurence Breiner to argue: "Though repatriation to Africa is its central tenet, it has no core of preserved African religion, and has not even adopted African elements from the surrounding culture to any considerable extent."[181] Breiner somewhat overstates his case, yet clearly Rastas idealize an almost entirely invented Africa, and rely more on Judeo-Christian scriptures channeled through a fundamentalist lens than any other source.

We have tended to think of enduring art as something found in books or buildings. So there is no model for nonwritten "Psalms." Marley's psalms are "new" because they are electronically mediated songs which cannot clearly be "placed" within or "owned" by one tradition or tribe. It is in their hybridity, and their pastiche-like construction, ironically, that Marley's "psalms" are most African.

Africa was postmodern before the modern. Long before postmodernists began theorizing about pastiche, Africans were assembling "found" objects into improvised co-creations, and using antiphony (call-and-response) in their styles of worship and artistic expression.[182] Which brings me to the link that Christianity provides between Africa and Marley's "Western" audiences. Christianity was for much of Africa and its diaspora an entry to modernity, during the same period in which Christianity signified a move away from modernity for many Europeans. European intellectuals and artists increasingly came to view Christianity as a vestige of premodern superstitions. Most modernists rejected Christianity as a source of legitimate tradition, and those intellectuals who have affirmed the potential validity of Judeo-Christian sources have often been ostracized. Modernists have turned to other invented traditions which they have invested with numinous/"religious" qualities: nationalism, or "progress." The trade-offs are wellknown: an unprecedented capacity for mass mobilization and the manufacture of short-term wealth, at the expense of a loss of a moral common ground, a sustainable life-style, and a sense of hope. Part of what is involved in the projection of Mosaic or Messianic qualities on to Marley emerges from a "primitivist" belief that moral or artistic regeneration in the "postmodern" world can only come from representatives of a "premodern" world who have not been "corrupted" by progress.[183]

Marley's humble origins endowed him with a moral authority which would be almost impossible to achieve for an artist from a "superpower." Moreover, Marley provided a means for his multiracial audience to reincorporate some of their Judeo-Christian heritage without having to acknowledge directly that this is in fact what they were doing. And in a broader sense, Marley's life and personal mythology followed an archtypal pattern of "heroes" which has worldwide resonance: he was an abandoned child who was "adopted" by royalty and later "died for his people."

During the course of his artistic career, Marley moved through a series of personas – from Rhyging to Moses to a Messianic figure – which increasingly seem to have been adapted to meet the needs of collective projections.[184] Within the seven years of his Island career these three personas are presented in "I Shot the Sheriff," "Exodus," and "Redemption Songs." What is lost in translation? Those personas tend to obscure other facets of Bob's art: Bob as street poet, "Soul Rebel," and a "Natural Mystic" who read the writing on the wall of late capitalism. My sense is that Bob tried mightily to resist the messianic projections of his audience. "I try to find the answers to all the questions they ask / But I know it's impossible to go living through the past," he sang in "Natural Mystic." In the end he had only the conviction that "our prophets" are still being killed, and that perhaps "... it's just a part of it / You've got to fulfill the book."

The chronic tendency in Afro-American history to invest leaders with Messianic or Mosaic qualities reveals itself as a vicious cycle of self-fulfilling prophecy. The sacrifice of prophets to appease the collective soul does not seem like a legacy that I would want to teach to my children. Still, in recent years I have read and heard people refer to Bob Marley as a Christ-figure so often that I have been driven to try to achieve a historical understanding of why Bob fulfills that archetype for so many. Something in our "psychological structure" seems to dictate that many human beings have to project greatness outside of themselves in order to find meaning in their life, or to maintain the hope of achieving greatness, or some type of immortality, in their own lives. And it has often been easiest for people to project unacknowledged or repressed messianic dreams on to "black culture heroes," who are, in fact, brown. This is an old story. "Don't forget that from the Jews, the most despised people of antiquity, living in [a] corner of Palestine or Galilee, came the redeemer of Rome," Jung reminded a seminar in 1930. And added, metaphorically: "Why should not our redeemer be a Negro? It would be logical and psychologically correct."[185]

In terms of the Ethiopianism in which Marley was rooted, I think it is safe to say that Marley represents the denouement of the tradition. As Bob interpreted Psalms 68:31, the lifting of Ethiopia's hand to God was no longer prophecy, but fulfillment. For Rastas, the "God within" reappeared in their own image to assist in the rebirth of a new world. The beauty of this legacy is that the representer and the representation of this God took a form in which all "races" could see themselves.[186]

For this, I say: "Thank you Bob. Want you to know, I am a rainbow too."

Afterthoughts: "integrative ancestors" for the future

> The wolf shall dwell with the lamb
> ... and a little child shall lead them.   (Isaiah 11:6)

It would be expected that as the author, I should try to draw some conclusions about this study of the "new culture" of Bob Marley, Ralph Ellison, and Frederick Douglass. I would like to challenge my readers to shift gears with me now while I attempt, in a more personal voice, a tentative summing up. I ask you to think along with me for a few pages without footnotes, in a more reflective mode, about how the issues that have been raised here might appear to a reader (or a nonreader) of a future generation.

In the preface, I posed something of a rhetorical question which has guided this project. If educators and political leaders treated figures such as Douglass, Ellison, and Marley as "integrative ancestors" who could be "claimed" by members of several ethno-racial groups, would this help us to envision how commonality and difference could coexist? Could such "integrative ancestors" give us some of the tools we need to construct a "multiracial democracy," or to see ourselves as co-creators of a "new culture" which was moving beyond the language of race?

Having contemplated variants of these questions for most of two decades, I have grown suspicious of sweeping generalizations. In a sense, my conclusions are inherent in the details of this "map." It is a *way of seeing* that I have suggested: a corrective to a blindness regarding our previously repressed or denied interracial heritage. Whether the reader finds that this perspective is recovered vision, or just projected desire, to a degree is in the details of the map itself. Yet in such a politicized domain, things are never so simple. This book also requires an effort at mutual imagining. So I am at the mercy of the reader: the degree to which he or she finds my account persuasive depends, first, on whether it has resonance in his or her own life experiences. And beyond that, whether or not my version of our-story rings true also depends on the reader's relative willingness to

221

take a "leap of faith" – to look at the world, at least briefly, without the blinders of racial mythology. In the final analysis, this involves an issue of trust: the reader must find the author a relatively trustworthy observer, if he or she is to look beyond the messenger to the message.

I remain convinced that, more than ever, these "big questions" are worth asking: "how do we build a multiracial democracy?" Or, "what kind of language do we need to build multi-ethnic coalitions?" And, "what cultural resources can we give our children to prepare them for the future?" We don't have a blueprint for these challenges. But the questions themselves serve as a horizon towards which it is important to orient ourselves. Douglass, Ellison, and Marley all believed that it was impossible to prepare for the future without having a thorough knowledge of the past. I obviously agree. Yet adhere to a sort of motto: don't forget your history, but don't get stuck in the rear-view mirror.

It is humbling to realize that the very language we choose to discuss the problems of the present may prevent us communicating with those of the future who – truth be told – would probably value a bit more clear thinking on our part, about how we created the various crises we have left for them to face. The crisis of "race" is just one of these messes. In the long run, I have to think that it really is a decoy.

I began writing the first version of this book shortly after my first child, Sela, came into this world. And I am completing it as she turns four. During the various revisions, I have often wondered if it were possible to write in a fashion that Sela would be able to understand, after she entered college around 2012. This may be just "entertaining a fantasy": engaging in contemporary theoretical or political debates, for instance, often requires a language that is incompatible with a college student of my own era, much less the future. Still, I have struggled with this idea throughout. If I am writing about the history of a multiracial community, or an interracial culture, then I also ought to be trying to make visible the relevance of this "story" to the offspring and the inheritors of that community and culture.

The thought of writing something that would one day be of value to my children has not been entirely self-willed. Because some of the "culture heroes" of this book are already a part of Sela's imagination, and she is already revising their stories, and asking for my feedback on these revisions.

As I mentioned in the Introduction, I have had life-sized portraits of Douglass and Marley above my desk ever since Sela was born. I wanted her to grow up surrounded with images of people who look like her. I wanted her to see that her cultural heritage is shared by both her mother and father. As I wrote earlier, by the time Sela was one, she was already speaking to these portraits, calling them "abuelo Fred" and "tio Bob," just as with her child's imagination, she spoke to other objects throughout the house – Mexican masks, pictures of her grandparents and cousins, etc.

I never explained to Sela anything about her "grandfather Frederick" or her "uncle Bob," other than that I was writing a book about them. (Although we have danced to Marley's music since she was an infant.) But around the time that she turned three, Sela suddenly "wrote" her own story about Frederick Douglass and Bob Marley, which she has repeated to me many times since. She began asking me, eventually, to repeat it back to her. Then she seemed to get the idea that this story existed somewhere outside of her: she would point to a book in my bookshelf, and ask if her story about Bob and Frederick was in there. Finally, she asked me if I was going to put her story in my own book. I told her that I would. It actually seemed like a good way to think about what different roles these "integrative ancestors" might play for their descendants in the future. I recount this story first in the language Sela used, Spanish, and then translate it to English.

Sela's Frederick Douglass and Bob Marley Story

Frederick Douglass y Bob Marley caminaban juntos en el camino. Frederick se convirtió en una estrella y Bob se transformó en un león. Un fantasma atacó a Frederick Douglass pero Bob Marley le salvó.

[*Frederick Douglass and Bob Marley were walking down a path together. Frederick transformed into a star and Bob changed into a lion. A ghost or an evil spirit attacked Frederick Douglass, but Bob Marley came to his rescue.*]

At first, as an adult, I wanted to know more. But when I asked her where the *fantasma* came from, she told me: "mi corazón no quiere hablar." Literally: my heart doesn't want to talk, which is what she tells me when she doesn't want to analyze something.

Well, out of the mouths of babes come some amazing things.

There was no way that a three-year-old could have known that the *North Star* was the name of Douglass' first paper. Nor could she have known about the great significance of the Lion of Judah in the music of Marley and the Rastas.

Sela most likely plucked these symbols, not from a *collective unconscious*, but from the cultural resources that her Mom and Dad put at her disposal. Sela's favorite story during her third year was *El Rey León*, or, The Lion King, which we read countless times in Spanish, and watched on video in both Spanish and English. In one scene, Simba, still a cub, asks his father Mufasa, the Lion King, if they would always be together.

Mufasa says that one day he will have to die, but that he will live on in the stars, always there to guide him. And after he has grown, Simba imagines that he sees Mufasa in the sky, and hears him calling him to remember who he is – to accept his destiny. Sela was full of questions about this scene, trying to comprehend the meaning of death. She seems to have come to understand my explanation that Mufasa lived inside of Simba, in his imagination, in his memory. She wanted to be constantly reassured that I also would always live inside of her. And she seemed to project these concerns into her little fable of the transformations of Frederick Douglass and Bob Marley.

One of Sela's other favorite books during her third year was *Follow the Drinking Gourd*, by Jeanette Winter (Knopf, 1988). This being in English, she read it with her mother, in fact requested it so often that we eventually had to hide it. She also watched the video version, which is narrated by Morgan Freeman, with music by Taj Mahal. This is a touching fable of the underground railroad, in which slaves are guided to freedom by the "drinking gourd" – the Big Dipper, whose cup points towards the North Star.

Teaching any child about the history of race relations is a daunting challenge. There are perhaps some unique dynamics for interracial families. My determination to present Douglass and Marley as "integrative ancestors" to Sela has had consequences I had not anticipated. During Sela's third year, she developed a deep interest in slavery, in variations of skin color, and in how skin color and slavery are connected. As an abolitionist parable, the *Drinking Gourd* is a tale that I, an "Irish-American" parent, find easy to identify with. Most of the "white" characters are sympathetic. Center stage is shared by Peg Leg Joe, a carpenter who travels from plantation to plantation teaching slaves a "freedom song," and by a family of escaping slaves. There are Quaker families who house the fleeing slaves, and a white boy who brings them food. Yet this is not what Sela fastened on. What fascinated and troubled her was the picture of a white overseer holding a whip, standing over slaves picking cotton. "Do all white people whip dark people?" she wanted to know.

Sela's library is filled with books about interracial families, "brown" families from Latin America, and varieties of skin color from the world over. But what drew her imagination, as she began to read stories about slavery, was an association of whiteness with cruelty. We bought her a "beginning biography" called *Frederick Douglass: Freedom Fighter* by Garnet Nelson Jackson (Cleveland: Modern Curriculum Press, 1993). Again, there are positive images of interraciality here – white children helping young Frederick learn how to read. But after Sela heard a line about Captain Anthony punishing slaves, her questions were: "Does Dad own slaves?" And, "white people are bad, right mom?"

Sela's images of white people as bad, I began to realize, came from many sources – from *Pocahontas*, for instance, which despite being a Disney film, has a strong anticolonial message, and which made it clear that "white men are dangerous." By contrast, contrary to conventional wisdom, I have found that with a little selective editing, it has been very easy to give Sela a very positive image of "black" and "brown" people. The real problem continues to be with a white/nonwhite binary, which is so deeply embedded in the culture that I have found it impossible to escape. I can only try to ameliorate it: I can hold my hand to a piece of white paper, to demonstrate the difference between the color white, and our concept of "whiteness." And I can show her the contrast between her mother's skin, and the black couch, to illustrate the difference between the color black and "blackness." By this means, I try to teach her that most if not all skin colors are really different shades of brown. And I hope that she will grow into an understanding of "the true interrelatedness of blackness and whiteness."

I think this story sheds light on my earlier question: what cultural resources can we give our children to prepare them for the future? For my academic peers, a Disney film would typically come under criticism for perpetuating negative "mainstream" values, while the story of Frederick Douglass would generally be placed in a "black box," as an example of resistance to this mainstream. But in my child's imagination, Disney and Douglass are not so easily separated into a "center" and a "margin." I think that the way in which she has fused themes from several sources shows that the world of a Disney cartoon and the backdrop of a deeper cultural history do not have to be mutually exclusive.

I have also recounted this story because I felt it said something about how differently the "integrative ancestors" I have presented in this book might speak to someone in the future. I feel certain that Douglass, Marley, and probably later Ralph Ellison, will continue to speak to Sela. But I have no idea what she will draw from them, what form her own vision will take.

Listening to Sela's questions about slavery, and about white people, I found myself thinking about the balances involved in trying to teach this history. How do you teach a child about the injustices of slavery, without painting all whites as being guilty of the atrocities of this system, or portraying all blacks as its victims? Is it possible to teach this history without forwarding the tendency to think in black and white, or divide the world between whites and "people of color?" When I hear questions about slavery and its legacy, from either my child, or my students, I have two thoughts. I think that it must be important to know that, at the height of slavery, only 10 percent of whites were slaveholders. And I simultaneously think of the voices of students I have heard at Berkeley, who said that they did not want some white teacher trying to tell them that things were really not so bad, after all. So, I know that there is no correct way of telling this integrative history. And I know that, in this era, it is usually not possible to separate the message from the messenger.

As both a parent and an educator, I am committed to synthesis, to striking a balance. As much as I want my children to know about slavery and racial discrimination, I feel it is equally important to let them know about resistance to race prejudice – and that people of all colors took part in this resistance. Surprising contradictions of the underground. I don't think the importance of either historical truth-telling, nor the importance of having positive models to emulate, can be overestimated. Another parent will want to focus on the brutality of slavery, and will not feel that it is important (or even possible) to give their children an image of whites other than "oppressor." Many more parents will not teach their children anything about slavery, or imperialism, whatsoever. What differences will this make in our respective children's attitudes about "race," and how they treat each other, when they later sit in the same classrooms, and compete for the same jobs? More big questions with no easy answers.

I have tried to present this map of the "new culture" of racial frontiers as one available worldview: not as the right choice, but an important perspective that I believe needs to be included in the mix. Both the "frightful wrongs" and the "great and beautiful things" that individuals and nations have done need to be remembered, Du Bois said. More simply, Bob Marley's words always echo in my ears: "tell the children the truth." Tell them the truth, "so far as the truth is ascertainable," in the words of Du Bois. Where "race" is concerned, I firmly believe that we need to give our children multiple perspectives, and then allow them to maintain multiple allegiances. We should give them the freedom to choose not to choose, should this be their choice. Such a freedom will require institutional recognition of multiracial formations. This is one policy-oriented recommendation I would be willing to make, at this moment, on the strength of the research I have undertaken in this book.

By way of leave-taking, I would like borrow Sela's image of Frederick Douglass and Bob Marley walking down the road together, toward the future, I presume. They change form, reappearing in a new face or form. They sometimes suffer attacks, and help each other out in moments of crisis. At the crossroads, they encounter Ralph Ellison. Like old friends, the three of them pick up on an old conversation that has no end. We listen in from time to time, and on the lower frequencies, they still speak to you and me. They have become a part of we.

Acknowledgments

This book is at root an outgrowth of my experiences in the music business in Austin, Texas, during the 1980s. The first-hand experience of living and working among the multi-ethnic audiences of popular cultures gave me a "grounding" which sustained me through the arduous resocializing process of graduate school. Two of my best friends in AusTex, Ron Johnson (alias DJ RJ) and Jay Trachtenberg, threw me a lifeline in the form of countless tapes of their radio shows on KUT and KAZI, during which they pumped up "bass culture" for the AusTex massive. They both brought back priceless treasures from Jamaica which have given me great entertainment, invaluable source material, and a moral compass. Jay gave me the journalistic assignment, back in 1982, which led to my songwriting career, and RJ has been my brother and musical alter ego since 1987. Respect to the maximum!

Thanks also to the many DJs from around the globe who have helped keep me semi-current: a-foreign, Danny "Pepperseed" Bouten for his marvelous "Dancehall Vibes" in The Netherlands; J. Moenen of "Reggae Vibes," and Jan-Allard Hummel (Souljah), also in Holland; Jess-I (Jesse Nonneman), "Chant Down Babylon," in Melbourne, Australia; Simon UK, "The Bassline," bridging London and Boston; in North America: Joshua B of WRBB and Heartbeat Records in Boston; Steve Radzi, "Reggae Beat East," WDNA, Miami; the deep roots of Robert Nelson on KRCL in Salt Lake City, and Papa Pilgrim's tireless promotion of Reggae Ambassadors Worldwide, also based in Salt Lake; StarCat (Larry Jones), for countless samples of Los Angeles radio; Daniel Frankston in San Francisco; Michael Rose and his dubwise "Echo Chamber" on KFAI in Minneapolis; "Ras" Adam Felleman in Syracuse and Michael Kuelker in St. Louis for Jamaican "talk radio"; Charles Fuller at Duke; Jah Nile (Rene Joseph Militello) in Lutz, Florida, and Michael DeGraf in Champaign, Illinois, both teenagers at this writing, for Marley tapes. A salute to Jerry Stevens of Root 1, songwriter extraordinaire and longtime friend in Austin. Heartfelt thanks to DJ, author, and Marley archivist Roger "Rojah" Steffens for support and guidance beyond the call of duty.

227

The following people at the University of California-San Diego tried to redirect this songwriter and journalist into an academic career. I am in debt to Michael Schudson of the Sociology and Communication Departments, who nurtured this project from an early stage. As dissertation cochair, he provided a rare combination of constructive criticism and contagious enthusiasm. Helene Keyssar, my other cochair, rescued me from the scrap heap of the Communication Department. The immediate genesis for this project came from a reading of Ellison which I did for her Culture seminar in the spring of 1993. Mike Cole held up the concept of "mediation" as a horizon which became a cornerstone of my thinking. Marta Sanchez in Literature provided a space within which to think about a "third space." Christine Hunefeldt in History dissected an early draft of eighteenth- and nineteenth-century material, and exposed me to a number of parallel "racial formations" in Latin America.

Portions of chapter 2 first appeared in a different form in *Communication Studies* 48:3 (Fall 1997). Thanks to Robert Levine for his reading of the Douglass chapter, and to William McFeely and John Callahan for encouraging words. The anonymous readers at Cambridge pushed me to clarify my terminology, and re-envision my intended audience. An earlier set of readers at Oxford UP also made important suggestions. I would like to express my gratitude to Catherine Max, my editor at Cambridge, for her steady long-distance dialogue through the wonders of e-mail and to her successor Elizabeth Howard, for stepping in to gracefully "ride herd" in the home stretch. Special thanks to my copy-editor Linda Randall for her remarkable attention to detail.

A tip of the hat to Maricia Battle for assistance in securing photos of Ellison; to Kim Gottlieb-Walker, for coming through in the clutch with lovely shots of Nesta Marley; to Valeria, for computer doctoring, and to Bea Velasco, for helping keep me afloat. Love and respect to my parents, Farrell Vernon and Rita Carol Stephens, for all the Bible stories which prepared me for Douglass and Marley, and for their encouragement during the long period of poverty in which this book was conceived and written.

Notes

PREFACE

1 Hollie West, "Ellison: Exploring the Life of a Not So Visible Man," *Washington Post*, Aug. 19–21, 1973, reprinted in *Conversations with Ralph Ellison*, ed. Maryemma Graham and Amritjit Singh (Jackson: University Press of Mississippi, 1995), 235. "Real revolutionaries": Marley's song "Zimbabwe." Marley's comments on "going soft" and his different approaches to different audiences are discussed at length in chapter 4. "On paper": *Frederick Douglass' Paper*, May 27, 1852, quoted in Robert Levine, *Martin Delany, Frederick Douglass, and the Politics of Representive Identity* (Chapel Hill: University of North Carolina Press, 1997), 79.

2 In a similar vein, John Edward Philips insists that "pride in their African heritage is something that white children should be taught along with blacks," and that "African culture among whites should not be treated as just an addendum to studies of blacks but must be included in the general curriculum of American studies": "The African Heritage of White America," in *Africanisms in American Culture*, ed. Joseph Holloway (Bloomington: Indiana University Press, 1990), 225–39.

3 Werner Sollors, *Beyond Ethnicity* (Oxford University Press, 1986), 263. Eric Hobsbawm and Terence Ranger, eds., *The Invention of Tradition* (Cambridge University Press, 1983).

4 This concept is discussed at length in chapter 1 of Gregory Stephens, "On Racial Frontiers" (PhD dissertation, University of California-San Diego, 1996).

5 "One repays a teacher badly if one remains only a pupil": Nietzsche, *Also Sprach Zarathustra*, part 1, sec. 3. *The Freud/Jung Letters*, ed. William McGuire (Princeton University Press, 1974), 491.

INTRODUCTION: THE CONTEMPORARY REAR-VIEW MIRROR

1 That is, a tradition "hidden" from our view, or previously invisible, until a new generation looks at cultural history through "new eyes." I owe this insight to an anonymous Cambridge reader, who draws a parallel to "the hidden tradition of black feminist thinking from Sojourner Truth to Anna Cooper to Audrey Lourde – a tradition that appears once the evidence for it is called to attention as it has been since the late 1980s." Nell Irvin Painter's biography *Sojourner Truth* (New York: Norton, 1996) illustrates many points of intersection be-

tween that tradition and my own study – specifically with Frederick Douglass' work on behalf of women's rights. For an overview of the black feminist tradition, in explicit opposition to the *"Driving Miss Daisy* syndrome" of white feminists, and their inexplicable fixation on Lacan and Freud, see Ann duCille, "The Occult of True Black Womanhood: Critical Demeanor and Black Feminist Studies," in *Female Subjects in Black and White,* ed. Elizabeth Abel, Barbara Christian, and Helene Moglen (Berkeley: University California Press, 1997), 21–56.

2 "Justification": Loring Brace, University of Michigan, speaking at AAS conference, Feb. 20, 1995, quoted *Los Angeles Times* editorial, Feb. 22, 1995. Census: *COSSA Washington Update,* Sept. 29, 1997. Kwame Anthony Appiah, "The Illusion of Race," from *In My Father's House* (New York: Oxford University Press, 1993), 37. Understanding the persistence of racialism requires us to "acknowledge that the categories of the imagination have a historical, cultural and ethnic dimension." Michael Vannoy Adams, *The Multicultural Imagination* (London: Routledge, 1996), 45–6. Adams tries to synthesize the work of Jung and Freud regarding the power of largely unconscious psychological structures in maintaining racialist patterns of thought. What Jung referred to as archetypal patterns or "categories of the *imagination*" (*Psychology and Religion* [Princeton University Press, 1958/1969], *Collected Works,* XI, 517–18), Freud calls *schema.* His perspective is quite "Jungian" in this regard, as when he comments: "We are often able to see the schema triumphing over the experience of the individual" (*Standard Edition of the Complete Psychological Works of Sigmund Freud* [London: Hogarth Press, 1974], XVII, 119). "Race" is a schema or imaginative category which trumps individual experience. Diminishing its power over us requires us to call into question the legitimacy of the binary categories on which it is based: black vs. white, etc.

"Ethno-racial pentagon": David Hollinger, *Postethnic America* (New York: Basic Books, 1995). I refer not only to institutional support of racial categories, but to the ever-more elaborate justifications of racialism (as practiced by nonwhites) as a form of "strategic essentialism." For a primer, see Diana Fuss, *Essentially Speaking* (London: Routledge, 1989). The usually clear-headed Paul Gilroy endorses an "anti-anti-essentialist" position in *The Black Atlantic* (Cambridge: Harvard University Press, 1993). Still, I understand the context against which Gilroy is reacting. In a piece on the intersections of US and British Cultural Studies, Manthia Diawara writes: "The anti-essentialism of this cultural studies has become an essentialism of its own kind": "Black Studies, Cultural Studies, Performative Acts," in *Race Identity and Representation in Education,* ed. Cameron McCarthy and Warren Crichlow (London: Routledge, 1993), 264.

3 The distinction between "his-story" – usually interpreted as the history of white males – and "our-story" was a pervasive trope in the early 1990s rap, and was also used during the 1980s by Gil Scott-Heron. I discuss rap's revisioning of his-story in "Interracial Dialogue in Rap Music: Call-and-Response in a Multicultural Style," *New Formations* 16 (Spring 1992).

Cycles: see William W. Freehling, *The Reintegration of American History* (New York: Oxford University Press, 1994). See also Thomas Bender, "Whole and Parts: The Need for Synthesis in American History," *Journal of American*

History 73 (June 1986). Much current history is a reaction against earlier Eurocentric whitewashing. This is a historically necessary corrective process, but such my-stories often do not move beyond the stage of reinscribing the histories of "marginalized" groups as if they existed in opposition to a center which continues to be defined in Eurocentric, patriarchal terms.

4 I have not referenced much of the burgeoning scholarship on "whiteness" and "white privilege" in my book as most of the people writing in this domain do not seem attentive to interracial and intersubjective dynamics. My own perspective is closest to that of Howard Winant, who questions the logic of calls for "the abolition of the white race." Although Winant values some of the historical and social constructionist work of "The New Abolitionist Racial Project," he has critiqued its reactionary stances. "Is the social construction of whiteness so flimsy that it can be repudiated by a mere act of political will, or even by widespread and repeated acts aimed at rejecting white privilege?" he asks. Winant argues that "rather than trying to repudiate [whiteness], we shall have to rearticulate it." Taking a position quite similar to that of Ralph Ellison, he stresses that "whiteness is a relational concept, unintelligible without reference to nonwhiteness." My own work illustrates Winant's observation that "rearticulation (or reinterpretation, or deconstruction) of whiteness can begin relatively easily . . . with the recognition that whiteness *already* contains substantial nonwhite elements." Howard Winant, "Behind Blue Eyes: Whiteness and Contemporary U.S. Racial Politics," in *Off White: Readings on Race, Power, and Society*, ed. Michelle Fine *et al.*, (London: Routledge, 1997), 48.

5 "Irishman": William S. McFeely, *Frederick Douglass* (New York: Norton, 1991), 280. "Cultivation of race": Waldo Martin, "Frederick Douglass: Humanist as Race Leader," in *Black Leaders of the Nineteenth Century*, ed. Leon Litwack and August Meier (University of Illinois Press, 1988), 82.

6 "Inter-relatedness": Ralph Ellison, "Change the Joke and Slip the Yoke," *Partisan Review* 25 (Spring 1958), reprinted in *Shadow and Act* (New York: New American Library, 1966), and *The Collected Essays of Ralph Ellison*, ed. with an Introduction by John F. Callahan (New York: Modern Library, 1995), 107. Albert Murray, *The Omni-Americans* (New York: Dutton, 1970), 112. Ellison typically conceived of vernacular culture as *both* black and *interracial*. After citing Ellison's passage in *Invisible Man* about residents of racial frontiers who are "running and dodging the forces of history," W. T. Lhamon Jr. notes: "Vernacular culture circulates and survives like weed seeds. It obeys no boundaries": *Raising Cain* (Cambridge, MA, and London: Harvard University Press, 1998), 64.

7 "God's side": *Time Will Tell* (Island, dir. Declan Lowney, 1991). "Songs of Freedom," a phrase from "Redemption Song," is the title of a Marley box set and book: *Songs of Freedom: From "Judge Not" to "Redemption Song,"* compiled by Trevor Wyatt and Neville Garrick (Tuff Gong/Island, 1992); Adrian Boot and Chris Salewicz, *Bob Marley: Songs of Freedom* (New York: Viking, 1995).

8 I use the designation Afro-American, rather than African-American, because it seems more inclusive of "Black Atlantic" cultures, and less chained to a specifically United States context. I also find Orlando Bagwell's point of view persuasive: "Afro-Americans are not Africans; they are among the most American of Americans, and the emphasis on their Africanness is both physically

inappropriate and culturally misleading. Furthermore, in light of increasing immigration of Africans from Africa to the U.S., it is best to reserve the term *African Americans* to describe this group": *The Ordeal of Integration* (Washington, DC: Civitas/Counterpoint, 1997), xi.

Four examples of early, mid-, and late twentieth century use of "biracial" to indicate a binary construction: Alain LeRoy Locke, *Race Contacts and Interracial Relations*, ed. Jeffrey C. Stewart (Washington, DC: Howard University Press, 1992; lectures delivered in 1916), 77; E. Franklin Frazier, *Race and Culture Contacts in the Modern World* (New York: Knopf, 1957); Joel Williamson, *New People* (New York: Free Press, 1980), 3, 87; Thomas Skidmore, "Racial Ideas and Social Policy in Brazil, 1870–1940," in *The Idea of Race in Latin America, 1870–1940*, ed. Richard Graham (Austin: University of Texas Press, 1990), 7. Frazier's work illustrates how biracial signified white dominance at mid-century: "When one studies the actual method of operation of a *biracial organization*, it is apparent that equality does not and cannot exist between white and colored people. [W]herever a biracial organization exists, there are discriminations in favor of the whites" (285), my emphasis.

9   "New cultures": Frazier, *Race and Culture Contacts*, 322, my emphasis. For similar uses of "new culture" from an anthropological perspective, see Charles Joyner, "Creolization," in *Encyclopedia of Southern Culture*, ed. Charles Reagan Wilson (Chapel Hill: University of North Carolina Press, 1989), 147–49; Sidney W. Mintz and Richard Price, *The Birth of African-American Culture* (Boston: Beacon, 1992), ix, *passim*. See also Lhamon, *Raising Cain*, 36, 72, on how interracial working-class interactions in the "Atlantic world" of 1825–50 spawned a "new blend." A summary of how Park's theories of racial contact influenced a new generation is R. Fred Wacker, "The Sociology of Race and Ethnicity in the Second Chicago School," in *A Second Chicago School? The Development of a Postwar American Sociology*, ed. Gary Alan Fine (University of Chicago Press, 1995), 136–63.

Mary Louise Pratt, "Criticism in the Contact Zone: Decentering Community and Nation," in *Critical Theory, Cultural Politics, and Latin American Narrative*, ed. Steven Bell *et al.* (University of Notre Dame Press, 1993). Pratt's theory of "contact zones," very different from Park's usage and mine, is discussed in chapter 1.

10 Eric Sundquist, *To Wake the Nations* (Cambridge: Belknap/Harvard, 1993), 9. Mestizo: Spanish anthropologist Claudio Esteva-Fabregat provides a hemispheric, historical overview in *Mestizaje in Ibero-America* (Tucson: University of Arizona, 1995).

11 Herder quoted in Gustav Jahoda, *Crossroads Between Culture and Mind: Continuities and Change in Theories of Human Nature* (Cambridge: Harvard University Press, 1993), 78.

12 John 1:14. The idea of "imagined communities" has been given its most influential rendering, of course, in Benedict Anderson's classic *Imagined Communities* (London: Verso, 1983/1991).

13 "Antagonistic cooperation": Ralph Ellison's phrase, originally applied to Irving Howe, at the end of the essay "The World and the Jug," in *Collected Essays*, 188. "Interracial dynamics": George Hutchinson, *The Harlem Renais-*

sance in Black and White (Cambridge, MA, and London: Belknap/ Harvard University Press, 1995/1997), 20.

My critique of the reactionary racial mythology in Spike Lee's film *Jungle Fever* appears in "Romancing the Racial Frontier: Mediating Symbols in Cinematic Interracial Representations," *Spectator* 16:1 (Fall/Winter 1995/ 1996), and a longer version in "On Racial Frontiers.: The Communicative Culture of Multiracial Audiences" (Dissertation, University of California-San Diego, 1996).

14 Michael Omi and Howard Winant, *Racial Formations in the United States* (New York and London: Routledge, 1986/1984). Omi and Winant use the concept of "racial formations" to demonstrate, among other things, how "racism" exists without "race." Whether or not individuals carry forward racist attitudes, they often participate in institutions which perpetuate racial inequality because preexisting racialized attitudes prestructure their mode of operation. Such is the force of our binary racial mythology that none of the many scholars who have adopted this concept, to my knowledge, balance it with the idea of "multiracial formations." Lhamon's *Raising Cain* is part of a growing body of scholarship which points to the deep historical roots of multiracial formations. For instance, regarding the early nineteenth century, he notes: "The marking of race was more observed by authorities than practised ... blacks and whites were clearly contracting intimate knowledge of each other ... Then as now, the ordinary people of these streets were attracted to one another well across 'race,' despite the fictions to which their doctors subscribed": *Raising Cain*, 19.

I have adapted the concept of multicentered public spheres from Craig Calhoun (ed.), *Habermas and the Public Sphere* (Cambridge: MIT Press, 1992). Especially useful re: "overlapping spheres" were Nancy Fraser's essay "Rethinking the Public Sphere" and Nicholas Garnham, "The Media and the Public Sphere," in ibid. See also *The Black Public Sphere* (University of Chicago Press, 1995).

15 Paul Gilroy, *Small Acts* (London: Serpent's Tail, 1993), 9.

16 "Allow": I am signifying here on Gloria Anzaldúa, who tells her fellow "women and men of color [who] do not want to have any dealings with white people": "I think we need to allow whites to be our allies." *Borderlands/La Frontera* (San Francisco: Spinsters/Aunt Lute Book Company, 1987), 85.

17 As Gayatri Spivak emphasizes, obsessive opposition to a European "other" or center in fact only serves to "reify" Euro-centric norms. *The Post-Colonial Critic* (London: Routledge, 1990).

18 "Angela Davis, a woman like that who defends something; me can appreciate that." This was Bob's answer when asked, after some sexist comments, if he admired any women. Stephen Davis, *Bob Marley* (Rochester, VA: Schenkman, 1990), 152. Davis' speech at the University of California-San Diego, Spring 1993, my emphasis. Angela Yvonne Davis, *Women, Race & Class* (New York: Random House, 1981).

19 David Hackett Fischer, *Historians' Fallacies* (New York: Harper, 1970), 3–39.
"Mental slavery": a line from Marley's "Redemption Songs."

20 Students have essentially racialized a utopian strain of oppositional thinking in cultural studies which has been in evidence since the beginnings of the

Frankfurt School. Scholars of audience studies have described a rather pervasive "fetishism of 'resistance'." Todd Gitlin, "The Politics of Communication and the Communication of Politics," in *Mass Media and Society*, ed. James Curran and Michael Gurevitch (London: Edward Arnold, 1991), 337. See also David Morley, *Television, Audiences and Cultural Studies* (London: Routledge, 1992), esp. 26–33 for a critique of the romance of "oppositional decodings."

21 Toni Morrison, "Unspeakable Things Unspoken: The Afro-American Presence in American Literature," *Michigan Quarterly Review* 28 (1989), 3. This is a familiar form of "racial censorship" since the 1960s. Hutchinson believes that recent attacks on Franz Boas, an influential antiracist anthropologist in the early twentieth century, "can be attributed to his choosing to attack the color line without being black himself": *Harlem Renaissance in Black and White*, 70. Morrison's view elides the extent to which racial categories have been a co-construction, first institutionalized by whites, but increasingly upheld by blacks. See Celeste Michelle Condit and John Louis Lucaites, F. James Davis, Wilson Jeremiah Moses, and David Hollinger (full citations in "Select bibliography"). Nelson Mandela, *Long Walk to Freedom* (Boston: Little, Brown, 1994). Mandela uses both "multiracial democracy" and "nonracial democracy," which I take to be an acknowledgment of the need for two strategies: "multiracial democracy" being the possible short-term goal, and "nonracial democracy" being the conceivable long-term goal. Nonraciality, a cornerstone of the African National Congress' ideology since the early twentieth century, has increasingly been questioned even among ANC loyalists, after the first blush of the downfall of apartheid, as the enduring strength of racialized and tribal divisions becomes more apparent.

22 "Imperial democracy": I have adapted this from Octavio Paz, "Mexico and the United States," in *The Labyrinth of Solitude and Other Writings* (New York: Grove, 1985), 375. "In many ways, ethnicity has become a residual category for people to fall back on when other projects and loyalties are found wanting": John Hutchinson and Anthony D. Smith (eds.), "Introduction," *Ethnicity* (Oxford University Press, 1996), 13. I am sympathetic to but not entirely convinced by authors who see the nation-state as the alternative to racialized tribalism. Michael Schudson, "The 'Public Sphere' and Its Problems: Bringing the State (Back) In," *Notre Dame Journal of Law, Ethics and Public Policy* 8:2 (1994); David Hollinger, "National Culture and Communities of Descent," *Reviews in American History* 26 (1998), 312–28; Michael Lind, *The Next American Nation* (New York: Free Press, 1996).

"Hold your corner & stay alive / and that's no jive": a lyric from British reggae singer Barrington Levy's "Teach the Youth."

23 "Ideal speech community": Jurgen Habermas, *Legitimation Crisis* (Boston: Beacon, 1975). For applications of Habermas' concept to pluralistic contexts, see Calhoun (ed.), *Habermas and the Public Sphere*; Charles Taylor et al., *Multiculturalism* (Cambridge, MA: MIT, 1994); *The Black Public Sphere*.

"Multicentric": Guillermo Gomez-Peña, "The Multicultural Paradigm," *High Performance* (Fall 1989); reprinted in *Warrior for Gringostroika* (St. Paul, MN: Graywolf Press, 1993), 45–54.

24 "True Democracy": this is also the title of a classic album by the British reggae group Steel Pulse (Elektra, 1982). Their song "Rally Round" envisions *True Democracy* through the lense of Ethiopianism, and Biblical passages such as Psalms 137 and Psalms 68:31.

"Systems of survival": by this I mean a sustainable life-style, and a political culture centered on sustainability. See Herman E. Daly, *Steady-State Economics* (Washington, DC, and Covelo, CA: Island Press, 1991). "System of Survival" is also a classic song by Earth, Wind, and Fire.

25 KRS on Douglass in Joe Wood, "Act Like Ya Know," *Vibe*, Aug. 9, 1995. Clarence Thomas on Douglass in *New York Times* on the Web, July 30, 1998. Many Marley tributes appeared after his fiftieth birthdate in 1995. There have been jazz renditions (Charlie Hunter Quartet, *Natty Dread*), pop and soul remakes (*One Love – a Tribute to Bob Marley* – mostly British artists), ambient dub (*Dreams of Freedom*, Island, prod. by Bill Laswell), jungle deconstructions, etc. Perhaps even more remarkable is the extent to which the riddims to Marley's songs are now being recycled in contemporary Jamaican "dancehall reggae." There must have been close to 100 songs released in 1996 which used the music to Marley's song "Heathen."

26 I was songwriter/manager for Austin-based singer Elouise Burrell. We won the 1984 Austin Music Umbrella Songwriting Competition; our band Trickle Down won the "Best New Band" award in the 1984–85 *Austin Chronicle* Music Poll. During the 1990s Burrell sang for the San Francisco Bay Area-based Amandla Poets.

27 Esteva-Fabregat, *Mestizaje in Ibero-America*. For a critique of celebrations of *mestizaje*, see Ernst Rudin, "New Mestizos: Traces of a Quincentenary Miracle in Old World Spanish and New World English," in *Cultural Difference and the Literary Text: Pluralism and the Limits of Authenticity in North American Literatures* (Iowa City: University of Iowa Press, 1996), ed. Winfried Siemerling and Katrin Schwenk (Iowa City: University of Iowa Press, 1996), 112–29.

28 "The so-called dominant culture is no longer dominant. Dominant culture is a meta-reality that only exists in the virtual space of the mainstream media and in the ideologically and aesthetically controlled spaces of the more established cultural institutions": Gomez-Peña, "The Multicultural Paradigm," 21.

29 The most relevant example of a use of the self-reflexive method, for my purposes, is Katya Givel Azoulay, *Black, Jewish, and Interracial* (Durham, NC: Duke University Press, 1997). The author is herself born to black and Jewish parents, which understandably provides both additional opportunities for informants, and insightful commentary. A good starting point on self-reflexive ethnography is *Writing Culture: The Poetics and Politics of Ethnography*, ed. James Clifford and George Marcus (Berkeley: University of California Press, 1986).

For a fascinating look at the deeper roots of self-reflexive ethnography, and an analysis of the links between fieldwork and cultural studies, see Gareth Stanton, "Ethnography, Anthropology and Cultural Studies: Links and Connections," in *Cultural Studies and Communications*, ed. James Curran, David Morley, and Valerie Walkerdine (London and New York: Arnold/St. Martin's, 1996), 334–58. Stanton's essay centers on what he sees as a transitional work between anthropology and cultural studies: Tom Harrison's *Savage Civilization* (London: Victor Gallancz, 1937).

I studied ethnographic writing under Smadar Lavie in the Anthropology Department, University of California-Davis, 1991–92, and participant observation under Mike Cole, University of California-San Diego, 1994.

On the importance of factoring subject positionality, see also Stuart Hall, "Culture, Media, and the 'Ideological Effect'," in *Mass Communication & Society*, ed. James Curran, Michael Gurevitch, and Janet Woollacott (Beverly Hills: Sage, 1979), 330.

30 I am thinking of *The Journey is the Destination: The Journals of Dan Eldon*, ed. Kathy Eldon (San Francisco: Chronicle Books, 1997). This remarkable multimedia document records the experiences of a young photographer whose worldview I would call "Afropean."

31 Talal Asad, "The Concept of Cultural Translation," in *Writing Culture*, ed. Clifford and Marcus, 156. Antonio Gramsci takes a similar approach in maintaining "contact with the simple" in the *Prison Notebooks* (New York: International Publishers, 1971), 330.

"Tell the children the truth": "Babylon System," *Survival*.

32 José Martí, "Gestación de Nuestra América," *Obras Completas*, II (La Habana, Cuba: Editorial Lex, 1946), 95–113. Martí mostly spent his adult life in New York, critiquing North American imperialism from within. Re Martí's use of "nuestra America" as both an oppositional, and a synthesizing concept, and for a critique of North America's perpetual assumption that "America" refers only to the United States, see José David Saldívar, *The Dialectics of Our America* (Durham, NC: Duke University Press, 1991), chapter 1.

33 Werner Sollors, *Neither Black nor White yet Both* (Oxford University Press, 1997), 62, 129.

34 "How black": Ellison, "Indivisible Man," in *Collected Essays*, 373. Robert Farris Thompson, "The Kongo Atlantic Tradition," lecture at the University of Texas, Austin, Feb. 28, 1992, quoted in Shelly Fisher Fishkin, *Was Huck Black?* (Oxford University Press, 1993), 132. Simon Frith, "Anglo-America and its Discontents," *Cultural Studies* 5:3 (Oct. 1991), 268.

C. Vann Woodward, "Clio with Soul," *Journal of American History* 1 (June 1969), 17. John Edward Philips, "The African Heritage of White America," in *Africanisms in American Culture*, ed. Joseph Holloway (Bloomington: Indiana University Press, 1990), 226.

For an excellent overview of some 100 pieces of recent scholarship that deal with themes of interraciality, see Shelley Fisher Fishkin, "Interrogating 'Whiteness,' Complicating 'Blackness': Remapping American Culture," *American Quarterly* 47:3 (Sept. 1995), 428–66. A longer version of this essay appears in *Criticism on the Color Line: Desegregating American Literary Studies*, ed. Henry Wonham (New Brunswick, NJ: Rutgers University Press, 1996).

1   INTERRACIALITY IN HISTORICAL CONTEXT: RETURN OF THE REPRESSED

1 Frederick Jackson Turner, "The Significance of the Frontier in American History," in *Early Writings of Frederick Jackson Turner*, ed. Everett Edwards and

Fulmer Mood (Madison, University of Wisconsin Press, 1938), 213. Staughton Lynd critiques Turner's view of slavery in *Class Conflict, Slavery, and the United States Constitution* (Indianapolis: Bobbs-Merrill, 1967). "Rendezvous model" and other revisionist frontier history: Patricia Nelson Limerick, *The Legacy of Conquest: The Unbroken Past of the American West* (New York: Norton, 1987); Richard White and Patricia Nelson Limerick, *The Frontier in American Culture*, ed. James Grossman (Chicago and Berkeley: Newberry Library and University of California Press, 1994); Richard Slotkin, *Gunfighter Nation: The Myth of the Frontier in 20th-Century America* (New York: Atheneum, 1992); Richard Slotkin, *Regeneration through Violence: The Mythology of the American Frontier, 1600–1860* (Middletown, CT: Wesleyan University Press, 1973). See also Richard Bernstein, "Unsettling the Old West," *New York Times Magazine*, Mar. 18, 1990.

John W. Cell, *The Highest Stage of White Supremacy* (Cambridge University Press, 1982), xiii. Howard Lamar and Leonard Thompson, *The Frontier in History* (New Haven: Yale University Press, 1981), 10.

2 Barbara Fields, "Ideology and Race in American History," in *Region, Race, and Reconstruction*, ed. J. Morgan Kousser and James M. McPherson (Oxford University Press, 1982), 143–77.

Samir Amin, *Eurocentrism* (New York: Monthly Review, 1989).

My discussion of the border-trespassing nature of discourses originating on racial frontiers has commonalities with the work of George Lipsitz. Even the most commercialized forms of culture have dual potentials, writes Lipsitz. They can erode "local knowledge or memory," but at the same time, they are capable of "bridging barriers of time, class, race, region, ethnicity, gender, and even nationality": *Time Passages: Collective Memory and American Popular Culture* (Minneapolis: University of Minnesota Press, 1990), 260–1.

One of the most compelling recent studies which traces the movement of interracial interaction from geographic to symbolic domains is Lhamon, *Raising Cain*. On the implications of symbolic interaction within electronically mediated domains: David Morley, *Television, Audiences and Cultural Studies* (London: Routledge, 1992), chapter 13, and J. Meyerowitz, *No Sense of Place* (Oxford University Press, 1985).

3 In Charles Chesnutt's 1900 novel *The House Behind the Cedars*, a mulatto character says: "You must take us for ourselves alone – we are new people." Joel Williamson uses this as the epigram of his study *New People*.

4 Anzaldúa, *Borderlands/La Frontera*, Preface and p. 80; Renato Rosaldo, *Culture and Truth* (Boston: Beacon, 1989); Saldívar, *The Dialectics of Our America*, and José David Saldívar, *Border Matters: Remapping American Cultural Studies* (Berkeley: University of California Press, 1997); Guillermo Gomez-Peña, *The New World Border* (San Francisco: City Lights, 1996); Gomez-Peña, *Warrior for Gringostroika*; Mary Louise Pratt, "Linguistic Utopias," in *The Linguistics of Writing*, ed. Nigel Fabb and Derek Attridge (New York: Methuen, 1987), 160–1.

"Interpenetration": Robert Park, *Race and Culture* (Glencoe, IL: Free Press, 1950), 373, my emphasis. "The interpenetration of . . . Euro-American and African-American . . . sectors poses one of the most . . . enigmatic questions to be weighed in examining the growth and character of so-called creole societies," Mintz and Price, *The Birth of African-American Culture*, 5.

While borders are thought of as a line in geographic space, frontiers are a more open-ended concept. (Borders in Spanish has a more elastic concept – *frontera* refers to a literal crossing line between nation-states, but also connotates a much more open-ended region. See Carlos Fuentes' treatment of borders-as-frontiers in *Gringo Viejo*.) And while borders usually have "official" sanction, frontiers often exist beyond state control. They are contested, fought over, and shared in a variety of ways. By situating interracial discourse on racial frontiers, I wish to retain the idea that racial "borders" are fluid. The expansion of racial frontiers can be seen as a liminal stage in which inhabitants of a community or region co-create a new culture with its own distinct linguistic practices. The concept of liminality, being in a state of transition between two worlds or two states of being, comes from Victor Turner's ethnographies and from Van Gennep's *Rites of Passage* (University of Chicago Press, 1960). A useful re-examination of the concept of liminality is in Dan Handelman, *Models and Mirrors: Towards an Anthropology of Public Events* (Cambridge University Press, 1990), 65ff. On Turner's elision in Cultural Studies, Donald Weber, "From Limen to Border: A Meditation on the Legacy of Victor Turner for American Cultural Studies," *American Quarterly* 47:3 (Sept. 1995), 525–36.

While residents of borders are *bilingual*, inhabitants of racial frontiers constitute an emergent *speech community*. Communication within racial frontiers cannot be understood without reference to "parent" cultures which have come into cooperation/conflict. But like a child, residents of racial frontiers are developing an identity distinct from their parents. In this sense, racial frontiers are less like borders or contact zones than a hybridized *region*, as with Paul Gilroy's *Black Atlantic*.

5 Locke, *Race Contacts*, and Leonard Harris (ed.), *The Philosophy of Alain Locke* (Philadelphia: Temple University Press, 1989), esp. chapters 14 and 19. Hutchinson, *Harlem Renaissance in Black and White*.

6 Park, "The Nature of Race Relations" (1939), in *Race and Culture*, 114. Seen "in the long historical perspective," twentieth-century race relations fusions appear "not merely unique but millennial" (116).

7 Everett Hughes and Helen Hughes, *Where Peoples Meet* (Glencoe, IL: Free Press, 1952), 19.

8 Frazier, *Race and Culture Contacts*, 314.

9 Michael Banton, *Racial Theories* (Cambridge University Press, 1987), 110. Herbert Blumer, "United States of America," *International Social Science Bulletin* 10 (1958), 403–47. Blumer was also trained in the "Chicago School" of Sociology co-founded by Park.

There are, of course, exceptions to the trend Banton notes. Jack Forbes, the long-time director of Native American Studies at the University of California-Davis, long ago noted that "the very essence of a frontier is the interaction of two or more peoples... Therefore, frontier studies must properly focus their attention upon interethnic behavior and problems arising therefrom": "Frontiers in American History and the Role of the Frontier Historian," *Ethnohistory* 15 (Spring 1963), 203–35. Forbes follows Hughes' paradigm (although it cannot be said that he bypasses the "prejudice–discrimination axis") in *Afri-*

cans and Native Americans: The Language of Race and the Evolution of Red-Black Peoples (Urbana: University of Illinois Press, 1993).

10 David Hollinger, *Postethnic America*, 169; Michael Rogin, *Blackface, White Noise: Jewish Immigrants in the Hollywood Melting Pot* (Berkeley: University of California Press, 1996), 37. Lott's best-known work, *Love and Theft* (Oxford University Press, 1993), is hardly an interracial utopia. Rogin's comment is clearly of the "I'm more hard-boiled than you" variety. This seems to be the inverse of black rappers calling each other "a white boy's hero" (Stephens, "Interracial Dialogue in Rap Music") – a competition or compulsion to prove oneself beyond the influence of, or unsusceptible to the longing for, interracial support or identification. Another manifestation of this phenomenon is critics accusing black writers of "being enthralled to white values," which, as Hutchinson observes, has been "a pervasive rhetorical ploy" among both black and white critics since the 1960s (*Harlem Renaissance in Black and White*, 20–1). All of these varieties of "the practice of scapegoating interracial dynamics that challenge the color line" reveal "a deeply institutionalized, and very American, cynicism about interracial relationships" (ibid., 20, 16). This phenomenon is also addressed in the Ellison chapter.

11 "the ideology of racial dualism and the resistance to interracial life ... are still more prevalent in the United States than are calls for hybridity": Werner Sollors, *Neither Black nor White yet Both*, 242.

Claims for the "permanence" of racism that infer a theory of white racism as a biological inheritance: following examples are from writers who are black, white, biracial, and Japanese-American, respectively: Derrick Bell, *Faces at the Bottom of the Well: The Permanence of Racism* (New York: Basic Books, 1992); Andrew Hacker, *Two Nations: Black and White, Separate, Hostile, Unequal* (New York: Scribner's, 1992); Lani Guinier, *The Tyranny of the Majority: Fundamental Fairness in Representational Democracy* (New York: Free Press, 1994); Mari Matsuda, "Public Response to Racist Speech: Considering the Victim's Story," in *Critical Race Theory, Assaultive Speech, & the First Amendment*, ed. Mari Matsuda, Charles Lawrence, Richard Delgado, and Kimberle Williams Crenshaw (Boulder: Westview Press, 1993).

For a reasoned critique of so-called critical race theorists which takes their claims seriously, see Henry Louis Gates, Jr., *et al.*, *Speaking of Race, Speaking of Sex: Hate Speech, Civil Rights, and Civil Liberties* (New York University Press, 1994).

12 Sollors, *Neither Black nor White yet Both*, 241. An example of this phenomenon is the fierce opposition among many black intellectuals to a "multiracial" census category. The logic employed often makes the threat of biraciality explicit: John Michael Spencer fears a multiracial category could "skim off" hundreds of thousands of black people, "steal black history," and so on: *The New Colored People* (New York University Press, 1997), 84, 89. In an interview with Katya Gibel Azoulay, an ethnographer of interraciality, Spencer claims that official recognition of multiracial identities would reinscribe "black" as a negative idea: *Black Jewish, and Interracial*, 7.

An antidote to this phobia about interraciality should focus primarily on cultural rather than biological miscegenation. I would point in particular to the work of Eric Sundquist, George Hutchinson, and Werner Sollors, who have written massive (and masterly) studies of the pervasive extent to which not only "black literature," but also much of the best of American literature and philosophy, is rooted in interracial contexts, and more generally, in racial ambiguity (Sundquist, *To Wake the Nations*; Hutchinson, *Harlem Renaissance in Black and White*; Sollors, *Neither Black nor White yet Both*). Their work should revolutionize the fields of literary and cultural studies. Sundquist and Shelly Fisher Fishkin, in another key work in this domain (*Was Huck Black?*), both say they are responding to Toni Morrison's call that readers become more aware of how central the Afro-American presence has been in "traditional" American literature: *Playing in the Dark* (Cambridge: Harvard University Press, 1992). The next step in this dialectical process, beyond tracing "white" influences on "black" culture, and "black" influences on "white" culture, is to move to synthesis – the study of interpenetrations. In this sense, Ralph Ellison is clearly the foundational model that Fishkin, Sundquist, Sollors, Hutchinson, and myself have all followed. Once this "true interrelatedness of blackness and whiteness" is understood (to repeat Ellison again), the fear of racial "theft" becomes less credible.

The most complete overview of recent scholarship on interraciality is Fishkin, "Interrogating 'Whiteness', Complicating 'Blackness'."

13 "From the 1920s to the 1940s there was a 'Copernican Revolution' in the way social scientists treated the concept of race," writes Michael Winston, in his foreword to Alain Locke's 1916 lectures on *Race Contacts*, ix. On the interracial networks in which Park, Locke, Boas, and other scholars of "race contacts" were situated, see Hutchinson, *Harlem Renaissance in Black and White*, chapters 1–3.

Frazier placed the "high stage" of attacks (verbal and physical) on Negroes from 1890 to 1915, although it should probably include the post-World War I race riots: *Race and Culture Contacts*. Cell, *The Highest Stage of White Supremacy*. But Frazier also places himself within a school of thought which recognizes that racism, and racialism, have passed through many distinct stages. Only historical amnesia (or the myopia induced by racial mythology) can allow observers to overgeneralize about its permanence and invariable characteristics. On the 1919 Chicago race riots, and the response from Park and his student Charles Johnson, see Martin Bulmer, *The Chicago School of Sociology* (University of Chicago Press, 1984), 64–88. Historian Rayford Logan called this era "The Nadir" of white racism: John Brace, Jr., August Meier, and Elliott Rudwick (eds.), *The Black Sociologists: The First Half Century* (New York: Wadsworth, 1971), 1.

14 Birth of NAACP: Louis R. Harlan, *Booker T. Washington* (Oxford University Press, 1983), 360ff; James M. McPherson, *The Abolitionist Legacy* (Princeton University Press, 1975).

Racism changing in response to demography, etc.: Jeffrey Stewart in Locke, *Race Contacts*, xxi. Du Bois came to believe that white racism was rooted in "subconscious trains of reasoning and unconscious nervous reflexes," which required a move from rational argument to "scientific propaganda." This is close to the belief in "genetic white racism" evident in much of 1990s scholarship. W. E. B. Du Bois, *Dusk of Dawn* (New York: Schoken, 1940/

1968), 171–72. Adolph L. Reed, Jr., *W. E. B. Du Bois and American Political Thought* (New York: Oxford University Press, 1997), 74.

Woodward and his students: see Kousser and McPherson, *Region, Race, and Reconstruction*.

"Diseased imagination": Frederick Douglass, "The Races," *Douglass Monthly* (August 1859), quoted in David Blight, "W. E. B. Du Bois and the Struggle for American Historical Memory," in *History & Memory in African-American Culture*, ed. Genevieve Fabre and Robert O'Meally (Oxford University Press, 1994), 52.

15 Ann Patton Malone, *Sweet Chariot: Slave Family and Household Structure in Nineteenth-Century Louisiana* (Durham, NC: Duke University Press, 1992), 257. "Bloody" historiography: Clarence Walker, "Black Reconstruction in America: W. E. B. Du Bois' Challenge to 'The Dark and Bloody Ground of Reconstruction Historiography'," in *Deromanticizing Black History* (Knoxville: University of Tennessee Press, 1991), 73–86; Bernard Weisberger, "The Dark and Bloody Ground of Reconstruction Historiography," *Journal of Southern History* 25:2 (Nov. 1959), 427–47; Eric Foner, "Preface," *A Short History of Reconstruction, 1863–1877* (New York: Harper & Row Perennial, 1990).

Todd Gitlin provides a useful overview of early twentieth-century antiracist scholarship, and of the multicultural "reaction" in the wake of the 1960s, in *The Twilight of Common Dreams* (New York: Metropolitan Books/Henry Holt, 1995).

16 Max Weber, "The Origin of Ethnic Groups," in *Ethnicity*, ed. Hutchinson and Smith, 35–40, my emphasis. On Vico and Herder's place in the genealogy of social constructionism, see Gustav Jahoda, *Crossroads Between Culture and Mind: Continuities and Change in Theories of Human Nature* (Cambridge, Harvard University Press 1993); Peter Burke, *Vico* (Oxford University Press, 1985); Isaiah Berlin, *Vico and Herder: Two Studies in the History of Ideas* (London and New York: Hogarth and Viking, 1976).

17 Stewart in Locke, *Race Contacts*, xxiv; Hutchinson, *Harlem Renaissance in Black and White*, 61–77; Franz Boas, "Instability of Human Types," in *Inter-Racial Problems: Papers from the First Universal Races Congress in London in 1911*, ed. G. Spiller (New York: Citadel Press, 1970); Franz Boas, *The Mind of Primitive Man*, intro. by Melville Herskovits (New York: Collier Books, 1911/1963).

The enormous influence that Boas had on mainstream institutions and intellectual thought is often "forgotten" by cultural studies scholars who are intent on finding racism under every rock in early twentieth-century American thought. A provocative critique of this tendency is Michael Schudson, "Paper Tigers: A Sociologist Follows Cultural Studies into the Wilderness," *Lingua Franca* 7:6 (August 1997), 49–56; and a longer version, Michael Schudson, "Cultural Studies and the Social Construction of 'Social Construction': Notes on 'Teddy Bear Patriarchy'," appears in *From Sociology to Cultural Studies*, ed. Elizabeth Long (London: Blackwell, 1997).

Park was a participant at the 1911 conference, where he seems to have met Locke. Park organized the "International Conference of the Negro" in 1912 at Tuskegee, where he met W. I. Thomas, which led to a job offer at the

University of Chicago. Bulmer, *The Chicago School of Sociology*, 61.

18 *The Melting Pot*/Zangwill and miscegenation: Gitlin, *Twilight of Common Dreams*, 55. Zangwill's 1913 revisions re miscegenation: W. J. Moses, *On the Wings of Ethiopia* (Ames: Iowa State University Press, 1990), 243. Jewish/ Aryan binary: Sollors, *Beyond Ethnicity*, 182ff. John Kerr, *A Most Dangerous Method: The Story of Jung, Freud, & Sabina Spielrein* (New York: Random House, 1993). Kallen and Bourne: Hollinger, *Postethnic America*, 91–104; Hutchinson, *Harlem Renaissance in Black and White*, 78–9, 102–05; Kallen's conversations with Locke: ibid., 85–87; Locke, *Race Contacts*, xxxvi–xxxviii. Horace Kallen, "Democracy Versus the Melting Pot," *Nation* 100 (Feb. 18–25, 1915); Horace Kallen, *Culture and Democracy in the United States* (New York: Boni & Liveright, 1924). Randolph Bourne, "Trans-National America," *Atlantic Monthly* 118 (July 1916), reprinted in *The American Intellectual Tradition*, ed. David Hollinger and Charles Capper (Oxford University Press, 1993), 179–88.

19 "We have to crush out the ... chameleon" and encourage "the realization of the race-self." Horace Kallen, "The Ethics of Zionism," *Maccabean* 11:2 (August 1906), 61–71. "Irishman ... Jew": Kallen, *The Structure of Lasting Peace* (Boston: Marshall Jones, 1918), 31. Sollors, *Beyond Ethnicity*, 182–3. "Salvation": Randolph Bourne, *War and the Intellectuals: Collected Essays, 1915–1919* (New York: Harper, 1964), 215. In "Trans-National America" Bourne refers to a "post-modern" America about seventy years early! *The Radical Will: Randolph Bourne – Selected Writings, 1911–1918* (New York: Urizen, 1977), 254–5. Bourne's view that "We are all foreign-born or the descendants of foreign-born, and if distinctions are to be made between us they should rightly be on some other grounds than indigenousness" arouses suspicion among 1990s multiculturalists. Gitlin, *Twilight of Common Dreams*, 14. Bourne, *Radical Will*, 249. Bourne's hostility towards the "Marginal Man": ibid., 254. Sollors, *Beyond Ethnicity*, 184–5.

20 "Colors run": Herder, previously cited (see Introduction, n. 11). David Hollinger refers to the American attachment to the essentialized categories of the "ethno-racial pentagon" (*Postethnic America*) as a "will to descend" ("National Culture and Communities of Descent").

21 Fred Matthews, *Quest for an American Sociology: Robert E. Park and the Chicago School* (Montreal: McGill-Queen's University Press, 1977); Hutchinson, *Harlem Renaissance in Black and White*, 50–58. "Diversity means": Troy Duster, "Diversity Report," University of California-Berkeley, 1990.

22 "Legacy": Harlan, *Booker T. Washington*, 201. To take a "guilt by association" view re Park's work with Washington is to project contemporary standards on to those who practiced a "politics of the possible" in a different era. I agree with Adolph Reed on the need to "confront past thinking as much as possible on its own terms, and that entails situating it within historical context": *Du Bois and American Political Thought*, 98. Although Du Bois criticized Washington fiercely, in some senses Washington was closer than Du Bois to conservative strains of black nationalism that emerged later, as in Garveyism, and the Nation of Islam. Washington's 1895 "Atlanta Compromise" speech won the support of West Indian black nationalist Edward Blyden, who "equated Washington's acquiescence in temporary segregation

with nationalist separatism" (ibid., 274). So it is not so simple to assign "correct" black influences on white scholars. Park's theories of assimilation, though influenced by his tenure with Washington, evolved through his associations with other black scholars and artists. Also, Park often played an "amelioratory" role with Washington: ghostwriting an exposé of Belgian atrocities in the Congo, organizing an International Conference on the Negro at Tuskegee in 1912, etc. (Harlan, *Booker T. Washington*, 271, 275). Park also became critical of what he viewed as Washington's American chauvinism, which he witnessed while traveling with Booker T. in Europe to research *The Man Down Under*, which he ghostwrote (ibid., 292).

Du Bois' critique of Washington: *The Souls of Black Folk* (New York: Penguin, 1903/1989), ch. 3. Adolph Reed covers Du Bois' view of Washington's accommodationism, and the elision of this part of Du Bois' thought by many late twentieth-century black intellectuals, in *Du Bois and American Political Thought*, 61–64. Reed makes too simple a dichotomy between Du Bois and Washington, in my view. Concerning problems in Washington's industrial education, and criticisms during his life, see James Anderson, *The Education of Blacks in the South, 1860–1935* (Durham, NC: Duke University Press, 1988), 42–44, 63–67, 75–77, 102–9, 216–17, 261–62; Louis R. Harlan, *Booker T. Washington: The Making of a Black Leader, 1856–1901*, I (Oxford University Press, 1972), 224–27, 227–28.

23 "Intentions": James Olney, "The Founding Fathers – Frederick Douglass and Booker T. Washington," in *Slavery and the Literary Imagination*, ed. Deborah McDowell and Arnold Rampersad (Baltimore: Johns Hopkins University Press, 1989), 14. Garvey in Louis R. Harlan, *Booker T. Washington: The Wizard of Tuskegee, 1901–1915* (Oxford University Press, 1983), 280. Numerous examples of people engaged in anticolonial struggles around the globe who found inspiration in Washington's book, many of whom came to study at Tuskegee, are cited in Harlan's chapter "Provincial Man of the World" (ibid., 266–94).

24 Booker T. Washington, *Frederick Douglass* (Philadelphia: George W. Jacobs, 1907). "Bland/Douglass of his Day": Olney, in *Slavery and the Literary Imagination*, ed. McDowell & Rampersad, 18, 15. In *My Larger Education*, Washington claims inheritance of Douglass' legacy in this way: "Frederick Douglass died in February, 1895. In September of the same year I delivered an address in Atlanta at the Cotton States Exposition" (New York: Doubleday, 1911), 242.

25 "Disgusted": Park quoted in Matthews, *Quest for an American Sociology*, 52. "Previous studies": "Autobiographical Note," in Park, *Race and Culture*, vii. "Treat Park as an equal": Harlan, *Booker T. Washington: Wizard of Tuskegee*, 291.

26 "Washington's Throne": "An American Dilemma: A Review" (1944), in *Collected Essays of Ellison*, 331. In introducing *Shadow and Act*, Ellison recalled "the humiliation of being taught in a class in sociology at a Negro college (from Park and Burgess, the leading textbook in the field) that Negroes represented the 'lady of the races.' This contention the Negro instructor passed blandly along to us without even bothering to wash his hands, much less his teeth": *Collected Essays*, 57. This passage, written in 1918, may be

offensive, but it is in keeping with what black intellectuals of the day were writing. In 1924 Du Bois romanticized the "sensuous, tropical love of life" among Afro-Americans, and declared that the Negro "is primarily an artist": *The Gift of Black Folk: The Negroes in the Making of America* (New York: Washington Square, 1924/1970), 178, 158. In the passage Ellison cited, Park used identical language: "The Negro . . . is primarily an artist." Park, "Education in its Relation to the Conflict and Fusion of Cultures" (1918), in *Race and Culture*, 280. Adolph Reed quotes both of these passages in different parts of his study of Du Bois, without noting their connection: *Du Bois and American Political Thought*, 58, 72, 118. Such assertions disappear from Park's later writings.

"Literate writers": David Remnick, "Visible Man," *New Yorker*, Mar. 14, 1994, in Graham and Singh, eds., *Conversations with Ralph Ellison*, 401.

27 Park writes that "cultural changes are not consolidated and transmitted biologically, or at least to only a very slight extent, if at all. Acquired characteristics are not biologically inherited": "Human Migration and the Marginal Man," *American Journal of Sociology* 33 (May 1928), in *Race and Culture*, 347.

Park contrasts a historical view of ethnic hybrids as normative, with "pigmentocracy"-derived views of race-mixing as abnormal or pathological. He lets Griffith Taylor voice his baseline perspective: "The whole teaching of ethnology shows that peoples of mixed race are the rule and not the exception." This is the *longue durée* view which, as we will see, was consistently expressed by Douglass. Griffith Taylor, *Environment and Race: A Study of the Evolution, Migration, Settlement, and Status of the Races of Man* (Oxford University Press, 1927), 336. Park, *Race and Culture*, 346.

28 As a journalist, Park was a strong critic of European imperialism. From 1900 to 1905 he published critiques of German militarism, and exposés of Belgian atrocities in the Congo. In a study of Park's early work, Stanford Lyman remarks that Park analogized "the political economy of capitalist imperialism [as a] preternatural vampire, who must roam the earth in search of its source of life-giving sustenance, human blood." Shades of Bob Marley: "Babylon System is the Vampire"! Stanford M. Lyman, *Militarism, Imperialism, and Racial Accommodation: An Analysis and Interpretation of the Early Writings of Robert E. Park* (Fayetville: University of Arkansas Press, 1992), xvii.

29 "Relations of power . . . generation": Banton, *Racial Theories*, 88–89. Similarly, Ralph Turner observes that "For all of his concern with race relations, it is striking that the achievement of social and economic equality never emerges as a dominant goal in Park's thought": *Robert E. Park on Social Control and Collective Behavior* (University of Chicago Press, 1967), xvii. Brace, Meier, and Rudwick, eds., *The Black Sociologists*, 6. "Conflicts of classes": Park, *Race and Culture*, 115. William Julius Wilson, *The Declining Significance of Race* (University of Chicago Press, 1980); William Julius Wilson, *The Truly Disadvantaged* (University of Chicago Press, 1987); William Julius Wilson, *When Work Disappears* (New York: Knopf, 1997). Orlando Patterson, *The Ordeal of Integration* (Washington, DC: Civitas/Counterpoint, 1997).

30 "Irreversible": Park, "Our Racial Frontier on the Pacific," *Survey Graphic* 9 (May 1926), in *Race and Culture*, 150. During the 1990s, the critique of assimilationist thought has largely refocused on the idea of integration itself. In extreme form, critics of integration attack even the ideal of inclusion as a sort of white cultural imperialism. See Michael Billig, "Nationalism and Richard Rorty: The Text as a Flag for *Pax Americana*," *New Left Review* 47 (Nov–Dec. 1993), and Abdul JanMohamed and David Lloyd, "Introduction," *The Nature and Context of Minority Discourse* (Berkeley: University of California Press, 1990).

31 See Adolph Reed's comments about Du Bois' essentially Anglocentric and Germanic cultural and philosophical affiliations, especially "Three Confusions about Du Bois: Interracialism, Pan-Africanism, Socialism," in *Du Bois and American Political Thought*. Numerous examples of Du Bois' racialized elitism can be found in Willard B. Gatewood, *Aristocrats of Color* (Bloomington: Indiana University Press, 1990).

32 "Electronically mediated": Mark Poster, *Mode of Information* (University of Chicago Press, 1990); "intensely miscegenated": Sollors, Introduction, *Beyond Ethnicity*.

"Pure opposition" is impossible, since any antithesis is constructed in opposition to a thesis, and must eventually resolve itself into a synthesis. Language is "tool," in the thought of Lev Vygotsky and C. G. Jung, used to construct these perpetual syntheses. So the idea of "using the master's tool's to dismantle the master's house" is "pointless – merely gestural." Gilroy, *Small Acts*, 9. "Our labour means that we have invested something of ourselves in its structure and that simple fact gives us a claim to ownership that we should not renounce too lightly" (ibid.).

Similar perspectives have been made, in different ways, by proponents of the "ethno-symbolic" school of ethnicity studies, by Bakhtinian literary analysis; and by psychologists such as C. G. Jung and Lev Vygotsky, with their emphasis on the "mediatory" capacity of symbols and cultural tools.

"Ethno-symbolic" school: John Armstrong, *Nations Before Nationalism* (Charlottesville: University of North Carolina Press, 1982); Anthony D. Smith, *The Ethnic Origins of Nations* (Oxford: Blackwell, 1986); Hutchinson and Smith, "Introduction," *Ethnicity*, 3–14.

Jung on mediating symbols: *Psychological Types* (Princeton University Press, 1921/1971), *Collected Works*, VI, 473–81, and "The Transcendent Function," in *The Structure and Dynamics of the Psyche* (Princeton University Press, 1969), *Collected Works*, VIII, 67–91. On academic blacklisting of Jung, and his relation to the broad sweep of Western (and non-Western) thought: Peter Homans, *Jung in Context* (University of Chicago Press, 1995), Kerr, *A Most Dangerous Method*, and George Hogenson's *Jung's Struggle With Freud* (Wilmette, IL.: Chiron, 1994); Christine Gallant's *Tabooed Jung* (New York University Press, 1996). On erroneous accusations of Jung's "Nazi sympathies," the most complete, balanced critical appraisal is Aryeh Maidenbaum and Stephen Martin, *Lingering Shadows: Jungians, Freudians, and Anti-Semitism* (Boston: Shambhala, 1991). Also Sonu Shamdasani, *Cult Fictions: C. G. Jung and the Founding of Analytical Psychology* (London: Routledge, 1998).

Vygotsky: *Mind in Society: The Development of Higher Psychological Process,* ed. Michael Cole *et al.* (Cambridge: Harvard University Press, 1978); James Wertsch, *Voices of the Mind: A Sociocultural Approach to Mediated Action* (Cambridge: Harvard University Press, 1991). Mikhail Bakhtin, *The Dialogic Imagination*, ed. Michael Holquist (Austin: University of Texas Press, 1981); Michael Holquist, *Dialogism: Bakhtin and His World* (London: Routledge, 1990).

33 George Devereux and Edwin Loeb, "Antagonistic Acculturation," *American Sociological Review* 8 (1943), 133–47; later elaborated in Fredrik Barth, *Ethnic Groups and Boundaries: The Social Organization of Cultural Difference* (Boston: Little, Brown, 1969). Albert Murray has said he introduced Ellison to the idea of "antagonistic cooperation" after reading it in Joseph Campbell's *The Hero With a Thousand Faces* (New York: Pantheon, 1949; 2nd edn Princeton University Press, 1972). Quoted in Dick Russell, "The Craft of Ralph Ellison," *Black Genius* (New York: Carrol & Graf, 1998), 40.

34 Devereux and Loeb, "Antagonistic Acculturation," 134ff. "overt hostility": R. Linton, *Acculturation in Seven American Indian Tribes* (New York: Appleton-Century, 1940), 498. Weber, "Origin of Ethnic Groups," in *Ethnicity*, ed. Hutchinson and Smith, 40, 37. W. J. Moses makes a similar point in an essay on E. Franklin Frazier. Black nationalism is often represented as a form of pure opposition to Eurocentrism, but is in fact "a result of the symbiotic relationship between whites and blacks in which blacks have become more like whites in the process of developing institutions to help them resist racism. Thus, black nationalism is a reactive movement much influenced by the forces against which it is reacting... [T]he process of acculturation endows blacks with a theory of nationalism and a religious framework to support it." *The Wings of Ethiopia*, 116–17.

35 Molefi Asante, *The Afrocentric Idea* (Philadelphia: Temple University Press, 1987), 56.

36 "Modern we are": Gilroy, *Small Acts*, 9. Ellison makes much the same point in his interview with James Alan McPherson. In Ellison, *Collected Essays*; Graham and Singh, eds., *Conversations with Ralph Ellison*; Kimberly Benston, ed., *Speaking for You* (Washington, DC: Howard University Press, 1987).

37 "Against one another": in Matthews, *Quest for an American Sociology*, 134. Park's quote of Simmel: "Human Migration and the Marginal Man," in *Race and Culture*, 351. Donald Levine compares uses and misuses of Simmel by Durkheim, Weber, Lukacs, Parsons, and Park in *Flight From Ambiguity* (University of Chicago Press, 1985). Although Simmel has been cited more for his writing on "the Stranger" that any other topic, this essay was originally an "excursus," a note to a chapter on "Space and the Spatial Ordering of Society." Although Park tends to collapse the "Stranger" and the "Marginal Man," the "Marginal Man" is really but one sub-type of the "stranger," as Simmel describes this type, according to Levine (73, 112–18).

38 Chinua Achebe, *Morning Yet on Creation Day* (New York: Doubleday, 1975), 76. See also Bill Ashcroft, Gareth Griffiths, and Helen Tiffin, *The Empire Writes Back: Theory and Practice in Post-Colonial Literatures* (London: Routledge, 1989), 78.

39 "Ambitious": Park, *Race and Culture*, 387. First delivered as an address at the Fourth Pacific Science Congress, May 1929.

40 "Mental endowment": Daniel Murray, a descendant of a prominent Maryland mulatto family, and a leading figure in Washington's so-called "black 400." His comments are from "The Power of Blood Inheritance," written about 1904, and quoted in Gatewood, *Aristocrats of Color*, 174.

41 Curlin quoted in Park, *Race and Culture*, 388. Shirlee Taylor Haizlip uses similar language, and makes similar claims, at the beginning of *The Sweeter the Juice: A Family Memoir in Black and White* (New York: Simon & Schuster, 1994).

42 There is a huge literature on the history of the "Tragic Mulatto." Rather than trying to cite a few representative samples, I will refer readers to Werner Sollors' insightful and thorough critical engagement with this literature: "Excursus on the 'Tragic Mulatto'; or, The Fate of a Stereotype," in *Neither Black nor White yet Both*, 220–45. Most useful, for my purposes, is Sollors' analysis of the ways in which the use of this concept has not only "helped to criticize an ideology of the past . . . but has also served as a vehicle of the ideological wish for a wholesale rejection of the representation of interracial life in literature" (242). He gives numerous examples of treatments of mulattos that do not fit this pattern, yet have been cut to size by critics' Procrustean use of this concept. I take a similar critical view of the notion of "tragic mulattos" in the Douglass chapter.

43 Du Bois wrote: "I am, in blood, about one half or more Negro, and the rest French and Dutch." David Levering Lewis, *W. E. B. Du Bois* (New York: Henry Holt, 1993), 120. "What, after all, was W. E. B. Du Bois but an Afro-Saxon?" asks Orlando Patterson, *The Ordeal of Integration*, 104.

44 James' impact on Du Bois and Pauline Hopkins: Sundquist, *To Wake The Nations*, 570–71, 684; Cynthia Schrager, "Pauline Hopkins and William James: The New Psychology and the Politics of Race," in Abel, Christian, and Moglen, eds., *Female Subjects in Black and White*, 307–29; Thomas J. Otten, "Pauline Hopkins and the Hidden Self of Race," *ELH* 59 (1992), 227–56.

James was a mentor of W. E. B. Du Bois beginning in 1888. Du Bois tells us that he was "repeatedly a guest in the house of William James." James may have been "predisposed" to take Du Bois under his wing, David Levering Lewis thinks (*Du Bois*, 91), by the fact that his own brother had served in the Massachusetts 54th Infantry Regiment. This is the same Civil War black regiment immortalized in the film *Glory*, for which Frederick Douglass had recruited, and supplied his own sons, Lewis and Charles. Du Bois, *Dusk of Dawn: An Essay Toward an Autobiography of a Race Concept* (New York: Schocken, 1940/1968), 38.

Adolph Reed says "Du Bois' double consciousness was embedded . . . in the neo-Lamarckian thinking about race, evolution, and social hierarchy that prevailed in a strain of reform-oriented, *fin-de-siècle* American social science." But he adamantly, and somewhat hypercritically, I think, rejects the notion that this idea came directly from James. Reed, *Du Bois and American Political Thought*, 91ff. James clearly influenced Du Bois, but "Du Bois, in turn, seems to have had a strong impact on James," as Hutchinson writes: *Harlem Renaissance in Black and White*, 36. James published an essay on "The Hidden Self" in 1890 which outlined a theory of "double selves," or multicentered consciousness. This was included in his 1897 book *The Will to Believe*. Both Du

Bois and Pauline Hopkins used James' essay to construct a version of diasporic "double consciousness" in their books *The Souls of Black Folk* and *One
Blood*, both published in 1903. James' theory of the hidden self reworks
themes from Alfred Binet's book *On Double Consciousness*, yet he wrote it
during a period in which he was a friend and mentor to Du Bois. Du Bois
would have been an important model of how "double consciousness" could
take form in an American, and interracial, context.

C. G. Jung's theory of "autonomous complexes" or "splinter pscyhes,"
which John Kerr and Peter Homans call an unacknowledged foundation of
modern psychoanalysis, drew on Binet and James. See Homans' assessment
in the provocative introduction to the second edition of his *Jung in Context*,
and Kerr's pioneering study *A Most Dangerous Method*. There are numerous
parallels between the work of James and Jung, and the theories of relational
selves developed by G. H. Mead and Lev Vygotsky. But although Vygotsky
and the Russian school read and cited Jung, Jung's work (and James') is
completely absent from the field of "cultural psychology," illustrating what
Homans calls "Jung's virtual erasure from the scholarly scene" (li). The most
complete synthesis of this field can be found in Michael Cole, *Cultural
Psychology: A Once and Future Discipline* (Cambridge: Belknap/Harvard University Press, 1996).

45 Boas on mulatto fertility in Williamson, *New People*, 123; W. G. Weatherby,
"Race and Marriage," *American Journal of Sociology* 15 (Jan. 1910), 544. John
Henderson, "The Forces Upon Which the Race Depends for Success,"
Colored American Magazine 14 (Jan. 1908), 71. The author attributes the
physical inferiority of mulattos to their being the issue of "lower-class" white
men. "Mulatto baiting": Willard Gatewood's chapter "The Color Factor,"
from *Aristocrats of Color*, 149–81, and Wilson Jeremiah Moses, *Alexander
Crummell* (Amherst: University of Massachusetts Press, 1992). Edward Byron
Reuter, *The Mulatto in the United States: Including a Study of the Role of
Mixed-Blood Races throughout the World* (Boston: Richard Badger, 1918). E.
Franklin Frazier, "Children in Black and Mulatto Families," *American Jour-
nal of Sociology* 39 (July 1933). Although C. G. Jung was usually quite
progressive regarding the union of opposites, he shared all the prejudices of
his age concerning miscegenation. In his Nietzsche seminar during the 1930s,
Jung claimed it was a "fact" that "a negro woman rarely conceives from a
white man." And mulattos will most often be a person of "bad character":
Nietzche's Zarathustra: Notes of the Seminar Given in 1934–1939 (Princeton
University Press, 1988), 643–44.

Spike Lee's work is a classic example of "the return of the repressed." Lee
grew up in an integrated neighborhood; his father remarried a white woman,
producing a biracial sibling. Lee's work has presented interracial relations as a
threat to black families, yet he returns obsessively to the theme of racial
ambiguity, both through the frequent presence and commentary on biracial
characters, and through commentaries on the racial ambiguity of Italians, as a
racially "liminal" group. I discuss this phenomenon in "Romancing the
Racial Frontier."

46 "Degeneration": Sundquist, *To Wake the Nations*, 395. In the 1990s "biracial" is often used to refer to people who were born to one parent considered

"white" and one parent considered "black." I use the term mainly in a cultural sense, but also sometimes employ the term to describe people who have a significant mixture of African and European ancestry, or a mixture of two other "national" origins, without in any way endorsing a numerical "quotient" or threshold at which a person could be considered "biracial."

47 In the plural I use the spelling "mulattos," which is truer to the word's linguistic roots, rather than "mulattoes." See Jack Forbes' discussion of this word's history in *Africans and Native Americans*, 131–50. "Passing" and integration with black population: Williamson, *New People*, 119, 209. Charles S. Johnson, "The Vanishing Mulatto," *Opportunity* 3 (Oct. 1925).

The best overview on passing is Werner Sollor's "Passing; or, Sacrificing a *Parvenu*," from *Neither Black nor White yet Both*, 246–84, with extensive sources. See also the sources from the 1880–1920 period listed in Gatewood, *Aristocrats of Color*, 379.

In the 1850–1920 period, the Census did not count mulattos in 1880 and 1900, while in 1890 "census takers were instructed . . . to distinguish between blacks, mulattoes, quadroons, and octoroons": Williamson, *New People*, 112.

48 Sigmund Freud, "Repression," in *The Freud Reader*, ed. Peter Gray (New York: Norton, 1989), 572. I am using "the return of the repressed" in a way similar to how Stuart Hall described the return of repressed ideological concerns, or how Henry Louis Gates speaks of the rediscovery and canonization of Zora Zeale Hurston as "a marvelous instance of the return of the repressed." Stuart Hall, "The Rediscovery of 'Ideology': Return of the Repressed in Media Studies," In Michael Gurevitch *et al.*, eds., *Culture, Society and the Media* (London: Methuen, 1982), 56–90; Henry Louis Gates, Jr., "Afterword," in Zora Neale Hurston, *Seraph on the Suwanee* (New York: HarperPerennial, 1948/1991), 357.

49 Tilden Edelstein, "*Othello* in America: The Drama of Interracial Marriage," in *Region, Race, and Reconstruction*, ed. Kousser and McPherson. There were early exceptions in Europe: New York-born black actor Ira Aldridge "received enthusiastic acclaim" in Europe during the 1830s, but he had both a white wife and a Swedish mistress, ensuring he would never appear in America (188). A few black Othellos appeared in America at minor theatres: James Hewlett in New York in 1821 with an all-black cast; an all-black cast in Greenwich Village in the 1880s; and another all-black cast with Edward Sterling Wright in the title role in New York and Boston in 1910 (188, 190–91).

The use of "One Blood" (Acts 17:26) in public equal rights discourse is discussed in the Marley and Douglass chapters.

50 Judges on "mixture": Williamson, *New People*, 18; Gary B. Mills, *The Forgotten People: Cane River's Creoles of Color* (Baton Rouge: Louisiana State University Press, 1977), xiii, 77–79. Many of the relative freedoms of Louisiana's free "creoles of color" were obtained under Spanish rule. See Kimberly S. Hanger, *Bounded Lives, Bounded Places: Free Black Society in Colonial New Orleans, 1769–1803* (Durham: Duke University Press, 1997), and "Conflicting Loyalties: The French Revolution and Free People of Color in Spanish New Orleans," in *A Turbulent Time: The French Revolution and the Greater Caribbean*, ed. David Barry Gaspar and David Patrick Greggus (Indiana University Press, 1997), 178–203.

51 Free mulattos: Williamson, *New People*, 65.

52 Fredricka Bremer, *The Homes of the New World: Impressions of America* (London: A. Hall, Virtue, & Co., 1853), 7–11. "White blood . . . could not cope": Williamson, *New People*, 72–73.

53 I am speaking here of a subset of a larger phenomenon: projection of white fears on to blacks (and other nonwhites).

Mulattos as symbols: Williamson, *New People*, 78; on the implications of the Plessy decision for the "One Drop" rule, see F. James Davis, *Who Is Black?* (University Park: Penn State University Press, 1991). Lillian Smith, *Killers of the Dream* (New York: Norton, 1949), quoted in Sundquist, *To Wake the Nations*, 392. Ellison to James Alan McPherson in *Collected Essays*, 377.

Crusade for Justice: The Autobiography of Ida B. Wells, ed. Alfreda M. Duster (University of Chicago Press, 1970). I discuss Douglass' comments on lynching in chapter 2.

Again, it is important to note exceptions to this racial psycho-pathology. Shelly Fishkin's work on Mark Twain gives a range of evidence of how some whites grew up in close contact with black playmates and maintained interracial contacts throughout their lives. Albert Barnes, a white "Africanist" during the Harlem Renaissance, is a dramatic example of the impact that black cultural traditions had on some white Americans during this time. Barnes traced his lifelong interest in Afro-American music to a black camp meeting he attended at age eight. He later reportedly "partially supported himself as a student in Heidelberg by singing Negro spirituals" (shades of Mark Twain!) (Hutchinson, *Harlem Renaissance in Black and White*, 45). Barnes, who grew up in poverty, later became a multi-millionaire, and built a factory in Philadelphia where he employed an interracial work force. He used William James' psychology in the workplace, and later studied modernist art under John Dewey at Columbia. Over the years, Barnes developed such an expertise on African and Afro-American art that Locke employed him as a "house expert on African aesthetics" at *Opportunity* (ibid., 45). He also began to teach his former teacher, Dewey, whose writing on art "is at least partly indebted to African and African American aesthetics as filtered through Barnes" (ibid., 46). Dewey in turn played several roles in the promotion of "cultural pluralism," serving as a mentor to the writer Anzia Yezierska, and writing an introduction to Claude McKay's *Selected Poems*. Mary V. Dearborn, *Pocahontas's Daughters* (Oxford University Press, 1986), 110–13.

54 "Internal miscegenation": Ralph Linton, "The Vanishing American Negro," *The American Mercury* 6 (Feb. 1947), 135. "Animus": Caroline Bond Day, *A Study of Some Negro-White Families in the United States* (Cambridge, MA: Peabody Museum of Harvard University, 1932), 109–10. "Mulatto-baiting": see for instance the discussion of the long career of attacks on mulattos by W. Calvin Chase, editor/publisher of the *Washington Bee*, and many other black editors, in Gatewood, *Aristocrats of Color*, 161–81.

Variations in time frame of growth of white racism: Roscoe Bruce (son of Blanche Bruce, the Reconstruction Mississippi Senator) stayed in the Harvard University dorm in 1903, but his son Roscoe Jr. was refused residence in 1923. The *New York Times* printed Bruce's letter of protest. Ibid., 146–48.

55 "Mulatto culture in America": Williamson, *New People*, 147.

56 Ibid., 25, 56–57, 86, 113. Pressure from white wives: Eugene D. Genovese, *Roll, Jordan, Roll* (New York: Random House/Vintage, 1974), 419. "A surprising number" of white women not only tolerated their spouses' second mulatto families, but "showed them tenderness and played the kind stepmother," Genovese adds. In an important work of synthesis, Ira Berlin divides the movements of blacks to the New World into three stages: the "charter generation," the "plantation generation," and the "revolutionary generation." Berlin points out that many in the first generations, which he refers to as "Atlantic Creoles," were cosmopolitan and multilingual. They were often descended from West African traders or interpreters, and many had spent time in Great Britain or other parts of the New World before coming to North America. Descendants of these Creoles and of blacks freed during the Revolution were an important part of Frederick Douglass' support group. Ira Berlin, *Many Thousands Gone: The First Two Centuries of Slavery in North America* (Cambridge, MA: Harvard University Press, 1998).

57 Du Bois, *Dusk of Dawn*, 115. "In common": Sundquist, *To Wake the Nations*, 460. For comments on the alienation of "staid, more or less dark New Englanders" from Southern blacks, see James Weldon Johnson, *Along This Way: The Autobiography of James Weldon Johnson* (New York: Viking, 1933/1968), 137–38. Darwin Turner, ed., *The Wayward and the Seeking: A Collection of Writings by Jean Toomer* (Howard University Press, 1980), 84. Williamson, *New People*, 149.

58 "Declaration," "American music," and "kingdom of culture": W. E. B. Du Bois, *The Souls of Black Folk*, in *Three Negro Classics* (New York: Avon, 1965), 220, 215. Ernest L. Tuveson, *Redeemer Nation* (University of Chicago Press, 1968). Adolph Reed makes similar points about the dual tendencies in Du Bois' thought, which distinguished between belief in integration – sometimes defined in assimilationist language – as a long-term horizon, and a recognition of the necessity of medium-term separation: *Du Bois and American Political Thought*, 58, 71–79. It was in opposition to Washington's view of assimilation that Du Bois defined his own version: "ultimate assimilation through self-assertion, and on no other terms." *Souls of Black Folk*, 86.

59 "Blackening": Hutchinson, *Harlem Renaissance in Black and White*, 145, my emphasis. W. J. Moses distinguishes between separatist and black nationalist strains in Afro-American thinking. Not only were many "separatist" movements not black nationalist, they often "amounted to little more than opportunistic collaboration with segregationists." Both E. Franklin Frazier and St. Clair Drake recognized that "separatist activity does not necessarily demonstrate a freedom from assimilationist values." Moses, *The Wings of Ethiopia*, 111, 114.

Ellison in Graham and Singh, eds., *Conversations with Ralph Ellison*, 336.

60 Johnson's 1917 speech: *Along This Way* (New York: Viking, 1933), 326–27. Seligman: Mary White Ovington, *The Walls Came Tumbling Down* (New York: Schocken Books, 1970), 108. Hutchinson, *Harlem Renaissance in Black and White*, 143–4.

61 Johnson as songwriter: Lewis, *Du Bois*, 523. James Weldon Johnson, *The Autobiography of an Ex-Colored Man* (New York: Hill & Wang, 1912/1960). Hurston from unpublished chapter of *Dust Tracks on the Road*, quoted in

Sollors, *Neither Black nor White yet Both*, 494. Gatewood discusses numerous mulatto aristocrats who found their racial identity questioned on both sides. Cyrus Fields Adams, often accused by blacks of trying to "pass" as white, replied that "My trouble is, all my life I have been trying to pass for colored": *Aristocrats of Color*, 173.

62 Prior to the Census' declaration of a formal black–white binary in 1920, there was considerable agitation in high places against more complex forms of American identity. In 1916 Woodrow Wilson had repudiated the "hyphenated vote"; in 1917 Theodore Roosevelt denounced "hyphenated Americans." Gitlin, *Twilight of Common Dreams*, 54.

Johnson, "The Vanishing Mulatto." Reuter, *The Mulatto in the United States*. Historian Laurence Glasco studied photos of Howard University students from 1912 to 1972 and found that during the 1920s there was a "sharp drop in representation among both the light and the black students": "The Mulatto: A Neglected Dimension of Afro-American Social Structure," Paper, Convention of the Organization of American Historians, April 17–20, 1974, pp. 22–26, 38. For a study showing similar results of increasing "brown-ness" in the professions, see Gilbert Edwards, *The Negro Professional Class* (New York: Free Press, 1958), 112–15. Charles S. Johnson's study of Southern Negro children showed that they viewed light brown skin most favorably, and saw black, white, and yellow as undesirable – the latter as "bad mixed blood": *Growing Up in the Black Belt: Negro Youth in the Rural South* (Washington, DC: American Council on Education, 1941), 258–66.

Native-born: Williamson, *New People*, 113. Melville J. Herskovits, *The Anthropometry of the American Negro* (Columbia University Press, 1930), 8–10. As an Oklahoman who married into a family from the Texas–Louisiana borderlands, I know that it is commonplace for whites and blacks throughout this region to claim Indian ancestry.

63 "Minimal": Williamson, *New People*, 188. *Statistical Abstract of the United States*, US Department of Commerce – Bureau of the Census, 1979–89. The US did not begin reporting interracial marriages until 1979, although it projected figures retroactively to 1970. Williamson presumably wrote without these figures.

64 Shirlee Taylor Haizlip, *The Sweeter the Juice. Secrets and Lies*, dir. Mike Leigh, 1996, starring Marianne-Jean Baptiste and Brenda Blethyn. *A Family Thing*, dir. Richard Pearce, 1995, starring Robert Duvall and James Earl Jones.

65 Sollors, *Neither Black nor White yet Both*, 62.
When you know the white yet hold on to the black,
You'll be the model for the country...
You'll return to the condition which has no limit.
Lao-Tzu, *Te-Tao Ching*, translated by Robert Henricks (New York: Ballantine, 1989), #28, p. 80.

66 August Wilson, "I Want a Black Director," *New York Times*, Aug. 26, 1990, and in *Spin* (Oct. 1990). Mr. Wilson is himself of mixed race, as one might suspect. People of mixed race, in overcompensation to prove their racial credentials, often develop "a kind of super-racial consciousness and zealousness," as Caroline Bond Day once wrote: *A Study of Some Negro-White Families*, 121–22. Day was a mulatto. Williamson, *New People*, 133.

Rap's predominantly nonblack audience: Stephens, "Interracial Dialogue in Rap Music." Chuck D has argued that sales are weighted to whites because most black youth tape ("pirate") the music. However, during the early 1990s there was plenty of testimony that Public Enemy's live shows had a largely white audience. Former Public Enemy "Minister of Information" Professor Griff commented: "We didn't attract black people; we had all-white audiences. Black people didn't want to hear what we had to say." *Daily Texan*, June 23, 1990.

67 Ann duCille, "The Occult of True Black Womanhood: Critical Demeanor and Black Feminist Studies," in *Female Subjects in Black and White*, ed. Abel *et al.*, 25, 23.

68 Spencer, *The New Colored People*, 89, 92, 86. The multiracialists Spencer referred to in this instance were myself and Naomi Zack, *Race and Mixed Race* (Philadelphia: Temple University Press, 1993).

69 Nathan Irvin Huggins, *Black Odyssey: The African-American Ordeal in Slavery* (New York: Vintage, 1990), xliv. "Slavery, especially in its plantation setting and in its paternalistic aspect, made white and black southerners one people while making them two," Genovese wrote: *Roll, Jordan, Roll*, xvi–xvii. "Masters and slaves shaped each other and cannot be discussed or analyzed in isolation."

70 "Central paradox": Edmund Morgan, *American Slavery, American Freedom* (New York: Norton, 1975), 4.

71 Small elite: Peter Kolchin, *American Slavery, 1619–1877* (New York: Hill and Wang, 1993), 34. Freehling, *Reintegration of American History*, 194.

72 "Run away ... make love": Morgan, *American Slavery, American Freedom*, 327. "Strength of that tendency": Howard Zinn, *A People's History of the United States* (New York: Harper and Row, 1980), 31.

73 "Existing order" and "servants": Zinn, *A People's History of the United States*, 37. "Racial contempt": Morgan, *American Slavery*, 328, my emphasis.

74 George Washington, "land they occupy": Mechal Sobel, *The World They Made Together* (Princeton University Press, 1987), 50–51. "Black world of work": ibid., 48–50. Thomas Jefferson later observed that "many [slaves] have been brought up to the handicraft arts, and from that circumstance have always been associated with the whites." *Notes on the State of Virginia* (New York (1785): Harper & Row, 1964), 134.

75 Williamson, *New People*, 10–11.

76 Ira Berlin, "Time, Space and Evolution of Afro-American Society," *American Historical Review* 85 (1980), 69. "Mulatto children": Sobel, *World They Made*, 284. Dickson Preston, *Young Frederick Douglass* (Baltimore: Johns Hopkins University Press, 1990), 13. A 1755 Maryland census listed 3,600 mulattos, of whom almost half were free – most apparently "ow[ing] their freedom to white maternity in the seventeenth century" (Williamson, *New People*, 13). James Hugo Johnston, *Race Relations in Virginia and Miscegenation in the South* (Amherst: University of Massachusetts Press, 1970). Also on attraction of poor white women to black men: Davis Brion Davis, *The Problem of Slavery in Western Culture* (Ithaca: Cornell University Press, 1966), 277. On similar relations (but more often involving upper-class white women) during slavery in Jamaica: Orlando Patterson, "Slavery and Slave Revolts: A Sociohistorical

Analysis of the First Maroon War, 1655–1740," *Social and Economic Studies* 19 (1970), 322; Edward Kamar Brathwaite, *The Development of Creole Society in Jamaica, 1770–1820* (Oxford: Clarendon Press, 188–91.

77 Blacks and whites both mixed with Indians, with less fuss. In fact, the popularity of captivity stories indicates that unions with Indians was somewhat idealized. Thomas Jefferson, who viewed blacks as a "blot" which had to be removed "beyond the reach of mixture," felt that Native Americans possessed "endowments" which would enable them, when crossed with Anglo-Saxons, to produce a new breed of Americans of "mixed blood." *Notes on the State of Virginia*, quoted in Ronald Takaki, ed., *From Different Shores* (Oxford University Press, 1987), 33; "mixed blood" in Appiah, *In My Father's House*, 49. "Shameful matches": Jeffrey Brackett, *The Negro in Maryland* (Freeport, NY: Books for Libraries Press, 1889/1969), 191–96. Captivity stories: Mary Dearborn, *Pocahontas's Daughters*. A similar pattern is observable in and around the Caribbean: relations between white women and black men leading to punitive legislation.

78 Eugene Genovese summarizes scholarship on miscegenation in *Roll, Jordan, Roll*, 413–41. See also Mintz and Price, *The Birth of African-American Culture*, 28–30, 91. Along with abundant evidence of the violence of slavery, including sexual violation, numerous examples of ex-slaves who remember loving relationships between their black mothers and white fathers can be found in the interviews conducted during the 1930s by the Federal Writers Project of the Works Project Administration, and published by George P. Rawick, ed., *The American Slave: A Composite Autobiography* (Westport, CT: Greenwood Press, 1972 –), V (3), 46; IX (3), 25–26; XV (2), 219; X (6), 97; XV (2), 230; XVII, 62; XVI, 77. Also, Joe Richardson, "A Negro Success Story: James Dallas Burruss," *Journal of Negro History* (Oct. 1965), 274; Norman Yetman, ed., *Life Under the "Peculiar Institution": Selections from the Slave Narrative Collection* (New York, 1970), 232, 259; Fisk University, *Unwritten History of Slavery: Autobiographical Accounts of Negro Ex-Slaves*, compiled and edited by Ophelia Settle Egypt, J. Masuoka, and Charles S. Johnson (Washington, DC, 1945/1968), 87; Johnston, *Race Relations and Miscegenation*. Genovese also notes that there exist numerous cases of white wives or daughters of slaveholders who took black lovers and bore their children. The most striking thing about these instances in the antebellum era, he writes, is that the black men involved were not lynched, which would surely have been the case in the postbellum era (422).

79 Arnold Rampersad, "The Color of His Eyes: Bruce Perry's *Malcolm* and Malcolm's Malcolm," in Joe Wood, *Malcolm X In Our Own Image* (New York: St. Martin's, 1992), 123. Rampersad is mostly convinced by Perry's evidence that Malcolm invented many details of his early life. Interviews with relatives in Grenada indicate that Malcolm's grandmother was never raped by a white man, as he claimed, but had a consensual relationship. Malcolm's description of Klan attacks (with which Spike Lee starts his film *Malcolm X)* also apparently never happened. Bruce Perry, *Malcolm: The Life of a Man Who Changed Black America* (New York: Station Hill Press: 1991). My reviews of this book are in the *San Francisco Chronicle Review*, Aug. 30, 1992, and *In These Times*, Oct. 28, 1992.

Bharati Mukherjee: David Armstrong, "An Immigrant Transformed," *San Francisco Examiner*, Oct. 28, 1993.

80 "Broken Speech"/dancing: Sobel, *World They Made*, 137, 167.

81 Parodies: ibid., 167. "half the night": James Haskins, *Black Dance in America* (New York: HarperCollins, 1990), 14. Lott, *Love and Theft*.

82 "Third race": Alexis de Tocqueville, *Democracy in America*, ed. J. P. Mayer (New York: Anchor/Doubleday, 1840/1969), 356, my emphasis. Sidney Andrews, *The South Since the War: As Shown by Fourteen Weeks of Travel and Observation in Georgia and the Carolinas* (1866), 229, quoted in Fishkin, *Was Huck Black?*, 28, with many similar observations in the notes, 161–62.

83 Douglass, "The U.S. Cannot Remain Half-Slave and Half Free" (Apr. 1883), in Philip S. Foner, ed., *The Life and Writings of Frederick Douglass* [hereafter *L&W*], IV (New York: International Publishers, 1955), 362.

84 Mechal Sobel, *Trabelin' On: The Slave Journey to an Afro-Baptist Faith* (Princeton University Press, 1979), and Sobel, *World They Made Together*.

85 One vote: Freehling, *Reintegration of American History*, 21. This ordinance was to have been post-dated to 1800.

86 "Slave labor": Morgan, *American Slavery*, 5. Morgan makes this statement after noting that we traded tobacco to France in return for warships. This twinning of slavery and freedom also raises the issue of how addictions have always fueled our liberties: not only addiction to slave labor, and to tobacco, but now, for instance, an addiction to petroleum, which fuels our personal freedom.

87 "Their rulers ... live slaves ... sin": Donald G. Nieman, *Promises to Keep* (Oxford University Press, 1991), 7–8. "Inhabited by slaves": Morgan, *American Slavery*, 3. "Constitutionality": John Phillip Reid, *The Concept of Liberty in the Age of the American Revolution* (University of Chicago Press, 1988), 49.

88 "White ancestors only": Nieman, *Promises to Keep*, 10. Seymour Drescher, *Capitalism and Anti-Slavery: British Mobilization in Comparative Perspective* (Oxford University Press, 1986); Robin Blackburn, *The Overthrow of Colonial Slavery, 1776–1848* (London: Verso, 1988); David Brion Davis, *The Problem of Slavery in the Revolution, 1776–1823* (Ithaca, NY: Cornell University Press, 1975); Gaspar and Geggus, eds., *A Turbulent Time*.

89 By 1800, eighteen years before Douglass' birth in Talbot County, the county had a higher percentage of free blacks than any other Maryland county, and "probably the highest ration of free to slave blacks of any similar area in America." Preston, *Young Frederick Douglass*, 19.

90 "Spirit of the Constitution": quoted in Gary Nash, *Race and Revolution* (Madison, WI: Madison House, 1990), 44. Yet for many of the founders, Montesquieu's emphasis upon a "familial" conception of civic virtue lent itself easily to exclusionary definitions of who would be eligible to shape the social compact of the new American republic. "The two key elements of commonality that the colonists perceived as necessary for a fruitful compact were Christianity and European bloodlines," as Celeste Michelle Condit and John Louis Lucaites write. *Crafting Equality* (University of Chicago Press, 1993), 60.

91 "Religious excitement": Sobel, *Trabelin' On*, 249.

92 "Mixed churches": Sobel, *World They Made*, 180. "Revival was exclusive": Winthrop D. Jordan, *White Over Black* (New York: Penguin, 1969), 212.

Ecstatic experiences: Willis Weatherford, *American Churches and the Negro* (Boston: Christopher, 1957). Censure against masters: William Warren Sweet, "The Churches as Moral Courts of the Frontier," *Church History* 2 (1933), 3–21. "Full members" and "victorious": Sobel, *Trabelin' On*, 181, 191, 196.

93 "Mass hysteria" and dating of Great Awakening: Sobel, *Trabelin' On*, 97, 88. *Black Orpheus*, dir. Marcel Camus, 1959; Maya Deren, 1953: *Divine Horsemen*; James Baldwin, *Go Tell It On the Mountain* (New York: Dell, 1953).

94 "Preblack Baptist pattern": Sobel, *Trabelin' On*, 98, my emphasis. "Bring down the spirit": ibid., Ulrich Phillips, *American Negro Slavery* (Baton Rouge: Louisiana State University Press, 1918/1966), 316.

95 Anglicism, "improvement": Sobel, *World They Made*, 178, 182.

96 "Respector of persons": ibid., 182. The allusion is to Acts 10:34. "Great countenance": Jordan, *White Over Black*, 181. The multiracial "Negro Plot": Lhaman, *Raising Cain*, 20, 35; Marcus Rediker, "'The Outcasts of the Nations of the Earth': The New York Conspiracy of 1841 in Atlantic Perspective," in Peter Linebaugh and Marcus Rediker, *The Many Headed Hydra* (Boston: Beacon, 1998).

97 John Woolman, *Some Considerations on the Keeping of Negroes* (Philadelphia: James Chattin, 1754). Sobel, *World They Made*, 238–39.

98 Invoking Benezet: many instances are in Dorothy Porter, ed., *Early Negro Writing, 1760–1837* (Boston: Beacon, 1971).

99 George Pilcher, ed., "Samuel Davies and the Instruction of the Negro in Virginia," *Virginia Magazine of History and Biography* 74 (1966), 293. "Abraham by faith," "sacred topography," "opened common ground": Sobel, *Trabelin' On*, 97, 125, 98. Davies' Ethiopian allusion is to Psalms 68:31. I trace the use of Psalms 68:31 by Davies, Benezet, and several dozen other writers and and performers from 1700 to the present in "Ethiopia is in the House: A Brief History of a Biblical Idea in Multiracial Context" (unpublished manuscript). "Whites and blacks alike": Sobel, *World They Made*, 200. See also Theophus Smith, *Conjuring Culture* (Oxford University Press, 1994).

100 "Discursive universes": Henry Louis Gates Jr., *The Signifying Monkey* (Oxford University Press, 1988), xxii.

101 "Common heritage": Sobel, *World They Made*, 222. "Israel and its heroes": Sobel, *Trabelin' On*, 153. Albert J. Raboteau makes the same points in *A Fire in the Bones* (Boston: Beacon, 1995), as does Theophus Smith in *Conjuring Culture*.

102 "Delight in Psalmody": Sobel, *World They Made*, 184.

103 Thomas Rankin in ibid., 204–5.

104 James Meacham in Sobel, *Trabelin' On*, 206, my emphasis.

105 Robert Farris Thompson, "An Aesthetic of the Cool: West African Dance," *African Forum* 2 (1966), 85–102, and Robert Farris Thompson, *Flash of the Spirit* (New York: Random House, 1983). Call-and-response: John Chernoff, *African Rhythm & African Sensibility* (University of Chicago Press, 1979); Lawrence Levine, *Black Culture and Black Consciousness* (Oxford University Press, 1977); John F. Callahan, *In the African-American Grain* (Urbana: University of Illinois Press, 1988); Dale Peterson, "Response and

Call: The African American Dialogue with Bakhtin," *American Literature* 65:4 (Dec. 1993), 761–75. I outline a theory of call-and-response as a communication paradigm for multiracial audiences in chapter 1 of the dissertation "On Racial Frontiers," and in "Interracial Dialogue in Rap Music."

106 On implications of nineteenth-century white "appropriation" of black cultural forms for "mainstream" American culture, see Lott, *Love and Theft*, and Lhamon, *Raising Cain*. Fraser, "Rethinking the Public Sphere."

107 Albert Raboteau, "Richard Allen and the African Church Movement," in *Black Leaders of the Nineteenth Century*, ed. Litwack and Meier, 1.

108 In 1785 Methodists sought Washington's support and petitioned the House of Delegates in Virginia to enact a general emancipation of slaves. The bill was dismissed, but not without "without an avowed patronage of its principle by sundry respectable members," according to James Madison. Nash, *Race and Revolution*, 15; James Madison to George Washington, in William Hutchinson and William Rachel, eds., *The Papers of James Madison*, VIII (University of Chicago Press, 1962), 403. See also Milton Sernett, *Black Religion and American Evangelicalism* (Metuchen, NJ: Scarecrow Press, 1975). "White discrimination": Raboteau, "Richard Allen and the African Church Movement," 2.

109 Rush's assistance: Sernett, *Black Religion and American Evangelicalism*, 117–18.

110 Albert Raboteau, "Richard Allen and the African Church Movement," in *Fire in the Bones*, 90–91.

111 There has been a long debate about the degree to which the models of government employed by the Five Nations (Mohawks, etc.) may have influenced the writers of the American Constitution. I am inclined to accept as plausible Vine DeLoria's commentary on this debate: "When we look at state–nation relations within the American constitutional framework we are looking at the Anglo adaptation of Iroquois thinking": Thomas Biolsi and Larry Zimmerman, eds., *Indians & Anthropology: Vine DeLoria & the Critique of Anthropology* (Tucson: University of Arizona Press, 1997), 217. See also "Forum: The 'Iroquois Influence' Thesis – Con and Pro," *William and Mary Quarterly* 53 (July 1996), 587–620.

Among the sources I have relied on for early examples of a black public sphere, and the centrality of white allies in its emergence, are Benjamin Brawley, *Early Negro American Writers* (New York: Dover, 1935/1970); George Brookes, *Friend Anthony Benezet* (Philadelphia: University of Pennsylvania Press, 1937); Cedric Cowing, *The Great Awakening & the American Revolution: Colonial Thought in the 18th Century* (Chicago: Rand McNally, 1971); George Crawford, *Prince Hall and His Followers* (New York: The Crisis/AMS Press, 1914/1971); Absolom Jones and Richard Allen, *A Narrative of the Proceedings of the Black People during the Late and Awful Calamity in Philadelphia, in the Year 1793* (Philadelphia: William Woodward, 1794; Early American Imprints, Microprint #17170); Porter, ed., *Early Negro Writing*; Adam Potkay and Sandra Burr, eds., *Black Atlantic Writers of the 18th Century* (New York: St. Martin's, 1995); Benjamin Quarles, *Frederick Douglass* (New York: Atheneum, 1948/1968); Raboteau, *A Fire in the Bones*; J. A. Rogers, *World's Great Men of Color*, ed. John Henrik Clark (New York: Collier, 1947/1972); Sernet, *Black Religion and American Evangelicalism*; Samuel Sewall, *The Selling of Joseph* (Boston: Bartholomew Green and John Allen, 1700).

"Contact zones": Pratt, "Linguistic Utopias."

112 On the influence that these camp meetings had on some whites, see n. 53, above, on Albert Barnes.

113 "Rhetorical culture" and "blacks and white": Condit and Lucaites, *Crafting Equality*, xii, 41, my emphasis.

114 Challenges: Genovese, *Roll, Jordan, Roll*, 204. "Earnestly": Jordan, *White Over Black*, 189. The deep-rootedness of Afro-American culture in Christian traditions show that dismissals of Christianity as the white man's religion are "merely gestural." E. Franklin Frazier, St. Clair Drake, and W. J. Moses, among others, have stressed the centrality of Western Christianity to the emergence of black political consciousness. St. Clair Drake, *The Redemption of Africa and Black Religion* (Chicago: Third World Press, 1970).

115 "Both sides": Sobel, *Trabelin' On*, 158.

116 I discuss multiple discursive strategies in the colonial era to the nineteenth century in Stephens, "On Racial Frontiers," chapter 2. "Suspect": Sobel, *Trabelin' On*, 143–44. There is a class connection here. Douglass came of age in "camp meetings" and the Zion African Methodist Episcopal church but later came to show discomfort with the "stomping" of black styles. McFeely, *Frederick Douglass*. But his writings on slave religion and music are perceptive and still relevant, Sterling Stuckey argues: *Going Through the Storm* (Oxford University Press, 1994), 52. Anti-music bias is still extant: the Church of Christ in which I was reared allowed no instruments (which may go a long ways towards explaining their traditionally lily-white congregations!).

117 Slave ship revolts also played a major role in polarizing public opinions about slavery in the antebellum era. Maggie Montesinos Sale has written about Douglass' dramatization of the *Creole* revolt (1841) in his only work of fiction, *The Heroic Slave* (1853), as well as the more indirect influence of the *Amistad* affair (1839) on Herman Melville's *Benito Cereno* (1855) in *The Slumbering Volcano* (Durham, NC: Duke University Press, 1997). *Amistad* was popularized in 1997 by a Steven Spielberg movie of the same name. On the links between the Haitian and French Revolutions, and their repercussions in the Atlantic world, see Gaspar and Geggus, *A Turbulent Time*, especially David Geggus, "Slavery, War, and Revolution in the Greater Caribbean, 1789–1815" (1–50); Michael Duffy, "The French Revolution and British Attitudes to the West Indian Colonies" (78–101); and David Geggus, "Slave Resistance in the Spanish Caribbean in the Mid–1790s" (131–55).

118 Frances Smith Foster, *Written by Herself* (Bloomington: Indiana University Press, 1993), 3–4. For biographical information: Marilyn Richardson, ed., *Maria W. Stewart* (Bloomington: Indiana University Press, 1987), and Sue E. Houchins, ed., *Spiritual Narratives* (Oxford University Press, 1988), and Marilyn Richardson, "'What if I Am a Woman?' Maria W. Stewart's Defense of Black Women's Political Activism," in *Courage and Conscience: Black and White Abolitionists in Boston*, ed. Donald M. Jacobs (Bloomington: Indiana University Press, 1993), 191–206.

119 "The grave" and "elevate us": Stewart, *Productions*, in Houchins, ed., *Spiritual Narratives*, 30, 60.

120 "Learn by experience" and "equals only": ibid., 48, 71.
121 "My breast" and "your spirits": ibid., 53, 19–20, my emphasis.
122 "Walker/Garrison": ibid., 20. "Israel from bondage": Douglass, *My Bondage and My Freedom* (New York: Dover, 1855/1969), 355; Douglass *Life and Times* (New York: Collier, 1892/1962), 213–14.
123 "Soul": Houchins, ed., *Spiritual Narratives*, 4. "Sing America": Foster, *Written by Herself*, 15.

2   FREDERICK DOUGLASS AS INTEGRATIVE ANCESTOR: THE CONSEQUENCES OF INTERRACIAL CO-CREATION

1 Philip S. Foner, ed., *L&W*, I (New York: International Publishers, 1950), Introduction; Gerald Fulkerson "Exile as Emergence: Frederick Douglass in Great Britain, 1845–1847," *Quarterly Journal of Speech* 60 (1974), 69–82; R. J. M. Blackett, *Building an Antislavery Wall* (Ithaca: Cornell University Press, 1989), 89ff.
2 Michael Lind, *The Next American Nation* (New York: Free Press Paperbacks, 1996), 378. While Douglass is a direct model for Lind's post-multicultural concept of diversity, he is an implicit model for David Hollinger's *Postethnic America*. KRS-One interview in Joe Wood, "Act Like Ya Know," *Vibe*, Aug. 9, 1995. In a speech to the National Bar Association on July 29, 1998, Supreme Court Justice Clarence Thomas, who has been denounced by many black leaders as a race traitor, "assert[ed] my right to think for myself, to refuse to have my ideas assigned to me as tho' I was an intellectual slave because I'm black ... I, like Frederick Douglass, believe that whites and blacks can live together and be blended into a common nationality": *New York Times* on the Web, July 30, 1998.
3 Rafia Zafar, "Franklinian Douglass: The Afro-American as Representative Man," in *Frederick Douglass*, ed. Eric J. Sundquist (Cambridge University Press, 1990), 99–117; Olney, "The Founding Fathers."
4 "Part Indian": McFeely, *Frederick Douglass*, 280. Douglass referred to himself as "a colored man of both Anglo-Saxon and African descent." Foner, ed., *L&W*, IV, 421.
5 I wish to call attention to the late Paul Goodman's *Of One Blood: Abolitionism and the Origins of Racial Equality* (Berkeley: University of California Press, 1998). This important work shows how racial mythology has plagued post-1960s scholarship on abolitionism, by demonstrating how interracialism spawned the resurgence of anti-slavery activism after 1830. Goodman focuses on how free black anti-colonization activists "converted" many important white abolitionists.
6 "Oppression studies": Manthia Diawara, "Black Studies, Cultural Studies: Performative Acts," *Afterimage* (Oct. 1993).
7 "Essentialized difference": Fuss, *Essentially Speaking*.
8 "Accusing position": Spivak, *The Post-Colonial Critic*, 156. "Merely gestural": Gilroy, *Small Acts*, 9. For a provocative critique of the ahistorical nature of too much of "oppositionality" in cultural studies, see Schudson, "Paper Tigers."
9 I have taken seminars at four California universities: San Francisco State, Cal-State, Hayward, University of California-Davis, and University of California-San Diego. I also spent considerable time at University of California-Berkeley, with the Berkeley area being my "home base" from 1989 to 1998.

10 Radical students dismiss Richard Rodriguez as a "sellout" because he embraces European elements of his Mexican American heritage. I discuss this in "Dancing with Richard Rodriguez' Shadow: On Multiracial Origins and the Limits of Oppositional Thinking," a paper written for the Simmons College Graduate Student Conference on "Marginality and Multiculturalism," 1995.

11 Hermeneutics of suspicion – *Semeia* 47 (1989). Paul Ricoeur used "hermeneutics of suspicion" to describe Freud's worldview and method in *Freud and Philosophy* (New Haven: Yale University Press, 1970), 32ff.

12 This cult of heroic opposition (oppositional utopias) has been critiqued by scholars of audience studies as a "fetishizing of difference." See John Corner, "Meaning, Genre and Context: The Problematics of 'Public Knowledge' in the New Audience Studies," and Todd Gitlin, "The Politics of Communication and the Communication of Politics," both in *Mass Media and Society*, ed. Curran and Gurevitch. Gitlin believes the "romance of audience resistance" is directly linked to the loss of real political power, in which "radical theories went searching for substitute proletariats, and found them in popular culture" (333–35).

13 Larene LaSonde, one of many mixed-race Americans interviewed by Lise Fundenburg, remarks: "We *are* Ralph Ellison's invisible men." *Black, White, Other: Biracial Americans Talk About Race and Identity* (New York: William Morrow, 1994), 336.

14 "House nigger": Wood, "Act Like Ya Know." "Sampling" – see KRS' mirroring of Malcolm's iconic with-gun-at-window pose on the cover of the Boogie Down Productions album *By Any Means Necessary* (Zomba/RCA, 1988).

15 "Thug life" – the late Tupac Shakur, son of a Black Panther, adopted this as his philosophy of life, tattooing the words on his belly. This "gangster" mentality became a self-fulfilling prophecy of an early death. Predictably, the cult of black revolution has turned Shakur into a messianic figure.

16 Respect to DJ RJ of KUT (AusTex) who sent me this interview.

17 Sterling Stuckey, *Slave Culture* (Oxford University Press, 1987). Waldo Martin, "Images of Frederick Douglass in the Afro-American Mind," in Sundquist, ed., *Frederick Douglass*.

18 Nat Turner/Uncle Tom: Wilson Jeremiah Moses, *Black Messiahs and Uncle Toms* (University Park: Pennsylvania State University Press, 1982), chapter 4, 49–66. Malcolm on why Douglass was not radical enough: Harold Cruse, *Crisis of the Negro Intellectual* (New York: Morrow, 1967), 429; Betty Shabazz, ed., *Malcolm X on Afro-American History* (New York: Pathfinder, 1970), 68.

19 "Lie-bury": KRS' term on *By Any Means Necessary*.

20 Ideal audience – KRS worked with reggae greats Sly & Robbie and had a broad multiracial audience. DJ RJ, my good friend in AusTex, became a vegetarian after hearing KRS' song "Beef" – an example of why I consider KRS' audience *my* ideal audience.

21 "Inclusion": Ellison, "What America Would Be Like Without Blacks," in *Collected Essays*, 582.

22 Michael Billig denounces (in reactive fashion) an "ethnocentrism of inclusion" in "Nationalism and Richard Rorty: The Text as a Flag for *Pax Americana*," *New Left Review* 47 (Nov.–Dec. 1993).

23 Cleveland convention/half white: Howard Holman Bell, *A Survey of the Negro*

Convention Movement 1830–1861 (New York: Arno Press, 1969), 101–2; "repulsive," white wife: Foner, ed., *L&W*, IV, 422, 427. Biraciality as refutation of "curse of Ham": Frederick Douglass, *Autobiographies*, ed. and with notes by Henry Louis Gates Jr. (New York: The Library of America/Penguin, 1845/1994), 17–18; Frederick Douglass, *Narrative of the Life of Frederick Douglass, an American Slave, Written by Himself*, ed. with an introduction by David Blight (Boston and New York: Bedford Books of St. Martin's Press, 1845/1993), 41.

24 Preston, *Young Frederick Douglass*, 9. "Indian boy": Douglass, *My Bondage and My Freedom*, 80. "Part Indian": Douglass, *Life and Times*, 513. "Known . . . as Indian": Frederick Douglass Papers, Manuscript Division, Library of Congress, container 33, microfilm reel 21.

25 Gates, *Signifying Monkey*, ix–xxv, writes of the impossibility of any text being "just black" because of the interpenetration between "parallel discursive universes." "Antagonistic cooperation": Ellison, *Shadow and Act*, 143. Anderson, *Imagined Communities*. Gregory P. Lampe, *Frederick Douglass* (East Lansing: Michigan State University Press, 1998), 13.

26 "Emancipate his slaves": Douglass, *My Bondage and My Freedom*, 194. Thomas Auld became Douglass' master, and Aaron his owner.

27 Ibid., my emphasis.

28 "Mystery": ibid., 51.

29 "Another Nat Turner": ibid., 200. Turner was hung after his bloodly uprising in Southampton County, Virginia (August 1831). The tremors of this, "the bloodiest slave revolt in Southern history," were obviously still being felt during Douglass' youth. Stephen B. Oates, *The Fires of Jubilee: Nat Turner's Fierce Rebellion* (New York: Harper and Row, 1975/1990), 4.

30 "As a child"; "running away with himself": Douglass, *My Bandage and My Freedom*, 142, 146. Gatewood, *Aristocrats of Color*.

31 "New republic": McFeely, *Frederick Douglass*, 34. As a journalist, his model was gleaned from the *Columbian Orator*. See Shelly Fishkin and Carla Peterson, "'We Hold These Truths to be Self-Evident': The Rhetoric of Frederick Douglass' Journalism," in Sundquist, ed., *Frederick Douglass*.

32 Intensely curious: McFeely, *Frederick Douglass*, 22.

33 Moses, *Black Messiahs and Uncle Toms*.

34 See Vincent Harding and Nell Irvin Painter's comments on the PBS program "When the Lion Wrote History."

35 Perry, *Malcolm*. See reactions in Wood, *Malcolm X*, esp. Arnold's Rampersad's essay "The Color of His Eyes: Bruce Perry's *Malcolm* and Malcolm's Malcolm."

36 "*Symballein*": Jolande Jacobi, *Complex/Archetype/Symbol* (Princeton University Press, 1959), 88.

37 Symbols vs. signs: Jung, *Psychological Types*, 473–81. By contrast, Freud, whose work never left its roots in "the vocabulary of racial science," makes comments on mixed-raced people which are similar to that of white supremacists such as Houston Stewart Chamberlain. Freud compares psychic contents of the preconscious to the *Mischling* or "half-breed": "We may compare them with individuals of mixed race who . . . resemble whites, but who betray their colored descent by some striking feature or other, and on that account are excluded from society and enjoy none of the privileges of white people." As Sander Gilman observes: "The inability to 'pass' is central here. The image

of individuals who attempt to cross racial lines but who inevitably reveal their difference is at the center of Freud's concern. One can convert, but one cannot hide": *Freud, Race, and Gender* (Princeton University Press, 1993), 17, 21. Sigmund Freud, "The Unconscious" (1915), in *The Standard Edition of the Complete Psychological Works of Sigmund Freud* (London: Hogarth Press, 1957), XIV, 191.

38 "More a symptom than a symbol": Jacobi, *Complex/Archetype/Symbol*, 96, emphasis in original. "Repressed antithesis": Jung, *Psychological Types*, 607. Although I am using Jung's theories to support a positive interpretation of interraciality, it must be acknowledged that Jung shared most of the prejudices of his day about mulattos. See Adams, *The Multicultural Imagination*, 130–31, and Jung's *Nietzsche's Zarathustra*, 643–44.

39 "Discursive universes": Gates, *Signifying Monkey*, xxii.

40 "Anglo-African" and "Irishman": McFeely, *Frederick Douglass*, 303, 280.

41 Benjamin Quarles, *Black Abolitionists* (Oxford University Press, 1973), and Benjamin Quarles, *Allies for Freedom: Blacks and John Brown* (Oxford University Press, 1973). Douglass is seldom seen in *Radical Abolitionism: Anarchy and the Government of God in Antislavery Thought*, published by Lewis Perry in 1973. In his preface to the 1995 reprint (Knoxville: University of Tennessee Press), Perry still equated radical abolitionism with Garrison. Douglass saw himself and Gerrit Smith as representatives of the "radical abolition" wing, and argued that Garrisonians' extreme political Puritanism actually left them in a quite reactionary position. "The Antislavery Movement" (1855), in Philip S. Foner, ed. *L&W*, (New York: International Publishers, 1950), II, 333–59.

42 In "The Antislavery Movement" (ibid., 350), Douglass classified abolitionsts in four main groups: (a) Garrisonians; (b) Anti-Garrisonians; (c) Political Abolitionists, or The Free Soil Party; (d) The Liberty Party, i.e., the Gerrit Smith School.

43 Jane Pease and William Pease, *They Who Would Be Free* (New York: Atheneum, 1974/1990), 15.

44 Mary Louise Pratt, "Linguistic Utopias," and Pratt, "Criticism in the Contact Zone." On abolitionism's interracial origins, see Goodman, *Of One Blood*.

45 Douglass, *My Bondage and My Freedom*, 194.

46 80 percent white subscribers: Pease, *They Who Would Be Free*, 117. In the early days of Garrison's paper, three-quarters of his subscribers were black: ibid., 31. Black writers published in the *Liberator*, but it did not have the same impact on "mainstream" politics – partly because of Garrisonians' self-righteous anti-political postures. Ralph Ellison noted the irony that white support "kept Frederick Douglass going ... just as a black sailmaker, a successful businessman in Philadelphia [James Forten], kept William Lloyd Garrison's paper, *The Liberator*, going in the name of Abolition": "Roscoe Dunjee & the American Language," in *Collected Essays*, 456.

Anna Richardson of Newcastle led the drive to purchase Douglass' freedom. He used additional funds from this drive to purchase his printing press. Blackett, *Building an Antislavery Wall*, 113.

47 Griffiths ... "his writing": Foner, *L&W*, I, 92.

48 "Indebted": Foner, ibid., 89. "Companion": Foner, ed., *L&W*, II, 47.
49 "Inexhaustible": Douglass, *Life and Times*, 706. Patterson, *The Ordeal of Integration*, 197. On Griffiths' contributions after 1855, see Blackett, *Building an Antislavery Wall*, 115. Maria Diedrich of the University of Munster is writing a biography of Otilia Assing, a German abolitionist who had a long relationship with Douglass. She committed suicide shortly after he married Helen Pitts in 1884.
50 James Smith: Douglass, *Autobiographies*, 1085–86; John Brown/"*impressions*": Douglas, *Life and Times*, 719, my emphasis.
51 Multiracial sphere: Stephens, "On Racial Frontiers," chapter 1; historical roots: Sobel, *World They Made*. In an intellectual climate in which oppositionality and the "hermeneutics of suspicion" is a fashion, seeing Judeo-Christian scriptures as having "redeemable" elements is a minority opinion. For a critique of reflexive dismissal of religious beliefs, see Stephen L. Carter, *The Culture of Disbelief* (New York: Basic Books, 1993). For a recent study of the "dark side" of Judaic scriptures: Regina Schwartz, *The Curse of Cain: The Violent Legacy of Monotheism* (University of Chicago Press, 1997). The scholar of religious expression who has most influenced me, Carl Jung, paid considerable attention to destructive, monologic, and patriarchal elements in Judeo-Christian scripture. See for instance his *Answer to Job* (London: Routledge & Paul, 1954) (and in *Psychology and Religion*). But Jung also insisted on interpreting the "dark side" of this tradition and its "redemptive" potential as two sides of the same coin. Of two recent Jung-inspired collections of Bible criticism, *Jung and the Monotheisms*, ed. Joel Ryce-Menuhin (London: Routledge, 1994), pays some attention to the "Us vs. Them" patterns Schwartz critiques, while *Jung and the Interpretation of the Bible*, ed. David L. Miller (New York: Continuum, 1995) focuses primarily on Biblical examples of psychological transformation.
52 The *North Star* declared its openness to all abolitionists, no matter their philosophical differences. Garrison did not tolerate deviations from his party line. But even after Garrisonians turned on him, Douglass still tried to mediate between Garrisonians and other abolitionists. See McFeely, *Frederick Douglass*, 175–76. On how Douglass' position between white and black abolitionists shaped his ideology, see Waldo Martin, *The Mind of Frederick Douglass* (Chapel Hill: University of North Carolina Press, 1984), 56–57.
53 This lends support to Nancy Fraser's theory that the dual character of counter-publics, both separatist and integrationist, gives them "emancipatory potential." However, the "emancipatory potential" of counter-publics depend heavily on the character of their spokespersons. Douglass' counter-public "redeemed" much of its emancipatory potential, because he consistently balanced themes of separation and integration: both oppositional critique, and articulation of potential common ground. Garrisonians voiced counter-publics of sheer opposition. As Puritans they were intent on separation from an enemy. Without being able to imagine integration they could not "redeem" liberatory potential or engage in politics. Fraser, "Rethinking the Public Sphere."
54 "Solutions [to problems facing] those who thought about ending slavery in America [depended] on a willingness to make economic sacrifices [and] an

ability to envision a truly biracial republic society": Nash, *Race and Revolution*, 35. "Among the . . . reasons for the Revolution's failure to cope with slavery were an inability to imagine a genuinely multiracial society, and an over-scrupulous regard for private property": Lynd, *Class Conflict, Slavery*, 180.

"Foundation": "The Dread Scott Decision," speech to American Anti-Slavery Society, May 11, 1857 (Foner, ed., *L&W*, II, 415, my emphasis). See also Nieman, *Promises to Keep*. "Practice followed": contrary to conventional wisdom, post-1877 antiracist activism continued and led directly to the founding of the NAACP and indirectly to the Civil Rights movement. See McPherson, *The Abolitionist Legacy*.

55 Gilroy, *Black Atlantic*. Hughes and Hughes, *Where Peoples Meet*.

56 "Congregation": David Paul Nord, "Tocqueville, Garrison and the Perfection of Journalism," *Journalism History* 13:2 (Summer 1986), 59; Robert Bellah, "Civil Religion in America," *Daedalus* 96 (1967), 1–21.

57 Garrison as Moses: Douglass, *Life and Times*, 213–14 (1994, 658–59). Jung to Freud, October 28, 1907: ". . . my veneration for you has something of the character of a 'religious' crush": *The Freud/Jung Letters*, ed. William McGuire, (Princeton University Press, 1974), 95.

58 "Justice": Martin, *The Mind of Frederick Douglass*, 20; "forces": Foner, ed., *L&W*, II, 333. "Even when secularized, the belief in natural rights retained the fervency – and authority – of the religious conviction from which they had arrived": Priscilla Ward, *Constituting Americans* (Durham: Duke University Press, 1995), 19.

59 Foster, *Written By Herself*, 21; Aileen Kraditor, *The Ideas of the Woman Suffrage Movement* (New York: Norton, 1981); Philip S. Foner, *Frederick Douglass on Women's Rights* (New York: Da Capo Press, 1992).

60 Condit and John Lucaites, *Crafting Equality*, 7; "sing America": Foster, *Written By Herself*, and Robert Branham, "'Of Thee I Sing': Contesting 'America'," *American Quarterly* 48:4 (Dec. 1996); "shareable language": Sundquist, *To Wake the Nations*.

61 "Assimilation": Ralph Ellison, "What America Would Be Like Without Blacks," *Time*, Apr. 6, 1970, in *Collected Essays*, 582; "racial Christianity": Moses, *Black Messiahs and Uncle Toms*, 46.

62 "Two religions": McFeely, *Frederick Douglass*, 84; "Zion church . . . bondage": ibid., 85; evangelical style: Moses, *Black Messiahs and Uncle Toms*, 46.

63 Foreshadows: Moses, *Black Messiahs and Uncle Toms*, 48. Eighteenth century: Sobel, *World They Made*. "Redeemable ideals": Sundquist, *Frederick Douglass*, 14–15.

64 "Black advances": Martin, *The Mind of Frederick Douglass*, 55.

65 "Calling card" and "charming": ibid., 24, 43; "repressed quest": McFeely, *Frederick Douglass*, 142.

66 "Agent": Douglass, *Life and Times* (1892, 264; 1994, 708). "De Foe": Henry Louis Gates, "Binary Oppositions in Chapter One of Douglass' *Narrative*," in *Critical Essays on Frederick Douglass*, ed. William L. Andrews (Boston: G. K. Hall & Co., 1991), 2.

67 "Popularity": Blackett, *Building an Antislavery Wall*, 106. "Colored their faces" and "Ethiopian lions": a correspondent for the *New York Express*, quoted in *National Anti-Slavery Standard*, July 1, 1847, and Blackett, *Building*

an Antislavery Wall, 39–40. "Accomplished women": Webb to Maria Chapmen, ibid., 112. "Half a Negro": FD to Francis Jackson, Jan. 29, 1846, in Foner, ed., *L&W*, I, 136. FD to Garrison, ibid., 127. Douglass' phrase "send back the money" (re Scottish churches accepting donations from Southern churches) was a "hit" in Scotland in 1846. See Fulkerson, "Exile as Emergence," and Blackett, *Building an Antislavery Wall*, 89ff.

68 "Child to parent": Douglass to Charles Sumner, Sept. 2, 1852: Charles Sumner Papers, Harvard University; Foner, ed., *L&W*, II, 210.

69 "Set him apart": Martin, *Mind of Frederick Douglas*, 56; Walker: Foner, ed., *L&W*, II, 22.

70 "Slavery churches": Martin, *Mind of Frederick Douglass*, 23.

71 "The axe . . . ": *North Star*, Mar. 10, 1848; "voice of . . . ": Bell, *A Survey of the Negro Convention Movement*, 98. "Race or color": quoted in Benjamin Quarles, "Abolition's Different Drummer: Frederick Douglass," in *The Antislavery Vanguard*, ed. Martin Duberman (Princeton University Press, 1965), 132–3.

72 Garnet's attacks/Douglass' response: *North Star*, Nov. 16, 1849.

73 "Themselves": Donald Gibson, "Faith, Doubt, and Apostasy: Evidence of Things Unseen in Frederick Douglass's *Narrative*," in Sundquist, *Frederick Douglass*, 91–2; "intervention": Fishkin and Peterson, "'We Hold These Truths to Be Self-Evident'," 194. "Solomon": Foner, ed., *L&W*, I, 380. Song of Songs 1:5.

74 "Senses": Martin, *Mind of Frederick Douglass*, 38; ambiguity: John McKivigan, "The Frederick Douglass–Gerrit Smith Friendship & Political Abolitionism in the 1850s," in Sundquist, ed., *Frederick Douglass*, 205–32. Some of Douglass' exchanges with other black leaders in his paper were quite critical. In 1849 he attacked Henry Highland Garnet for advocating emigration. In 1850 he chided Ward for speaking at a segregated antislavery rally. But in general, Douglass acted as moderator and mediator, and even when he and other blacks did engage in mutual criticism, "Douglass comes off as the more measured and community-concerned writer": Levine, *Politics of Representative Identity*, 56.

75 James McCune Smith/"mulatto identity": Martin, *Mind of Frederick Douglass*, 58.

76 "White friends": *North Star*, Dec. 3, 1847. "Break down the walls": Douglass, *Life and Times*, 453. Lewis Hyde interprets Douglass' role of interracial mediator as that of a trickster in "Frederick Douglass and Eshu's Hat," in *Trickster Makes This World* (New York: Farrar, Straus & Giroux, 1998), 226–51.

77 "Oppressed . . . whites as well": Martin, *Mind of Frederick Douglass*, 94.

78 David Blight, *Frederick Douglass' Civil War* (Baton Rouge: Louisiana State University Press, 1989), 47.

79 McFeely, *Frederick Douglass*, 73. David R. Chesebrough, *Frederick Douglass* (Westport, CT: Greenwood Press, 1998), 47. Similar assessments of this speech are in Sundquist, ed., *Frederick Douglass*, 14, and in Andrews, ed., *Critical Essays on Frederick Douglass*, 58, 60.

80 Gerald Fulkerson, "Frederick Douglass and the Kansas-Nebraska Act: A Case Study in Agitational Versatility," *Central States Speech Journal* 23

(1972), 261. Chesebrough, *Frederick Douglass*; Lampe, *Frederick Douglass*. Robert Felgar, "The Rediscovery of Frederick Douglass," *Mississippi Quarterly* 35 (Fall 1982), 427–31.

81 Abolitionist speaker: Thomas Harwood, "Great Britain and American Anti-Slavery" (PhD dissertation, University of Texas, 1959), 386; antebellum orator: Robert Oliver, *History of Public Speaking in America* (Boston: Allyn & Bacon, 1965), 246.

82 "Cadences": George Whitfield, "Frederick Douglass: Negro Abolitionist," *Today's Speech* (1963), 7; "eloquence of Frederick Douglass": ibid., 24; "florid prose": Fulkerson, "Exile as Emergence," 70.

83 Pamphlets: Foner, ed., *L&W*, II, 95. Summaries: Fulkerson, "Frederick Douglass and the Kansas-Nebraska Act," 265.

84 Stephen Douglas: Fulkerson, "Frederick Douglass and the Kansas-Nebraska Act," 267–8.

85 "White editors": Russ Castronovo, *Fathering the Nation* (Berkeley: University of California Press, 1995), 197. "Speaking to white men": Peter Walker, "Frederick Douglass: Orphan Slave," in *Moral Choices* (Baton Rouge: Louisiana State University Press, 1978), 242.

86 On the preference for the *Narrative* over *My Bondage and My Freedom*, see Wilson Moses, "Dark Forests and Barbarian Vigor: Paradox, Conflict, and Africanity in Black Writing before 1914," *American Literature* 1 (1989), 637–42.

87 Levine, *Politics of Representative Identity*, 242, n. 16. 1852–55 was transitional, among other reasons, because in 1851 Douglass had renamed his paper, and officially broken with Garrisonians. He was also becoming radicalized in response to the 1850 Fugitive Slave Law.

88 "Appropriative reader": ibid., 73. Levine, "*Uncle Tom's Cabin* in *Frederick Douglass' Paper*: An Analysis of Reception," *American Literature* 64 (1992), 71–93.

89 "Working assumption": Levine, *Politics of Representative Identity*, 82.

90 William Andrews, "The 1850s: The First Afro-American Literary Renaissance," in *Literary Romanticism in America* (Baton Rouge: Louisiana State University Press, 1981), 42. Sacvan Bercovitch, *The American Jeremiad* (Madison: University of Wisconsin Press, 1978). Genevieve Fabre, "African-American Commemorative Celebrations in the Nineteenth Century," in *History and Memory in African-American Culture*, ed. Genevieve Fabre and Robert O'Meally (Oxford University Press, 1994), 72–91.

91 "Spokesmen/myth making/symbols": Andrews, *Literary Romanticism*, 46–7. A valuable recent book which critically reviews a long history of attempts to debunk reports on Jefferson's personal miscegenation is Annette Gordon-Reed, *Thomas Jefferson and Sally Hemings: An American Controversy* (Virginia University Press, 1997).

92 "Third place"/race over nation/emigration based on Exodus archetype/Manifest Destiny: Levine, *Politics of Representative Identity*, 60, 64, 67.

93 "Sunlight": *Frederick Douglass' Paper*, May 27, 1852, quoted in ibid., 259. "Modify" and "such display": ibid., 77, 79. Paul Gilroy's claim that attempts to be purely oppositional are "merely gestural" (*Small Acts*, 9) echoes Douglass' comments.

94 "Abolitionizing ... mind" and "white and black reasons": Foner, ed., *L&W*, II, 482, 414.
95 "White audience ... a colored man ... horizon ... crisis": ibid., 243, 246. "At one with his people": Blight, *Frederick Douglass' Civil War*, 47.
96 Even the most oppositional of writers and artists in antebellum America tended to unconsciously replicate many aspects of imperialist thought, as Wai-chee Dimock persuasively illustrates in *Empire for Liberty: Meville and the Poetics of Individualism* (Princeton University Press, 1989). My own thinking on the link between slavery and freedom, and between empire and liberty, has been influenced by Orlando Patterson's *Freedom in the Making of Western Culture* (London: I. B. Tauris, 1991), Paz' critique of North America as a monologic "imperial democracy" in *Labyrinth of Solitude*, and Morgan's magisterial study, *American Slavery*. On American millennialism, a good starting point is Tuveson's *Redeemer Nation*. The millennial nature of Douglass' thought is explored in Blight's *Frederick Douglass' Civil War*.
97 "Hero worship/adoration": Douglass, *My Bondage and My Freedom*, 354, 394. Reappraising patriarchs: Castonovo, *Fathering the Nation*; Donald Gibson, "Christianity and Individualism: (Re-)Creation and Reality in Frederick Douglass' Representation of Self," *African-American Review 26* (1992), 591–603. On medical roots of the word "projection" and both Freud's and Jung's differing adaptations, see George Hogenson, *Jung's Struggle with Freud* (Wilmette, IL: Chiron Press, 1994), 120ff. Some of Jung's comments on the dangers of unrecognized projections: *The Structure and Dynamics of the Psyche* (Princeton University Press, 1969), *Collected Works*, VIII, 265; *Psychology and Religion* (Princeton University Press, 1958/ 1969), *Collected Works*, XI, 12. On the withdrawal of projections: ibid., 83–85. See also Marie-Louise von Franz, *Projection and Re-Collection in Jungian Psychology* (La Salle and London: Open Court, 1980).
98 "Bigoted in spirit": Foner, ed., *L&W*, II, 210.
99 I have used the text of this speech in ibid. The full speech also appears in Carter Woodson, *Negro Orators & Their Orations* (Washington, DC: Associated Publishers, 1925), and William Andrews, ed., *The Oxford Frederick Douglass Reader* (Oxford University Press, 1996), 108–39. The short edit seems to follow the extract Douglass printed in an Appendix to *My Bondage and My Freedom*.
100 "Mediatory symbols": Jung, *Psychological Types*, 473–81. A symbol created out of a collision between opposites, and having "bipolar" meaning capable of mediating between binaries and creating a third space or "third thing." Jung, *Structure and Dynamics of the Psyche*, 90; C. G. Jung, *Alchemical Studies* (Princeton University Press, 1968), *Collected Works*, XIII, 134.
101 Delany/Douglass' use of "your revolutionary fathers": Levine, *Politics of Representative Identity*, 61. "Invoking fathers": Castronovo, *Fathering the Nation*, 42. "Prominent ... heroic fathers": Priscilla Ward, "Neither Citizen nor Alien: National Narratives, Frederick Douglass, and the Politics of Self-Definition," in *Constituting Americans*, 64.
102 Bercovitch, *American Jeremiad*, 191. Castronovo, *Fathering the Nation*, 194–5.
103 Castronovo points out a fascinating parallel in the language used by both

Douglass and apologists for slavery in attempting to prove that they were following the model of the founders. In *My Bondage and My Freedom*, Douglass made this argument in favor of the slave's use of violence: "If he kills his master, he imitates only the heroes of the revolution" (1855: 191). Chief Justice Roger Taney, in rejecting Dred Scott's suit for freedom, opined that in holding human beings in bondage, the slaveholder *"imitates only the heroes* of revolution" (*Dred Scott* v. *Sanders*, 703, quoted in Castronovo, *Fathering the Nation*, 196), my emphasis.

104 "Entire winter": Douglass, *Life and Times*, 708.

105 "Free of blackness"; Scotland; "his tongue": Walker, "Frederick Douglass: Orphan Slave," 257, 256, 242. Anthony/"father image": Preston, *Young Frederick Douglass*, 23, 25. "For a time I was made to forget that my skin was dark and my hair cripped," Douglass recalled of his early Garrisonian days. Gates thinks Douglass "graft[ed] himself onto his nameless white father's heritage, here displaced in the white Garrisonians": "Frederick Douglass and the Language of the Self," in *Figures in Black* (Oxford University Press, 1987), 119–20.

106 "Antitype . . . prophecy": Smith, *Conjuring Culture*, 55.

107 Moses types: Sollors, *Beyond Ethnicity*; Levine, *Politics of Representative Identity*.

108 the Melodians' 1973 song "Rivers of Babylon" is available on the compilation *Groove Yard* (Mango/Island, 1979). Steel Pulse's "Rally Round" is from *True Democracy* (Elektra, 1980). A traditional version of "Rivers of Babylon" also appears on the *Wingless Angels* albums produced by Keith Richards (1997).

109 "Not so white after all": Levine, *Politics of Representative Identity*, 38. In a speech at Harvard in 1973, Ralph Ellison remarked that he did not recognize "any white culture. I recognize no American culture which is not a partial creation of black people." Graham and Singh, eds., *Conversations with Ralph Ellison*, xiii.

110 Sale, *The Slumbering Volcano*, 195. "Post-Revolutionary generation/truer 'son'": Sundquist, *Frederick Douglass*, 14–15. Also Wald, *Constituting Americans*, 92. I make two allusions here: to Bob Marley's song "Zimbabwe": "Now we'll find out who are the real revolutionaries"; and to the invisibility of Afro-Americans as social actors, which becomes, of course, the theme of Ellison's *Invisible Man*.

111 "Self-fathering": Sundquist, *Frederick Douglass* 12. In some ways the manner in which Douglass interacts with his white audience is a forerunner of what Shelby Steele has called a "harrangue-flagellation ritual" in the 1960s – in *The Content of our Character* (New York: St. Martin's, 1990).

112 "Quoted verse": Raboteau, *A Fire in the Bones*, 42. On political applications of Psalms 68:31, see George Frederickson's excellent survey "'Ethiopia Shall Stretch Forth Her Hands': Black Christianity and the Politics of Liberation," in *Black Liberation* (Oxford University Press, 1995), 57–93.

113 Tuveson, *Redeemer Nation*. I trace historical usage of Psalms 68:31, to argue for racial equality and later a messianic destiny for black people, in "Ethiopia is in the House: A Brief History of a Biblical Idea in Multiracial Context," in

manuscript. Ola Elizabeth Winslow, *Samuel Sewall of Boston* (New York: MacMillan, 1964). See also Sewall, *The Selling of Joseph*, and Jones and Allen, *A Narrative*, available on microfiche. On the lines between Sewall and the Boston abolitionists for whom Douglass was an agent, see Donald Jacobs, "David Walker and William Lloyd Garrison: Racial Cooperation and the Shaping of Boston Abolition," and James Brewer Stewart, "Boston, Abolition, and the Atlantic World, 1820–1861," in *Courage and Conscience*, ed. Jacobs.

114 Yekutiel Gershoni, *Black Colonialism* (Boulder: Westview Press, 1985); Levine, *Politics of Representative Identity*, chapter 2, esp. 63ff: "a colonizing, or imperial, desire guides [Delany's] Central American vision, one not so very different from that of the filibusterer William Walker." "Glimpse": Gibson, "Christianity and Individualism," 600.

115 These are McFeely's words: *Frederick Douglass*, 158.

116 Douglass refers to the "higher law" controversy. New York clergy had set aside Dec. 12, 1850 for sermons upholding the Compromise of 1850. They advised acquiescence and denounced the "higher law" doctrine which argued that scriptures insisting on the commonality of all humanity should take precedent over unjust human laws. Many of these sermons were published, such as John C. Lord's *The Higher Law in its Application to the Fugitive Slave Bill* (New York: 1851). Foner, ed., *L&W*, II, 561–62.

117 A good overview of how Psalms 68 and the theme of "father for the fatherless" has been used in Afro-American religious history is Cheryl Townsend Gilkes, "'Mother to the Motherless, Father to the Fatherless': Power, Gender, and Community in an Afrocentric Biblical Tradition," *Semeia* 47 (1989), 57–85.

118 "Perfectionist philosophy": McKivigan, "The Frederick Douglass–Gerrit Smith Friendship & Political Abolitionism in the 1850s," 206.

119 Douglass tried to educate his contempories, who were inclined to view Garrison as the "founder" of abolitionism, about the deep roots of the antislavery movement in the eighteenth century and beyond: "the oldest abolitionist of to-day is but the preacher of a faith framed and practised long before he was born": Foner, ed., *L&W*, II, 337.

120 Nineteenth-century black egalitarians often employed the Declaration "as a rhetorical fulcrum to give leverage to Equality as a primary commitment of the community, promoting it to the status of the prevailing and competing constitutive values of Liberty and Property": Condit and Lucaites, *Crafting Equality*, 88.

121 On the use of Acts 17:26 ("One Blood") in multiethnic context: Sollors, *Beyond Ethnicity*, 60–65. Abolitionist use: Goodman, *Of One Blood*.

122 Condit and Lucaites see the "One Blood" ideal as being "white abolitionist"/Christian: *Crafting Equality*, 79. My research on eighteenth- and nineteenth-century use of the Bible to argue for racial equality suggests otherwise.

123 Anne Weaver Teabeau cited in *Jet*, Nov. 22, 1979, 30.

124 "Not unforgiveable": Waldo Martin, "Images of Frederick Douglass in the Afro-American Mind," in Sundquist, ed., *Frederick Douglass*, 281.

125 "Anti-nationalist" and Fanon, etc.: Wilson Jeremiah Moses, *The Golden Age*

of Black Nationalism, 1850–1925 (New York: Oxford University Press, 1978), 84, 282.

126 Opposition and "decline": August Meier, *Negro Thought in American, 1880–1915* (Ann Arbor: University of Michigan Press, 1988), 54, 76. Surveys: Andrews, "Introduction," in *Critical Essays on Frederick Douglass*; Martin, "Images of Frederick Douglass in the Afro-American Mind," in Sundquist, ed., *Frederick Douglass*, 271–85. On Malcolm's comments: *By Any Means Necessary: Speeches, Interviews*, ed. George Breitman (New York: Pathfinder, 1970), 3–14. This list of "race leaders" with white wives also includes Douglass' contemporaries: Charles Purvis and Archibald Grimke. Washington's biography of Douglass: Wilson J. Moses, "Frederick Douglass and the Constraints of Racialized Writing," in Sundquist, ed., *Frederick Douglass*, 77. The "closeting" of white spouses by black men in public positions continues. It would have been almost impossible to tell from Richard Wright's work that he was married to a white woman: his legitimacy depended upon claiming an unbridgeable divide between himself, as representative of an oppressed people, and his white audience. Calling attention to his own interracial positionality could have undermined his ability to arouse guilt among his white readers.

127 The mistrust of the desire to have official recognition of both sides of a mixed heritage is in part a reaction to historical claims of privilege by some mulattos (see Gatewood, *Aristocrats of Color*). There is also a widely expressed fear that official recognition of mixed-race people would be used as a "wedge" between blacks and whites: reflecting a recognition that political power comes from numbers. The end result is that the old "One Drop" rule, which held that any African ancestry made one black, is now being perpetuated primarily by Afro-Americans. Patterson, *The Ordeal of Integration*, 194. Lenny Kravitz quote in Lynn Norment, "Am I Black, White or In Between: Is There a Plot to Create a 'Colored' Buffer Race in America?" *Ebony* (Aug. 1995), 110–12. The author ends the article by writing: "Some biracial brothers and sisters might do well to heed advice from Lenny Kravitz . . . 'In this world, if you have one spot of Black blood, you are *Black*. So get over it'." Lisa Jones, *Bullet-Proof Diva* (New York: Doubleday, 1994). Hostility towards interracial couples by black women writers is widespread and generally uncriticized, considering that similar attitudes would be roundly condemned if voiced by whites. See the rather virulent view of black men who date white women in Sister Souljah's *No Disrespect* (New York: Times Books, 1994), or Aliona Gibson's *Nappy: Growing Up Black and Female in America* (New York: Harlem River Press/Writers and Readers Publishing, 1995). My sense is that this phenomenon is pervasive. *The Chronicle of Higher Education* ran a cover story about black women at Brown University who ignited a campus controversy by posting a "Wall of Shame" – which listed famous black men who had married white women, as well as black male students dating white women. Ben Gose, "Public Debate over a Private Choice," May 10, 1996.

Gloria Wade-Gayles has provided a thoughtful personal view on (and gentle critique of) the widespread hostility among young black women towards black men who marry white women in "A Change of Heart about

Matters of the Heart: An Anger Shift from Interracial Marriages to Real Problems," in *Rooted Against the Wind* (Boston: Beacon, 1997), 87–131.

Recent works among black intellectuals which reflect a distrust of, and often a hostility to, the movement for recognition of biracial identity include Jon Michael Spencer, *The New Colored People: The Mixed-Race Moment in America* (New York University Press, 1997); Itabari Njeri, *The Last Plantation: Color, Conflict, and Identity. Reflections of a New World Black* (Boston: Houghton Mifflin, 1997).

128 Wilson J. Moses, "Frederick Douglass and the Constraints of Racialized Writing," in Sundquist, ed., *Frederick Douglass*, 66–83.

129 "Political insight"; "defective"; "ordinary Negro": Waldo Martin, *The Mind of Frederick Douglass*, 91, 72, 74. Dickson Preston documents that Douglass' difficulties with identifying with lower-class blacks are rooted in his own extended Maryland family in *Young Frederick Douglass*.

130 Moses, *Black Messiahs and Uncle Toms*.

131 Reminders of slavery: McFeely, *Frederick Douglass*, 211–12. Douglass' relentless criticisms of "lynch law" and of slanders of blacks in the press preceded his association with Ida B. Wells-Barnett by two decades, and refute the charge that he had lost his critical edge. See his critique of "Ku-Kluxism" in "Demands of the Hour" and "Barbarism Against Civilization," both from *New National Era*, Apr. 6, 1871, reprinted in Foner, ed., *L&W*, IV, 241–44. Note also his documentation of mob violence against blacks in "Address to the People of the U.S.," delivered in Louisville, Kentucky, on Sept. 24, 1883 (ibid., 373–92); his 1886 letter to Francis Grimke (ibid., 428–29), or the scathing 1886 speech on "Southern Barbarism" (ibid., 430–42). Both Douglass and Ida B. Wells tended to accept that many Negroes who had been lynched "were weak enough to accept favors from white women," but heatedly denied the charges of rape. Wells pointed out the hypocrisy of such charges coming from "white men who had created a race of mulattoes by raping and consorting with Negro women" and "were still doing so wherever they could": *Crusade for Justice* (University of Chicago Press, 1970), 71. See also Douglass, "Why is the Negro Lynched?" (from the pamphlet *The Lesson of the Hour*, 1894), in Foner, ed., *L&W*, IV, 491–523.

132 Moses, in Sundquist, ed., *Frederick Douglass*, 78; Martin, *The Mind of Frederick Douglass*, 100; Meier, *Negro Thought in America*, 76.

133 "Earth will remain" and "drive out the Negro": Michael Meyer, ed., *Frederick Douglass* (New York: Modern Library, 1984), 388, 390, and Howard Brotz, ed., *Negro Social and Political Thought 1850–1920* (New York: Basic Books, 1966), 307.

134 "Become Englishmen": Meyer, *Frederick Douglass* 391, and Brotz, *Negro Social and Political Thought*, 308.

135 "Pressures": McFeely, *Frederick Douglass*, 182. Griffiths' UK activism: see Blackett, *Building an Antislavery Wall*, 115.

136 "Honeymoon," "encouraging intermarriages," and social intercourse: Pease, *They Who Would Be Free*, 83, 6, 68.

137 Visits to Hopedale and Florence: McFeely, *Frederick Douglass*, 97.

138 Carolyn L. Karcher, *The First Woman in the Republic* (Durham, NC: Duke University Press, 1994).

139 "Two White Women": Meyer, *Frederick Douglass*, 294–98. See Richard
    Webb's comments on upper-class white women "patting" Frederick Doug-
    las in Blackett, *Building an Antislavery Wall*, 112. Douglass' piece on
    "American Colorphobia," published in May 1848, reflects the new vantage
    England gave him on the insularity of US racial obsessions. Meyer, *Frederick
    Douglass*, 273–76.

140 At the 1848 Seneca Falls Convention, Douglass' support enabled passage by
    one vote of Elizabeth Stanton's resolution urging women to seek "elective
    franchise." Garrison opposed it. McFeely, *Frederick Douglass*, 156. Douglass
    introduced similar language at the 1848 Cleveland Negro Convention.
    Griffiths and Auld: Moses, in Sundquist, ed., *Frederick Douglass*, 77.

141 "Every inch a man": Martin, *The Mind of Frederick Douglass*, 43. In a letter to
    Elizabeth Cady Stanton, shortly after his second marriage, Douglass impli-
    citly references the illiteracy of his first wife, Anna. "How good it is to have a
    wife who can read and write, and who can as Margaret Fuller says cover one
    in all his range." Foner, ed., *L&W*, IV, 411.

142 Pitts' background and Douglass regaining his "political bearings": McFeely,
    Frederick Douglass, 311–13.

143 Marriage ceremony by Grimke: ibid., 319. Katherine Du Pre Lumpkin, *The
    Emancipation of Angela Grimke* (Chapel Hill: University of North Carolina
    Press, 1974). On Grimke and the "mulatto elite" in DC, see Gatewood,
    Aristocrats of Color.

144 Color contrast: Foner, ed., *L&W*, IV, 477, in Martin, *The Mind of Frederick
    Douglass*, 100. "False friends": Douglass, *Life and Times*, 534. Letter about
    invitations in PBS program *When the Lion Wrote History*.

145 "Curse of Ham" myth: quoted by Gates, in Andrews, ed., *Critical Essays on
    Frederick Douglass*, 89–90. Samuel Sewall had pointed out in 1700 that this
    "curse" could not be read racially based on the passage in question, Genesis
    9:20–27. The curse was directed at Canaan, one of Ham's four sons. Two
    other sons, Egypt and Cush, are supposed to be the ancestors of Egypt,
    Sudan, and Ethiopia. "Pleasing to God": Foner, ed., *L&W*, II, 40. White
    half: Bell, *A Survey of the Negro Convention Movement*, 101–2. Rynders in
    George William Curtis, "Frederick Douglass," *Harper's Weekly* 27:1405
    (Nov. 24, 1883), p. 743.

146 "Pure race": Moses, *Golden Age*, 86. "Something of an Irishman": written in
    1873, quoted in McFeely, *Frederick Douglass*, 280. "Intermediate race":
    "Future of the Negro," *North American Review* (July 1884), in Foner, ed.,
    L&W, IV, 412, and Meyer, *Frederick Douglass*, 391.

147 Response to marriage and Douglass' refusal to be black role model: Martin,
    The Mind of Frederick Douglass, 100. Refuses amalgamation model: ibid.,
    221. "Judicial decisions": Foner, ed., *L&W*, IV, 116. "No division/
    blended/A painter": John Blassingame and John McKivigan, eds., *The
    Frederick Douglass Papers*, V (Yale University Press, 1992), 146–47, 240.

148 "The Future of the Colored Race," *North American Review* (May 1886), in
    ibid., 193–96. Foner dates this piece as 1866, but Douglass' reference to
    "twenty years of semi-freedom" indicates that the correct dating would be
    1886, as it appears in Brotz, ed., *Negro Social and Political Thought*, 308–10;
    and Meyer, ed., *Frederick Douglass*, 389–91.

149 Ibid., my emphasis.
150 Meyer, *Frederick Douglass*; Brotz, ed., *Negro Social and Political Thought*; Foner, ed., *L&W*, IV, 196; Martin, *The Mind of Frederick Douglass*, 220.
151 Immanuel Wallerstein, *Unthinking Social Science* (London: Polity Press, 1991), 146. Wallerstein adapts the concept from Braudel's "too-long time," a meta-cycle of history, and the Greek term *kairos* Paul Tillich used to distinguish between "qualitative" and "quantitative" time: *The Protestant Era* (University of Chicago Press, 1984), 33. A millennial *Right Time* appears in many reggae songs, as on the Mighty Diamonds album of the same name. "Ruling archetype" discussed in my "Romancing the Racial Frontier" (1995), and in longer form, 1996.
152 "Time Will Tell" – allusion to Bob Marley's song on the *Kaya* album. The US Census was changed in 1980 to note that "Hispanics can be of any race."
153 "American description": Foner, ed., *L&W*, IV, 124–25; Martin, *The Mind of Frederick Douglass*, 206. Egypt visit also recounted in McFeely, *Frederick Douglass*, 329–32. Douglass wrote about Europe's earlier dependency on Egypt, foreshadowing a favorite theme of Afrocentrists, but he also noted the paradox of Egypt's contemporary dependency on the "West."
154 Du Bois, "self-assertion": *The Souls of Black Folk*, 86.
155 Brotz, ed., *Negro Social and Political Thought*, 311–28. In a letter to W. H. Thomas (July 16, 1886), Douglass says: "what you call the *Negro* problem is a misnomer. It were better called a white man's problem": Foner, ed., *L&W*, IV, 443.
156 I have seen this paraphrase in numerous contexts, such as the PBS program *When the Lion Wrote History* and a poster I own. The full text reads: "The real problem . . . is whether American justice, American liberty, American civilization, American law and American Christianity can be made to include and protect . . . all American citizens in the rights which, in a generous moment in the nation's life, have been guaranteed to them by the . . . law of the land": Brotz, ed., *Negro Social and Political Thought*, 314.
157 Note similar usage of Jer. 13:23 in "The Color Line," *North American Review* (June 1881), in Foner, ed., *L&W*, IV, 347. In this essay Douglass refers to racialism as a "moral disease."
158 My emphasis. To give black, biracial, and white examples of "racism-is-eternal" critical race theorists: Derrick Bell, *Faces at the Bottom of the Well: The Permanence of Racism* (New York: Basic Books, 1992); Lani Guinier, *The Tyranny of the Majority: Fundamental Fairness in Representational Democracy* (New York: Free Press, 1994); Andrew Hacker, *Two Nations: Black and White, Separate, Hostile, Unequal* (New York: Scribner's, 1992).
159 Martin, *The Mind of Frederick Douglass*, 195. This echoes the "don't dip on the black side/white side" quote beginning my Bob Marley chapter.
160 Gadamer referred to this process as a "fusion of horizons." Charles Taylor writes that this fusion depends on and is enacted through mutually created "vocabularies of comparison." That horizons fuse means that they intersect, not that one supersedes the other. These horizons, functioning in "parallel discursive universes," interpenetrate, seed each other, and become a mutually created language. H. G. Gadamer, *Wahrheit und Methode* (Tubingen: Mohr, 1975), 238. Taylor *et al.*, *Multiculturalism*, 67. Mutually created

language: Stephens, "Interracial Dialogue in Rap Music: Call-and-Response"; "discursive universes": Gates, *Signifying Monkey*.

161 My view of FD as an integrative ancestor is informed by scholarship on "Site of memory": Pierre Nora, "Between History and Memory: *Les Lieux de Mémoire,*" *Representations* 26 (Spring 1989), 7–25. For valuable essays applying Nora's concept to "black" history, see Fabre and Robert O'Meally, eds., *History and Memory*.

162 Freehling, *Reintegration of American History*.

163 "Our country": McFeely, *Frederick Douglass*, 167. This again reflects the dual stragegy of Jeremiads noted by Bercovitch, *American Jeremiad*, 191.

164 "Insignificant," "color-blind institutions," and "everlasting . . . false foundation": Waldo Martin, "Frederick Douglass: Humanist as Race Leader," in *Black Leaders of the Nineteenth Century*, ed. Litwack and Meier, 59, 72, 82, and Brotz, ed., *Negro Social and Political Thought*, 316. "Our noisy assertions of equality with the Caucasian race": Martin, *The Mind of Frederick Douglass*, 98; Brotz, ed., *Negro Social and Political Thought*, 314.

165 Nathan Irwin Huggins, "Introduction," *Black Odyssey: The African-American Ordeal in Slavery* (New York: Vintage, 1990).

166 Gary Nash, "The Great Multicultural Debate," *Contention* 1 (1992).

167 Roy P. Basler, *The Lincoln Legend: A Study in Changing Conceptions* (New York: Octagon, 1935/1969), 306.

168 Frederick Turner quoted in Sollors, *Beyond Ethnicity*, 42.

169 "Our Canaan": Douglass, *My Bondage and My Freedom*, 178; Douglass, *Life and Times*, 156–60. Frederick Douglass' wish to escape the language of race: Moses, "Racialized Writing," in Sundquist, ed., *Frederick Douglass*.

170 "Equal terms": McFeely, *Frederick Douglass*, 300. "Her people": Foner, ed., *L&W*, II, 47.

171 Freud and Hurston in "Select bibliography." For an excellent discussion of "racial" ambiguity in the history of European thought on Moses, see Yosef Hayim Yerushalmi, *Freud's Moses* (New Haven: Yale University Press, 1991), and Jan Assmann, *Moses the Egyptian: The Memory of Egypt in Western Monotheism* (Harvard University Press, 1997).

172 Sundquist, ed., *Frederick Douglass*, 3.

173 That is, unless one includes Charles Chestnutt in this group. Werner Sollors, ed., *The Invention of Ethnicity* (Oxford University Press, 1989) xvii, and Sundquist, *To Wake the Nations*.

3 INVISIBLE COMMUNITY: RALPH ELLISON'S VISION OF A MULTIRACIAL "IDEAL DEMOCRACY"

1 "Blurb" on cover of the Vintage edition of *Invisible Man*. Impossibility of Afro-American discourse being "just black": Gates, *Signifying Monkey*, xxiii–xv. On Ellison's hero as a trickster: T. V. Reed, "Invisible Movements, Black Powers: Double Vision & Trickster Politics in *Invisible Man*," in *Fifteen Jugglers, Five Believers: Literary Politics and the Poetics of American Social Movements* (Berkeley: University of California Press, 1992). A forceful statement of Ellison's determination to claim a much broader identity than "black protest writer" is made by Stanley Crouch, "The Measure of the

Oklahoma Kid," in *The All-American Skin-Game* (New York: Pantheon, 1995), 83–92. One significant exception to the "black box" tendency is Mark Busby, who calls *Invisible Man* "the *Moby Dick* of the 20th century," and makes Ellison's use of "frontier mythology" and border symbols a central part of his analysis: *Ralph Ellison* (Boston: Twayne, 1991), 39.

2 "Temptation," "sanctuary of race": Introduction, *Shadow and Act*, in *Collected Essays*, 57, 58.

3 John F. Callahan, "Chaos, Complexity, and Possibility: The Historical Frequencies of Ralph Waldo Ellison," in Benston, ed., *Speaking for You*, 131. "Indian Nations"/Bessie Smith: "Going to the Territory," in *Collected Essays*, 600–01. Oklahoma as racial frontier: this notion was central to Ellison's thinking. For instance, in "Going to the Territory," he wrote: "Today most of the geographical frontier is gone, but the process of cultural integration continues along the lines that mark the hierarchal divisions of the United States": *Collected Essays*, 604. See also references to Oklahoma in Quintard Taylor, *In Search of the Racial Frontier* (New York: W. W. Norton, 1998). The theme of Oklahoma as a "black state" also appears in Toni Morrison's novel *Paradise* (Knopf, 1998).

4 "Breaks": "That Same Pain, That Same Pleasure," interview with Richard Stern, in *Collected Essays*, 71. Edna Ferber, *Cimarron* (New York: Bantam, 1929/1963). See discussion of interracial dynamics of this novel in Dearborn, *Pocahontas's Daughters*, pp. 128–30. Oklahoma was more commonly thought of as Southwestern in the early twentieth century, and is sometimes still referred to as part of the Southwest. Hence, Ellison differentiates between his "Southern experience" (at Tuskegee) and "my South-Southwestern identity": "An Extravagance of Laughter," *Collected Essays*, 658.

5 Family background: Robert G. O'Meally, *The Craft of Ralph Ellison* (Cambridge, MA, and London: Harvard University Press, 1980), 7. "Ginger-colored": Ralph Ellison, *Invisible Man* (New York: Vintage, 1982), 22. Ellison usually referred to mixing in a cultural sense, although he was clearly aware that biological and cultural miscegenation were often interrelated. For instance, in an essay reflecting on his Oklahoma heritage, "Going to the Territory," he wrote that "by ignoring such matters as the sharing of bloodlines and cultural traditions by groups of widely differing ethnic groups . . . we misconceive our cultural identity": *Collected Essays*, 595–96. In what seems to be a cultural sense, he refers to "my mixed background" in the Introduction to *Shadow and Act* (*Collected Essays*, 56). Charles Davis, "The Mixed Heritage of the Modern Black Novel: Ralph Ellison and Friends," in Benston, ed., *Speaking for You*, 272–82. Eleanor Lyons, "Ellison's Narrator as Emersonial Scholar," in Susan Resneck Parr and Pancho Savery, eds., *Approaches to Teaching Ellison's "Invisible Man"* (New York: Modern Language Association, 1989). Ellison learned many years later of "my father's hope that I would become a poet": *Collected Essays*, 50.

6 "Middle-class/warm relations": "That Same Pain," *Collected Essays*, 71. "White friends": Hollie West interview, Graham and Singh, eds., *Conversations with Ralph Ellison*, 255.

7 "I recall that much of so-called Kansas City jazz was actually brought to perfection in Oklahoma by Oklahomans." Intro to *Shadow and Act*, in *Collected Essays*, 51.

8 Models for budding "Renaissance Men": ibid., 52–53.

Although the psychologist Ellison most often mentions as an influence is Freud, his understanding of myth, and of psychological projection, is usually closer to Jung's position. Here, his sense of "projecting archetypes" as a process of perpetual reinvention is more like Jung's own position than either Jung's critics or many of his followers. Both opponents and "fans" of Jung often describe his theory of archetypes as describing biologically inherited, universally valid, and static forms. Jung himself argued that an archetype, like a genre, is a heuristic idea which cannot be perceived directly, and which only takes on visible form as an "archetypal idea," when it is "born anew from the human psyche" and has "come to independent life" within a specifical social, cultural, and psychological context. C. G. Jung, "After the Catastrophe" (1945), *Civilization in Transition*, CW10 (Princeton University Press, 1970), 217. "Independent life": C. G. Jung, *Modern Man in Search of a Soul* (New York: Harcourt, Brace & World/Harvest, 1933), 242.

9 "Boyish ideal": *Collected Essays*, 55. Ellison's apprenticeship as a writer involved a four-year gig with the Federal Writers Project from 1938 to 1942. Better federal money was never spent than his $103 monthly salary during those years! On this, and Ellison's attraction to, and later rejection of, the Communist Party, see chapters 2 and 3 of O'Meally, *The Craft of Ralph Ellison*.

10 Douglass school: Graham and Singh, eds., *Conversations with Ralph Ellison*, 152.

11 "Roscoe Dunjee and the American Language," *Collected Essays*, 456–59. The wealthy black sailmaker from Philadelphia Ellison refers to is James Forten.

12 Alain Locke Symposium, Harvard University, Dec. 1, 1973. *Collected Essays*, 447.

13 "Alain Locke," *Collected Essays*, 441–42, 445. Despite the conventional wisdom, which one still hears, that the Harlem Renaissance had died out by the 1930s, Locke himself argued that it had only really come of age during the 1930s. Alain Locke, "Jingo, Counter-Jingo and the U.S.," *Opportunity* (Jan. 1938), 4–5. On the strength of the Renaissance in the 1930s and its continuing influence into the present, see also Hutchinson, *Harlem Renaissance in Black and White*. Frederick Douglas Patterson; Locke at Tuskegee: O'Meally, *The Craft of Ralph Ellison*, 16, 18–20. An anonymous reader of my book in manuscript pointed out that "W. E. B. Du Bois *was* the New Negro – before Locke." However, it was Douglass who was the dominant model (of "Negro" and mixed-race American achievement) in Ellison's imagination from boyhood on.

14 "Link together": *Collected Essays*, 71. "Our style": ibid., 446. One very humorous example of the role of Ellison's Oklahoma upbringing in his tendency to see all American culture as "racially hybrid" is in his "Portrait of Inman Page," ibid., 587. "Insidious confusion": "Going to the Territory," in *Collected Essays*, 606.

15 James Alan McPherson, "Indivisible Man," originally published in *Atlantic Monthly* 226 (Dec. 1970). This citation in reprints in Bentson's *Speaking for You*, 15, in Graham and Singh, eds., *Conversations with Ralph Ellison*, 174, and in Ellison's *Collected Essays*, 356. Busby, *Ralph Ellison*, 39, 141.

16 "Pure stream": "Alain Locke," *Collected Essays*, 443. Hollie I. West, "Ellison:

Exploring the Life of a Not So Visible Man," *Washington Post*, Aug. 19–21, 1973, in Graham and Singh, eds., *Conversations with Ralph Ellison*, 250. "In spilling out his heart's blood in his contest with the machine, John Henry was asserting a national value as well as a Negro value": Ellison, "Some Questions and Answers" (1958), in *Collected Essays*, 299.

17 Robert B. Stepto and Michael S. Harper, "Study and Experience: An Interview with Ralph Ellison," *Massachusetts Review* 18 (1977), in Graham and Singh, eds., *Conversations with Ralph Ellison*, 319ff.

18 "Father/son metaphors . . . Speaking of fathers": ibid., 322–23.

19 The trauma of the death of Ellison's mother, Ida, is dealt with at length by John Callahan in his introduction to the posthumous collection of Ellison stories, *Flying Home and Other Stories* (New York: Random House/Vintage, 1996).

20 Ishmael Reed, Quincy Troupe, and Steve Cannon, "The Essential Ellison," *Y'Bird Magazine* 1 (Autumn 1977); Graham and Singh, eds., *Conversations with Ralph Ellison*, 361–62.

21 "Self-fathering": Sundquist, ed., *Frederick Douglass*, 12.

22 Many critics have been less concerned with hagiography or demonization than with claiming Ellison as an "icon" in a larger, transracial literary tradition. The two studies along these lines I have found most useful are Alan Nadel, *Invisible Criticism* (Iowa City: University of Iowa Press, 1988), and O'Meally, *The Craft of Ralph Ellison*. See also Valerie Bonita Gray, "*Invisible Man*"*'s Literary Heritage: "Benito Cereno" and "Moby Dick"* (Amsterdam: Rodopi, 1978); Robert N. List, *Dedalus In Harlem* (Washington, DC: University Press of America, 1982); Michael Lynch, *Creative Revolt: A Study of Wright, Ellison, and Dostoevsky* (New York: Peter Lang, 1990).

But a division between celebration and attack is one feature of Ellison criticism, especially for the two decades following *Invisible Man*'s publication. One can also see differing emphases between Afro-American critics, and European and Euro-American critics. A good overview of Ellison's place in black intellectual history, and his battles with his peers who condemned him for being insufficiently oppositional, is Jerry Gafio Watts, *Heroism and the Black Intellectual* (Chapel Hill: University of North Carolina Press, 1994). Watts' study contains many of the unresolved tensions of Afro-American politics and cultural criticism. He provides a sorely needed critique of Harold Cruse's *The Crisis of the Negro Intellectual*, with its "reified consciousness" (10). His criticism of how many black nationalists became deeply invested in a "victim status" (16ff), centering on a demand for recognition from white intellectuals, is perceptive, and in fact is Ellison's critique of Wright and Baldwin. And Watts' determination to "critically confront in Ellison a sacred icon of the Afro-American intellectual world" (xi) is admirable. But the further one proceeds in Watts' study, the more it becomes evident that Watts has internalized many black nationalist and Marxist assumptions about the proper role of the artist. By the last footnote, Watts can speak of Ellison's view of heroism as "myopic, selfish, and thoroughly disgusting" (144–45).

Other studies of Ellison as "black literature" include Donald Petesch, *A Spy in the Enemy's Country* (Iowa City: University of Iowa Press, 1989); Addison Gayle, *The Way of the World* (New York: Doubleday, 1975); Richard

Kostelanetz, *Politics in the African American Novel* (New York: Greenwood, 1991); Berndt Ostendorf, *Black Literature in White America* (New Jersey: Barnes and Nobles, 1982); and Fred Lee Hord, with a rather reductionist chapter on Ellison in *Reconstructing Memory* (Chicago: Third World Press, 1991).

A good starting point for Ellison's reception among "white" critics is Jacqueline Covo, *The Blinking Eye: Ralph Waldo Ellison and His American, French, German, and Italian Critics, 1952–1971* (Metuchen, NJ: Scarecrow Press, 1974). Covo notes that most early European critics questioned Ellison's technical competence.

Two volumes of essays from which I have drawn which include both "black" and cross-cultural/comparative perspectives are Benston, ed., *Speaking for You*, and Parr and Savery, eds., *Approaches*. Studies which treat interracial themes include David Britt, "The Image of the White Man in the Fiction of Hughes, Wright, Baldwin, and Ellison" (PhD dissertation, Emory University, 1968); Kerry McSweeney, *"Invisible Man": Race and Identity* (Boston: Twayne, 1988); Eric Sundquist, ed., *Cultural Contexts for Ralph Ellison's "Invisible Man"* (Boston: Bedford Books/St. Martin, 1995); Robert O'Meally, *New Essays on Invisible Man* (Cambridge University Press, 1988).

Irving Howe's attack on Ellison is in "Black Boys and Native Sons," in *Dissent* 10 (Autumn 1963), 353–68. Howe's view of the proper role of the black writer as a sort of quasi-messianic "black wrath of retribution" is typical of white leftist projections. He praised Richard Wright's "clenched militancy" and suggested Ellison had betrayed Wright's cause (and his race). Ellison's side of this celebrated exchange is in "The World and the Jug." He acerbically observes that "Howe feels that unrelieved suffering is the only 'real' Negro experience, and that the true Negro writer must be ferocious": *Collected Essays*, 159.

23 Moses, "The Wings of Ethiopia: Consensus History and Literary Allusion in Ralph Ellison's *Invisible Man*," in *The Wings of Ethiopia*, 275–6. A slightly different version of this essay appears in Parr and Savery, eds., *Approaches*. The tone here, I believe, is tongue-in-cheek. Moses' essay is not really a critique of Ellison, but a meditation on the challenges of teaching *Invisible Man*.

24 George E. Kent, "Ralph Ellison and Afro-American Folk and Cultural Tradition," in Benston, ed., *Speaking for You*, 95. Ellison and Hyman, "The Negro Writer in America: An Exchange," *Partisan Review* (Spring 1958). See also Stanley Edgar Hyman, *The Promised End* (Cleveland: World Publishing, 1963).

25 "Change the Joke and Slip the Yoke," *Collected Essays*, 101, 103–04, 109. On Ellison's use of trickster themes, see Reed, "Invisible Movements, Black Powers," and Houston Baker, "To Move Without Moving: An Analysis of Creativity and Commerce in Ralph Ellison's Trueblood Episode," in Benston, ed., *Speaking for You*. Ellison seems to have read Paul Radin's classic study *The Trickster: A Study in American Indian Mythology* (London: Routledge & Kegan Paul, 1955), which included Jung's essay "On the Psychology of the Trickster Figure."

The best study of blackface which considers its interracial dynamics is Lhamon, *Raising Cain*.

26 Kenneth Burke, "The Negro's Pattern of Life," in *The Philosophy of Literary Form* (Berkeley: University of California Press, 1973), 366–67. "Circumstance": Ellison, "Change the Joke," 101. On parallels between Ellison's thought, and Jung's theory of archetypes, see n. 8. For sources regarding academic "blacklisting" of Jung and (erroneous) accusations that he was anti-Semitic, see chapter 1 nn. 32, 44.

27 Stepto and Harper, in Graham and Singh, eds., *Conversations with Ralph Ellison*, 330–35. "Life wouldn't be worth living if you just repeated the formulas of your success forever and ever. I've lost audiences, I've recovered them. I've been thrashed by the critics – I love having critics for breakfast. I've been having them for 30 years in Mexico, just eating them like chicken, and then throwing their bones away. They have not survived, and I have." "Crossing Borders: The Journey of Carlos Fuentes." Narrated by Luis Valdez. Films Inc. Co.

28 "Glib talk . . . stylistic elements": *Collected Essays*, 587. "Defend politically": Watts, *Heroism and the Black Intellectual*, 13.

29 In my dissertation chapter on Ellison, I critique Abdul JanMohamed and David Lloyd's *The Nature and Context of Minority Discourse* at some length. See Gilles Deleuze and Felix Guattari, "What Is a Minor Literature?" *Mississippi Review* 11:3 (1983), 13–33; and Gilles Deleuze and Felix Guattari, *Kafka: Toward a Minor Literature* (Minneapolis: University of Minnesota Press, 1986). But there is an older genealogy in anti/postcolonial studies. Albert Memmi speaks of an irrevocably hostile relationship between colonizer and colonized in which "neither one nor the other will ever change." *The Colonizer and the Colonized* (Boston: Beacon, 1967), 71–72. Nancy Hartsock cites this passage approvingly in "Rethinking Modernism: Minority vs. Majority Theories," in *Minority Discourse*, ed. JanMohamed & Lloyd, 23.

30 Renato Rosaldo, "Politics, Patriarchs, and Laughter," in *Minority Discourse*, ed. JanMohamed & Lloyd, 126. Other important texts on border cultures are Anzaldúa, *Borderlands/La Frontera*; and Gomez-Peña, *New World Border*.

31 Gomez-Peña, "The Multicultural Paradigm." Esteva-Fabregat, *Mestizaje in Ibero-America*. For a bracing if overly cynical critique of mestizo-faddism, see Ernst Rudin, "New Mestizos: Traces of a Quincentenary Miracle in Old World Spanish and New World English," in *Cultural Difference and the Literary Text*, ed. Siemerling and Schwenk.

Among books I consulted for historical perspectives on "mixed blood" and mulatto identity: J.A. Rogers, *Nature Knows no Color Line* (privately printed, 1952); Murray, *The Omni-Americans*; Williamson, *New People*; Davis, *Who is Black?*; Maria P. P. Root, ed., *Racially Mixed People in America* (Newbury Park, CA.: Sage, 1992); Sollors, *Neither Black nor White but Both*.

32 Despite my sympathy with "multicentric" theories, I am still in agreement with a recent trend in literary criticism that treats ethnic, "racial," or gender-based canons as "*an intermediary stage* on the way towards a more comprehensive literary criticism." Gayle Greene and Coppelia Kahn, "Feminist Scholarship & the Social Construction of Woman," in *Making a Difference: Feminist Literary Criticism*, ed. Greene and Kahn (London: Routledge, 1988), 1–36. This stage should not be mistaken for an orienting horizon. Like Werner

Sollors, I believe that such categories are "a very partial, temporal, and insufficient characterization at best" ("A Critique of Pure Pluralism," in *Reconstructing American Literary History*, ed. Sacvan Bercovitch [Cambridge: Harvard University Press, 1986]). But like some critics who have taken Sollors' critique as a departure point, I am inclined to see these groupings as an inevitable and necessary historical corrective. Siemerling and Schwenk, eds., *Cultural Difference and the Literary Text*. My criticism is directed not so much at the idea of a "minority" canon itself, as at the reification of a "dominant" or "majority" culture which often accompanies this self-defined "otherness." Spivak, *The Post-Colonial Critic*.

33 "Product of damage": JanMohamed and Lloyd, eds., *The Nature and Context of Minority Discourse*, 4. A more historically accurate view is that languages created by interethnic collisions emerged from contexts in which there existed "attraction and repulsion on both sides," as Bharati Mukherjee puts it: David Armstrong, "An Immigrant Transformed," *San Francisco Examiner*, Oct. 28, 1993.

34 Condit and Lucaites, *Crafting Equality*. "Mutually created language": Stephens, "Interracial Dialogue in Rap Music," and Fishkin, *Was Huck Black?*

35 Callahan, *In the African-American Grain*, 15–19.

36 Nieman, *Promises to Keep*. Condit and Lucaites, *Crafting Equality*. Douglass, *My Bondage and My Freedom*.

37 "Necessary fiction": Habermas, *Legitimation Crisis*. See also Fraser, "Rethinking the Public Sphere."

38 "Was emerging": "Change the Joke and Slip the Yoke," *Partisan Review* 25 (Spring 1958). *Collected Essays*, 107.

39 Although some critics still tag Ellison as a "conservative," his background as a radical in the late 1930s and early 1940s is well documented – writing for *New Masses*, etc. John Callahan quotes a letter to Richard Wright on October 27, 1937 from Ellison during what he called his "exile" in Dayton Ohio, in which the "self-described young radical" complained: "there is no *Daily* [*Worker*] nor [*New*] *Masses* to be had here … all I have is the *New Republic* and the radio." Introduction, *Flying Home*, xiii.

40 Ellison, *Invisible Man*, xviii.

41 Of course, several previous Afro-American writers had created black characters with "intellectual depth," including Charles Chestnutt, James Weldon Johnson, W. E. B. DuBois, and Nella Larsen.

    Robert List affirms: "Joyce was Ellison's stylistic mentor because Joyce experimented with literary technique in order to assert ethnic identity as a member of an oppressed culture (or race)": *Dedalus in Harlem*, cited in Nadel, *Invisible Criticism*, 25. Ellison's claims for "literary ancestors" are sometimes invented, according to Robert O'Meally, "The Rules of Magic: Hemingway as Ellison's 'Ancestor'," *Southern Review* 21:3 (Summer 1985). See also chapter 4 of Busby, *Ralph Ellison*.

42 Habermas' orienting horizon is an "ideal speech community." Such a community "is *conceivable* only if the dichotomy between in-group and out-group morality disappears" in an intersubjective arena "free from constraints of domination" in which "there is an effective equality of chances to assume

dialogue roles": Habermas, *Legitimation Crisis*, 87, xvii.
43 "Understated": Ellison, *Shadow and Act*, 165–66. "Slavery is perhaps the central intellectual challenge, other than the Constitution itself, to those who would understand the meaning of America": McDowell and Rampersad, eds., *Slavery and the Literary Imagination*, viii.
44 "Two-toned": Gates, *Signifying Monkey*, xxiii–xv. This is derived from Bakhtin's work on heteroglossia and double-voiced language: *The Dialogic Imagination*.
45 Anderson, *Imagined Communities*.
46 Nadel notes that in *Golden Day* Lewis Mumford only devotes 500 words to the "Negro question": *Invisible Criticism*, 92.
47 Meyer, ed., *Frederick Douglass*, 274.
48 Martin Bernal, *Black Athena: The Afroasiatic Roots of Classical Civilization* (New Brunswick: Rutgers University Press, 1987). Critical evaluations of Bernal: Mary Lefkowitz and Guy MacLean Rogers, eds., *Black Athena Revisited* (Durham: Duke University Press, 1996).
49 "Justice": Booker T. Washington, *Up From Slavery*, in *Three Negro Classics*, introduced by John Hope Franklin, New York: Avon, 1901/1965, 224.
50 Hyde, "Frederick Douglass and Eshu's Hat."
51 This moment echoes the Garrisonian advice to Douglass that he leave the philosophy to his white "handlers."
52 "Racial unity": Gayle, *The Way of the World*, 213. Irving Howe, "Black Boys and Native Sons."
53 "Resisting": Callahan, *In the African-American Grain*, 184, my emphasis.
54 "Group/cooperation": Ellison, *Shadow and Act*, 234, 143, my emphasis.
55 "Biracial culture": Sundquist, *To Wake the Nations*, 9. "Kingdom of culture": Du Bois, *The Souls of Black Folk*, 5.
56 Ellison's comments on "antagonistic cooperation" come at the end of a rejoinder to Irving Howe – a powerful critique of those who imagine a pure oppositionality is possible, and especially those who project this oppositional burden on to Afro-Americans. "The World and the Jug," in Ellison, *Collected Essays*, 155–88.
57 Michael Lind calls Douglass "the greatest American" who can be a standard-bearer for a postracial twenty-first-century "trans-America": *The Next American Nation*, 379.
58 Fraser, "Rethinking the Public Sphere." On the impossibility of "meta-narratives" being universally valid: Jean-Francois Lyotard, *The Post-Modern Condition* (Minneapolis: University of Minnesota Press, 1984).
59 "Regroupment" and "emancipatory": Fraser, "Rethinking the Public Sphere." "Discursive redemption": Habermas, *Legitimation Crisis*. "Black nationalism is, in essence, a variety of religious experience": Moses, *The Wings of Ethiopia*, 120.
60 Gomez-Peña, *New World Border*.

4 BOB MARLEY'S ZION: A TRANSRACIAL "BLACKMAN REDEMPTION

1 "Grand Canyon": Roger Steffens, in Bruce Talamon and Roger Steffens, *Bob Marley: Spirit Dancer* (New York: Norton, 1994), 15. Testimony of song-

writers in Timothy White, "Give Thanks and Praises: The Music Community Remembers Bob Marley," *The Beat* 8:3 (1989). *Legend* itself has sold 10 million units in the US; 6 million abroad. Island Records sales of Marley recordings probably exceed 50 million units. Yet if one includes small labels and the ubiquitous bootlegs in the global market, then hundreds of millions of copies of Marley's music have been sold. And the music itself is only the tip of the iceberg, compared to the cottage industry of Marley-as-icon.

2   Ethiopianism: see Moses, *Black Messiahs and Uncle Toms*; Frederickson, *Black Liberation*; Raboteau, *Fire in the Bones*; Leonard E. Barrett, *The Rastafarians* (Boston: Beacon, 1977/1988). I included an overview of Ethiopia's historical use of the myth of Solomonic descent in order to justify imperial expansion in the longer chapter on Marley in my dissertation. "Racial Armageddon": Richard D. E. Burton, *Afro-Creole* (Ithaca: Cornell University Press, 1997), 112.

3   There have been countless reggae songs with themes of racial unity, such as Junior Reid's anthem "One Blood." This is probably the face of reggae best known to an international audience. However, "inna de yard" (in Jamaica) "black supremacy" is still invoked as a matter of course. As an example, I have a debate between "dub poet" Mutabaruka and the Bobo Shanti, a popular contemporary Rasta sect (popularized through singers such as Sizzla and Anthony B), taped from IRIE-FM on June 7, 1997.

4   Messianic mindset: Barry Chevannes, *Rastafari* (Syracuse University Press, 1994), and Barry Chevannes, ed., *Rastafari and Other African-Caribbean World-views* (London: MacMillan, 1995; New Brunswick, NJ: Rutgers University Press, 1998); Burton, *Afro-Creole*. Theorizing global culture: Simon During, "Popular Culture on a Global Scale: A Challenge for Cultural Studies?" *Critical Inquiry* 23 (Summer 1997), 808ff.

5   "Ocean": Talamon and Steffens, *Bob Marley*, 30. Testimony on Marley's global influence in *The Beat* 14:3 (1995), 54–59.

6   "Riches": Roger Steffens, *The Beat* 12:3 (1993). "Modern music": Steffens in Talamon and Steffens, *Bob Marley*, 31.

7   "New psalms" and "new world": Talamon and Steffens, *Bob Marley*, 16, 30. Steffens attributes the "new psalms" quote to Marley's art director Neville Garrick in "Bob Marley: Rasta Warrior," in *Chanting Down Babylon*, ed. Nathaniel Samuel Murrell, William David Spencer, and Adrian Anthony McFarlane (Philadelphia: Temple University Press, 1998), 251. Garrick compares Marley to King David as a psalmist in the Island video *The Bob Marley Story*.

8   Some early books about Rastafarianism I have used are Barrett, *The Rastafarians*; Derek Bishton, *Blackheart Man* (London: Chatto & Windus, 1986); Horace Campbell, *Rasta and Resistance* (Trenton, NJ: Africa World Press, 1987); Stephen Davis and Peter Simon, *Reggae International* (New York: R&B, 1982); Virginia Lee Jacobs, *Roots of Rastafari* (San Diego: Avant Books, 1985); Tracy Nicholas and Bill Sparrow, *Rastafari* (New York: Doubleday/Anchor, 1979); Anita M. Waters, *Race, Class, and Political Symbols* (New Brunswick, NJ: Transaction Publishers, 1985); Adrian Boot and Michael Thomas, *Jamaica: Bablylon on a Thin Wire* (London: Schoken, 1976). Works released close to Marley's fiftieth birthday: *Songs of Freedom: From "Judge Not" to*

"Redemption Song," compiled by Trevor Wyatt and Neville Garrick (Tuff Gong/Island, 1992); Boot and Salewicz, *Bob Marley*; Talamon, *Bob Marley*.

9 Chevannes, *Rastafari*, and *Rastafari and Other African-Caribbean Worldviews*. Carolyn Cooper, *Noises in the Blood: Orality, Gender, and the "Vulgar" Body of Jamaican Popular Culture* (Durham, NC: Duke University Press, 1995). Jack A. Johnson-Hill, a pastor in Jamaica in the late 1970s and early 1980s, has written a study of the "social ethics" of Rastafarian religious culture: *I-Sight* (Metuchen, NJ, and London: American Theological Library Association and Scarecrow Press, 1995); Burton, *Afro-Creole*. Carole D. Yawney, "Rasta Mek a Trod: Symbolic Ambiguity in a Globalizing Religion," in *Alternative Cultures in the Caribbean*, ed. Ulrich Fleischmann and Thomas Bremer (Frankfurt am Main: Vervuert, 1993), 161–68. John P. Homiak, "Dub History: Soundings on Rastafari Livity and Language," in *Rastafari and Other African-Caribbean Worldviews*, ed. Chevannes, 127–81. I would like to call attention to William F. Lewis, *Soul Rebels* (Prospect Heights, IL: Waveland Press, 1993). This slender volume, published posthumously, has an immediacy often missing in more formal ethnographies. Murrell *et al.*, eds., *Chantry Down Babylon*, was published just before my book went to press.

10 Johnson-Hill, *I-Sight*, 29.

11 Carter, *Culture of Disbelief*. Jenny Franchot, "Invisible Domain: Religion and American Literary Studies," *American Literature* 67:4 (Dec. 1995), 833–42. Black Atlantic studies "is one of the very few contemporary locations for interesting work on religion," Franchot notes (838). For a critique of the lack of attention to religion in American Studies which richly documents the connection between "Christian existentialism" and civil rights activism among white youth around 1960, see Doug Rossinow, "'The Break-through to New Life': Christianity and the Emergence of the New Left in Austin, Texas, 1956–1964," *American Quarterly* 46:3 (Sept. 1994), 309–40.

12 Jung's *Aion* (Princeton University Press, 1959), Collected Works, IX, ii, surveys the history of "god within" beliefs, beginning with the Gnostics and the Monophysites. "God above" – alludes to Marley songs "Baldhead" and "Get Up Stand Up."

13 The impact of this first visit to Jamaica is evident in Stephens, "Fashion Dread Rasta: On the One in Jamaica with Bob Marley's Children," *Whole Earth Review* (Summer 1988). Vine DeLoria, Jr., *God Is Red: A Native View of Religion* (2nd edn, Golden, CO: North American Press, 1992; first published by New York: Grosset & Dunlap, 1973).

14 Dogma vs. numinous experience: Jung, *Psychology and Religion*, 9. Homans, *Jung in Context*, 186–87.

15 On the claims of Selassie, and his Amhara ethnic group, to be descended from Solomon, see Harold G. Marcus, *Haille Sellassie* (Berkeley: University of California Press, 1987), and Harold G. Marcus, *A History of Ethiopia* (Berkeley: University of California Press, 1994). Arguments for and against Selassie's supposed divinity are an ongoing (and often blinkered) part of the internet reggae conference group known as RMR (rec.music.reggae). One of the best critical assessments of the Amharas' invention of a "Solomonic dynasty," and its reinventions by the Rastas, is Nathaniel Samuel Murrell and Lewis Williams, "The Black Biblical Hermeneutics of Rastafari," in *Chanting*

Down Babylon, ed. Murrell *et al.*, 326–48. The authors are critical of the Rastas for their racialized fundamentalism, yet rightly observed that the Rastas do not need to justify their beliefs "any more than the Native Americans or the Torajas of Indonesia" (340). Christianity and Rastafari are merely two of many possible "fulfillments" of Old Testament prophecy, and "Selassie is alive for the Rastafarians in the same way that Christ is alive for Christians." See also Clinton Chisholm, "The Rasta–Selassie–Ethiopian Connections," in ibid., 166–77.

16 "Rasta" is a term used within the culture as a shortened version of Rastafarian, but also as a personification of the collective consciousness. On Biblical endorsement of lay prophecy, see Moses' admonition, "Would that all the Lord's people were prophets" (Numbers 11:29), and I Corinthians 14. History of the Ethiopian church: Jacobs, *Roots of Rastafari*; Ephraim Isaac, *The Ethiopian Church* (Boston: H.N. Sawyer, 1968).

Jack Johnson-Hill calls Rasta "a broadly based, distinctive religious consciousness – of one's self, life-style, and vision of good": *I-Sight*, 22. Political and religious expression have been even more closely intertwined in Jamaica than in the US. What Stanley Crouch calls the "evangelical humanism at the center of modern democracy" is very much in evidence in Marley's music: *The All-American Skin Game*, xiii.

17 In addition to Harold Marcus' summary of the Amharas' invention of a Biblical lineage, see Bonnie Holcomb and Sisai Ibssa, *The Invention of Ethiopia* (Trenton, NJ: Red Sea Press, 1990), and Peter Sorenson, *Imagining Ethiopia* (New Brunswick, NJ: Rutgers University Press, 1993).

18 Robert Hill, ed., *Marcus Garvey* (Berkeley: University of California Press, 1987), xvi. Barrett, *The Rastafarians*, 67. Rupert Lewis, "Garvey's Significance in Jamaica's Historical Evolution," *Jamaica Journal* 20:3 (1987), 56–65. "In the thinking of the Rastafarians after Garvey's death in 1940, he assumed mythic proportions, second only to Haile Selassie." Rupert Lewis, "Marcus Garvey and the Early Rastafarians: Continuity and Discontinuity," in *Chanting Down Babylon*, ed. Murrell *et al.*, 156.

19 "Fascism": Hill, ed., *Marcus Garvey*, lviii. "Shortcomings": Moses, *Black Messiahs and Uncle Toms*, 125. Clarence Walker, "The Virtuoso Illusionist: Marcus Garvey," in *Deromanticizing Black History*, 34–55. Walker calls Garvey "racist and reactionary" (xxv, 35) and a "megalomaniac" (49), but concludes that although Garvey's movement was "proto-fascist," he was not himself a fascist (54). C. L. R. James' view of Garvey is more complex. As a young man, he heckled Garvey when he spoke at Hyde Park in London, along with George Padmore, who called Garveyism "the most reactionary expression [of] Negro bourgeois nationalism." Yet he came of age reading Garvey's *Negro World* in Trinidad. James' writings were generally sympathetic to Garvey's aims, yet some critics felt he focused too much on Garvey's "Fascist demagoguery." Robin D. G. Kelley, "The World the Diaspora Made: C. L. R. James and the Politics of History," in *Rethinking C. L. R. James*, ed. Grant Garrell (Oxford: Blackwell, 1996), 114–15. In "From Toussaint l'Overture to Fidel Castro" (1962), James' ambiguity is evident. He called Garvey's mass appeal "one of the propagandistic miracles of this century," and noted: "Garvey never set foot in Africa. He spoke no African language. His concep-

tions of Africa seemed to be a West Indian island and West Indian people multiplied times over." Yet "Garvey managed to convey to Negroes everywhere . . . his passionate belief that Africa was the home of a civilization which had once been great and would be great again": *The C. L. R. James Reader*, ed. Anna Grimshaw (Oxford: Blackwell, 1992), 300.

20 Anita Waters shows how mainstream Garvey has become in Jamaica – despite some ambivalence about his legacy – by documenting how both the left-of-center People's National Party and the right-of-center Jamaican Labour Party engaged in an "unseemly contest over the remains of Marcus Garvey," as a *Gleaner* columnist put it, in an effort to market themselves to poor black voters. Edward Seaga of the JLP got a lot of mileage in 1976 and 1980 trumping up his role in returning Garvey's remains from England. Waters, *Race, Class, and Political Symbols*, 225.

21 Garvey established two newspapers during his 1910–12 sojourn in Central America – *La Nacionale* in Costa Rica and *La Prensa* in Panama. During his first stay in England he wrote for the *African Times and Orient Review*, where he came into contact with many West Africans. When Garvey established his own US paper, the *Negro World*, it spanned continents and generations – employing respected black journalists from Africa, the Caribbean, and Latin America, as well as older American journalists such as William Ferris and Thomas Fortune, who had links to Alexander Crummell and Frederick Douglass. Bishton, *Blackheart Man*, 86; Campbell, *Rasta and Resistance*, 58. There was a large influx of Jamaicans into Central America beginning in the 1880s, who later played an important role in the dissemination of Rastafarianism in Latin America. Chevannes, *Rastafari*, 15.

22 Wilson Moses has often tried to call attention to similarities between Crummell and Garvey. They both hated mulattos, worshiped at the altar of classical European culture, and quoted Psalms 68:31 incessantly. They used a rigidly essentialized definition of race, and were both Puritanical in their tastes and moral philosophy. Crummell's influence on Garvey is much larger than is usually acknowledged, Moses insists, at least indirectly through members of Crummell's American Negro Academy such as Thomas Fortune, Duse Mohamed, and William Ferris who went on to work with Garvey. A good overview of this continuity is in *The Wings of Ethiopia*, 201–22. "Achilles heel": Bishton, *Blackheat Man*, 88. "Enduring symbols": Bishton, *Blackheart Man*, 88. The scam-like nature of Garvey's movement has found its expression in Afro-American art, as in Chester Himes' novel *Cotton Comes to Harlem*. "Charlatan": Walker, *Deromanticizing Black History*, xxv.

23 Conservative racialism drew the largest black audience (as with the novels of Sutton Griggs), yet was itself rooted in a racist European ethnology. "Bohemian" racialism came to be seen as the "real" black culture of America, and continues to be portrayed as such by literary and cultural critics today. Moses, *The Wings of Ethiopia*, 201ff. In his review of Claude McKay's *Home to Harlem*, Du Bois decried the longing of "a certain decadent section of the white American world" for "fierce and unrestrained passions" which "it wants to see written out in black and white and saddled on black Harlem": ibid., 213. Hutchinson challenges this conventional wisdom in *Harlem Renaissance in Black and White*. Two scholars who echo it: David Lewis, *When*

Harlem Was in Vogue (New York: Vintage, 1982); Nathan Huggins, *Harlem Renaissance* (Oxford University Press, 1971).

24 Myth of poverty: Bishton, *Blackheart Man*, 86. Stonemason: Moses, *Black Messiahs and Uncle Toms*, 125.

25 Garvey wrote: "Spiritual and Jazz Music are credited to the Negro … Simply because we did not know better music": Walker, *Deromanticizing Black History*, 38. Tennyson in Hill, *Marcus Garvey*, xxxi.

26 Garvey's philosophy fused fundamentalist Christianity, a worship of military conquerors, and an adaptation of late-Victorian self-help books. Garvey "identified with the extreme authoritarianism of the supreme leader," Hill notes (*Marcus Garvey*, xxx, xliii). He also identified with Dale Carnegie-style advice for self-made men. Garvey's thought replicated much of so-called "New Thought," a branch of the mental healing phenomenon associated with Christian Science. In 1920 Hodge Kirnon observed that "the Negro" had been so taken with this "New Thought" that "he has designated himself under the name of The New Negro" ("The New Negro and His Will to Manhood and Achievement," *Promoter* 1 [Aug. 1920], 4, in Hill, *Marcus Garvey*, xxviii). Garvey offered a "black version of New Thought" for the next two decades. For black people "to rise out of this racial chaos *new thought* must be injected into the race" (ibid., xl, xxix, my emphasis). Yet the "new thought" Garvey drew on was inevitably European and Euro-American.

27 Hill, *Marcus Garvey*, 203–4.

28 Ibid., 204–05, 194.

29 Ibid., 193–94, my emphasis.

30 Amilcar Cabral, *Return to the Source* (New York: Monthly Review Press, 1973), 51.

31 "Traumatic one": Moses, *Black Messiahs and Uncle Toms*, 125–26. Garvey's account of his white girlfriend first appeared in "The Negro's Greatest Enemy," *Current History* (Sept. 1923); reprinted in Amy Jacques-Garvey, ed., *Philosophy and Opinions of Marcus Garvey* (New York: Atheneum, 1980), 124ff.

32 "Degenerates"; "mulatto-hating": Moses, *Black Messiahs and Uncle Toms*, 140, 132. "Monstrosities": Walker, *Deromanticizing Black History*, 51. Jervis Anderson, *This Was Harlem* (New York: Farrar, 1982). Quoted in Walker, *Deromanticizing Black History*.

33 Garvey's inconsistency also extended to Jews, who early on patronized him, before he began demonizing Jews and making overtures to the anti-Semitic Ku Klux Klan. Garvey's ties to Jewish supporters began in Jamaica. Hill, *Marcus Garvey*, lv. UNIA's Jewish patrons, McKay, Padmore; Jacques-Garvey, *Philosophy and Opinions*, liii–lvii.

34 "Kingdom/help to make them": Walker, *Deromanticizing Black History*, 37, my emphasis. On Ethiopia's invention of a Biblical past to legitimate imperial conquest, see Sorenson, *Imaging Ethiopia*, and Harold Marcus, *A History of Ethiopia*.

35 Bernard Lewis, *History Remembered, Recovered, Invented* (Princeton University Press, 1975), 96–97.

36 Sollors, ed., *Invention of Ethnicity*, xv. For a critical examination of Rasta's ideological roots, see Murrell and Williams, "The Black Biblical Her-

meneutics of Rastafari," in *Chanting Down Babylon*, ed. Murrell *et al.*, 326–48.

37 E. Franklin Frazier, "Garvey: A Mass Leader," *Nation* 123 (Aug. 18, 1926), 147–48. Bellah, "Civil Religion in America." Randall Burkett, *Garveyism as a Religious Movement: The Institution of a Black Civil Religion* (Metuchen, NJ: Scarecrow Press, 1978). Moses, *Black Messiahs and Uncle Toms*, 124, 138. "New religion": *Negro World*, Oct. 16, 1920, in Hill, *Marcus Garvey*, xxxvi.

38 Henry McNeal Turner, *Voice of the Missions*, Feb. 1, 1898, quoted in Moses, *Black Messiahs and Uncle Toms*, 134. "Spectacles of Ethiopia": Jacques-Garvey, *Philosophy and Opinions*, 34; Barrett, *The Rastafarians*, 77.

39 In 1920 the UNIA adapted "Ethiopia, Thou Land of our Fathers" ("The Universal Ethiopian Anthem") as an anthem sung at all UNIA gatherings. Chevannes compares the impact of this song, later adapted by the Rastas, to the emotions aroused in South Africa by the singing of "Nkosi Sikele i Africa," the anthem of the African National Congress: *Rastafari*, 41. One line, "Thou land where the Gods love to be," echoes testimony by the Greeks (such as in the *Odyssey*) that the Ethiopians were "beloved of the gods," and Diodorus of Sicily, who wrote that Ethiopians were "deemed the most religious of all men." Barrett, *The Rastafarians*, 74. The image of being "led by the red, black and green" foreshadows a theme that continues in reggae and rap music to the present day.

40 "Our hymns": Jacques-Garvey, *Philosophy and Opinions*, 201. Madonna: Campbell, *Rasta and Resistance*, 61. "Hopes … Solomon … her hands": editorial, *Blackman*, Oct. 25, 1930. Campbell, *Rasta and Resistance*, 65, my emphasis. Garvey's belief that Ethiopia's "imperial authority" could be "repossessed" is an endorsement of the Solomonic legend the Amhara elite were circulating in the West. Marcus, *Haille Sellassie* and *A History of Ethiopia*. Garvey alludes to Psalms 68:31. "Pan-African solidarity": Rupert Lewis, "Marcus Garvey and the Early Rastafarians," in *Chanting Down Babylon*, ed. Murrell *et al.*, 146.

41 "[My people are] the direct descendants of the inhabitants of Meroe. We [wait] for the coming of our king who shall restore to the Ethiopian race its ancient glory." Pauline Hopkins, "Of One Blood, or the Hidden Self," *Colored American Magazine* 6:7 (July 1903), 492. Quoted in Moses, *Golden Age*, 200. Webb: Timothy White, *Catch a Fire: The Life of Bob Marley* (New York: Henry Holt & Co., 1989), 4–5.

42 "Coronation of Selassie": Chevannes, *Rastafari*, 95. C. L. R. James believed that one reason why Garvey was deported in 1926 was that the Japanese government was trying to finance and control his Back-To-Africa movement in order "to embarrass and disrupt the imperialist empires in Africa." Quoted in Walton Look Lai, "Trinidadian Nationalism," in *C. L. R. James's Caribbean*, ed. Paget Henry and Paul Buhle (Durham, NC: Duke University Press, 1992), 192.

43 "Contempt": White, *Catch a Fire*, 4. "Crazy": Bishton, *Blackheart Man*, 120.

44 "Prophecy fulfill": a common phrase in Rasta reggae. See Smith, *Conjuring Culture*, on a "black" tradition of interpreting Biblical "types" as being fulfilled in the present.

45 Geographic: Barrett, *The Rastafarians*, 82. "Come to pass": a quote from

Burning Spear's 1975 song "Marcus Garvey" (on album of same name). "Him black": Chevannes, *Rastafari*, 115.

46 "Lobby": Bishton, *Blackheart Man*, 117.

47 "Preemptive action": Chevannes, *Rastafari*, 43. K. W. J. Post, "The Bible as Ideology: Ethiopianism in Jamaica, 1930–38," in *African Perspectives*, ed. C. H. Allen & R. N. Johnson (Cambridge University Press, 1970), 204.

48 *Voice of Ethiopia*: Barrett, *The Rastafarians*, 77.

49 Hibbert: Chevannes, *Rastafari*, 124–26; Bishton, *Blackheart Man*, 119; Gayraud S. Wilmore, *Black Religion and Black Radicalism* (Maryknoll, NY: Orbis Books, 1998), 180. Liele: Barrett, *The Rastafarians*, 40, 76; Wilmore, *Black Religion*, 105; Chevannes, *Rastafari and Other African-Caribbean Worldviews*, 7–8, 33, 47, 57, 64.

50 Howell: Chevannes, *Rastafari*, 121–22. "Crucified": Bishton, *Blackheart Man*, 111.

51 Bedward: Chevannes, *Rastafari*, 78–80, 108–09, 126–27. "Quarter century": Bishton, *Blackheart Man*, 120. "Negro rules": Wilson Jeremiah Moses, ed., *Classical Black Nationalism* (New York University Press, 1996), 244. The *Rastafari Movement*, written by Rex Nettleford and others in 1960, partly responded to the destruction of Howell's Compound in 1954–55, and ensuing clashes between Rastas and the police. Bishton, *Blackheart Man*, 109. On the wearing of sackcloth and other anti-materialistic "folkways" of some early Rastas, see Homiak, "Dub History."

Howell treated as Messiah; "white wall": Ken Post, *Arise Ye Starvelings: The Jamaican Labour Rebellion of 1938 and Its Aftermath* (The Hague: Martinus Nijhoff, 1978), 165, 7; Patrick Bryan, *The Jamaican People: Race, Class and Social Control* (London: Macmillan, 1991), 45. Travels beyond Jamaica as Moses/Jesus in wilderness: Burton, *Afro-Creole*, 140–44.

52 Garvey myths and legends: Chevannes, *Rastafari*, 99–110.

53 "Mental slavery" – according to Rex Nettleford, Garvey used this line in a speech at Menelik Hall, Nova Scotia, in 1937: "Discourse on Rastafarian Reality," in *Chanting Down Babylon*, ed. Murrell *et al.*, 313. See also Marley's former art director Neville Garrick in Boot and Salewicz, *Songs of Freedom*, 247. I discuss Bogle's rebellion and his biracial sponsor in the next section.

54 "House of Prayer": Isaiah 56:7. "Cornerstone": Psalms 118:22.

55 *Time Will Tell*, dir. by Declan Lowney, Rock Oldham, Prod., Executive Producer Neville Garrick and Malcolm Garrie (Initial Film and Television/ Island, 1991). All of my subsequent quotes of Marley not cited otherwise come from this film. R. A. Allen, *Carribean Times*, interview in London, late July 1975, cited in Davis, *Bob Marley*, 152.

56 Ambivalence: Burton, *Afro-Creole*, 113.

57 Waters, *Race, Class, and Political Symbols*, 40. "Ears of the masters": Campbell, *Rasta and Resistance*, 26. John Bigelow, *Jamaica in 1850* (Westport, CT: Negro Universities Press, 1851/1970), 157. In Waters, *Race, Class, and Political Symbols*, 35. Cynric Williams, *Tour through the Island of Jamaica* (London: Hunt & Clarke, 1826), 27, quoted in Burton, *Afro-Creole*, 68.

58 Archetypal figures/"Good White Man": Burton, *Afro-Creole*, 114, 106–07, 56; Abigail Bakan, *Ideology and Class Conflict in Jamaica: The Politics of Rebellion* (Montreal: McGill-Queen's University Press, 1990), 7–8.

59 "Lowly blacks": Paul Blanshard, *Democracy and Empire in the Caribbean* (London: Macmillan, 1974), 52. On Gordon, see Waters, *Race, Class, and Political Symbols*, and Barrett, *The Rastafarians*, 52–58. Manley and Bustamante as "savior figures": Burton, *Afro-Creole*, 144–47.

60 "Brown Babylonians": M. G. Smith, Roy Augier, and Rex Nettleford, *The Rastafari Movement in Kingston, Jamaica* (Mona: Jamaica, University College of the West Indies, Institute of Social and Economic Research, 1960). Castro as indigenous: Chevannes, *Rastafari*, 249. This view was voiced by Black Rock Rastas. "Brown-Man Supremacy": Barrett, *The Rastafarians*, 149. C. L. R. James: Waters, *Race, Class, and Political Symbols*, 79. "Premature integration": a separatist view of culture espoused by JanMohamed and Lloyd, eds., in *The Nature and Context of Minority Discourse*, 7.

61 "White father... never make it": Boot and Salewicz, *Songs of Freedom*, 10, 48.

62 "Him a white man": Davis, *Bob Marley*, 36; Boot and Salewicz, *Songs of Freedom*, 63. "Light-skin people": ibid., 59. Also, Steffens in Talamon, *Bob Marley*, 17.

63 Benjamin Foot in Boot and Salewicz, *Song of Freedom*, 114. From listening to public feedback over the years to my published columns on Marley, from talking to Ziggy Marley on his 1988 "Conscious Party" tour, and from reading Ziggy's heated denials that his dad was "half-white," I know that any assertions that Bob was other than "fully black" will arouse intense resistance among some reggae lovers, while being fully embraced by others.

64 "Sacrifices... successful"; "black and white thing": ibid., 128, 112. Rupert Lewis writes: "Rastafari needs to be seen in the context of... social and racial struggles over a Jamaican identity that is heir to both British and African cultures." Marley's life and art dramatizes this struggle for a British/African synthesis in a personal way. "Marcus Garvey and the Early Rastafarians," in *Chanting Down Babylon*, ed. Murrell *et al*. 155.

65 "Massive" is a Caribbean term which refers to a mass audience or collective, most often the audience of a speaker or singer. It signifies a collective identity/ support group. "Mass" is used in a similar sense in Trinidad. In an interview on *Time Will Tell*, Marley gestures to his surroundings and says: "Me and this massive is a revolutionary... fighting single-handed with music." He refers most directly to the large Wailers touring entourage, but the Wailers as a massive are situated within a much larger massive – the Rastafarians, who are in turn just the tip of an iceberg, so to speak, of all Africans "at home and abroad." The collective self-concept of Rastas is revealed in their use of "I and I" as a language tool. This term refers not only to the unity between human beings, but to the "eye" within the "I" – the unity between humans and the God within. Thus Rastas refuse to engage in what they see as "Babylonian" individualism: for "conscious" Rastas, the different people within a massive are united by the common divine spirit that dwells within them. See Marley's discourse on the meaning of "I & I" in Malika Whitney and Dermott Hussey, *Bob Marley* (Rohnert Park, CA: Pomegranate, 1984), 86; explanations by other Rastas in Nicholas and Sparrow, *Rastafari*, 38–39; Davis and Simon, *Reggae International*, 62; Barrett, *The Rastafarians*, 144–5: and Adrian Anthony McFarlane, "The Epistemological Significance of 'I-an-I' as a Response to Quashie and Anancyism in Jamaican Culture," in *Chanting Down*

Babylon, ed. Murrell *et al.* 107–21.

66 In 1958 Blackwell was in a boat with friends near Hellshire when they developed engine trouble and ran aground on a coral reef. Six hours later, Blackwell found the hut of a Rasta fisherman, who motioned him inside and gave him water. Blackwell fell asleep and when he awoke at night he was surrounded by Rastas, who fed him, and talked to him about the Bible. After a twelve-hour stay they put Blackwell in a canoe and paddled five miles to Port Royal to get help. Blackwell claimed this experience gave him lasting goodwill towards Rastas. White, *Catch a Fire*, 238.

67 Michael Thelwell, *The Harder They Come* (New York: Grove, 1980).

68 "Movie": Boot and Salewicz, *Songs of Freedom*, 100.

69 "Hippest event": ibid., 106.

70 White, *Catch a Fire*, 133. White's tendency to hagiography and fictionalized recreations limits his reliability.

71 Rhyging act: ibid., 292; Davis, *Bob Marley*, 178. "I don't come to bow, I come to Conquer": Marley in *Time Will Tell*. "Rule this land": from the single "Jail House," 1965/66.

72 "Natchul man": Zora Neale Hurston, *Jonah's Gourd Vine* (New York: Lippincott/Perennial, 1934/1990).

73 "Pocomania" and "forever": interview with Fikisha Cumbo, June 20, 1975, in Whitney and Hussey, *Bob Marley*, 92, 88. This has Biblical precedent too: "My words will never pass away" (Mark 13:31).

74 See Bunny Wailer's discussion of these early influences in interview with Roger Steffens, *The Beat* 12:3 (1993), 44–48. Bunny describes the Impressions as "our loved ones." The song "It Hurts to be Alone" was directly modeled on Curtis Mayfield's "I'm So Proud," he notes. The Wailers first came to Studio One "more or less as the Impressions" – Johnny More in Boot and Salewicz, *Song of Freedom*, 66.

75 Hendrix, Kong, etc., Davis, *Bob Marley*, 71, 77. On Bob's rock influences, and the tensions this caused within the Wailers of the early 1970s, and the efforts of Bob's black audience to push him away from perceived "white" styles, see Mark Gorney, "Fire on the Wire: Earl 'Wya' Lindon," *The Beat* 17:3 (1998), 60–62.

76 Sims in ibid., 76. At least by late 1970, Marley's songs begin to refer explicitly to Rastafari. On "Small Axe," recorded with Perry in 1970, Bob sings: "The goodness of Jah Jah endureth for I-ver [forever]" (Psalms 52). Some songs from this period can be interpreted through either a Christian or Rastafarian lense, such as the line "I've got to reach Mt. Zion" on "Duppy Conqueror."

77 Perry's inspiration for the new style of music he forged with the Wailers came from attending a Trench Town Pocomania church. Marley's "rebirth," he claimed, occurred "when Bob drop into my hands" (ibid., 81). Rita Marley and others in Boot and Salewicz, *Songs of Freedom*, corroborate Perry's role in Bob's "rebirth" (92–97). White comments on Bob's "dated rhythmic base" in the songs he brought back from Delaware. Marley's later heavy reliance on Aston Barrett and Tyrone Downie as musical arrangers indicates that Bob was cut out of a "folk" singer/songwriter mold.

78 Elsewhere Garrick says more colloquially: "bad pronunciation created an iration" (*Songs of Freedom* box set booklet, page 36). Bob on his sense of

"knotty": Davis, *Bob Marley*, 138. Discussion of change from *Black Survival* also in Davis.

"The Lord is with me as a *dread warrior*": Jeremiah 20:11. Barry Chevannes believes the adaptation of a "dread warrior" image was copied from the matted hair of derelicts, around 1955, as an explicit attempt to advertise the more radical Rastas' rejection of Jamaican society. At this time beards, which had been the Rastas' previous symbol of radical other-ness, had become a fad in "mainstream" culture. "The Origin of the Dreadlocks," in Chevannes, *Rastafari and Other Africa-Caribbean Worldviews*, 89. See also Chevannes' "The Phallus and the Outcast: The Symbolism of the Dreadlocks in Jamaica," in ibid., 97–126, and John Homiak, "Soundings on Rastafari Livity and Language," in ibid., 127–81.

79 Sims and others note that Marley's revolutionary lyrics emerged in conjunction with Michael Manley's election as prime minister in 1972. In a sense Manley's democratic socialism and the flowering of Rastafarianism spearheaded by Marley were mutually constituted phenomena. Manley had visited Ethiopia in 1970, and brought back a "walking stick" he said was a gift from Emperor Selassie. He called this the "Rod of Correction," a Biblical term already employed by Rastas. This "rod" became a central legitimating symbol in Manley's 1972 campaign. A. W. and N. L. Singham note that Manley's PNP "appropriated very heavily the cultural forms of the Rastafarians, the most alienated group in the society... In the 1972 election the PNP came to victory after ten years in opposition using the Rasta language and music in almost undisguised form": "Cultural Domination and Political Subordination: Notes towards a Theory of the Caribbean Political System," *Comparative Studies in Society and History* 15:3 (1973), 281. Bob and Rita had played on the "PNP Musical Bandwagon" in 1971–72. Davis, *Bob Marley*, 96. Marley's support for Manley, officially denied, was an open secret, and probably factored into the 1976 assasination attempt.

Given the (repressed) symbiotic relationship between Manley and Marley, Leonard Barrett's assessment is suggestive: "In no other politician has the spirit of G. W. Gordon been so thoroughly reincarnated as it is in Michael Manley": *The Rastafarians*, 65. Gordon, like Manley, was "brown," and a forerunner of Marley as a biracial Jamaican who supported "black liberation."

80 "I am Natty Dread": Davis, *Bob Marley*, 150. I got a close-up glimpse of how offensive a term like "Fashion Dread" could be to those who think they are on a divine mission during a face-off with Ziggy Marley in Austin on the 1988 *Conscious Party* Tour. I had given the band a copy of my article "Fashion Dread" (1988) in Houston. In Austin, as I was interviewing Dallol, the Ethiopian backing band, Rita Marley called me into Ziggy's hotel room. Ziggy was vexed by the article, thinking that the title referred to him. Rita wanted to know what I meant by the term. I explained it as a marketing concept, which she seemed to understand, but Ziggy kept reading one quote after another from the article, barking into my face, spit flying from his mouth, while his teenaged brother Stephen winked at me. My article had been intended to illustrate how dance hall reggae had become "mainstream," but Ziggy, who was used to hearing people talk about his Dad as a prophet or a Christ-figure, did not want to believe that fashion had anything to do with his own popular-

ity. This incident came to mind when I heard Ziggy's 1995 tune "Never Get a Righteous Man Vex."

81 On the "performative," see Judith Butler, *Excitable Speech: A Politics of the Performative* (London: Routledge, 1997).

82 In a passage that could be applied to Marley's efforts to deflect messianic projections, Richard Webster writes of "the characteristic insecurity of the messianic personality who, doubting his own divine calling, feels compelled to project his sense of election onto others": *Why Freud Was Wrong: Sin, Science, & Psychoanalysis* (New York: Basic Books, 1995), 302.

83 This view has been challenged by James Lincoln Collier. See his *Jazz: The American Theme Song* (Oxford University Press, 1993). Jamaican musicians/ leaders have often had to come "back from foreign" before gaining respect at home. Burton, *Afro-Creole*, 141, 144.

84 "Just spread": Boot and Salewicz, *Songs of Freedom*, 147.

85 Rasta "blossoming": Morris in ibid., 165.

86 Jaffe's whiteness: Davis, *Bob Marley*, 149.

87 Marley told Dennis Morris that it was a "system," and "not a black and white thing" he was fighting. Boot and Salewicz, *Song of Freedom*, 112. Much of the media was picking up on the interracial mediating quality of Marley's music. In *Black Music* magazine, Carl Gayle called "Natty Dread" "the soul rebel from Kingston and Ethiopia" who "is breaking down the colour barrier." Davis, *Bob Marley*, 149.

88 Laurence Breiner, "The English Bible in Jamaican Rastafarianism," *Journal of Religious Thought* 42:2 (Fall/Winter 1985/1986), 30–43. Barrett refers to the "ambivalent routinization" of Rastafarian thought: *The Rastafarians*, 146. He adapts this concept from the explanation of "routinization" in Anthony F. C. Wallace, "Revitalization Movement," *American Anthropologist* 58 (1956).
See Timothy White's discussion of the Twelve Tribes and its impact on Marley's Hope Road scene: *Catch a Fire*, 279–82. Barry Chevannes writes that the "Twelve Tribes . . . is symbolic of the kind of 'shift in consciousness' . . . that has been forced on the Jamaican middle class by the Rastafarian movement": "Rastafari and the Exorcism of Racism," in *Chanting Down Babylon*, ed. Murrell *et al.*, 67.

89 In fact, "up to the very recent past the belief that Rastafari cannot die was very strong," as Chevannes writes. The death of Selassie in 1975 and of Marley in 1981 were pivotal events, after which some Rastas began to acknowledge "that man is put on earth only for a time." However, as Chevannes observes, this "is not the majority view": *Rastafari and Other African-Caribbean World-views*, 37.

90 Smith, *Conjuring Culture*, 55–56. Sollors, *Beyond Ethnicity*. The belief in a literal exodus has modulated, especially among urban Rastas, who "attempt to create 'Zionic' conditions within their respective 'exodus' communities," notes Randall Hepner. He observes that US Rastas envision "the emergence of a new Zionlike society, symbolized by collective memories of an ancient Africa (Ethiopia) . . . If they cannot be transported (repatriated) to Zion, then Zion must somehow be brought to or created within the societies in which Rastafarians have been forced to dwell." Randall Hepner, "Chanting Down Babylon in the Belly of the Beast: The Rastafarian Movement in the

Metropolitan United States," in *Chanting Down Babylon*, ed. Murrell *et al.*, 211–12.

91 "Moses ... work to do": Nicholas and Sparrow, *Rastafari*, 75. This should not be seen as a product of an individual messianic self-concept, since all Rastas believe in a "God within". Ras Hu-I, interviewed by Nicholas, says: "Rasta is sent to do a job ... Each and every man have Ras Tafari in them, therefore have divinity in them": ibid., 34. Hence on "Ride Natty Ride" Marley sings: "Dready's got a job to do / And he's got to fulfill that mission."

92 "Paved the way ... support": Davis, *Bob Marley*, 183. This fusion led directly to the "two-tone" movement of interracial ska bands around 1980, and has inspired countless spin-offs in contemporary British music. Letts later played keyboards in a reggae-influenced Clash spin-off group, Big Audio Dynamite.

93 "Jungle music/drop one on it": Neville Garrick in Whitney and Hussey, *Bob Marley*, 160–61.

94 "Prisoner": Davis, *Bob Marley*, 197. Bob links *Kaya* to Jamaican violence: Boot and Salewicz, *Songs of Freedom* 214. In a 1980 interview with Stephen Davis, Marley expressed admiration for Bob Dylan's *Saved*, whose Biblical themes critics disliked. "There come a time when an artist just cyaan follow the crowd," Marley observed. "You got to mek the crowd follow you." "Like Two Rolling Stones," *The Beat* 11:3 (1992), 45. Criticism of *Rastaman Vibration*: Davis, *Bob Marley*, 163.

95 Marley continued to use a variety of approaches to try and connect with different elements of his audience. The use of a dual "star guitar" sound on *Babylon by Bus* was another move on Bob's part to internationalize his sound. Davis, *Bob Marley*, 204–5. At the same time, to prove he had not "sold out," Marley recorded songs in 1978 with Lee Perry designed for his "roots" Jamaican audience (such as "Rastaman Live Up" and "Blackman Redemption").

96 "Careless Ethiopian": Chevannes, *Rastafari*, 244–45, 249.

97 "White men": Davis, *Bob Marley*, 204.

98 "Prejudice?": ibid.

99 C. J. Jung, *Analytical Psychology*, ed. William McGuire (Princeton University Press, 1989), 91. "Small people one day must get big" Bob's son Ziggy sang on the album *Jahmekya* (Virgin, 1991). In a December 1979 interview Marley says he is "*vexed with Africa*" because of anti-Selassie sentiment he witnessed in Ethiopia. Because of this, he expresses doubt that Ethiopia will be the country in Africa to which Jamaican Rastas repatriate. Jeff Cathrow, "Marley Speaks: A Conversation with Rastafari's Reggae Prophet," *Reggae Report* 8:4 (1990), 21–23.

Two major transformations in the last year of Malcolm X's life foreshadowed Marley, and were a repudiation of the Nation of Islam, which shared ideological roots with the Rastas. Malcolm "discovered" the humanity of whites, and he determined that the advice of Garvey and Elijah Muhammad to go "back to Africa" should be interpreted metaphorically. Whereas Malcolm never came to terms with his own partial "whiteness," Marley began with the understanding that he could not be prejudiced against whites without being prejudiced against himself.

100 In June 1975, Marley referred to Selassie as "the perfect father for me." Whitney and Hussey, *Bob Marley*, 93. Zion/Babylon as systems of good/evil: Murrell and Williams, "The Black Biblical Hermeneutics of Rastafari," in *Chanting Down Babylon*, ed. Murrell *et al.*, 343.

101 This echoes the line in "Road Block" from *Natty Dread*: "Why can't we roam this open country?"

102 Ethiopian Amharas and Afro-American emigrationists, both models for the Rastas, shared similar imperialist assumptions. See Gershoni, *Black Colonialism*; Holcomb and Ibssa, *The Invention of Ethiopia*; Levine, *Politics of Representative Identity*.

103 In an interview with black journalist Greg Broussard, June 22, 1977, Marley says Africa is underdeveloped because it is waiting for Rastas to come lead the way. "And so dem seh Africa nuh develop. Why? Because Africa wait fi we." Greg Broussard, "Bob Marley's Message: Africans Unite!" *The Beat* 9:3 (1990), 27.

104 Foner, ed., *L&W*, IV, 341, my emphasis.

105 "Healing fiction": Jung, *Psychology and Religion*, 131. Mario Jacoby sees "longing for paradise" as "an archetypal pattern necessary to human development." Projecting this image "creat[es] a nostalgia the intensity of which is in inverse proportion to the amount of external fulfillment encountered in the earliest phase of life." Mario Jacoby, *Longing for Paradise* (Boston: Sigo, 1985), 8. The strength of Marley's projection on to Selassie as divine ruler of an African Zion was clearly fueled by the absence of his father.

106 "Earth will remain": Foner, ed., L&W, IV, 411.

107 Erich Auerbach, *Mimesis: The Representation of Reality in Western Literature* (New York: Anchor/Doubleday, 1952). Quoted in Smith, *Conjuring Culture*, 70. On the Rastas' "blackening" of the Bible, see Murrell and Williams, "Black Biblical Hermeneutics of Rastafari," in *Chanting Down Babylon*, ed. Murrell *et al.*, 333.

108 "Baldheads" is usually interpreted as a reference to whites, but it is also applied to non-dreads in a generic sense: i.e., "careless Ethiopians" or blacks who are not following a "natural" life-style. Rastas also developed a vocabulary to take into account intermediate groups; for instance, blacks who live a positive life but have not allowed their hair to dread are called "combsome." It is fairly common now to refer to "conscious" whites as "Rasta." Like much of Rastafarian vocabulary, "baldhead" has its roots in racial formations, but has partly transcended race.

    The mandate to let one's hair grow naturally is located in Leviticus 21:5: "They [priests] shall not make baldness upon their head, neither shall they shave off the corner of their beard, nor make any cuttings in their flesh." The latter law was cited by Marley as a reason he would not allow his toe to be amputated when it developed cancer.

    Some participants in the 1865 Morant Bay uprising declared that their intention was "to beat all the brown and white off the island." Gad Heuman, *"The Killing Time": The Morant Bay Rebellion in Jamaica* (Knoxville: University of Tennessee Press, 1994), 88–89; Burton, *Afro-Creole*, 113.

109 "Word/Sound/Power" is something of a holy trinity for Rastas: the combination of conscious words and appropriate sounds used repetitively equals

power. Note that this belief is implicit in Garvey's advice to engage in "whispering campaigns." Word/Sound/Power is a form of "conjuring" and shares common points of reference with magical rituals of many "indigenous" peoples. Chevannes, *Rastafari*, 227; Nicholas and Sparrow, *Rastafari*, 38.

110 "Worship freedom": Du Bois, *Souls of Black Folk*, 47, my emphasis.

111 "Conscious lyrics": a line by KRS-One, on an album he produced for Jamaica's "riddim twins," Sly Dunbar and Robbie Shakespeare, *Silent Assassin* (Island, 1989).

112 "Father's command": Garnet Silk, "The Rod." Garnet died in a house fire in 1995. In reggae's self-mythologizing process, Silk has already entered into a state of prophetic "sonship": for instance, in Macka B's single, "Tribute to Garnet Silk," released in Great Britain, 1996. "Colonizing space": Cornel West, "The New Cultural Politics of Difference," *October* 53 (Summer 1990).

113 "Messenger": Jean Comaroff, *Body of Power, Spirit of Resistance: The Culture and Resistance of a South African People* (University of Chicago Press, 1985), xi–xiii. "God within": "Each and every man have . . . divinity in them": Ras Hu-I, in Nicholas and Sparrow, *Rastafari*, 34.

114 "Self": Smith, *Conjuring Culture*, 62, my emphasis.

115 "Transposes Africa": Nicholas and Sparrow, *Rastafari*, 28. "Last shall be first": Mark 10:31/ Matthew 20:16/ Luke 13:30.

116 "Abandoned child": Davis, *Bob Marley*, 20. Otto Rank, *The Myth of the Birth of the Hero: A Psychological Interpretation of Mythology* (New York: R. Brunner, 1914/1957). Jung notes that abandonment is a central motif of the "child god" archetype: *Archetypes of the Collective Unconscious* (Princeton University Press, 1959/1968), *Collected Works*, IX, i, 166. Jung elsewhere observes that the hero normally comes "from something humble and forgotten," from a "wholly improbable source" (ibid., 141). In a comment applicable to how many of Marley's audience viewed him, Jung interprets the child savior motif as "a symbol who unites the opposites; a mediator, bringer of healing" (ibid., 164). The Moses myth inverts the more common "birth of the hero" scenario, in which an abandoned child of royal birth is raised by a humble family (or even by animals). Jan Assmann, *Moses the Egyptian* (Cambridge: Harvard University Press, 1997), 150.

117 "Black sheep": Davis, *Bob Marley*, "Citizen": White, *Catch a Fire*, 53. Cedella Booker with Anthony Winkler, *Bob Marley* (London: Penguin, 1996), 13–30, 34–5, 38–47. On the sexual chauvinism of Jamaican men in general and Rastas in particular, see especially Carole D. Yawney, "Moving with the Dawtas of Rastafari: From Myth to Reality," in *The Caribbean and Latin America: Third Interdisciplinary Colloquium about the Caribbean*, ed. Ulrich Fleischmann and Ineke Thaf (Berlin: Verlag Klaus Dieter Verwoerd) and "To Grow a Daughter: Cultural Liberation and the Dynamics of Oppression in Jamaica," in *Feminism*, ed. Angela Miles and Geraldine Finn (Montreal: Black Rose Books, 1989). Many treatments of gender roles in the Caribbean start from a critique of Peter Wilson's typology of a division between a female, private sphere of "respectability" and a male, public sphere of "reputation": *Crab Antics: The Social Anthropology of English-*

Speaking Negro Societies of the Caribbean (New Haven: Yale University Press, 1973). Jean Besson, "Reputation and Respectability Reconsidered: A New Perspective on Afro-Caribbean Peasant Women," in *Women and Change in the Caribbean*, ed. Janet H. Momsen (Bloomington: Indiana University Press, 1993), 15–37.

Chevannes views the emergence of dreadlocks as symbolizing "both a rejection of social control as well as a triumph of male power over the female": *Rastafari and Other African-Caribbean Worldviews*, 97. This view is seconded by Jean Besson, "Religion as Resistance in Jamaican Peasant Life: The Baptist Church, Revival Worldview and Rastafari Movement," in ibid., 44. J. P. Homiak's ethnographic work includes testimony from older Rastas indicating that many of their ideological innovations and folkways were developed not only in opposition to a "female sphere," but often during periods of celibacy that could last for years: "Dub History."

118 Norval disinherited: Davis, *Bob Marley*, 12. Norval named Bob after a brother, but no one knows where Norval got the name Nesta, which was originally Bob's first name until a US immigration officer switched the order. "Give to Bob": ibid., 17. Norval did manage to sire another child by a like-skinned woman before dying (ibid., 61). According to Cedella, when she brought bigamy charges against Norval, they were dismissed on the grounds that he was senile. When Cedella confronted "the new so-called Mrs. Marley" in the street and demanded that she give Bob some of his father's money, this woman insisted: "He don's have one thing to offer me! He has nothing to call his own!" Booker, *Bob Marley*, 47–48.

When Bob later developed melanoma cancer, he felt it might have been inherited from his biological father, because this was supposedly a rare type of melanoma among black people. Allan "Skill" Cole, in Whitney and Hussey, *Bob Marley*, 189.

119 "Bad man . . . his way": Davis, *Bob Marley*, 21–22. Booker, *Bob Marley*, 196.

120 "Fatherless Nesta": Boot and Salewicz, *Songs of Freedom*, 42.

121 "Obey no one": Davis, *Bob Marley*, 23. "Stubborn": Booker, *Bob Marley*, 52.

122 "Selah" – a musical notation added to some Psalms. In the black Christian oral tradition it means "stop and meditate."

123 Higgs' influence: Davis, *Bob Marley*, 31, White, *Catch a Fire*, 150–55, Boot and Salewicz, *Song of Freedom*, 59–61. Higgs replaced Bunny Wailer on Marley's 1974 US tour.

124 *Rockers* is a Jamaican film starring reggae drummer Leroy "Horsemouth" Wallace. Arguments over absentee Jamaican fathers often occur on the Internet discussion group rec.music.reggae. Bob's grandfather Omeriah fathered twenty to thirty children by various women outside his marriage, according to a memoir by Bob's mother, Cedella Booker. Bob himself sired eleven children by seven mothers – all of whom he supported financially. His sons are carrying on this tradition – with Lauryn Hill of the popular group The Fugees bearing a child to Rohan Marley being the most publicized example.

125 "Give you": White, *Catch a Fire*, 214; Davis, *Bob Marley*, 65. Cedella Booker recounts this incident in a less dramatic manner in her memoir: *Bob*

Marley, 108–09. This tiny diamond on the ring would appear to represent the "scintilla" or the seed of the "light within."

126 "Blessin' now": White, *Catch a Fire*, 215.

127 Hagiography – the projection of divine qualities and elision of human weaknesses – is of course a tendency in writing about most culture heroes, from Buddha to Martin Luther King, Jr.

Meeting with Wossen; "just like Christ": ibid., 295, 298. See Roger Steffens' 1993 interview with Ibis Pitts, a friend of Bob's in Delaware (*The Beat* 12:3 [1993], 39). Steffens reports that Cedella Booker (Bob's mother) had told him that Ibis and Dion, another Delaware friend of Bob's, had heard him prophesy in 1969 that he would die at age thirty-six. Pitts is fuzzy on the details, telling Steffens that he remembered something of the sort, but that it was was Dion who remembered the specifics after Bob died. Timothy White records this prediction as having happened in 1977 while Bob was sitting in a tree with his friends. Cindy Breakspeare describes Bob as choosing not to believe his doctors, repressing his awareness of the cancer as "something that he really didn't want to deal with." Whitney and Hussey, *Bob Marley*, 184. After Bob's death, members of the Twelve Tribes mounted an intense campaign to try and recover Bob's Lion of Judah ring. White, *Catch a Fire*, 314–15.

128 These lyrics are from "Redemption Song." Perhaps Marley, who overcame expectations that browns were normally white-identitified, fulfilled both the black martyr and colored redeemer archetype for Jamaicans.

129 "We fly a color": Whitney and Hussey, *Bob Marley*, 93–94.

130 The portion of Selassie's speech set to music by Marley is: "until the philosophy which holds one race superior and another inferior is finally and permanently discredited and abandoned; . . . until the colour of a man's skin is of no more significance than the the the colour of his eyes; that until the basic human rights are equally guaranteed to all, without regard to race – until that day, the dream of lasting peace and world citizenship and the rule of international morality will remain but a fleeting illusion, to be pursued but never attained. And until the ignoble and unhappy regimes that hold our brothers in Angola, in Mozambique and in South Africa in sub-human bondage have been toppled and destroyed . . . until that day the African continent will not know peace. We Africans will fight, if necessary and we know that we shall win, as we are confident in the victory of good over evil."

131 "Third force": Davis, *Bob Marley*, 217–18.

132 Coexistence of faith and critique: see almost any of Cornel West's writings; also Yerushalmi, *Freud's Moses*, 116.

133 "Black Hebrews": Nichols and Sparrow, *Rastafari*, 34. "The Giant Nile," Pt. II, directed by Chris Monty (Blue Bird Films/Atlas Video, 1990).

134 "A study . . . coming of Christ": Isaac, *The Ethiopian Church*, 46.

135 Higginson in Lawrence Levine, *Black Culture and Black Consciousness*, 50. Also Robert Levine, *Politics of Representative Identity*, 13. The Jamaican Ethiopian Baptist Church was founded by George Lisle in 1784. An émigré from South Carolina, he had been baptized by a disciple of Great Awakening preacher George Whitefield.

136 Boot and Salewicz, *Songs of Freedom* 44, 67, 115, 160. Barrett, *The Rastafar-*

ians, 214. "Poetic biblicism": Smith, *Conjuring Culture*, 129. "Literary sensibility": Cooper, *Noises in the Blood*, 76. Cedella Booker's memoir (*Bob Marley*) and Allan Cole's interview in Whitney and Hussey (*Bob Marley*, 190) note that Bob still read the Bible daily while dying in Germany.

137 "Which nation": *Reggae Report* 8:4 (1990), 22.

138 Breiner, "The English Bible in Jamaican Rastafarianism," 30, 33. See also Murrell and Williams, "Black Biblical Hermeneutics of Rastafari," in *Chanting Down Babylon*, ed. Murrell *et al.*, 327–28. There are of course many different Bibles which vary considerably. The Protestant Bible itself has been in flux for most of the Christian era; the Catholic Bible includes many books considered "apocryphal" by Protestants. The Eastern Orthodox and Ethiopian churches have their own Bibles. The huge literature on the "Dead Sea Scrolls" is making increasingly clear how multicentered was the tradition of sacred texts among the Hebrews of Jesus' time, and, correspondingly, how impossible it is to determine the borders of a "sacred canon." A good starting point for study of the many layers of composition and revision in Judaic scriptures: Richard Friedman, *Who Wrote the Bible?* (New York: Perennial/Harper & Row, 1987).

139 Manley quoted in Davis and Simon, *Reggae International*, 59.

140 "Spiritual diagnosis": Nicholas and Sparrow, *Rastafari*, 30, my emphasis.

141 "Enter": Luke 18:17. "Little child": Isaiah 11:6.

142 Bob's 1978 reading habits: Boot and Salewicz, *Bob Marley*, 214. The Jamaica-born Garrick had an Art Design degree from UCLA and had been a "disciple" of Angela Davis before becoming Bob's art director in 1975. He seems certain to have had an impact upon Marley's awareness of Afro-American intellectual and cultural currents: in 1975 Marley named Angela Davis as a woman he admired: "a woman like that who defends something: Me can appreciate that." Davis, *Bob Marley*, 152.

143 "Time a really a run out": *The Beat* 9:3 (1990), 27. Interview June 22, 1977.

144 "Careless Ethiopians": a term among Rastas for blacks who are unconcerned about their African heritage. See Chevannes, *Rastafari*, 228, or the reference by the group The Abyssinians on their song "Peculiar Number," from *Satta Massagana*.

145 "Meaning to a man": Basil Wilson and Herman Hall, "Marley in His Own Words: A Memorable Interview," *Everybody's Magazine* 5:4 (1981): 24. Cooper, *Noises in the Blood*, 118.

146 "Black yuh out": *The Beat* 9:3 (1990), 28.

147 "Psychic spur": Davis, *Bob Marley*, 217. The *Wingless Angels* was an album of traditional Nyabinghi chants, produced by Keith Richards of the Rolling Stones, and released in 1997.

148 "Literary text" and Brathwaite in Cooper, *Noises in the Blood*, 117, 1. Linton Kwesi Johnson, *Bass Culture* (Island/Mango, 1980). "One harmony": *Time Will Tell*.

149 There is an echo of Garvey here, who wrote: "the Negro's chance will come when the smoke from the fire and ashes of twentieth-century civilization has blown off." Hill, *Marcus Garvey*, xxiv.

150 "Sonship": Barrett, *The Rastafarians*, 111. Tony Rebel on Island promotional video for Buju Banton. There is a parallel for Bob Marley here: as

Jesus was born without the benefit of an earthly father (according to later theological insertions), so Bob bypasses his physical father through "divine sonship" with a perfect Ethiopian father.

151 Marley often said that the use of guns was counter-productive in the West, although he called for an armed uprising in Zimbabwe. Marley's "truest" sense of what was a "real revolutionary" seems to be summed up in the famous lines in "Redemption Songs": "Emancipate yourself from mental slavery / None but ourselves can free our minds." In interviews he elaborated on his particularly religious view of the psychological roots of freedom: "To have freedom I must be free within myself. My mind must be free. The only time my mind can be free is when I praise Rastafari."

152 On the Amharas' invention of Solomonic ancestry, and their racial ambiguity, see Marcus, *A History of Ethiopia*, and Sorenson, *Imagining Ethiopia*. The use of real and imagined persecution as a unifying tool is a common theme – especially in "black history." See for instance Robert Levine's excellent study of Martin Delany's use of what we would now call "strategic essentialism," in opposition to Frederick Douglass' transracialism: *Politics of Representative Identity*.

153 "Bell hooks" (a *nom de plume*) is consistently reductionist about "white" participation in "black" forms. She reports on a Jimmy Cliff concert in which whites did not join in the slogan "Africa for the Africans." "There was suddenly a hush in the room, as though the listeners finally heard the rebellion against white supremacy, against imperialism in the lyrics. They were silent, unable apparently to share in this gesture of affirming black solidarity." In *Talking Back: Thinking Feminist, Thinking Black* (Boston: South End, 1989), 14.

154 Douglass' last words of advice to a group of young Afro-Americans were: "Agitate, agitate." This advice is echoed in Marley's words: "Rebel, rebel." See King's allusions to Isaiah 63 and "The Battle Hymn of the Republic," in "Our God is Marching On," in *I Have a Dream: Writings and Speeches that Changed the World*, ed. James W. Washington (New York: HarperCollins, 1992), 119–24.

155 This Old Testament story has been popular among Rastas. See the Abyssinians' song "Abendigo" from the classic *Satta Massagana*, and the Congos, "La La Bam Bam," from *Heart of the Congos*.

156 This "roof chamber open to Jerusalem" evokes the Rasta "higher consciousness," which in the midst of exile is open to their Zion, Africa. Thus Marley sings on "Roots": "There's nothing they can do to separate I and I / from the love of our father / You see, blood is thicker than water." The mythologized blood ties with Solomon – which Bob celebrated on "Blackman Redemption" – transcend the separation by water.

157 Although Marley always disclaimed any messianic self-concept, such themes reappear in his work. In the 1980 song "Trenchtown," he asks rhetorically: "Can anything good come out of Trenchtown?" This echoes John 1:45, in which Nathanael voices doubt that Jesus could be the Messiah: "Can anything good come out of Nazareth?" However, Marley is explicitly talking about collective liberation. He sings "we free the people with music." It is a massive, a collective who emerged out of Trenchtown, whom Marley be-

lieves will be able, against all odds to "free the people with music." So in this sense Marley's use of Messianic themes seems intended to refer to a group redeemer rather than an individual messiah.

"Own country": also in John 4:44. Isaiah also refers to the Daniel story when he records the promise: "you will walk through fire, and you will not be scorched, through flames, and they will not burn you" (43:2).

"Man's house": another instance of Bob recycling the Bible. The original passage reads: "The rain falls on the just and the unjust."

158 Handouts: Boot and Salewicz, *Song of Freedom*, 222; *The Beat* 10:3 (1991), 32; Davis, *Bob Marley*. Chris Blackwell estimates that Bob was responsible for the support of 4,000 people. Colin Leslie, the Tuff Gong manager responsible for cutting checks to Bob's supplicants, believes the number was higher. *The Beat* 14:3 (1995), 57–8.

Asked why he thinks Bob died at thirty-six, Desmond Smith commented: "I figure he was probably bearing too much burden, 'cause when he died, he really know how much thing he was dragging around. See what happened? Everyt'ing collapsed": *The Beat* 11:3 (1993), 53. Alan Cole was Marley's trainer as well as best friend through 1976, when he moved to Ethiopia to coach a soccer team. His friends reported that since 1977 so many friends were "exploiting the situation" that "Bob stop eat, him couldn't get no time to eat, the people them 'round him so much . . . when him come to Africa [in December 1978] me see a tired man . . . Them work Bob too much . . . Look like everybody 'round him was on a trip": Whitney and Hussey, *Bob Marley*, 188. Malika Whitney observed that "some people didn't seem to have any discretion, just in terms of his time. He seemed to be saturated by their needs and wants." Judy Mowatt notes "he was always giving himself. I have never seen that man take any time off for himself. He's always giving." Ibid., 193. In the 1990s this *giving* is called co-dependency.

159 Mark 9:35; Mark 10:43.

160 Mowatt in Whitney and Hussey, *Bob Marley*, 192–93.

161 Early 1979 depression: Davis, *Bob Marley*, 209–10. Disturbed by Ethiopia: *Reggae Report* 8:4 (1990), 23. Kinsey: Davis, *Bob Marley*, 220.

162 Stephen Davis, "Bob Marley's Lost Tapes," *The Beat* 9:3 (1990), 31–33, 46. An example of these themes is the "Wounded Lion in the Jungle" rehearsal tapes, circulated among Marley collectors.

163 "Wider than that": Richard Cromelin, "Bob Marley: Talkin' Revolution," *The Beat* 14:3 (1995), 47. "Vexed . . . in your consciousness": Cathrow, "Marley Speaks." Object of faith/act of faith: the idea of religious objects as a part of our "psychological structure" is discussed in Moshe Halevi Spero, *Religious Objects as Psychological Structures* (University of Chicago Press, 1992).

164 Devil as friend: *The Beat* 14:3 (1995), 48. Ziggy's denial of his father's biraciality: interviewing Ziggy, Roger Steffens commented, "your dad was black and white." "My father was black and white?" Ziggy responded. "No, mon. Him father was white, but him no black and white." *The Beat* 12:3 (1993), 36.

165 Douglass used the same metaphors to try to "keep hope alive" during seemingly hopeless times: in the wake of the Dred Scott decision in 1857, he

wrote: "David ... looked small and insignificant when going to meet Goliath, but looked larger when he had slain his foe." Blight, *Frederick Douglass' Civil War*, 22.

166 "All people": Isaiah 56:7. Universal/national god: Friedman, *Who Wrote the Bible?*, 154.

167 Barrett, *The Rastafarians*, 213. Wesley was responsible for directing Methodism towards an international audience. Gentiles: Chevannes, *Rastafari*, 270.

168 *The Five Gospels: The Search for the Authentic Words of Jesus*, transl. Robert W. Funk, Roy W. Hoover, and the Jesus Seminar (New York: Pole Bridge Press/MacMillan, 1993). "Rivers of Babylon" in Ireland: White, *Catch a Fire*, 332.

169 See Roger Steffens in Talamon, *Bob Marley*, 14.

170 Lebanese *Natty Dread* in Tibet: *The Beat* 10:3 (1991), 34. Blackwell in Bali: ibid.

171 Isaac Selassie on Bob as Yahred, Bob as Vishnu in Nepal; Sandanistas: *The Beat* 14:3 (1995), 56–59. Austin, Texas, DJ Sista Irie posted a report on the prevalence of Marley's image and music on the Havasupai reservations at the bottom of the Grand Canyon on Aug. 21, 1998 (raw @ databack.com) titled "A Grand Revelation – Havasupai and Rastafari – I."

172 Himmelfarb and WASPafarians: Chevannes, *Rastafari*, 271. On Marley's impact in Japan and contemporary Japanese love of reggae: Boot and Salewicz, *Songs of Freedom*, 218–19; Neville Garrick in *The Beat* 9:3 (1990), 36.

173 "White people"/"word go out": *The Beat* 9:3 (1990), 25, 28. I have a tape of Mutabaruka's "Running African" show (IRIE-FM, Sept. 29, 1996) in which he discusses how European African music shows "full up" with white people, as a reproach to black Jamaicans' comparative lack of interest in African culture.

174 "Suspicion": Davis, *Bob Marley*, 161. "Black, white, china": *Time Will Tell*.

175 "Trivilialization": Yawney, "Rasta Mek a Trod," 79. Many of both poorer Rastas and middle-class Jamaicans thought the crowd at Marley's Hope Road complex was hypocritical: they talked about being sufferers, yet lived an opulent life-style. However, most Rastas seemed not to have held this against Marley – whom they called "Nesta" – perhaps in part because of his legendary generosity. Lewis, *Soul Rebels*, 32, 78.

176 "Slaves": Albert J. Raboteau, *Slave Religion* (Oxford University Press, 1980), 311. Sollors, *Beyond Ethnicity*.

177 Zora Neale Hurston, *Moses, Man of the Mountain* (Urbana: University of Illinois Press, 1939/1984), and Sigmund Freud, *Moses and Monotheism* (New York: Knopf, 1939). See Yerushalmi, *Freud's Moses*, on the long history of Jewish scholars' questioning of the ethnicity of Moses, in which he discusses Freud's original plan to classify his book on Moses as a historical novel.

178 Loss of sacred: Robert Bellah, *Habits of the Heart: Individualism and Commitment in American Life* (New York: Harper & Row, 1986), and Michael Smith, *Psychotherapy and the Sacred: Religious Experience and Religious Resources in Psychotherapy* (Chicago: Center for the Scientific Study of Religion, 1995). "Consensual community": Yawney, "Rasta Mek a Trod," 79. The

projection of divinity on Selassie seems part of a wider trend in diasporic African thought (at least in Afrocentric variants) in which slaves and their movements often arouse less interest than the Pharaohs of Northeast Africa. Favoring the imperial kingdoms of Northeast Africa over the tribal cultures of sub-Saharan Africa enables the assumption of God-like qualities.

179 "Heritage," "symbolic ambiguity"; "echo of allegiance": Yawney, "Rasta Mek a Trod," 83. On the ritual construction of community ("Communitas"), see Victor Turner, *Dramas, Fields, & Metaphors: Symbolic Action in Human Society* (Ithaca: Cornell University Press, 1974), 274; Victor Turner, *The Ritual Process: Structure and Anti-Structure* (Ithaca: Cornell University Press, 1969), 96–113. On Turner's virtual elision in 1990s cultural studies: Donald Weber, "From Limen to Border: A Meditation on the Legacy of Victor Turner for American Cultural Studies," *American Quarterly* 47:3 (Sept. 1995).

Rasta symbols, as formulated by Marley, were both Judeo-Christian and anti-Christian. As an alternative "nuclear myth" constructed in "antagonistic cooperation" with European cultural myths, Rasta was both anti-Oedipus and anti-Christ: pro-father rather than anti-father; opposed to the idea that human beings need a mediator to access the divinity.

180 Global sales figures on Marley are hard to tally. Island has released fifteen Marley albums, and of *Legend* alone has sold (as of 1998) 10 million copies in the US and 6 million "abroad." Island alone has probably sold around 50 million units of "official" Marley recordings. This figure does not include the many other labels which have released Marley albums, such as CBS and Trojan, much less the international bootlegs, which would easily push the figure into the hundreds of millions.

181 Breiner, "The English Bible in Jamaican Rastafarianism," 30. This is a claim that would arouse resistance among many writers accustomed to viewing Rasta reggae as a transplant of African traditions. Breiner's claim is not entirely accurate: the *burru* rhthyms on which reggae was built have been identified as an African survivalism. And as I have noted, Rastas adapted elements of Ethiopia's "indigenous" Christianity. Yet as Chevannes illustrates, Rastas have often tried to repress the variants of Revival such as Pocomania which manifest clear African survivalisms.

182 On the collage style of West African art and performance, see Thompson, "An Aesthetic of the Cool"; Thompson, *Flash of the Spirit*. I have drawn a parallel between West African performance art and rap music as "postmodern" collages in Stephens, "Rap Music's Double-Voiced Discourse: A Crossroads for Interracial Communication," *Journal of Communication Inquiry* 15 (1991), 70–91.

183 "Thinking of christ as non-black in the 20th century is as theologically impossible as thinking of him as non-Jewish in the first century": James Cone, *Black Theology and Black Power* (New York: Seabury, 1969), 69. This rang true when I first read it in 1989, but seems too Afrocentric now. Marley has become an alternative for those who want to imagine a divinity in non-binary colors.

184 Von Franz, *Projection and Re-Collection*.

185 Marley wanted union with his father, not Oedipal destruction. The Christ

archetype is anti-Oedipus, Paul Vitz notes: the son loves, not hates his father; seeks perfect union, not separation; redemption, not alienation: *Sigmund Freud's Christian Unconscious* (New York: Guilford, 1988), 168–9. C. J. Jung, *Dream Analysis: Notes of the Seminar Given in 1928–1930*, ed. William McGuire (Princeton University Press, 1984), 706.

186 The King James Version was a misleading translation. This passage actually refers to a period of imperial conquest, in which Egypt and Ethiopia must pay tribute to Jerusalem. The millennial tone is present only in the King James Version; most subsequent translations convey the sense of Israel's enemies having to subjugate themselves. Gilkes, "Mother to the Motherless, Father to the Fatherless."

Select bibliography

Abel, Elizabeth, Christian, Barbara, and Moglen, Helene, eds., *Female Subjects in Black and White: Race, Psychoanalysis, Feminism*, Berkeley: University of California Press, 1997.

Adams, Michael Vannoy, *The Multicultural Imagination: "Race", Color, and the Unconscious*, London: Routledge, 1996.

Anderson, Benedict, *Imagined Communities: Reflections on the Origin and Spread of Nationalism*, London: Verso, 1983/1991.

Andrews, William L., ed., *Critical Essays on Frederick Douglass*, Boston: G. K. Hall & Co., 1991.

Anzaldúa, Gloria, *Borderlands/La Frontera: The New Mestiza*, San Francisco: Spinster/Aunt Lute Book Company, 1987.

Appiah, Kwame Anthony, *In My Father's House: Africa in the Philosophy of Culture*, New York: Oxford University Press, 1993.

Asante, Molefi, *The Afrocentric Idea*, Philadelphia: Temple University Press, 1987.

Asante, Molefi and Gudykunst, William, eds., *Handbook of International and Intercultural Communication*, Newbury Park, CA: Sage, 1989.

Assmann, Jan, *Moses the Egyptian: The Memory of Egypt in Western Monotheism*, Cambridge: Harvard University Press, 1997.

Azoulay, Katya Gibel, *Black, Jewish, and Interracial: It's Not the Color of Your Skin, but the Race of Your Kin, and Other Myths of Identity*, Durham, NC: Duke University Press, 1997.

Bakhtin, Mikhail, *The Dialogic Imagination*, ed. Michael Holquist, Austin: University of Texas Press, 1981.

Banton, Michael, *Racial Theories*, London: Cambridge University Press, 1987.

Barrett, Leonard E., *The Rastafarians: Sounds of Cultural Dissonance*, Boston: Beacon, 1977/1988.

Bell, Howard Holman, *A Survey of the Negro Convention Movement 1830–1861*, New York: Arno Press and the New York Times, 1953/1969.

Bellah, Robert, "Civil Religion in America," *Daedalus* 96 (1967), 1–21.

Benston, Kimberly, ed., *Speaking for You: The Vision of Ralph Ellison*, Washington, DC: Howard University Press, 1987.

Bercovitch, Sacvan, *The American Jeremiad*, Madison: University of Wisconsin Press, 1978.

Bernal, Martin, *Black Athena: The Afroasiatic Roots of Classical Civilization*, New Brunswick: Rutgers University Press, 1987.

Besson, Jean, "Reputation and Respectability Reconsidered: A New Perspective on Afro-Caribbean Peasant Women," in *Women and Change in the Caribbean: A Pan-Caribbean Perspective*, ed. Janet H. Momsen, Bloomington: Indiana University Press; London: James Currey, 1993, 15–37.

Bishton, Derek, *Blackheart Man: A Journey into Rasta*, London: Chatto & Windus, 1986.

Black Public Sphere Collective, eds., *The Black Public Sphere*, University of Chicago Press, 1995 (series ed. Houston A. Baker).

Blackett, R. J. M., *Building an Antislavery Wall: Black Americans in the Atlantic Abolitionist Movement, 1830–1860*, Ithaca: Cornell University Press, 1989.

Blight, David, *Frederick Douglass' Civil War: Keeping Faith in Jubilee*, Baton Rouge: Louisiana State University Press, 1989.

Bogle, Donald, *Toms, Coons, Mulattoes, Mammies and Bucks: An Interpretive History of Blacks in American Films*, New York: Continuum, 1973/1989.

Booker, Cedella with Winkler, Anthony, *Bob Marley: An Intimate Portrait by His Mother*, London: Penguin, 1996.

Boot, Adrian and Salewicz, Chris, *Bob Marley: Songs of Freedom*, New York: Viking, 1995.

Boot, Adrian and Thomas, Michael, *Jamaica: Babylon on a Thin Wire*, London: Schoken, 1976.

Brawley, Benjamin, *Early Negro American Writers*, New York: Dover, 1935/1970.

Breiner, Laurence, "The English Bible in Jamaican Rastafarianism," *Journal of Religious Thought* 42:2 (Fall/Winter 1985/1986), 30–43.

Brookes, George, *Friend Anthony Benezet*, Philadelphia: University of Pennsylvania Press, 1937.

Brotz, Howard, ed., *Negro Social and Political Thought 1850–1920*, New York: Basic Books, 1966.

Burton, Richard D. E., *Afro-Creole: Power, Opposition, and Play in the Caribbean*, Ithaca: Cornell University Press, 1997.

Calhoun, Craig, ed., *Habermas and the Public Sphere*, Cambridge: MIT Press, 1992.

Callahan, John F., *In the African-American Grain: The Pursuit of Voice in Twentieth-Century Black Fiction*, Urbana: University of Illinois Press, 1988; repr. Middleton, CT: Wesleyan University Press, 1990.

Campbell, Horace, *Rasta and Resistance: From Marcus Garvey to Walter Rodney*, Trenton, NJ: Africa World Press, 1987.

Carter, Stephen L. *Reflections of an Affirmative Action Baby*, New York: Basic Books, 1991.

    The Culture of Disbelief: How American Law and Politics Trivialize Religious Devotion, New York: Basic Books, 1993.

Castronovo, Russ, *Fathering the Nation: American Genealogies of Slavery and Freedom*, Berkeley: University of California Press, 1995.

Cell, John W., *The Highest Stage of White Supremacy: The Origins of Segregation in South Africa and the American South*, Cambridge University Press, 1982.

Chernoff, John, *African Rhythm & African Sensibility*, University of Chicago Press, 1979.

Chesebrough, David R., *Frederick Douglass: Oratory from Slavery*, Westport, CT, and London: Greenwood Press, 1998.

Chevannes, Barry, *Rastafari: Roots and Ideology*, Syracuse University Press, 1994.

Chevannes, Barry, ed., *Rastafari and Other African-Caribbean Worldviews*, New Brunswick, NJ: Rutgers University Press, 1998; originally published London: MacMillan, 1995.

Collins, John J., *The Apocalyptic Imagination: An Introduction to the Jewish Matrix of Christianity*, New York: Crossroads, 1984/1987.

Condit, Celeste Michelle and Lucaites, John Louis, *Crafting Equality: America's Anglo-African Word*, University of Chicago Press, 1993.

Cone, James, *Black Theology and Black Power*, New York: Seabury Press, 1969.

Cooper, Carolyn, *Noises in the Blood: Orality, Gender, and the "Vulgar" Body of Jamaican Popular Culture*, Durham, NC: Duke University Press, 1995.

Cornelius, Janet Duitsman, *When I Can Read My Title Clear: Literacy, Slavery, and Religion in the Antebellum South*, Columbia: University of South Carolina Press, 1991.

Crouch, Stanley, *The All-American Skin Game, or, The Decoy of Race*, New York: Pantheon, 1995.

Curran, James, and Gurevitch, Michael, *Mass Media and Society*, London: Routledge, 1992.

Dasenbrock, Reed Way, "Intelligibility and Meaningfulness in Multicultural Literature in English," *Modern Language Association* 102 (1987).

Davis, David Brion, *The Problem of Slavery in Western Culture*, Ithaca: Cornell University Press, 1966.

Davis, F. James, *Who Is Black? One Nation's Definition*, University Park: Penn State University Press, 1991.

Davis, Stephen, *Bob Marley*, Rochester, VA: Schenkman, 1983/1990.

Davis, Stephen and Simon, Peter, *Reggae International*, New York: R&B, 1982.

Dearborn, Mary V., *Pocahontas's Daughters: Gender & Ethnicity in American Literature*, Oxford University Press, 1986.

Dillon, Merton L., *The Abolitionists: The Growth of a Dissenting Minority*, De Kalb: Northern Illinois University Press, 1974.

Douglass, Frederick, *Narrative of the Life of Frederick Douglass, an American Slave, Written by Himself*, ed. with an introduction by David Blight, Boston and New York: Bedford Books of St. Martin's Press, 1845/1993.

My Bondage and My Freedom, New York: Dover, 1855/1969.

Life and Times, New York: Collier, 1892/1962.

Autobiographies, ed. and with notes by Henry Louis Gates, Jr., New York: The Library of America/Penguin, 1994.

Du Bois, W. E. B., *The Souls of Black Folk*, New York: Penguin, 1903/1989.

Black Reconstruction, New York: Harcourt Brace, 1935.

Ellison, Ralph, *Invisible Man*, New York: Vintage, 1952/1982.

Shadow and Act, New York: New American Library, 1966.

Going to the Territory, New York: Random House/Vintage, 1986.

The Collected Essays of Ralph Ellison, ed. with an introduction by John F. Callahan, New York: Modern Library, 1995.

Flying Home and Other Stories, ed. with an Introduction by John F. Callahan, New York: Random House, 1996.

Esteva-Fabregat, Claudio, *Mestizaje in Ibero-America*, Tucson and London: University of Arizona Press, 1995; translation by John Wheat of *El mestizaje en*

Iberoamérica, Madrid: Alhambra Longman, 1987.

Fabre, Genevieve and O'Meally, Robert, eds., *History and Memory in African-American Culture*, Oxford University Press, 1994.

Farrand, Max, *The Fathers of the Constitution*, New Haven: Yale University Press, 1921.

Finkelman, Paul, "Slavery & the Constitutional Convention: Making a Covenant With Death," in *Beyond Confederation*, ed. Richard Beeman *et al.*, Chapel Hill: University of North Carolina Press, 1987.

Fischer, David Hackett, *Historians' Fallacies: Toward a Logic of Historical Thought*, New York: Harper, 1970.

Fishkin, Shelly Fisher, *Was Huck Black? Mark Twain and African American Voices*, Oxford University Press, 1993.

"Interrogating 'Whiteness,' Complicating 'Blackness': Remapping American Culture," *American Quarterly* 47:3 (Sept. 1995), 428–66; also in *Criticism on the Color Line: Desegregating American Literary Studies*, ed. Henry Wonham, New Brunswick, NJ: Rutgers University Press.

Fishkin, Shelly and Peterson, Carla, "'We Hold These Truths to be Self-Evident': The Rhetoric of Frederick Douglass's Journalism," in *Frederick Douglass: New and Literary and Historical Essays*, ed. Eric Sundquist, Oxford University Press, 1990.

Foner, Eric, *A Short History of Reconstruction, 1863–1877*, Harper & Row/Perennial, 1990.

Foner, Philip S., ed., *The Life and Writings of Frederick Douglass*, I: *Early Years, 1817–1849*, New York: International Publishers, 1950.

The Life and Writings of Frederick Douglass II: *Pre-Civil War Decade*, New York: International Publishers, 1950.

The Life and Writings of Frederick Douglass, IV: *Reconstruction and After*, New York: International Publishers, 1955.

Frederick Douglass on Women's Rights, New York: Da Capo Press, 1976/1992.

Foster, Frances Smith, *Written By Herself: Literary Production by African American Women, 1746–1892*, Bloomington: Indiana University Press, 1993.

Franklin, Benjamin, "Observations Concerning the Increase of Mankind" (1751), in *The Papers of Benjamin Franklin*, ed. Leonard Labaree, New Haven: Yale University Press, 1959.

von Franz, Marie-Louise, *Projection and Re-Collection in Jungian Psychology*, La Salle and London: Open Court, 1980.

Fraser, Nancy, "Rethinking the Public Sphere," in *Habermas and the Public Sphere*, ed. Craig Calhoun, Cambridge: MIT Press, 1992.

Frazier, E. Franklin, *Race and Culture Contacts in the Modern World*, New York: Knopf, 1957.

Fredrickson, George, *A Comparative Study on American and South African History*, Oxford University Press, 1981.

Black Liberation: A Comparative History of Black Ideologies in the United States and South Africa, New York: Oxford University Press, 1995.

Fredrickson, George, ed., *A Nation Divided: Problems and Issues of the Civil War and Reconstruction*, Minneapolis, MN: Burgess Publishing, 1975.

Freehling, Alison Goodyear, *Drift Toward Dissolution: The Virginia Slavery Debate of 1831–32*, Baton Rouge: Louisiana State University Press, 1982.

Freehling, William W., *The Reintegration of American History: Slavery and the Civil War*, New York: Oxford University Press, 1994.

Freud, Sigmund, *Moses and Monotheism*, New York: Knopf, 1939.

Frey, Sylvia R., *Water From the Rock: Black Resistance in a Revolutionary Age*, Princeton University Press, 1991.

Friedman, Richard Elliott, *Who Wrote the Bible?*, New York: Perennial/Harper & Row, 1987.

Fulkerson, Gerald, "Frederick Douglass and the Kansas-Nebraska Act: A Case Study in Agitational Versatility," *Central States Speech Journal* 23 (1972), 262–69.

"Exile as Emergence: Frederick Douglass in Great Britain, 1845–1847," *Quarterly Journal of Speech* 60 (1974), 69–82.

Fuller, Robert, *Naming the Antichrist: The History of an American Obsession*, New York: Oxford University Press, 1995.

Fuss, Diana, *Essentially Speaking: Feminism, Nature, and Difference*, London: Routledge, 1989.

Gadamer, H. G., *Wahrheit und Methode*, Tubingen: Mohr, 1975; translated by J. Cumming as *Truth and Method*, New York: Seabury, 1975.

Gates, Henry Louis, Jr., *Figures in Black: Words, Signs, and the "Racial" Self*, Oxford University Press, 1987.

The Signifying Monkey: A Theory of Afro-American Literary Criticism, Oxford University Press, 1988.

Gatewood, Willard B., *Aristocrats of Color: The Black Elite, 1880–1920*, Bloomington: Indiana University Press, 1990.

Gay, Peter, ed., *The Freud Reader*, New York: Norton, 1989.

Gayle, Addison, *The Way of the World: The Black Novel in America*, New York: Doubleday, 1975.

Geertz, Clifford, *The Interpretation of Cultures*, New York: Basic Books, 1973.

Genovese, Eugene D., *Roll, Jordan, Roll: The World the Slaves Made*, New York: Random House/Vintage, 1974.

Gershoni, Yekutiel, *Black Colonialism: The Americo-Liberian Scramble for the Hinterland*, Boulder: Westview Press, 1985.

Gibson, Donald, "Christianity and Individualism: (Re-)Creation and Reality in Frederick Douglass' Representation of Self," *African-American Review* 26 (1992), 591–603.

Gilkes, Cheryl Townsend, "'Mother to the Motherless, Father to the Fatherless': Power, Gender, and Community in an Afrocentric Biblical Tradition," *Semeia* 47 (1989), 57–85.

Gilroy, Paul, *The Black Atlantic: Modernity and Double Consciousness*, Cambridge: Harvard University Press, 1993.

Small Acts: Thoughts on the Politics of Black Cultures, London: Serpent's Tail, 1993.

Gitlin, Todd, *The Twilight of Common Dreams: Why America is Wracked by Culture Wars*, New York: Metropolitan Books/Henry Holt, 1995.

Gomez-Peña, Guillermo, "The Multicultural Paradigm," *High Performance* (Fall 1989).

Warrior for Gringostroika, St. Paul: Graywolf Press, 1993.

The New World Border: Prophecies, Poems, and Loqueras for the End of the Century,

San Francisco: City Lights, 1996.

Goodman, Paul, *Of One Blood: Abolitionism and the Origins of Racial Equality*, Berkeley: University of California Press, 1998.

Graham, Maryemma and Singh, Amritjit, eds., *Conversations with Ralph Ellison*, Jackson: University Press of Mississippi, 1995.

Habermas, Jurgen, *Legitimation Crisis*, Boston: Beacon, 1975.

Hall, Stuart, "The Emergence of Cultural Studies and the Crisis of the Humanities," *October* 53 (Summer 1990).

Harlan, Louis R., *Booker T. Washington: The Wizard of Tuskegee, 1901–1915*, Oxford University Press, 1983.

Harris, Cheryl I., "Whiteness as Property," *Harvard Law Review* 106:8 (June 1993).

Harwood, Thomas, "Great Britain and American Anti-Slavery," PhD dissertation, University of Texas, 1959.

Haskins, James, *Black Dance in America: A History Through Its People*, New York: HarperCollins, 1990.

Hill, Robert, ed., *Marcus Garvey: Life and Lessons*, Berkeley: University of California Press, 1987.

Hobsbawn, Eric and Ranger, Terence, eds., *The Invention of Tradition*, Cambridge University Press, 1983.

Holcomb, Bonnie and Ibssa, Sisai, *The Invention of Ethiopia*, Trenton, NJ: Red Sea Press, 1990.

Hollinger, David, *Postethnic America: Beyond Multiculturalism*, New York: Basic Books, 1995.

"National Culture and Communities of Descent," *Reviews in American History* 26 (1998), 312–28.

Holquist, Michael, *Dialogism: Bakhtin and His World*, London: Routledge, 1990.

Homans, Peter, *Jung In Context: Modernity and the Making of a Psychology*, University of Chicago Press, 1995.

Homiak, John P., "Dub History: Soundings on Rastafari Livity and Language," in *Rastafari and Other African-Caribbean Worldview*, ed. Barry Chevannes, New Brunswick: Rutgers University Press, 1998, 127–81.

Hord, Fred Lee, *Reconstructing Memory: Black Literary Criticism*, Chicago: Third World Press, 1991.

Horsman, Reginald, *Race and Manifest Destiny*, Cambridge: Harvard University Press, 1981.

Houchins, Sue E., ed., *Spiritual Narratives*, Oxford University Press, 1988.

Hughes, Everett and Hughes, Helen, *Where Peoples Meet: Racial and Ethnic Frontiers*, Glencoe, IL: Free Press, 1952.

Hurston, Zora Neale, *Moses, Man of the Mountain*, Urbana: University of Illinois Press, 1939/1984.

Hutchinson, George, *The Harlem Renaissance in Black and White*, Cambridge, MA, and London: Belknap/Harvard University Press, 1995/1997.

Hutchinson, John and Smith, Anthony D., eds., *Ethnicity*, Oxford University Press, 1996.

Hyde, Lewis, "Frederick Douglass and Eshu's Hat," in *Trickster Makes This World: Mischief, Myth, and Art*, New York: Farrar, Stras & Giroux, 1998.

Isaac, Ephraim, *The Ethiopian Church*, Boston: H. N. Sawyer, 1968.

Jacobi, Jolande, *Complex/Archetype/Symbol*, Princeton University Press, 1959.

Jacobs, Donald, M., ed., *Courage and Conscience: Black and White Abolitionists in Boston*, Bloomington: Indiana University Press, 1993.

Jacobs, Virginia Lee, *Roots of Rastafari*, San Diego: Avant Books, 1985.

Jacoby, Mario, *Longing for Paradise: Psychological Perspectives on an Archetype*, Boston: Sigo, 1985.

JanMohamed, Abdul and Lloyd, David, eds., *The Nature and Context of Minority Discourse*, Berkeley: University of California Press, 1990.

Jefferson, Thomas, *Notes on the State of Virginia* (1785), New York: Harper & Row, 1964.

Jensen, Merrill, ed., *Tracts of the American Revolution 1763–1776*, Indianapolis: Bobbs Merrill, 1977.

Johnson-Hill, Jack A., *I-Sight: The World of Rastafari: An Interpretive Sociological Account of Rastafarian Ethics*, Metuchen, NJ, and London: American Theological Library Association and Scarecrow Press, 1995.

Jones, Absolom and Allen, Richard, *A Narrative of the Proceedings of the Black People during the Late and Awful Calamity in Philadelphia, in the Year 1793*, Philadelphia: William Woodward, 1794; Early American Imprints, Microprint #17170.

Jordan, Winthrop D., *White Over Black: American Attitudes Toward the Negro, 1550–1812*, Chapel Hill: University of North Carolina Press, 1968/New York: Penguin, 1969.

Jung, C. G., *Psychological Types*, Princeton University Press, 1921/1971, *Collected Works*, VI.

   Archetypes of the Collective Unconscious, Princeton University Press, 1959/1968, *Collected Works*, IX, i.

   Aion: Researches into the Phenomenology of the Self, Princeton University Press, 1959, *Collected Works*, IX, ii.

   Psychology and Religion: East and West, Princeton University Press, 1958/1969, *Collected Works*, XI.

   The Symbolic Life, Princeton University Press, 1976, *Collected Works*, XVIII.

   Analytical Psychology: Notes on the Seminar Given in 1925, edited William McGuire, Princeton University Press, 1989.

Kapuscinski, Ryszard, *The Emperor*, New York: Vintage, 1978/1983.

Karcher, Carolyn, *The First Woman in the Republic: A Cultural Biography of Lydia Maria Child*, Durham, NC: Duke University Press, 1994.

Kolchin, Peter, *American Slavery, 1619–1877*, New York: Hill and Wang, 1993.

Kousser, J. Morgan and McPherson, James M., eds., *Region, Race, and Reconstruction*, Oxford University Press, 1982.

Kraditor, Aileen, *The Ideas of the Woman Suffrage Movement*, New York: Norton, 1981.

Lamar, Howard and Thompson, Leonard, *The Frontier in History: North America and South Africa Compared*, New Haven: Yale University Press, 1981.

Lampe, Gregory P., *Frederick Douglass: Freedom's Voice, 1818–1845*, East Lansing: Michigan State University Press, 1998.

Levine, Lawrence, *Black Culture and Black Consciousness*, Oxford University Press, 1977.

Levine, Robert, *Martin Delany, Frederick Douglass, and the Politics of Representative Identity*, Chapel Hill: University of North Carolina Press, 1997.

Lewis, David Levering, *W. E. B. Du Bois: Biography of a Race, 1868–1919*, New York: Henry Holt, 1993.

Lewis, William F., *Soul Rebels: The Rastafari*, Prospect Heights, IL: Waveland Press, 1993.

Lhamon, W. T., Jr., *Raising Cain: Black Performance from Jim Crow to Hip Hop*, Cambridge, MA, and London: Harvard University Press, 1998.

Lienesch, Michael, "Thomas Jefferson and the American Democratic Experience," in *Jeffersonian Legacies*, ed. Peter Onuf, Charlottesville: University Press of Virginia, 1993.

Lind, Michael, *The Next American Nation: The New Nationalism & the Fourth American Revolution*, New York: Free Press Paperbacks, 1996.

List, Robert N., *Dedalus in Harlem: The Joyce–Ellison Connection*, Washington, DC: University Press of America, 1982.

Litwack, Leon and Meier, August, eds., *Black Leaders of the Nineteenth Century*, Urbana: University of Illinois Press, 1988.

Locke, Alain LeRoy, *Race Contacts and Interracial Relations*, ed. Jeffrey C. Stewart, Washington, DC: Howard University Press, 1916/1992.

Locke, John, *Two Treatises of Government*, ed. Peter Laslett, New York: Basic Books, 1965.

Lott, Eric, "Love and Theft: The Racial Unconscious of Blackface Minstrelsy," *Representations* 39 (Summer 1992), 23–50.

Lovejoy, David S., *Religious Enthusiasm in the New World: Heresy to Revolution*, Cambridge: Harvard University Press, 1985.

Lynd, Staughton, *Class Conflict, Slavery, and the United States Constitution*. Indianapolis: Bobbs-Merrill, 1967.

Lyotard, Jean-Francois, *The Post-Modern Condition*, Minneapolis: University of Minnesota Press, 1984.

McCoy, Drew R., *The Last of the Fathers: James Madison and the Republican Legacy*, New York: Cambridge University Press, 1989.

McDowell, Deborah and Rampersad, Arnold, eds., *Slavery and the Literary Imagination*, Baltimore: Johns Hopkins University Press, 1989.

McFeely, William S., *Frederick Douglass*, New York: Norton, 1991.

McGinn, Bernard, *Antichrist: Two Thousand Years of the Human Fascination with Evil*, New York: HarperCollins, 1994.

McKivigan, John, "The Frederick Douglass–Gerrit Smith Friendship & Political Abolitionism in the 1850s," in *Frederick Douglass: New Literary and Historical Essays*, ed. Eric J. Sundquist, New York: Cambridge University Press, 1990.

McPherson, James M., *The Abolitionist Legacy: From Reconstruction to the NAACP*, Princeton University Press, 1975.

Mandela, Nelson, *Long Walk to Freedom: The Autobiography*, Boston: Little, Brown, 1994.

Marcus, Harold G., *Haille Sellassie*, Berkeley: University of California Press, 1987.

A History of Ethiopia, Berkeley: University of California Press, 1994.

Martin, Clarice, "A Chamberlain's Journey and the Challenge of Interpretation for Liberation," *Semeia* 47 (1989), 105–35.

Martin, Tony, ed., *African Fundamentalism: A Literary and Cultural Anthology of Garvey's Harlem Renaissance*, Dover, MA: Majority Press, 1991.

Martin, Waldo, *The Mind of Frederick Douglass*, Chapel Hill: University of North Carolina Press, 1984.

Marty, Martin E., *Pilgrims in Their Own Land: 500 Years of Religion in America*, New York: Penguin, 1984.

Meier, August, *Negro Thought in America, 1880–1915*, Ann Arbor: University of Michigan Press, 1963/1988.

Memmi, Albert, *The Colonizer and the Colonized*, Boston: Beacon, 1967.

Meyer, Michael, ed., *Frederick Douglass: The Narrative and Selected Writings*, New York: Modern Library, 1984.

Miller, David L., ed., *Jung and the Interpretation of the Bible*, New York: Continuum, 1995.

Mintz, Sidney W. and Price, Richard, *The Birth of African-American Culture: An Anthropological Perspective*, Boston: Beacon, 1976/1992.

Morgan, Edmund S., *American Slavery, American Freedom: The Ordeal of Colonial Virginia*, New York: Norton, 1975.

Inventing the People: The Rise of Popular Sovereignty in England and America, New York: Norton, 1988.

Morrison, Toni, *Playing in the Dark: Whiteness and the Literary Imagination*, Cambridge: Harvard University Press, 1992.

Moses, Wilson Jeremiah, *The Golden Age of Black Nationalism, 1850–1925*, New York: Oxford University Press, 1978.

Black Messiahs and Uncle Toms: Social and Literary Manipulations of a Religious Myth, University Park: Pennsylvania State University Press, 1982.

On the Wings of Ethiopia: Studies in African-American Life and Letters, Ames: Iowa State University Press, 1990.

Alexander Crummell: A Study of Civilization and Discontent, Amherst: University of Massachusetts Press, 1992.

Moses, Wilson Jeremiah, ed., *Classical Black Nationalism: From the American Revolution to Marcus Garvey*, New York University Press, 1996.

Mullane, Deirdre, ed., *Crossing the Danger Water: Three Hundred Years of African-American Writing*, New York: Anchor/Doubleday, 1993.

Murray, Albert, *The Omni-Americans: New Perspectives on Black Experience and American Culture*, New York: Dutton, 1970.

Murrell, Nathaniel Samuel, Spencer, William David, and McFarlane, Adrian Anthony, eds., *Chanting Down Babylon: The Rastafari Reader*, Philadelphia: Temple University Press, 1998.

Nadel, Alan, *Invisible Criticism: Ralph Ellison and the American Canon*, Iowa City: University of Iowa Press, 1988.

Nash, Gary, *Race and Revolution*, Madison, WI: Madison House, 1990.

"The Great Multicultural Debate," *Contention* 1 (1992).

Nicholas, Tracy and Sparrow, Bill, *Rastafari: A Way of Life*, New York: Doubleday/Anchor, 1979.

Nieman, Donald G., *Promises to Keep: African-Americans and the Constitutional Order, 1776 to the Present*, Oxford University Press, 1991.

Nord, David Paul, "Tocqueville, Garrison and the Perfection of Journalism," *Journalism History* 13:2 (Summer 1986).

Oliver, Robert, *History of Public Speaking in America*, Boston: Allyn & Bacon, 1965.

Olney, James, "The Founding Fathers – Frederick Douglass and Booker T. Washington," in *Slavery and the Literary Imagination*, ed. Deborah McDowell and Arnold Rampersad, Baltimore: Johns Hopkins University Press, 1989.

O'Meally, Robert G., *The Craft of Ralph Ellison*, Cambridge and London: Harvard University Press, 1980.

Omi, Michael and Winant, Howard, *Racial Formations in the United States*, New York and London: Routledge, 1986/1994.

Painter, Nell Irvin, *Sojourner Truth: A Life, a Symbol*, New York: Norton, 1996.

Park, Robert, *Race and Culture*, Glencoe, IL: The Free Press, 1950.

Parr, Susan Resneck and Savery, Pancho, eds., *Approaches to Teaching Ellison's "Invisible Man,"* New York: Modern Language Association, 1989.

Patterson, Orlando, *Freedom in the Making of Western Culture*, London: I. B. Tauris, 1991.

  The Ordeal of Integration: Progress and Resentment in America's "Racial" Crisis, Washington, DC: Civitas/Counterpoint, 1997.

Paz, Octavio, *The Labyrinth of Solitude and Other Writings*, New York: Grove, 1961/1985.

Pease, Jane and Pease, William, *They Who Would Be Free: Blacks' Search for Freedom, 1830–1861*, New York: Atheneum, 1974/1990.

Perry, Bruce, *Malcolm: The Life of a Man Who Changed Black America*, New York: Station Hill Press, 1991.

Peters, John Durham, "Distrust of representation: Habermas on the Public Sphere," in *Media Culture and Society* 15 (1993).

Petesch, Donald, *A Spy in the Enemy's Country: The Emergence of Modern Black Literature*, Iowa City: University of Iowa Press, 1989.

Pilcher, George, ed., "Samuel Davies and the Instruction of the Negro in Virginia," *Virginia Magazine of History and Biography* 74 (1966).

  The Reverend Samuel Davies Abroad, Urbana: University of Illinois Press, 1967.

Porter, Dorothy, ed., *Early Negro Writing 1760–1837*, Boston: Beacon, 1971.

Poster, Mark, *Mode of Information*, University of Chicago Press, 1990.

Potash, Chris, ed., *Reggae, Rasta, Revolution: Jamaican Music from Ska to Dub*, New York: Schirmer Books/Prentice Hall International, 1997.

Potkay, Adam and Burr, Sandra, eds., *Black Atlantic Writers of the 18th Century: Living the New Exodus in England and the Americas*, New York: St. Martin's, 1995.

Pratt, Mary Louise, "Linguistic Utopias," in *The Linguistics of Writing*, ed. Nigel Fabb and Derek Attridge, New York: Methuen, 1987.

  "Criticism in the Contact Zone: Decentering Community and Nation," in *Critical Theory, Cultural Politics, and Latin American Narrative*, ed. Steven Bell, *et al.*, University of Notre Dame Press, 1993.

Preston, Dickson, *Young Frederick Douglass: The Maryland Years*, Baltimore: Johns Hopkins University Press, 1990.

Quarles, Benjamin, *Frederick Douglass*, New York: Atheneum, 1948/1968.

  The Negro in the American Revolution, Chapel Hill: University of North Carolina Press, 1961; repr. New York: Norton, 1973.

Black Abolitionists, Oxford University Press, 1973.

Raboteau, Albert J., *A Fire in the Bones: Reflections on African-American Religious History*, Boston: Beacon, 1995.

Redkey, Edwin S., *Black Exodus: Black Nationalist and Back-to-Africa Movements, 1890–1910*, New Haven: Yale University Press, 1969.

Reed, Adolph L., Jr., *W. E. B. Du Bois and American Political Thought: Fabianism and the Color Line*, New York: Oxford University Press, 1997.

Reid, John Phillip, *The Concept of Liberty in the Age of the American Revolution*, University of Chicago Press, 1988.

Richardson, Marilyn, ed., *Maria W. Stewart: America's First Black Woman Political Writer*, Bloomington: Indiana University Press, 1987.

Ringer, Benjamin, *"We the People" and Others: Duality and America's Treatment of its Racial Minorities*, New York and London: Tavistock Publications, 1983.

Robinson, Donald L., *Slavery in the Structure of American Politics, 1765–1820*, New York: Harcourt Brace Jovanovich, 1971.

Rodriguez, Richard, *Days of Obligation: An Argument with my Mexican Father*, New York: Viking Penguin, 1992.

Rogers, J. A., *World's Great Men of Color*, ed. John Henrik Clark, New York: Collier, 1947/1972.

Root, Maria P. P., ed., *Racially Mixed People in America*, Newbury Park, CA: Sage, 1992.

The Multiracial Experience: Racial Borders as the New Frontier, Thousand Oaks, CA: Sage, 1996.

Rosaldo, Renato, *Culture and Truth*, Boston: Beacon, 1989.

Roux, Edward, *Time Longer Than Rope: A History of the Black Man's Struggle for Freedom in South Africa*, Madison: University of Wisconsin Press, 1948/1966.

Saldívar, José David, *The Dialectics of Our America: Genealogy, Cultural Critique and Literary History*, Durham, NC: Duke University Press, 1991.

Sale, Maggie Montesinos, *The Slumbering Volcano: American Slave Ship Revolts and the Production of Rebellious Masculinity*, Durham, NC: Duke University Press, 1997.

Samuels, Andrew, *The Political Psyche*, London: Routledge, 1993.

Sanders, James A. *Canon and Community: A Guide to Canonical Criticism*, Philadelphia: Fortress, 1984.

Saxton, Alexander, *The Rise and Fall of the White Republic: Class Politics and Mass Culture in Nineteenth-Century America*, London: Verso, 1990.

Schatz, Tom, *Hollywood Genres: Formulas, Filmmaking and the Studio System*, Philadelphia: Temple University Press, 1981.

Schudson, Michael, "The 'Public Sphere' and Its Problems: Bringing the State (Back) In," *Notre Dame Journal of Law, Ethics and Public Policy* 8:2 (1994).

"Paper Tigers: A Sociologist Follows Cultural Studies into the Wilderness," *Lingua Franca* 7:6 (Aug. 1997), 49–56.

Scott, William, "And Ethiopia Shall Stretch Forth Her Hands: The Origins of Ethiopianism in Afro-American Thought 1767–1896," *Umoja* (Spring 1978).

Sernett, Milton, *Black Religion and American Evangelicalism: White Protestants, Plantation Missions, and the Flowering of a Negro Christianity, 1787–1865*,

Metuchen, NJ: Scarecrow Press, 1975.

Sewall, Samuel, *The Selling of Joseph*, Boston: Bartholomew Green and John Allen, 1700.

Shepperson, George, "Ethiopianism: Past and Present," in *Christianity in Tropical Africa*, ed. C. G. Baeta, New York and London: Oxford University Press, 1968, 249–64.

Shields, John C., ed., *The Collected Works of Phillis Wheatley*, New York: Oxford University Press, 1988; 1st edn, 1773.

Shklar, Judith, *American Citizenship: The Quest for Inclusion*, Cambridge: Harvard University Press, 1991.

Siemerling, Winfried and Schwenk, Katrin, eds., *Cultural Difference and the Literary Text. Pluralism and the Limits of Authenticity in North American Literatures*, Iowa City: University of Iowa Press, 1996.

Smith, Rogers M., "The 'American Creed' and American Identity: The Limits of Liberal Citizenship in the United States," *Western Political Quarterly* 41:2 (1988).

Smith, Theophus H., *Conjuring Culture: Biblical Formations in Black America*, Oxford University Press, 1994.

Sobel, Mechal, *Trabelin' On: The Slave Journey to an Afro-Baptist Faith*, Princeton University Press, 1979.

The World They Made Together: Black and White Values in Eighteenth-Century Virginia, Princeton University Press, 1987.

Sollors, Werner, *Beyond Ethnicity: Consent and Descent in American Culture*, Oxford University Press, 1986.

"A Critique of Pure Pluralism," in *Reconstructing American Literary History*, ed. Sacvan Bercovitch, Cambridge: Harvard University Press, 1986.

Neither Black nor White yet Both: Thematic Explorations in Interracial Literature, Oxford University Press, 1997.

ed., *The Invention of Ethnicity*, Oxford University Press, 1989.

Sorenson, Peter, *Imagining Ethiopia: Struggles for History and Identity in the Horn of Africa*, New Brunswick, NJ: Rutgers University Press, 1993.

Spero, Moshe Halevi, *Religious Objects as Psychological Structures*, University of Chicago Press, 1992.

Spivak, Gayatri, *The Post-Colonial Critic*, London: Routledge, 1990.

Stephens, Gregory, "Fashion Dread Rasta: On the One in Jamaica with Bob Marley's Children," *Whole Earth Review* (Summer 1988).

"Rap Music's Double-Voiced Discourse: A Crossroads for Interracial Communication," *Journal of Communication Inquiry* 15 (1991).

"Interracial Dialogue in Rap Music: Call-and-Response in a Multicultural Style," *New Formations* 16 (Spring 1992).

"Romancing the Racial Frontier: Mediating Symbols in Cinematic Interracial Representation," *Spectator* 16:1 (Fall/ Winter 1995/1996), 58–71.

"On Racial Frontiers: The Communicative Culture of Multiracial Audiences," PhD dissertation, University of California-San Diego, 1996.

"Frederick Douglass' Multiracial Abolitionism: 'Antagonistic Cooperation' and 'Redeemable Ideals' in the July 5 Speech," *Communication Studies* 48:3 (Fall 1997), 1–19.

"'You Can Sample Anything': *Zebrahead*, 'Black' Music, and Multiracial

Audiences," *New Formations*, forthcoming.

Stewart, Maria W., *Productions*, originally published by Friends of Freedom and Virtue, Boston, 1835; reprinted in Sue E. Houchins, ed., *Spiritual Narratives*, New York: Oxford University Press, 1988.

Stuckey, Sterling, *The Ideological Origins of Black Nationalism*, Boston: Beacon, 1972.

Slave Culture: Nationalist Theory and the Foundations of Black America, Oxford University Press, 1987.

Going Through the Storm: The Influence of African American Art in History, Oxford University Press, 1994.

Sundquist, Eric, *To Wake the Nations: Race in the Making of American Literature*, Cambridge: Belknap/Harvard, 1993.

Sundquist, Eric J., ed., *Frederick Douglass: New Literary and Historical Essays*, Cambridge University Press, 1990.

Swearingen, C. Jan, "Dialogue and Dialectic: The Logic of Conversation and the Interpretation of Logic," in *The Interpretation of Dialogue*, ed. Tulio Maranhao, University of Chicago Press, 1990.

Sweet, William Warren, "The Churches as Moral Courts of the Frontier," *Church History* 2 (1933), 3–21.

Swift, David E., *Black Prophets of Justice: Activist Clergy Before the Civil War*, Baton Rouge: Louisiana State University Press, 1989.

Takaki, Ronald, ed., *From Different Shores*, Oxford University Press, 1987.

Talamon, Bruce, *Bob Marley: Spirit Dancer*, New York: Norton, 1994.

Taylor, Charles, *et al.*, *Multiculturalism: Examining the Politics of Recognition*, ed. Amy Gutmann, Cambridge, MA: MIT, 1994.

Taylor, Quintard, *In Search of the Racial Frontier: African Americans in the American West, 1528–1990*, New York: W. W. Norton, 1998.

Thelwell, Michael, *The Harder They Come*, New York: Grove, 1980.

Thompson, Robert Farris, "An Aesthetic of the Cool: West African Dance," *American Forum* 2 (1966), 85–102.

Flash of the Spirit: African and Afro-American Art and Philosophy, New York: Random House, 1983.

de Tocqueville, Alexis, *Democracy in America*, ed. J. P. Mayer, New York: Anchor/Doubleday, 1840/1969.

Turner, Frederick Jackson, "The Significance of the Frontier in American History" (1893), in *Early Writings of Frederick Jackson Turner*, ed. Everett Edwards and Fulmer Mood, Madison: University of Wisconsin Press, 1938.

Turner, Terisa with Ferguson, Bryan, eds., *Arise Ye Mighty People! Gender, Class & Race in Popular Struggles*, Trenton, NJ: Africa World Press, 1994.

Tuveson, Ernest L., *Redeemer Nation: The Idea of America's Millennial Role*, University of Chicago Press, 1968.

Vasconcelos, José, *The Cosmic Race/La raza cósmica*, bilingual edition, translated by Didier T. Jaen, Baltimore and London: Johns Hopkins University Press, 1925/1997.

Vincent, Theodore G., *Voices of a Black Nation: Political Journalism in the Harlem Renaissance*, Trenton, NJ: Africa World Press, 1973/1990.

Wald, Priscilla, "Neither Citizen nor Alien: National Narratives, Frederick Douglass, and the Politics of Self-Definition," in *Constituting Americans: Cultural*

Anxiety and Narrative Form, Durham, NC, and London: Duke University Press, 1995, 14–105.

Walker, Clarence, *Deromanticizing Black History*, Knoxville: University of Tennessee Press, 1991.

Walker, David, *Appeal to the Coloured Citizens of the World*, ed. Charles Wiltse, New York: Hill and Wang, 1829/1965.

Walker, Peter, "Frederick Douglass: Orphan Slave," in *Moral Choices: Memory, Desire, and Imagination in 19th-Century Abolitionism*, Baton Rouge: Louisiana State University Press, 1978.

Walker, Robbie Jean, *The Rhetoric of Struggle: Public Address by African American Women*, New York: Garland, 1992.

Wallerstein, Immanuel, *Unthinking Social Science: The Limits of Nineteenth-Century Paradigms*, London: Polity Press, 1991.

Washington, Booker T., *Up From Slavery*, in *Three Negro Classics*, introduced by John Hope Franklin, New York: Avon, 1901/1965.

Waters, Anita M., *Race, Class, and Political Symbols: Rastafari and Reggae in Jamaican Politics*, New Brunswick, NJ: Transaction Publishers, 1985.

Watts, Jerry Gafio, *Heroism and the Black Intellectual: Ralph Ellison, Politics, and Afro-American Intellectual Life*, Chapel Hill: University of North Carolina Press, 1994.

Weatherford, Willis, *American Churches and the Negro: A Historical Study from Early Slave Days to the Present*, Boston: Christopher, 1957.

Wells, Ida B., *Crusade for Justice: The Autobiography*, ed. Alfreda M. Duster, Chicago and London: University of Chicago Press, 1970.

West, Cornel, "The New Cultural Politics of Difference," *October* 53 (Summer 1990).

White, Timothy, *Catch a Fire: The Life of Bob Marley*, New York: Henry Holt & Co., 1983/1989.

Whitefield, George, *George Whitefield's Journals* (1747), Gainesville, FL: Scholar's Fascimiles and Reprints, 1969.

Whitfield, George, "Frederick Douglass: Negro Abolitionist," *Today's Speech* 11 (1963), 6–8.

Whitney, Malika and Hussey, Dermott, *Bob Marley: Reggae King of the World*, Rohnert Park, CA: Pomegranate, 1984.

Williams, Raymond, "Base and Superstructure in Marxist Cultural Theory," in *Problems in Materialism and Culture*, London: Verso, 1980.

Williamson, Joel, *New People: Miscegenation and Mulattoes in the United States*, New York: The Free Press, 1980.

Wilmore, Gayraud, *Black Religion and Black Radicalism: An Interpretation of the Religious History of African Americans*, 3rd edn, Maryknoll, NY: Orbis Books, 1998.

Wilmore, Gayraud, ed., *African American Religious Studies: An Interdisciplinary Anthology*, Durham, NC: Duke University Press, 1989.

Wilson, William Julius, *The Truly Disadvantaged: The Inner City, the Underclass, and Public Policy*, University of Chicago Press, 1987.

When Work Disappears: The World of the New Urban Poor, New York: Knopf, 1997.

Winslow, Ola Elizabeth, *Samuel Sewall of Boston*, New York: Macmillan, 1964.

Witvliet, Theo, *The Way of the Black Messiah*, Oak Park: Meyer-Stone, 1987.

Wood, Joe, ed., *Malcolm X In Our Own Image*, New York: St. Martin's, 1993.

Woodson, Carter, *Negro Orators & Their Orations*, Washington, DC: Associated Publishers, 1925.

Woolman, John, *Some Considerations on the Keeping of Negroes: Recommended to the Professors of Christianity, of Every Denomination*, Philadelphia: James Chattin, 1754.

Wright, Jeremiah A., Jr., *Africans Who Shaped our Faith*, Chicago: Urban Ministries, 1995.

Yawney, Carole D., "Moving with the Dawtas of Rastafari: From Myth to Reality," in *The Caribbean and Latin America: Third Interdisciplinary Colloquium about the Caribbean*, ed. Ulrich Fleischmann and Ineke Thaf, Berlin: Verlag Klaus Dieter Verwoerd, 1987.

"To Grow a Daughter: Cultural Liberation and the Dynamics of Oppression in Jamaica," in *Feminism: From Pressure to Politics*, ed. Angela Miles and Geraldine Finn, Montreal: Black Rose Books, 1989, 177–202.

"Rasta Mek a Trod: Symbolic Ambiguity in a Globalizing Religion," in *Alternative Cultures in the Caribbean*, ed. Ulrich Fleischmann and Thomas Bremer, Frankfurt am Main: Vervuert, 1993; reprinted in Terisa Turner, ed., *Arise Ye Mighty People! Gender, Class & Race in Popular Struggles*, Trenton: Africa World Press, 1994.

Yerushalmi, Josef Hayim, *Freud's Moses: Judaism Terminable and Interminable*, New Haven: Yale University Press, 1991.

Young, Robert Alexander, *The Ethiopian Manifesto* (1829), in Sterling Stuckey, *Ideological Origins of Black Nationalism*, Boston: Beacon, 1972, and Wilson Jeremiah Moses, *Classical Black Nationalism*, New York University Press, 1996.

Zinn, Howard, *A People's History of the United States*, New York: Harper and Row, 1980.

Index

abolitionism   36, 40–45, 49
  black abolitionists   74–75, 84, 87,
    91–92, 99
  in Britain   74–75
  and Douglass   55, 57, 67–78, 81–82,
    83–84, 86, 87, 91–92, 108
  European   41
  and the Great Awakenings   40, 42–45,
    93
  and miscegenation   98
  North American   41
  rhetorical strategies of abolitionists
    49–50, 51–53
  as a "secular church"   71–72, 72–73
  see also slavery
Achebe, Chinua   23
African Civilization Society   103
African culture, in the United States   11
African Fundamentalism, and Garvey
    161
African Zion, and Marley   182–83
Afrocentrism, and Marley   182
Allen, Richard   47, 48, 49, 91
AME (African Methodist Episcopal)
    church   48, 51
Anderson, Alpharita see Marley, Rita
Anderson, Jervis   159
Andrews, Sidney   39
Andrews, William   82
Anglicanism, and the Great Awakening
    43–44
antagonistic cooperation   22–3
  and Douglass   59, 61, 72, 78, 91, 94,
    108
  and Ellison   22, 145, 146, 147
Anthony, Aaron   60, 88
anticolonial movements   15
Anzaldúa, Gloria   14, 23
Appiah, Kwame   1
archetypal figures
  and Ellison   116–17, 119, 122–23, 147
  in Jamaica   168

Asad, Talal   10
Asante, Molefi   22
assimilation, and Douglass   105, 108
Auerbach, Erich   185
Auld, Sophia   62, 99
Auld, Thomas   61, 62

"Babylon System"
  and Marley   183, 204–45
  and Rastafarianism   151–52, 218
Bailey, Betsy   60
Bakhtin, M.   135
Baldwin, James   43
Banton, Buju   205, 217
Banton, Burru, "Bible Again"   196
Banton, Michael   15, 21, 24
Barrett, Aston "Familyman"   176, 203
Barrett, Carlton   176, 203
Barrett, Leonard   155, 196, 213
Basler, Roy P.   112
"Battle Hymn of the Republic"   207
Bedward, Alexander   165
Benezet, Anthony   44–45, 73
Bercovitch, Sacvan   87
Berlin, Ira   37
Bethel African church, Philadelphia   48
Bibb, Henry   77
Bible, the
  and black Americans as the Children of
    Israel   89–91
  Book of Daniel   208–09
  and the "curse of Ham" myth   60,
    103
  and Douglass   22, 61, 67, 76–77, 78,
    86, 87–88, 89–91, 94, 103, 106, 109
  and Ellison   130, 146
  and Ethiopia   91–92, 195–96, 197
  and Garvey   154–55, 159
  and the Great Awakening   45
  and interracial call-and-response   125
  and Jamaican culture   195–96
  and Maria Stewart   52–53